the wisden
guide to
international
cricket 2011

edited by
steven lynch

First published in the UK in 2010 by
John Wisden & Co
An imprint of A & C Black Publishers Ltd
36 Soho Square, London W1D 3QY
www.wisden.com
www.acblack.com

ISBN: 978 14081 2916 6

Cover by James Watson
Cover photographs © Getty Images
Inside photographs © Getty Images

A CIP catalogue record for this book is available from the British Library.

This book is produced using paper that is made from wood
grown in managed, sustainable forests. It is natural, renewable and
recyclable. The logging and manufacturing processes conform to the
environmental regulations of the country of origin.

Typeset in Mendoza Roman and Fruitiger
by Saxon Graphics Ltd, Derby

Printed by MPG Books Ltd, Bodmin, Cornwall

INTRODUCTION

Welcome to the **Wisden Guide to International Cricket 2011**, which includes – in words and pictures, facts and figures – details of 200 leading players, telling you *how* they play as well as where they come from. You will also find a rundown on the players from other leading non-Test-playing nations – including Canada for the first time – and a handy guide to upcoming international fixtures. To help you identify everyone on the field or in the dressing-room, there are photographs and short descriptions of the international umpires, coaches and referees. Finally there is a section containing records for all international matches – Tests, one-dayers, Twenty20s and the World Cup – with a country-by-country breakdown too.

Many of the profiles in the book are edited versions from ESPN Cricinfo's player pages, used with their kind permission. We have tried to include every player likely to appear in international cricket in 2010 – but, like all selectors, we will undoubtedly have left out someone who should have been included. Details of anyone who managed to escape our selectorial net can be found on www.cricinfo.com.

The statistics have been updated to **September 23, 2010**, the end of the international season in England. The abbreviation 'S/R' in the batting tables denotes runs per 100 balls; in the bowling it shows the balls required to take each wicket. A dash (–) in the records usually indicates that full statistics are not available (such as details of fours and sixes, or balls faced, in all domestic matches).

Thanks are due to Christopher Lane of Wisden, Charlotte Atyeo and Becky Senior at A&C Black, Rob Brown and the typesetting team at Saxon, James Watson who designed the cover, and Cricinfo's technical wizards Robin Abrahams and Travis Basevi.

Finally, I couldn't have managed without the support of my wife Karina, who puts up with this annual intervention into our lives with amazing patience, and our sons Daniel and Mark.

Steven Lynch, September 2010

CONTENTS

PLAYER INDEX

PLAYER INDEX

ABDUL RAZZAQ

Full name	**Abdul Razzaq**
Born	**December 2, 1979, Lahore, Punjab**
Teams	**Lahore, Zarai Taraqiati Bank, Hampshire**
Style	**Right-hand bat, right-arm fast-medium bowler**
Test debut	**Pakistan v Australia at Brisbane 1999-2000**
ODI debut	**Pakistan v Zimbabwe at Lahore 1996-97**
T20I debut	**Pakistan v England at Bristol 2006**

THE PROFILE Abdul Razzaq was once rapid enough to open the bowling, and remains composed enough to bat anywhere, although the lower order suits him nicely. His bowling is characterised by a galloping approach, accuracy, and reverse-swing, but it is his batting that is more likely to win matches. He is particularly strong driving through cover and mid-off. He has two gears: block or blast. Cut off the big shots and he can get bogged down, although he is very patient, as demonstrated by a match-saving 71 in almost six hours against India at Mohali in March 2005. Just before that he had batted bewilderingly slowly at Melbourne, scoring 4 in 110 minutes – but when the occasion demands he can slog with the best of them. After a mid-career bowling slump he rediscovered some of his old guile, if not his nip. And if the pitch is helpful to seam – as Karachi's was for his only Test five-for in 2004, and also against India there in January 2006 – he can still be a danger. Razzaq's allround performance in that win over India was easily his most emphatic: he made 45 and 90 and took seven wickets. He missed the 2007 World Cup with a knee injury, then joined the unauthorised Indian Cricket League. His international career seemed over when all the ICL players were banned, but after an amnesty he was the first to reappear in official internationals, reinforcing the World Twenty20 squad in England in June 2009, taking three wickets in the final victory over Sri Lanka. He remained a steady limited-overs contributor, spanking Tim Bresnan's last five balls of the innings at Lord's in September 2010 for fours.

THE FACTS Abdul Razzaq took a hat-trick against Sri Lanka at Galle in June 2000: he is one of only four players to have scored a hundred and taken a hat-trick in Tests (after England's Johnny Briggs, Wasim Akram of Pakistan and the New Zealander James Franklin) ... Razzaq took 7 for 51 – still his best figures – on his first-class debut, for Lahore City v Karachi Whites in the Quaid-e-Azam Trophy final in November 1996 ... He made 203 not out for Middlesex v Glamorgan in 2003 ... His record includes four ODIs for the Asia XI ...

THE FIGURES to 23.9.10   ᴇSᴘᴨcricinfo.com

Batting & Fielding	M	Inns	NO	Runs	HS	Avge	S/R	100	50	4s	6s	Ct	St
Tests	46	77	9	1946	134	28.61	41.04	3	7	230	23	15	0
ODIs	243	210	53	4726	112	30.10	80.40	2	22	354	112	33	0
T20Is	21	19	8	268	46*	24.36	124.07	0	0	14	13	2	0
First-class	116	182	27	5195	203*	33.51	–	8	27	–	–	32	0

Bowling	M	Balls	Runs	Wkts	BB	Avge	RpO	S/R	5i	10m
Tests	46	7008	3694	100	5–35	36.94	3.16	70.08	1	0
ODIs	243	10329	8103	258	6–35	31.40	4.70	40.03	3	0
T20Is	21	261	300	14	3–20	21.42	6.89	18.64	0	0
First-class	116	18516	10778	340	7–51	31.70	3.49	54.45	11	2

ABDUR RAZZAK

Full name	**Khan Abdur Razzak**
Born	**June 15, 1982, Khulna**
Teams	**Khulna**
Style	**Left-hand bat, slow left-arm orthodox spinner**
Test debut	**Bangladesh v Australia at Chittagong 2005-06**
ODI debut	**Bangladesh v Hong Kong at Colombo 2004**
T20I debut	**Bangladesh v Zimbabwe at Khulna 2006-07**

THE PROFILE Another of Bangladesh's seemingly never-ending supply of left-arm spinners, Abdur Razzak (no relation to the similarly named Pakistan allrounder) first made his mark when he helped unheralded Khulna to their first-ever National Cricket League title in 2001-02. Tall, with a high action, "Raj" played for the A team against Zimbabwe early in 2004, and took the opportunity well with 15 wickets, including a matchwinning 7 for 17 in the third encounter on the batting paradise of Dhaka's old Bangabandhu National Stadium. He has an uncanny ability to pin batsmen down, although his action has often been questioned, most recently late in 2008, when he was suspended by the ICC after tests showed he sometimes flexed his elbow by almost twice the permitted amount. After remedial work, he was cleared to resume playing in March 2009. He was immediately hurried back, playing in the World Twenty20 in England then taking seven wickets in Bangladesh's rare one-day clean sweep against a depleted West Indies side in the Caribbean in July. Razzak took 3 for 17 on his one-day debut against Hong Kong in the Asia Cup in July 2004, but his action was reported for the first time after the next game. He made his Test debut in April 2006, against Australia on a turning track at Chittagong (even the Aussies played three spinners), but failed to take a wicket, and has continued to struggle for penetration in Tests. But he has become an automatic one-day selection, maintaining a miserly economy-rate, and was the only Bangladeshi signed up for the first year of the Indian Premier League in 2008, although he did not return for the second season.

THE FACTS Abdur Razzak took 5 for 29 in an ODI against Zimbabwe at Mirpur in December 2009 ... He took 7 for 11 (10 for 62 in the match) for Khulna at Sylhet in 2003-04 ... During 2008 Razzak became the third Bangladeshi, after Mohammad Rafique and Mashrafe Mortaza, to take 100 ODI wickets ...

THE FIGURES to 23.9.10   **ESPNcricinfo.com**

Batting & Fielding	M	Inns	NO	Runs	HS	Avge	S/R	100	50	4s	6s	Ct	St
Tests	8	15	5	160	33	16.00	55.36	0	0	24	1	3	0
ODIs	103	66	28	548	33	14.42	70.43	0	0	39	14	24	0
T20Is	13	9	5	11	5	2.75	32.35	0	0	0	0	2	0
First-class	49	81	14	1387	83	20.70	58.03	0	7	–	–	17	0

Bowling	M	Balls	Runs	Wkts	BB	Avge	RpO	S/R	5i	10m
Tests	8	1881	1079	16	3–93	67.43	3.44	117.56	0	0
ODIs	103	5421	4092	144	5–29	28.41	4.52	37.64	2	0
T20Is	13	294	328	20	4–16	16.40	6.69	14.70	0	0
First-class	49	10889	4987	157	7–11	31.76	2.74	69.35	5	1

HASHIM **AMLA**

Full name	**Hashim Mahomed Amla**
Born	**March 31, 1983, Durban, Natal**
Teams	**Dolphins, Nottinghamshire**
Style	**Right-hand bat, occasional right-arm medium-pacer**
Test debut	**South Africa v India at Kolkata 2004-05**
ODI debut	**South Africa v Bangladesh at Chittagong 2007-08**
T20I debut	**South Africa v Australia at Brisbane 2008-09**

THE PROFILE An elegant, wristy right-hander with a fine temperament, Hashim Amla was the first South African of Indian descent to reach the Test team. His elevation was hardly a surprise after he reeled off four centuries in his first eight innings in 2004-05, after captaining the Dolphins (formerly Natal) at the tender age of 21. He toured with the Under-19s in 2000-01, captained South Africa at the 2002 Youth World Cup and, after starring for the A team, made his Test debut against India late in 2004. He was not an instant success, with serious questions emerging about his technique as he mustered only 36 runs in four innings against England later that season, struggling with an ungainly crouched stance and a bat coming down from somewhere in the region of gully. But he made his second chance count, with 149 against New Zealand at Cape Town in April 2006, followed by big hundreds against New Zealand (again) and India in 2007-08, before a fine undefeated 104 helped save the 2008 Lord's Test. After a consistent home series against England in 2009-10 Amla came into his own in India early in 2010 with a monumental 253 not out to set up victory at Nagpur, followed by valiant twin centuries in defeat at Kolkata. Not originally seen as a one-day player, he was tried at the end of 2008 and, after slamming 140 against Bangladesh, made 80 not out and 97 in consecutive victories over Australia to make his place safe. Amla, a devout Muslim whose beard matches Pakistan's Mohammad Yousuf's as the most impressive in the game, is a strong candidate to become South Africa's captain one day.

THE FACTS Amla scored 253 not out at Nagpur, and 114 and 123 not out at Kolkata in the two-Test series in India in February 2010: his series average of 490 has been exceeded only by England's Wally Hammond (563.00 v New Zealand in 1932-33) ... Amla averages 104.80 in Tests against New Zealand, but 17.25 v Sri Lanka ... His older brother Ahmed also plays for the Dolphins ...

THE FIGURES *to 23.9.10*   **ESPncricinfo.com**

Batting & Fielding	M	Inns	NO	Runs	HS	Avge	S/R	100	50	4s	6s	Ct	St
Tests	46	81	6	3383	253*	45.10	48.67	10	16	427	3	37	0
ODIs	29	28	3	1371	140	54.84	88.56	3	8	131	8	11	0
T20Is	2	2	0	52	26	26.00	104.00	0	0	4	1	0	0
First-class	132	219	20	9688	253*	48.68	–	29	48	–	–	100	0

Bowling	M	Balls	Runs	Wkts	BB	Avge	RpO	S/R	5i	10m
Tests	46	42	28	0	–	–	4.00	–	0	0
ODIs	29	0	–	–	–	–	–	–	–	–
T20Is	2	0	–	–	–	–	–	–	–	–
First-class	132	315	224	1	1–10	224.00	4.26	315.00	0	0

JAMES **ANDERSON**

Full name	**James Michael Anderson**
Born	**July 30, 1982, Burnley, Lancashire**
Teams	**Lancashire**
Style	**Left-hand bat, right-arm fast-medium bowler**
Test debut	**England v Zimbabwe at Lord's 2003**
ODI debut	**England v Australia at Melbourne 2002-03**
T20I debut	**England v Australia at Sydney 2006-07**

THE PROFILE When the force is with him, James Anderson is capable of irresistible spells, seemingly able to swing the ball round corners at an impressive speed. New Zealand were blown away in Nottingham in 2008 (Anderson 7 for 43); the following May the West Indies looked clueless in Durham (nine wickets in the match); and back at Trent Bridge in 2010 Pakistan's inexperienced batsmen could hardly lay a bat on him (5 for 54 and 6 for 17). And then there are the bad days, when the ball isn't coming out quite right and refuses to swing: Anderson can then sometimes look downcast, and the purists start murmuring about an action in which he seems to be looking at the ground at the moment of delivery, rather than down the pitch at the target as the MCC coaching manual advocates. Anderson had played only occasionally for Lancashire when he was hurried into England's one-day squad in Australia in 2002-03 as cover for Andy Caddick. He didn't have a number – or even a name – on his shirt, but ten overs for12 runs in century heat at Adelaide earned him a World Cup spot. There was a five-for in his debut Test, against Zimbabwe in 2003, and a one-day hat-trick against Pakistan ... but then a stress fracture sidelined him for most of 2006 before suddenly, in the absence of the entire Ashes-winning attack in the second half of 2007, Anderson looked the part of pack leader again. His batting has also steadily improved: one of his unlikelier landmarks was going 54 Test innings before collecting a duck, an England record. At Cardiff in 2009 he survived for 69 nail-chewing minutes to help stave off defeat by Australia. He is also a superb fielder.

THE FACTS Anderson was the first man to take an ODI hat-trick for England, against Pakistan at The Oval in 2003 ... He took the first six wickets to fall on his way to career-best figures of 7 for 43 for England v New Zealand at Nottingham in 2008 ... Anderson went 54 Test innings before being out for a duck at The Oval in 2009, an English record (previously Geraint Jones's 51); only AB de Villiers (78), Aravinda de Silva (75) and Clive Lloyd (58) have started with more duckless innings in Tests ...

THE FIGURES to 23.9.10   **ESPN cricinfo.com**

Batting & Fielding	M	Inns	NO	Runs	HS	Avge	S/R	100	50	4s	6s	Ct	St
Tests	52	71	31	502	34	12.55	35.90	0	0	61	1	21	0
ODIs	133	56	29	159	15	5.88	39.35	0	0	10	0	36	0
T20Is	19	4	3	1	1*	1.00	50.00	0	0	0	0	3	0
First-class	111	132	54	792	37*	10.15	–	0	0	–	–	44	0

Bowling	M	Balls	Runs	Wkts	BB	Avge	RpO	S/R	5i	10m
Tests	52	10777	5970	188	7–43	31.75	3.32	57.32	10	1
ODIs	133	6564	5429	179	5–23	30.32	4.96	36.67	1	0
T20Is	19	422	552	18	3–23	30.66	7.84	23.44	0	0
First-class	111	20736	11342	409	7–43	27.73	3.28	50.69	22	3

RAVICHANDRAN **ASHWIN**

Full name	**Ravichandran Ashwin**
Born	**September 17, 1986, Madras (now Chennai)**
Teams	**Tamil Nadu, Chennai Super Kings**
Style	**Right-hand bat, offspinner**
Test debut	**No Tests yet**
ODI debut	**India v Sri Lanka at Harare 2010**
T20I debut	**India v Zimbabwe at Harare 2010**

THE PROFILE A tall offspinner with a high action, Ravichandran Ashwin – who is studying to be an engineer – has some similarities with another tall international spinner from Tamil Nadu, Srinivasaraghavan Venkataraghavan, although for the moment the comparison with Venkat – who took 156 wickets in 57 Tests spanning almost 20 years – should end there. Ashwin made big strides in his debut season, 2006-07, taking 31 wickets at less than 20: 11 of them came in only his fourth first-class game, against Baroda. He showed promise with the bat as well the following season, although he was restricted by injury, and made his maiden first-class hundred in 2009-10. He was signed by Chennai Super Kings for the first IPL in 2008, and by the third instalment of the 20-over league in 2010 proved to be the most economical regular bowler on view, going for 6.10 an over, miserly in Twenty20 terms. He often opened the bowling, and finished the IPL season with 13 wickets and a much-enhanced reputation. Ashwin had continued to perform consistently for Tamil Nadu, and captained them to the domestic one-day title in 2008-09. He earned a central contract that season, but did not break into the national squad until the one-dayers at home against South Africa early in 2010, when Harbhajan Singh was unavailable. He didn't actually play then, but when Harbhajan was one of several senior players to give a triangular one-day series in Zimbabwe a miss later in the year, Ashwin finally got his chance. He started his 50-overs international career with an important 38 and two wickets against Sri Lanka, then had a couple of Twenty20 outings against the hosts.

THE FACTS Ashwin was the most economical regular bowler in the third season of the IPL, going for 6.10 runs per over ... He took 5 for 65 and 6 for 64 for Tamil Nadu v Baroda in Chennai in January 2007, in only his fourth first-class match ... Ashwin made 107 not out for Tamil Nadu v Himachal Pradesh at Dharmasala in November 2009 ... He took a wicket (Tatenda Taibu of Zimbabwe) with his third ball in Twenty20 internationals ...

THE FIGURES to 23.9.10   **ESPn cricinfo.com**

Batting & Fielding	M	Inns	NO	Runs	HS	Avge	S/R	100	50	4s	6s	Ct	St
Tests	0	0	–	–	–	–	–	–	–	–	–	–	–
ODIs	1	1	0	38	38	38.00	118.75	0	0	4	1	0	0
T20Is	2	0	–	–	–	–	–	–	–	–	–	0	0
First-class	28	41	11	1085	107*	36.16	55.35	2	6	164	0	13	0

Bowling	M	Balls	Runs	Wkts	BB	Avge	RpO	S/R	5i	10m
Tests	0	0	–	–	–	–	–	–	–	–
ODIs	1	60	50	2	2–50	25.00	5.00	30.00	0	0
T20Is	2	48	70	2	1–22	35.00	8.75	24.00	0	0
First-class	28	6837	3032	103	6–64	29.43	2.66	66.37	7	2

AZHAR ALI

Full name	**Azhar Ali**
Born	**February 19, 1985, Lahore**
Teams	**Lahore, Khan Research Laboratories**
Style	**Right-hand bat, legspinner**
Test debut	**Pakistan v Australia at Lord's 2010**
ODI debut	**No ODIs yet**
T20I debut	**No T20Is yet**

THE PROFILE Usually an opener, Azhar Ali made steady progress in domestic cricket after a stuttering start in which he played only eight first-class matches in five seasons following his debut in 2001-02. Promotion to open paid off, though, and he made 409 runs at 68 in 2006-07 – with his first two hundreds – and swelled that to 603 in 2007-08 and 788 the following season, impressive figures in a country where opening has long been difficult. He toured Australia with the A team in 2009, and twice batted for more than five hours for seventies against an attack including Doug Bollinger and Clint McKay. Azhar has a compact and correct technique, and although he has had a few problems against the shorter ball he seemed to have addressed them by the end of the 2010 tour of England, during which he was unlucky to miss a maiden Test century at The Oval, stranded on 92 after batting for more than four hours. Azhar was selected for that ultimately controversial tour – which included two Tests against Australia and four against England – after the selectors decided they could do without Younis Khan and Mohammad Yousuf (although Yousuf was eventually called up). Azhar started off batting at No. 3, and although his inexperience showed at first he played two important innings (30 and 51) as Pakistan beat Australia in the second Test at Headingley. "Before I became a cricketer, I was a fan," he said. "As both a fan and a cricketer there was always a desire to see Pakistan beat the best team in the world." Nonetheless, Azhar looked more at home when Yousuf belatedly arrived and he could ease down to No. 5.

THE FACTS Azhar Ali scored 153 not out for Khan Research Labs against Sui Southern Gas in Rawalpindi in December 2009 ... After not making a century in his first nine first-class matches, spread over five seasons, he scored nine in his next 17 games ... Azhar took 14 for 128 for Lahore Greens against Azad Jammu & Kashmir in a Quaid-e-Azam Trophy Grade 2 (not first-class) match in October 2000 ...

THE FIGURES *to 23.9.10*   ESPNcricinfo.com

Batting & Fielding	M	Inns	NO	Runs	HS	Avge	S/R	100	50	4s	6s	Ct	St
Tests	6	12	1	291	92*	26.45	39.75	0	2	36	0	3	0
ODIs	0	0	–	–	–	–	–	–	–	–	–	–	–
T20Is	0	0	–	–	–	–	–	–	–	–	–	–	–
First-class	56	92	12	3080	153*	38.50	–	11	11	–	–	51	0

Bowling	M	Balls	Runs	Wkts	BB	Avge	RpO	S/R	5i	10m
Tests	6	6	9	0	–	–	9.00	–	0	0
ODIs	0	0	683	15	3–31	45.53	4.79	56.93	0	0
T20Is	0	0	–	–	–	–	–	–	–	–
First-class	56	996	639	18	4–34	35.50	3.84	55.33	1	0

ADRIAN **BARATH**

Full name	**Adrian Boris Barath**
Born	**April 14, 1990, Chaguanas, Trinidad**
Teams	**Trinidad & Tobago, Kings XI Punjab**
Style	**Right-hand bat, occasional offspinner**
Test debut	**West Indies v Australia at Brisbane 2009-10**
ODI debut	**West Indies v Zimbabwe at Providence 2009-10**
T20I debut	**West Indies v Zimbabwe at Port-of-Spain 2009-10**

THE PROFILE Adrian Barath, a diminutive right-hander who usually opens, was long seen as one of the Caribbean's brightest batting talents, and he fulfilled that promise with a superb century on Test debut at Brisbane in November 2009. He was only 19, and became West Indies' youngest centurion, breaking a record previously held by George Headley. Barath cut and carved like a veteran – but unfortunately his team-mates could muster only 73 runs between them, and West Indies still lost heavily. Barath's batting is based on orthodoxy: "As a youngster my dad saw me playing straight, which is unusual," he told Cricinfo. "Normally players begin by hitting across the line, but I was playing straight without anyone teaching me. Maybe it was because of television. I used to watch a lot and try and emulate what I saw." One of the best examples of those he was watching, Brian Lara, became an early mentor – he invited Barath to join him at Lord's for a function honouring Lara's contribution to cricket. Barath was originally chosen for the series against Bangladesh in mid-2009, but joined the senior players in boycotting the matches in a row over contracts. Earlier in 2009 he had showed his mettle by making 132 against England for West Indies A in St Kitts, sharing a partnership of 262 with Lendl Simmons. Not long after that Barath – who hit centuries in his second and third first-class matches when still a few months short of his 17th birthday – made a career-best 192 for Trinidad & Tobago against the Leeward Islands in St Augustine. He injured his knee early in 2010, and required surgery, but he'll be back.

THE FACTS Barath was the 12th man to make a century in his first Test for West Indies, scoring 104 v Australia at Brisbane in November 2009 ... At 19 years 228 days he was West Indies' youngest Test century-maker, beating George Headley (20 years 230 days in 1929-30) ... After making 73 on his first-class debut in January 2007 when still only 16, Barath hit 131 in his second match (against the Leeward Islands) and 101 in his third (against the Windwards) ...

THE FIGURES to 23.9.10   ᴇSᴘᴨcricinfo.com

Batting & Fielding	M	Inns	NO	Runs	HS	Avge	S/R	100	50	4s	6s	Ct	St
Tests	2	4	0	139	104	34.75	61.23	1	0	25	0	2	0
ODIs	5	5	0	131	50	26.20	57.45	0	1	13	1	1	0
T20Is	1	1	0	8	8	8.00	42.10	0	0	1	0	1	0
First-class	26	46	3	1963	192	45.65	–	6	10	–	–	17	0

Bowling	M	Balls	Runs	Wkts	BB	Avge	RpO	S/R	5i	10m
Tests	2	6	4	0	–	–	4.00	–	0	0
ODIs	5	0	–	–	–	–	–	–	–	–
T20Is	1	0	–	–	–	–	–	–	–	–
First-class	26	12	4	0	–	–	2.00	–	0	0

IAN **BELL**

Full name	**Ian Ronald Bell**
Born	**April 11, 1982, Walsgrave, Coventry**
Teams	**Warwickshire**
Style	**Right-hand bat, right-arm medium-pace bowler**
Test debut	**England v West Indies at The Oval 2004**
ODI debut	**England v Zimbabwe at Harare 2004-05**
T20I debut	**England v Pakistan at Bristol 2006**

THE PROFILE Ian Bell was earmarked for greatness long before he was drafted into the England squad in New Zealand in 2001-02, aged 19, as cover for the injured Mark Butcher. Tenacious and technically sound, Bell is in the mould of Michael Atherton, who was burdened with similar expectations on his debut a generation earlier and was similarly adept at leaving the ball outside off. Bell had played only 13 first-class matches when called into that England squad, and his form dipped while he was under the spotlight, but by 2004 he was on the up again. He finally made his Test debut against West Indies that August, stroking 70 at The Oval, before returning the following summer to lift his average to an obscene 297 against Bangladesh. Such rich pickings soon ceased: found out by McGrath and Warne, like so many before him, Bell mustered just 171 runs in the 2005 Ashes. But he bounced back better for the experience, collecting 313 runs in three Tests in Pakistan, including a classy century at Faisalabad. And when Pakistan toured in 2006, Bell repeated the dose, with elegant hundreds in each of the first three Tests. He improved his record against the Aussies in 2006-07 without going on to the big score, and continued to look good in 2008, hitting 199 against South Africa at Lord's. However, he was dropped after an unproductive winter and missed the start of the 2009 Ashes, returning only when Kevin Pietersen was injured. A fine 140 followed at Durban, plus two tons against Bangladesh. Bell seemed set fair again – but broke his foot in a one-dayer in mid-2010 and missed most of the rest of the season.

THE FACTS After three Tests, and innings of 70, 65 not out and 162 not out, Bell's average was 297.00: he raised that to 303.00 before Australia started getting him out – only Lawrence Rowe (336), David Lloyd (308) and "Tip" Foster (306) have ever had better averages in Test history ... Bell was the first Englishman to be out for 199 in a Test, against South Africa at Lord's in 2008 ... He averages 158.25 in Tests against Bangladesh – but 24.66 v India ... Bell made 262 not out for Warwickshire v Sussex at Horsham in May 2004 ...

THE FIGURES to 23.9.10

ESPNcricinfo.com

Batting & Fielding	M	Inns	NO	Runs	HS	Avge	S/R	100	50	4s	6s	Ct	St
Tests	57	100	10	3863	199	42.92	50.18	11	23	445	17	50	0
ODIs	83	80	8	2622	126*	36.41	72.33	1	16	262	11	24	0
T20Is	5	5	1	109	60*	27.25	110.10	0	1	14	1	4	0
First-class	171	290	27	11575	262*	44.01	–	31	60	–	–	126	0

Bowling	M	Balls	Runs	Wkts	BB	Avge	RpO	S/R	5i	10m
Tests	57	108	76	1	1–33	76.00	4.22	108.00	0	0
ODIs	83	88	88	6	3–9	14.66	6.00	14.66	0	0
T20Is	5	0	–	–	–	–	–	–	–	–
First-class	171	2809	1564	47	4–4	33.27	3.34	59.76	0	0

SULIEMAN **BENN**

Full name	**Sulieman Jamaal Benn**
Born	**July 22, 1981, Haynesville, St James, Barbados**
Teams	**Barbados**
Style	**Left-hand bat, slow left-arm orthodox spinner**
Test debut	**West Indies v Sri Lanka at Providence 2007-08**
ODI debut	**West Indies v Sri Lanka at Port-of-Spain 2007-08**
T20I debut	**West Indies v Australia at Bridgetown 2008**

THE PROFILE Not many players can look down on Chris Gayle, but at 6ft 7ins (200cm) Sulieman Benn towers over his captain and makes some of his team-mates look like schoolboys. Built like a fast bowler, and with the fiery attitude of one, Benn is also no stranger to on-field controversies. In 2007, he was involved in an ugly incident in a club game, and two years later had a heated on-field argument with Brad Haddin and Mitchell Johnson in the Perth Test. There were more charges to come, as Benn was sent off the field in Dominica by Gayle during South Africa's one-day whitewash in 2010, after apparently refusing to bowl over the wicket, and in the Tests that followed he was involved in several colourful exchanges with Dale Steyn. But between the controversies came consistent performances which made clear Benn's passion, determination and skill as a bowler, and he has become West Indies' most reliable spinner in years. His height gives him a curious aspect not unlike a windmill when he delivers, but it also makes facing him on a dry track a daunting prospect. He has been economical without being spectacular in one-day cricket, but did register the remarkable figures of 4 for 6 in a Twenty20 international against Zimbabwe at Port-of-Spain early in 2010 – a match which West Indies still managed to lose. He picked up eight wickets in the first Test against England at Kingston in February 2009 to help set up what was ultimately a Test-series win, although his efforts were overshadowed as Jerome Taylor sent England crashing to 51 all out in the second innings.

THE FACTS Benn took 6 for 81 (from 46.4 overs) in a Test against South Africa at Bridgetown in June 2010 ... His eight wickets against England at Kingston in February 2009 were the most by any West Indian spinner in a Test since Lance Gibbs took nine in 1974-75 ... Benn took 3 for 16 as the Stanford Superstars beat England in a Twenty20 challenge in November 2008 ... Benn's highest score is 79 for Barbados v Windward Islands in Grenada in January 2009 ...

THE FIGURES to 23.9.10   **ESPncricinfo.com**

Batting & Fielding	M	Inns	NO	Runs	HS	Avge	S/R	100	50	4s	6s	Ct	St
Tests	15	25	2	352	42	15.30	58.76	0	0	42	8	7	0
ODIs	18	10	1	87	31	9.66	82.07	0	0	8	1	1	0
T20Is	17	7	4	37	13*	12.33	88.09	0	0	5	1	7	0
First-class	62	95	13	1645	79	20.06	–	0	7	–	–	41	0

Bowling	M	Balls	Runs	Wkts	BB	Avge	RpO	S/R	5i	10m
Tests	15	4255	2046	50	6–81	40.92	2.88	85.10	3	0
ODIs	18	900	648	13	2–23	49.84	4.32	69.23	0	0
T20Is	17	354	414	15	4–6	27.60	7.01	23.60	0	0
First-class	62	14512	6646	208	6–81	31.95	2.74	69.76	8	0

DOUG **BOLLINGER**

Full name	**Douglas Erwin Bollinger**
Born	**July 24, 1981, Baulkham Hills, Sydney**
Teams	**New South Wales, Chennai Super Kings**
Style	**Left-hand bat, left-arm fast-medium bowler**
Test debut	**Australia v South Africa at Sydney 2008-09**
ODI debut	**Australia v Pakistan at Dubai 2008-09**
T20I debut	**No T20Is yet**

THE PROFILE   Until 2007-08 it looked as if Doug Bollinger's career would be an uneventful one. But he shrugged off a disappointing time with Worcestershire to star for New South Wales, and by early 2008 had his first national contract, a new wife ... and a fresh head of hair, courtesy of the same company which rethatched Shane Warne and Graham Gooch (that also led to a new nickname, "Doug the Rug" replacing the old "Bald Eagle"). Finally, just as he was preparing to depart on his honeymoon, Bollinger heard that he was a late addition to the Test squad to tour the West Indies in May 2008. He was unlucky not to have been named in the first place after topping the Pura Cup wicket-takers with 45 at 15.44, an especially good return considering he missed the last three games of New South Wales's successful campaign with a broken foot. A combative left-armer who mixes sharp pace with a consistent line and length, Bollinger finally won a Test cap at home at the SCG early in 2009, and ended up on the winning side against South Africa – but soon found himself overtaken by the likes of Ben Hilfenhaus and Peter Siddle in the return series. In England in 2009 Hilfenhaus was narrowly preferred at the start of the Ashes series, and bowled so well that Bollinger was a back number by the end of the tour, but injuries to others let him back in, and he made the most of his reprieve, taking 37 wickets in seven Tests in 2009-10, and utterly dominating the dangerous Chris Gayle in one-dayers.

THE FACTS   Bollinger has twice taken 5 for 35 in ODIs – against Pakistan in Abu Dhabi in May 2009, and v India at Guwahati the following November ... He took a one-day hat-trick for NSW v South Australia at Canberra in December 2004, dismissing Numbers 3, 4 and 5 in the order for ducks ... He also took 6 for 47 for NSW v South Australia at Sydney in December 2008 ... For Worcestershire in 2007 Bollinger took only 16 first-class wickets at 44.56 ...

THE FIGURES to 23.9.10   **ESPN**cricinfo.com

Batting & Fielding	M	Inns	NO	Runs	HS	Avge	S/R	100	50	4s	6s	Ct	St
Tests	10	10	4	42	21	7.00	34.71	0	0	6	0	2	0
ODIs	26	4	2	4	3	2.00	66.66	0	0	0	0	5	0
T20Is	0	0	–	–	–	–	–	–	–	–	–	–	–
First-class	64	69	30	301	31*	7.71	–	0	0	–	–	23	0

Bowling	M	Balls	Runs	Wkts	BB	Avge	RpO	S/R	5i	10m
Tests	10	2083	1085	44	5–28	24.65	3.12	47.34	2	0
ODIs	26	1288	930	42	5–35	22.14	4.33	30.66	3	0
T20Is	0	0	–	–	–	–	–	–	–	–
First-class	64	11574	6324	222	6–47	28.48	3.27	52.13	12	2

RAVI **BOPARA**

ENGLAND

Full name	**Ravinder Singh Bopara**
Born	**May 4, 1985, Forest Gate, London**
Teams	**Essex, Kings XI Punjab**
Style	**Right-hand bat, right-arm medium-pace bowler**
Test debut	**England v Sri Lanka at Kandy 2007-08**
ODI debut	**England v Australia at Sydney 2006-07**
T20I debut	**England v New Zealand at Manchester 2008**

THE PROFILE Ravi Bopara has had an up-and-down Test career. Uniquely he followed three successive ducks (against Sri Lanka late in 2007, including an embarrassing first-ball run-out) with three successive centuries against West Indies in 2009, despite being dropped after his maiden hundred in Barbados. His success against West Indies meant he was inked in at No. 3 against Australia for the 2009 Ashes – helping usher Michael Vaughan into retirement – but his wristy technique proved too loose, and he made only 105 runs in seven innings before being dropped. His usually excellent fielding wavered too, as he dropped a couple of relative sitters, while his energetic medium-pacers proved toothless. He reacted to the chop by making 201 for Essex against Surrey, and was back for the chastening one-day series against Australia, making several starts without going on to a big score. Bopara has packed a lot in since he signed for Essex at 17 in 2002. A good county season in 2006 won him a place in the Academy squad which was based in Perth during that winter's Ashes whitewash. When Kevin Pietersen broke a rib in the first match of the one-day tournament, Bopara was summoned: not worried about having such big boots to fill, he made his debut in front of the Sydney Hill, and bowled Australia's "finisher", Michael Hussey, as England began the amazing turnaround that eventually won them that series. In the 2007 World Cup Bopara showed impressive resolve in making 52, which almost conjured an unlikely victory against eventual finalists Sri Lanka, and has been consistent in one-dayers ever since.

THE FACTS Bopara hit 229 for Essex v Northamptonshire at Chelmsford in June 2007, putting on 320 for the third wicket with Grant Flower ... He made 104 (at Bridgetown), 143 (at Lord's) and 108 (at Chester-le-Street) in successive Test innings, all against West Indies, in 2009; his previous three Test innings had all been ducks ... Bopara scored 201 not out for Essex in the Friends Provident Trophy at Leicester in June 2008 ...

THE FIGURES *to 23.9.10* **ᴇѕᴘɴcricinfo.com**

Batting & Fielding	M	Inns	NO	Runs	HS	Avge	S/R	100	50	4s	6s	Ct	St
Tests	10	15	0	502	143	33.46	53.63	3	0	64	2	5	0
ODIs	54	50	10	1140	60	28.50	73.45	0	4	101	16	18	0
T20Is	11	10	0	191	55	19.10	100.52	0	1	19	1	4	0
First-class	103	172	22	6332	229	42.21	54.04	17	25	–	–	67	0

Bowling	M	Balls	Runs	Wkts	BB	Avge	RpO	S/R	5i	10m
Tests	10	296	199	1	1–39	199.00	4.03	296.00	0	0
ODIs	54	391	331	10	4–38	33.10	5.07	39.10	1	0
T20Is	11	0	–	–	–	–	–	–	–	–
First-class	103	6946	4585	107	5–75	42.85	3.96	64.91	3	1

LOOTS **BOSMAN**

Full name	**Lungile Loots Bosman**
Born	**April 14, 1977, Kimberley**
Teams	**Dolphins, Derbyshire**
Style	**Right-hand bat, right-arm medium-pace bowler**
Test debut	**No Tests yet**
ODI debut	**South Africa v Zimbabwe at Bloemfontein 2006-07**
T20I debut	**South Africa v Australia at Johannesburg 2005-06**

THE PROFILE A hard-hitting opener and the archetypal Twenty20 batsman, Loots Bosman was born in the Cape Province, where he was raised by his grandfather, and – after starring in local cricket for a club called Yorkshire – made his first-class debut in November 1997, making 96 in his first innings and 77 in his second. But a century was three years away, and he seemed destined for a quiet provincial career until Twenty20 cricket reached South Africa in 2003-04. Bosman, by now playing for the Eagles franchise, topped the lists with 219 runs at a strike-rate of 120.99. He started with 84 not out from 44 balls against the Dolphins in April 2004: the following season he thrashed the Lions for a 44-ball hundred, with nine sixes. And when Bosman tamed the Lions again, with a 22-ball half-century in February 2006, the selectors could ignore him no longer and included him in the Twenty20 team against Australia. He has remained a 20-overs regular, the highlight coming with 94 from just 45 balls against England at Centurion in November 2009 – including nine more sixes – in a record opening stand of 170 in 13 overs with Graeme Smith. But Bosman has had less success at 50-overs cricket, and his first-class record is puzzlingly modest. He missed the first World Twenty20, officially injured (although he claimed he was fit), and finally reached the world stage in the West Indies in 2010 ... but failed to fire, with 15 runs in four innings. He made a good start to a T20 stint with Derbyshire in 2010, biffing 94 off Yorkshire in his second match, but tailed off a little after that.

THE FACTS Bosman and Graeme Smith shared an opening stand of 170 – a Twenty20 international record – against England at Centurion in November 2009 ... Bosman scored 140 for Griqualand West v Western Province at Kimberley in September 2002 ... On his first-class debut for Griquas in November 1997 Bosman scored 96 against Free State at Bloemfontein ...

THE FIGURES *to 23.9.10*   **ESPN**cricinfo.com

Batting & Fielding	M	Inns	NO	Runs	HS	Avge	S/R	100	50	4s	6s	Ct	St
Tests	0	0	–	–	–	–	–	–	–	–	–	–	–
ODIs	14	12	0	301	88	25.08	98.68	0	2	37	9	3	0
T20Is	10	10	1	272	94	30.22	150.27	0	3	22	17	0	0
First-class	94	169	12	4568	140	29.09	–	5	23	–	–	50	0

Bowling	M	Balls	Runs	Wkts	BB	Avge	RpO	S/R	5i	10m
Tests	0	0	–	–	–	–	–	–	–	–
ODIs	14	0	–	–	–	–	–	–	–	–
T20Is	10	0	–	–	–	–	–	–	–	–
First-class	94	576	343	8	3–25	42.87	3.57	72.00	0	0

JOHAN **BOTHA**

SOUTH AFRICA

Full name	**Johan Botha**
Born	**May 2, 1982, Johannesburg**
Teams	**Warriors**
Style	**Right-hand bat, offspinner**
Test debut	**South Africa v Australia at Sydney 2005-06**
ODI debut	**South Africa v India at Hyderabad 2005-06**
T20I debut	**South Africa v Australia at Brisbane 2005-06**

THE PROFILE Determined and fiercely competitive, Johan Botha started off as a rather ordinary medium-pacer, but one day Mickey Arthur – now South Africa's coach – spotted something else, and Botha dropped his ambitions for speed. He became an offspinner, and started studying the *doosra*. A year later he was touring Sri Lanka with South Africa A, scoring a few runs as well as taking key wickets. He made a promising Test debut in India late in 2005, gating Irfan Pathan during six tidy overs at Hyderabad, and when the selectors later suspected that the Sydney Test pitch would turn, Botha (who was already due to go to Australia for the one-dayers) was flown in early. He managed a couple of wickets, but delight turned to dismay when his jerky action was reported, and he was banned by the ICC on suspicion of throwing. After remedial work he made a low-key international return in the Afro-Asia Cup in India in June 2007, but remains in the frame – especially in one-dayers and Twenty20 games, where he has the priceless ability to keep it tight. He also proved a canny stand-in captain when Graeme Smith was injured in Australia early in 2009, skippering his side to a 4-1 victory in the one-day series. But his *doosra* was reported again, and after tests showed his right elbow flexed by 26.7 degrees – nearly twice the permitted limit of 15 – Botha was told not to bowl his wrong'un again by the ICC. Even without it, he played a useful role in South Africa's World Twenty20 campaign in England, and late in 2010 he became the permanent T20 captain when Smith stood down.

THE FACTS Botha's best bowling remains 6 for 42, for Eastern Province v Northerns at Port Elizabeth in March 2004, when still a medium-pacer ... He made 109 98 for Warriors v Dolphins at Port Elizabeth in October 2009 ... Botha made 101 for South Africa in an Under-19 Test v New Zealand (for whom Brendon McCullum made 186) in February 2001 ... He has captained South Africa in eight ODIs, winnings seven ... Botha's record includes two ODIs for the Africa XI ...

THE FIGURES to 23.9.10

ESPNcricinfo.com

Batting & Fielding	M	Inns	NO	Runs	HS	Avge	S/R	100	50	4s	6s	Ct	St
Tests	3	3	1	54	25	27.00	33.12	0	0	5	0	2	0
ODIs	57	31	10	352	46	16.76	81.48	0	0	33	1	26	0
T20Is	21	13	7	113	28*	18.83	122.82	0	0	9	5	10	0
First-class	63	105	16	3087	109	34.68	–	1	22	–	–	46	0

Bowling	M	Balls	Runs	Wkts	BB	Avge	RpO	S/R	5i	10m
Tests	3	464	280	11	4–56	25.45	3.62	42.18	0	0
ODIs	57	2772	2143	52	4–19	41.21	4.63	53.30	0	0
T20Is	21	420	422	22	3–16	19.18	6.02	19.09	0	0
First-class	63	8835	4503	147	6–42	30.63	3.05	60.10	4	1

MARK **BOUCHER**

Full name	**Mark Verdon Boucher**
Born	**December 3, 1976, East London, Cape Province**
Teams	**Warriors, Bangalore Royal Challengers**
Style	**Right-hand bat, wicketkeeper**
Test debut	**South Africa v Pakistan at Sheikhupura 1997-98**
ODI debut	**South Africa v New Zealand at Perth 1997-98**
T20I debut	**South Africa v New Zealand at Johannesburg 2005-06**

THE PROFILE A man to go to war with, but never against, Mark Boucher packs all the archetypical attributes of the South African cricketer into his short, stocky frame. He is relentlessly competitive, invariably aggressive, and as hard and uncompromising as the new ball. He makes a point of "walking onto the field as if you own the place". He has tucked most of international cricket's wicketkeeping records under his belt, passing 500 Test dismissals during 2010, with 1000 in sight all told. He's played more than 130 Tests, too, although probably his most significant achievement came in only his second one, against Pakistan at Johannesburg in February 1998, when he helped Pat Symcox add 195, a Test ninth-wicket record, from a desperate 166 for 8. Boucher had made his debut a few months previously, still not 21, rushing to Pakistan to replace the injured Dave Richardson, who retired after the Australian tour that followed. Boucher was not everyone's first choice, but once he got his hands into the gloves he refused to let them go, scrapping successfully to regain his spot when occasionally a form dip did cost him his place. He returned just as safe behind the stumps, and adapted his attacking batting to become a one-day "finisher" – qualities he has often transferred to the Test arena, notably helping Graeme Smith to anchor a tense series-clincher at Edgbaston in 2008. Boucher might now be in the autumn of his career, but his commitment to his conditioning should earn him extra years at the top.

THE FACTS Boucher has more dismissals than anyone else in Tests, and only Adam Gilchrist (472) currently heads him in ODIs ... Boucher reached his century against Zimbabwe at Potchefstroom in September 2006 in only 44 balls, the second-fastest in all ODIs ... His 75 consecutive Tests between 1997-98 and 2004-05 is a South African record ... His figures include one Test for the World XI and five ODIs for the Africa XI ...

THE FIGURES to 23.9.10　　　　　　　　　　　ESPNcricinfo.com

Batting & Fielding	M	Inns	NO	Runs	HS	Avge	S/R	100	50	4s	6s	Ct	St
Tests	134	189	22	5171	125	30.96	50.06	5	33	613	20	482	22
ODIs	292	218	56	4664	147*	28.79	84.72	1	26	354	83	400	22
T20Is	25	21	6	268	36*	17.86	97.45	0	0	22	2	18	1
First-class	196	285	40	8279	134	33.79	–	9	51	–	–	660	36

Bowling	M	Balls	Runs	Wkts	BB	Avge	RpO	S/R	5i	10m
Tests	134	8	6	1	1–6	6.00	4.50	8.00	0	0
ODIs	292	0	–	–	–	–	–	–	–	–
T20Is	25	0	–	–	–	–	–	–	–	–
First-class	196	26	26	1	1–6	26.00	6.00	26.00	0	0

DARREN **BRAVO**

Full name	**Darren Michael Bravo**
Born	**February 6, 1989, Santa Cruz, Trinidad**
Teams	**Trinidad & Tobago**
Style	**Left-hand bat, occasional left-arm medium-pacer**
Test debut	**No Tests yet**
ODI debut	**West Indies v India at Kingston 2009**
T20I debut	**West Indies v Zimbabwe at Port-of-Spain 2009-10**

THE PROFILE Darren Bravo is the younger half-brother of allrounder Dwayne, but although he can bowl a bit it is his batting – and quicksilver fielding, like Dwayne's – which aroused the interest of the regional selectors. A left-hander, Bravo junior has a style reminiscent of Brian Lara – not a bad role model – as Chris Gayle, who captained Darren in his first internationals, spotted. "There are some similarities, like the batting technique, and they look alike a bit," said Gayle. "Brian is his idol, and he now has the ability to go from strength to strength. He didn't show any form of nerves in the dressing-room – maybe it was his brother who calmed him down a bit – and he did well in the outfield as well." Bravo himself (who is actually a distant relative of Lara's, on his mother's side, and, like Lara, was born in Santa Cruz in Trinidad) has a mature approach to any lofty comparisons: "I go out there and play my game, the Darren Bravo game, and if in the eyes of the people it looks like Lara, then that is their judgment. At the end of the day it is just my game." Bravo scored 605 runs at 45 in 2008-09, his first full season for Trinidad & Tobago, including centuries against Barbados and the Windward Islands. This pushed him to the fringes of the West Indian side, and he made his debut alongside Dwayne in the short one-day series against India in June, scoring 19 and 21 in the only two innings the weather allowed him. And Darren kept his name in the frame with some eye-catching performances for West Indies A in 2010.

THE FACTS Darren Bravo made his debut for West Indies, alongside his half-brother Dwayne, in the ODI series against India at home in June 2009 ... He made 105 for Trinidad & Tobago v Windward Islands in January 2009, and 111 against Barbados the following month, when he and Kieron Pollard (174) put on 250 for the fourth wicket ... Bravo played in the Under-19 World Cup in Malaysia in 2008, scoring 59 against Papua New Guinea ...

THE FIGURES to 23.9.10   ESPNcricinfo.com

Batting & Fielding	M	Inns	NO	Runs	HS	Avge	S/R	100	50	4s	6s	Ct	St
Tests	0	0	–	–	–	–	–	–	–	–	–	–	–
ODIs	10	8	2	219	74	36.50	83.90	0	1	15	5	3	0
T20Is	1	1	0	0	0	0.00	0.00	0	0	0	0	0	0
First-class	17	26	1	918	111	36.72	–	3	2	–	–	21	0

Bowling	M	Balls	Runs	Wkts	BB	Avge	RpO	S/R	5i	10m
Tests	0	0	–	–	–	–	–	–	–	–
ODIs	4	0	–	–	–	–	–	–	–	–
T20Is	0	0	–	–	–	–	–	–	–	–
First-class	15	22	9	1	1–9	9.00	2.45	22.00	0	0

DWAYNE **BRAVO**

Full name	**Dwayne John Bravo**
Born	**October 7, 1983, Santa Cruz, Trinidad**
Teams	**Trinidad & Tobago, Mumbai Indians, Victoria**
Style	**Right-hand bat, right-arm fast-medium bowler**
Test debut	**West Indies v England at Lord's 2004**
ODI debut	**West Indies v England at Georgetown 2003-04**
T20I debut	**West Indies v New Zealand at Auckland 2005-06**

THE PROFILE   A genuine allrounder (a rare breed, especially in the Caribbean), Dwayne Bravo was born in Santa Cruz, like Brian Lara, and made his one-day debut in April 2004, on the tenth anniversary of Lara's 375. He won his first Test cap at Lord's three months later, aged 20, and took three wickets with his medium-paced swingers. He also displayed a cool, straight bat even though his team was facing a big total. By the end of the series, West Indies were down and out, but at least they knew they had unearthed a special talent. Bravo hit his maiden century against South Africa in Antigua in April 2005, and played an even better innings the following November, 113 at Hobart against the rampant Australians. He continued to chip in with useful runs, while a selection of slower balls makes him a handful in one-dayers, if less so in Tests. He's also electric in the field. Bravo missed the 2009 home Tests against England with a niggling ankle injury, then was left out for the Tests in England that followed – despite being fit enough to play in the Indian Premier League – although he did lift the side visibly in both one-day series. Back in Australia at the end of 2009, he made another century, at Adelaide, then – after recovering from a broken thumb – batted consistently at home against South Africa in June 2010. The previous year Bravo had been one of several players who boycotted the home series against Bangladesh as a contracts dispute festered, and the worry is that, financially secure with Twenty20 deals in Australia and India, he might turn his back on regular international cricket.

THE FACTS   Dwayne Bravo's second Test century – 113 at Hobart late in 2005 – came during a stand of 182 with his fellow-Trinidadian Denesh Ramdin, the day after Trinidad & Tobago qualified for the football World Cup for the first time ... Bravo averages 30.72 with the ball in Tests against Australia – but 81.66 v Pakistan ... He played 27 Tests before finally finishing on the winning side, against Sri Lanka at Port-of-Spain in April 2008 ... Bravo's half-brother Darren has also played for West Indies ...

THE FIGURES *to 23.9.10*   **ᴇsᴨᴨcricinfo.com**

Batting & Fielding	M	Inns	NO	Runs	HS	Avge	S/R	100	50	4s	6s	Ct	St
Tests	37	68	1	2175	113	32.46	48.61	3	13	266	20	39	0
ODIs	107	87	16	1715	112*	24.15	82.13	1	5	138	28	44	0
T20Is	22	20	5	344	66*	22.93	123.29	0	2	22	15	5	0
First-class	94	173	7	5193	197	31.28	–	8	29	–	–	81	0

Bowling	M	Balls	Runs	Wkts	BB	Avge	RpO	S/R	5i	10m
Tests	31	5139	2771	70	6–55	39.58	3.23	73.41	2	0
ODIs	99	3832	3382	114	4–19	29.66	5.29	33.61	0	0
T20Is	15	224	341	14	4–38	24.35	9.13	16.00	0	0
First-class	87	9268	5036	154	6–11	32.70	3.26	60.18	7	0

TIM **BRESNAN**

Full name	**Timothy Thomas Bresnan**
Born	**February 28, 1985, Pontefract, Yorkshire**
Teams	**Yorkshire**
Style	**Right-hand bat, right-arm fast-medium bowler**
Test debut	**England v West Indies at Lord's 2009**
ODI debut	**England v Sri Lanka at Lord's 2006**
T20I debut	**England v Sri Lanka at Southampton 2006**

ENGLAND

THE PROFILE The stocky Tim Bresnan was tipped for higher honours in 2001 after becoming the youngest to play for Yorkshire for 20 years. He quickly progressed to England's youth team, and played in two Under-19 World Cups. The potential took a few years to ripen, but in 2005 he was given more responsibility in a transitional Yorkshire team, and responded with 47 wickets with swinging deliveries which, if a shade short of being truly fast, travel at a fair rate. He can also bat, making three first-class centuries in 2007, the highest an undefeated 126 for England A against the Indians, when he and Stuart Broad put on 129 for the eighth wicket. A good start to the previous season had resulted in a place in a new-look one-day squad against Sri Lanka in June 2006, but Bresnan fell victim to the flashing blades of Sanath Jayasuriya and friends, and took only two wickets in four appearances in what became a clean sweep for the tourists. He then suffered a back injury, and was not in serious consideration for a World Cup spot. He responded well with the bat in 2007, although his form with the ball dipped a little (34 wickets at 34), before a return to bowling form the following year eventually led to a one-day recall. He did finally make his Test debut against West Indies in May 2009, but failed to shine and had to make way for Andrew Flintoff in the Ashes series. Since then, though, he has quietly become a one-day regular.

THE FACTS Bresnan made all three of his first-class centuries during 2007, including 126 not out for England A against the Indian tourists at Chelmsford ... His 80 against Australia at Centurion in October 2009 is the highest score by an England No. 8 in ODIs ... His best bowling figures are 5 for 42 for Yorkshire at Worcester in July 2005 ... Bresnan made his Yorkshire debut in a National League match in 2001, when he was just 16 ...

THE FIGURES to 23.9.10   ■■■■■ cricinfo.com

Batting & Fielding	M	Inns	NO	Runs	HS	Avge	S/R	100	50	4s	6s	Ct	St
Tests	5	3	0	125	91	41.66	36.54	0	1	9	0	3	0
ODIs	33	27	11	408	80	25.50	96.45	0	1	48	1	8	0
T20Is	14	8	4	50	23*	12.50	116.27	0	0	5	0	5	0
First-class	96	127	22	2882	126*	27.44	47.64	3	14	–	–	41	0

Bowling	M	Balls	Runs	Wkts	BB	Avge	RpO	S/R	5i	10m
Tests	5	986	492	14	3–45	35.14	2.99	70.42	0	0
ODIs	33	1599	1415	36	4–28	39.30	5.30	44.41	0	0
T20Is	14	262	334	9	3–10	37.11	7.64	29.11	0	0
First-class	96	15723	8109	250	5–42	32.43	3.09	62.89	4	0

STUART **BROAD**

Full name	**Stuart Christopher John Broad**
Born	**June 24, 1986, Nottingham**
Teams	**Nottinghamshire**
Style	**Left-hand bat, right-arm fast-medium bowler**
Test debut	**England v Sri Lanka at Colombo 2007-08**
ODI debut	**England v Pakistan at Cardiff 2006**
T20I debut	**England v Pakistan at Bristol 2006**

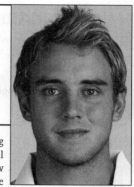

THE PROFILE Stuart Broad was shaping up to be an opening bat just like his dad, Chris, until he suddenly shot up. Already well over six feet with England Under-19 caps under his belt, he grew three inches over the winter of 2005-06. The previous summer he had taken 30 first-class wickets at 27.69 for Leicestershire, his first county. And it got even better in 2006, as he collected four five-fors before an increasingly inevitable summons to England's full one-day side. Brisk, with a smooth action that helps him swing the ball, he made an impressive start to his international career, keeping a cool head in the mayhem of a Twenty20 match, then claiming an early wicket on his one-day debut. He just missed out on initial selection for the World Cup, but stepped in when Jon Lewis returned home, and nervelessly hit the winning runs against West Indies in England's last game. Nerves were also notably absent later in 2007 when Broad and Ravi Bopara spirited England to an unlikely one-day win over India at Old Trafford, and he even kept reasonably cool shortly afterwards when being swatted for six sixes in an over by Yuvraj Singh in the World Twenty20. In the 2009 Ashes he was unimpressive at first, but kept his place, and silenced the critics with a superb spell to set up England's series-winning victory at The Oval. Broad can bat, too, and made up for a disappointing spell by collecting a superb 169 – a long-overdue maiden first-class century – against Pakistan at Lord's in August 2010, during a Test-record eighth-wicket stand with Jonathan Trott.

THE FACTS Broad scored 169 – the highest by an England No. 9 in Tests – and shared a record eighth-wicket partnership of 332 with Jonathan Trott, against Pakistan at Lord's in 2010 ... He took 5 for 23 as South Africa were bowled out for 83 in an ODI at Trent Bridge in August 2008 ... Broad took 6 for 91 (and scored 61) in the fourth Test against Australia at Leeds in 2009 ... Broad's father, Chris, played 25 Tests for England in the 1980s, scoring 1661 runs with six centuries – he's now a match referee (see page 221) ...

THE FIGURES *to 23.9.10*   **ESP∩cricinfo.com**

Batting & Fielding	M	Inns	NO	Runs	HS	Avge	S/R	100	50	4s	6s	Ct	St
Tests	32	45	6	1096	169	28.10	59.33	1	5	141	7	9	0
ODIs	73	43	14	372	45*	12.82	72.37	0	0	24	5	17	0
T20Is	29	11	5	36	10*	6.00	124.13	0	0	3	1	13	0
First-class	73	94	18	1905	169	25.06	53.37	1	11	–	–	21	0

Bowling	M	Balls	Runs	Wkts	BB	Avge	RpO	S/R	5i	10m
Tests	32	6274	3328	97	6–91	34.30	3.18	64.68	3	0
ODIs	73	3710	3187	124	5–23	25.70	5.15	29.91	1	0
T20Is	29	611	755	35	3–17	21.57	7.41	17.45	0	0
First-class	73	13017	7342	253	8–52	29.01	3.38	51.45	12	1

MICHAEL **CARBERRY**

Full name	**Michael Alexander Carberry**
Born	**September 29, 1980, Croydon, Surrey**
Teams	**Hampshire**
Style	**Left-hand bat, occasional offspinner**
Test debut	**England v Bangladesh at Chittagong 2009-10**
ODI debut	**No ODIs yet**
T20I debut	**No T20Is yet**

THE PROFILE Michael Carberry's decision to move to Hampshire, after becoming frustrated with a lack of opportunities at Kent and Surrey (where he made just one appearance in the strong 2002 Championship-winning side), seemed to provide just the spark he needed to reignite his career. In 2007 Carberry, a talented left-hand opener, passed 1000 runs in the Championship, which earned him an England Lions tour of India early in 2008. He did well there, scoring two hundreds, and was also one of three centuries for the Lions against New Zealand at home at the Rose Bowl a few months later. His reputation in domestic cricket continued to grow, and in 2009 he scored 1251 runs at 69.50 in 12 Championship matches – the highlight a fluent 204 against Warwickshire – before a broken finger ended his season. Still, he had done enough to earn himself a stint with the England Performance Programme in South Africa. He made a century against Gauteng, and was added to the full squad for the third Test at Cape Town as cover for Paul Collingwood, who had dislocated a finger. Collingwood recovered in time to play, but Carberry's consolation was a tour place for the Test series in Bangladesh early in 2010. With Andrew Strauss giving the trip a miss Carberry made his debut as Alastair Cook's partner in the first Test at Chittagong, letting no-one down with 34 and 30, but the adaptable Jonathan Trott opened in the second match. Carberry, who is one of the best fielders in the county game, kept his name in the frame by averaging over 50 again in 2010.

THE FACTS Carberry scored 204 for Hampshire v Warwickshire at Southampton in July 2009: his previous-highest score of 192 not out also came against Warwickshire at the Rose Bowl, in 2007 ... His maiden first-class century was for Surrey against Cambridge UCCE in 2002: his second was also at Fenner's, but for Kent in 2003 ...

THE FIGURES to 23.9.10   **ESFN**cricinfo.com

Batting & Fielding	M	Inns	NO	Runs	HS	Avge	S/R	100	50	4s	6s	Ct	St
Tests	1	2	0	64	34	32.00	45.71	0	0	9	0	1	0
ODIs	0	0	–	–	–	–	–	–	–	–	–	–	–
T20Is	0	0	–	–	–	–	–	–	–	–	–	–	–
First-class	112	198	18	7832	204	43.51	52.10	23	36	–	–	50	0

Bowling	M	Balls	Runs	Wkts	BB	Avge	RpO	S/R	5i	10m
Tests	1	0	–	–	–	–	–	–	–	–
ODIs	0	0	–	–	–	–	–	–	–	–
T20Is	0	0	–	–	–	–	–	–	–	–
First-class	112	1201	873	13	2–85	67.15	4.36	92.38	0	0

SHIVNARINE **CHANDERPAUL**

Full name	**Shivnarine Chanderpaul**
Born	**August 16, 1974, Unity Village, Demerara, Guyana**
Teams	**Guyana, Lancashire**
Style	**Left-hand bat, occasional legspinner**
Test debut	**West Indies v England at Georgetown 1993-94**
ODI debut	**West Indies v India at Faridabad 1994-95**
T20I debut	**West Indies v New Zealand at Auckland 2005-06**

THE PROFILE Crouched and crabby at the crease, Shivnarine Chanderpaul proves there is life beyond the coaching handbook. He never seems to play in the V, or off the front foot, but uses soft hands, canny deflections and a whiplash pull to maintain an average nudging 50 over more than 120 Tests. Early on he had a problem converting fifties into hundreds, and also missed a lot of matches, to the point that some thought him a hypochondriac. That was rectified when a large piece of floating bone was removed from his foot in 2000: suitably liberated, he set about rectifying his hundreds problem too, and now has 22 (five each against England, India and South Africa, and four against Australia), including 104 as West Indies successfully chased a world-record 418 to beat the Aussies in Antigua in May 2003. In England the following year he put his first bad trot behind him, narrowly missing twin tons in the Lord's Test. In 2005 he became captain during the first of several acrimonious disputes between the players and the West Indian board, and celebrated with 203 at home in Guyana, although he was too passive in the field to prevent South Africa taking the series. He stood down after an Australian tour where he struggled with bat and microphone, and in England in 2007 he was back to his limpet best, top-scoring in each of his five innings, and going more than 1000 minutes without being out in Tests for the third time in his career (he did it again in 2008). It's not all defence, though: he can blast with the best when he needs to.

THE FACTS Chanderpaul averages 71.86 in Tests against India, but only 28.77 v Zimbabwe ... He scored 303 not out for Guyana v Jamaica at Kingston in January 1996 ... At Georgetown in April 2003 Chanderpaul reached his century against Australia in only 69 balls – the fourth-fastest in Test history by balls faced ... He averages 58.46 in Tests at home, and 41.75 away ... He once managed to shoot a policeman in the hand in his native Guyana, mistaking him for a mugger ...

THE FIGURES to 23.9.10   **ESPNcricinfo.com**

Batting & Fielding	M	Inns	NO	Runs	HS	Avge	S/R	100	50	4s	6s	Ct	St
Tests	126	215	33	8969	203*	49.28	42.78	22	54	1008	27	52	0
ODIs	261	245	38	8648	150	41.77	71.11	11	59	718	83	73	0
T20Is	22	22	5	343	41	20.17	98.84	0	0	34	5	7	0
First-class	254	412	75	18424	303*	54.67	–	53	93	–	–	143	0

Bowling	M	Balls	Runs	Wkts	BB	Avge	RpO	S/R	5i	10m
Tests	126	1680	845	8	1–2	105.62	3.01	210.00	0	0
ODIs	261	740	636	14	3–18	45.42	5.15	52.85	0	0
T20Is	22	0	–	–	–	–	–	–	–	–
First-class	254	4634	2453	56	4–48	43.80	3.17	82.75	0	0

DINESH **CHANDIMAL**

Full name	**Lokuge Dinesh Chandimal**
Born	**November 18, 1989, Balapitiya**
Teams	**Nondescripts, Ruhuna**
Style	**Right-hand bat, wicketkeeper**
Test debut	**No Tests yet**
ODI debut	**Sri Lanka v Zimbabwe at Bulawayo 2010**
T20I debut	**Sri Lanka v New Zealand at Providence 2009-10**

THE PROFILE Dinesh Chandimal is a batsman who can keep wicket, like one of his heroes Romesh Kaluwitharana. He's taller than the diminutive "Kalu", though, at 5ft 9ins (175cm), and has grabbed a full national contract after a seamless run through Sri Lanka's age-group sides. First-class cricket also seemed to pose few terrors: he scored a century in his second match, against the New Zealand tourists in August 2009, and added two more in his next five games. He finished his first full home season with 895 runs at 52.64, and did well enough in limited-overs cricket to earn selection for the World Twenty20 in the West Indies early in 2010. He played in three of the matches there as a batsman, and was called up to keep wicket for the 50-overs team in a tri-series in Zimbabwe in June while Kumar Sangakkara took a rest. Still only 20, Chandimal did a passable impersonation of Sangakkara behind the stumps – and in front of them, too, spanking a superb 111 in only his second ODI, against India at Harare. Cricinfo observed: "He impressed with his shot-selection, his footwork and his aggressive bent of mind: he walked down the track to lift Pankaj Singh over mid-on, welcomed Pragyan Ojha into the attack with a six over long-off and later smashed him over long-on, and crashed Ravichandran Ashwin over long-off and long-on. All these sashays down the pitch were made possible because he used the crease well, often dropping well back to create his own length for his cut shots against the spinners." A fine future beckons for one of Sri Lanka's brightest prospects.

THE FACTS Chandimal scored 111 in an ODI against India at Harare in June 2010 ... He made 64 on his first-class debut, and 109 in his second match, both against the New Zealand tourists in August 2009 ... He hit 164 for Nondescripts v Colombo CC in October 2009 ... Chandimal scored 143 in an Under-19 Test against India when he was 17, and 184 v Bangladesh U-19 in April 2009 ...

THE FIGURES to 23.9.10   **ESPNcricinfo.com**

Batting & Fielding	M	Inns	NO	Runs	HS	Avge	S/R	100	50	4s	6s	Ct	St
Tests	0	0	–	–	–	–	–	–	–	–	–	–	–
ODIs	4	4	2	143	111	71.50	85.11	1	0	9	5	4	1
T20Is	4	3	0	57	29	19.00	103.63	0	0	2	2	0	0
First-class	20	30	3	1577	244	58.40	71.94	5	7	177	37	34	6

Bowling	M	Balls	Runs	Wkts	BB	Avge	RpO	S/R	5i	10m
Tests	0	0	–	–	–	–	–	–	–	–
ODIs	4	0	–	–	–	–	–	–	–	–
T20Is	4	0	–	–	–	–	–	–	–	–
First-class	20	6	1	0	–	–	1.00	–	0	0

PIYUSH **CHAWLA**

Full name	**Piyush Pramod Chawla**
Born	**December 24, 1988, Aligarh, Uttar Pradesh**
Teams	**Uttar Pradesh, Kings XI Punjab**
Style	**Left-hand bat, legspinner**
Test debut	**India v England at Mohali 2005-06**
ODI debut	**India v Bangladesh at Dhaka 2006-07**
T20I debut	**India v South Africa at Gros Islet 2010**

THE PROFILE   Less than a month after he was one of the stars of the Youth World Cup early in 2006, 17-year-old Piyush Chawla was making his Test debut against England, dismissing Andrew Flintoff for 51 as India glided to a nine-wicket win at Mohali. Chawla had always been a young achiever: he first hit the headlines for Uttar Pradesh's Under-14s, scoring 121 then taking 15 wickets for 69 in the demolition of Rajasthan's juniors. In October 2005 he bamboozled Sachin Tendulkar with a googly in the final of the Challenger Trophy (a trial tournament for India's one-day team), and dismissed MS Dhoni and Yuvraj Singh as well, then he led the wicket-takers at the Under-19 World Cup in Sri Lanka. Chawla, who is also no slouch with the bat, has a well-disguised googly and a flipper, and is not afraid to give the ball air. In 2007, he had an extended run in the one-day team, replacing Anil Kumble who retired from the shorter game after the World Cup, and did well against England. He was among the leading wicket-takers in the inaugural IPL season early in 2008, which helped him regain his one-day place for the Asia Cup in Pakistan that June. But apart from taking 4 for 23 against Hong Kong he was disappointing there, and was packed off back to domestic cricket to polish his variations. By 2009-10 he had been bumped down from a Grade B national contract to Grade D, and it was a surprise when he was chosen as the second spinner for the World Twenty20 in the West Indies in 2010.

THE FACTS   Piyush Chawla was 17 years 75 days old when he made his Test debut in March 2006: the only younger Indian debutant was Sachin Tendulkar ... He took 4 for 12 and 6 for 46 as India A hammered a Zimbabwe Select XI at Bulawayo in July 2007 ... Chawla scored 102 not out – his maiden first-class century – for Sussex v Worcestershire at New Road in June 2009: later in the match he took 6 for 152 ...

THE FIGURES to 23.9.10   ᴇꜱᴘɴcricinfo.com

Batting & Fielding	M	Inns	NO	Runs	HS	Avge	S/R	100	50	4s	6s	Ct	St
Tests	2	2	0	5	4	2.50	23.80	0	0	1	0	0	0
ODIs	21	10	5	28	13*	5.60	65.11	0	0	2	0	9	0
T20Is	3	0	–	–	–	–	–	–	–	–	–	2	0
First-class	61	89	9	2257	102*	28.21	–	1	17	–	–	29	0

Bowling	M	Balls	Runs	Wkts	BB	Avge	RpO	S/R	5i	10m
Tests	2	205	137	3	2–66	45.66	4.00	68.33	0	0
ODIs	21	1102	911	28	4–23	32.53	4.96	39.35	0	0
T20Is	3	66	69	2	1–14	34.50	6.27	33.00	0	0
First-class	61	13519	6753	247	6–46	27.34	2.99	54.73	15	2

MICHAEL **CLARKE**

AUSTRALIA

Full name	**Michael John Clarke**
Born	**April 2, 1981, Liverpool, New South Wales**
Teams	**New South Wales**
Style	**Right-hand bat, left-arm orthodox spinner**
Test debut	**Australia v India at Bangalore 2003-04**
ODI debut	**Australia v England at Adelaide 2002-03**
T20I debut	**Australia v New Zealand at Auckland 2004-05**

THE PROFILE Michael Clarke was being touted as an Australian captain before he'd even played a Test. And when he marked his eventual debut with 151 against India in October 2004, his future looked even brighter than the yellow motorbike he received as Man of the Match. Another thrilling century followed on his home debut, and his first Test season ended with the Allan Border Medal. Then came the fall. Barely a year later he was dropped after 15 centuryless Tests. He was told to tighten his technique, especially early on against swing. Clarke remained a one-day regular, but had to wait until the low-key Bangladesh series early in 2006 to reclaim that Test spot. He cemented his place with two tons in the 2006-07 Ashes whitewash, did well in the World Cup, and scored a century in each of Australia's three Test series in 2007-08: he has been a fixture ever since. In England in 2009 Clarke was the classiest batsman on show, finishing with two centuries and a near-miss (93). Soon afterwards he was entrusted with the Twenty20 captaincy, and further responsibility can't be far off. He started as a ravishing shotmaker who did not so much take guard as take off: he radiated a pointy-elbowed elegance reminiscent of the young Greg Chappell or Mark Waugh, who both also waited uncomplainingly for Test openings then started with hundreds. His bouncy fielding and searing run-outs, add to his value, while his slow left-armers can surprise (they once shocked six Indians in a Test at Mumbai). A cricket nut since he was in nappies, "Pup" honed his technique against the bowling machine at his dad's indoor centre.

THE FACTS Clarke scored a century on his Test debut, 151 v India at Bangalore in 2004-05, and the following month added another in his first home Test, 141 v New Zealand at Brisbane: only two other batsmen (Harry Graham and Kepler Wessels) have done this for Australia ... Clarke averages 63.50 in Tests against Pakistan, but only 15.50 v Scotland (and 0.00 v Ireland) ...

THE FIGURES to 23.9.10   ESPncricinfo.com

Batting & Fielding	M	Inns	NO	Runs	HS	Avge	S/R	100	50	4s	6s	Ct	St
Tests	62	101	12	4514	168	50.71	53.52	14	19	495	19	61	0
ODIs	178	162	34	5509	130	43.03	77.62	4	42	456	29	69	0
T20Is	33	27	5	472	67	21.45	103.96	0	1	28	9	13	0
First-class	120	204	20	8475	201*	46.05	–	28	34	–	–	118	0

Bowling	M	Balls	Runs	Wkts	BB	Avge	RpO	S/R	5i	10m
Tests	62	1636	782	20	6–9	39.10	2.86	81.80	1	0
ODIs	178	2234	1886	52	5–35	36.26	5.06	42.96	1	0
T20Is	33	156	225	6	1–2	37.50	8.65	26.00	0	0
First-class	120	2816	1470	31	6–9	47.41	3.13	90.83	1	0

PAUL **COLLINGWOOD**

Full name	**Paul David Collingwood**
Born	**May 26, 1976, Shotley Bridge, Co. Durham**
Teams	**Durham, Dehli Daredevils**
Style	**Right-hand bat, right-arm medium-pace bowler**
Test debut	**England v Sri Lanka at Galle 2003-04**
ODI debut	**England v Pakistan at Birmingham 2001**
T20I debut	**England v Australia at Southampton 2005**

THE PROFILE A natural athlete, with a happy-go-lucky temperament, Paul Collingwood became the first England captain ever to capture a global tournament when England won the World Twenty20 in Barbados in 2010. It was reward for nine years of uncomplaining professionalism, in which time he scrapped his way past several seemingly more talented rivals to make himself indispensable in both forms of the game. He had made the one-day side in 2001, but four years and numerous tours later had won only three Test caps, although the third of those was the 2005 Ashes decider at The Oval. He still seemed destined to be the uncomplaining stand-in – but that winter struck 96 and 80 at Lahore, and added a brilliant century against India, as England struggled with injuries. Then a superb 186 against Pakistan at Lord's booked a middle-order place at last, and Collingwood later joined rarefied company with an Ashes double-century at Adelaide. By 2008 his technique looked in need of a 50,000-mile service, although a defiant 135 against South Africa at Edgbaston probably saved his Test career. The following season his 344-minute 74 did much to save the first Ashes Test at Cardiff, but he looked careworn by the end of that series, making only 112 more runs in the remaining four Tests. Collingwood remains a superb fielder, capable of breathtaking moments at backward point or in the slips. His bowling, which verges on the dibbly-dobbly, is negligible in Tests, but given the right conditions he can be irresistible in one-dayers – as at Trent Bridge in 2005, when he followed a century against Bangladesh with 6 for 31.

THE FACTS Collingwood's century and six wickets in the same match – against Bangladesh at Nottingham in 2005 – is unmatched in ODI history: his 6 for 31 that day are also England's best one-day bowling figures ... He made 206 at Adelaide in December 2006, England's first double-century in a Test in Australia since Wally Hammond in 1936-37 ... In September 2006 he became the 11th man to play 100 ODIs for England ...

THE FIGURES to 23.9.10   ᴇsᴘⁿcricinfo.com

Batting & Fielding	M	Inns	NO	Runs	HS	Avge	S/R	100	50	4s	6s	Ct	St
Tests	63	109	10	4176	206	42.18	46.44	10	20	462	24	87	0
ODIs	189	173	35	4978	120*	36.07	76.57	5	26	359	72	105	0
T20Is	33	31	2	561	79	19.34	130.76	0	3	35	24	12	0
First-class	188	325	26	10977	206	36.71	–	24	56	–	–	214	0

Bowling	M	Balls	Runs	Wkts	BB	Avge	RpO	S/R	5i	10m
Tests	63	1719	945	15	3–23	63.00	3.29	114.60	0	0
ODIs	189	4898	4095	106	6–31	38.63	5.01	46.20	1	0
T20Is	33	222	329	16	4–22	20.56	8.89	13.87	0	0
First-class	188	9665	4928	121	5–52	40.72	3.05	79.87	1	0

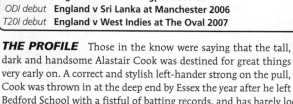

ALASTAIR **COOK**

ENGLAND

Full name	**Alastair Nathan Cook**
Born	**December 25, 1984, Gloucester**
Teams	**Essex**
Style	**Left-hand bat, occasional offspinner**
Test debut	**England v India at Nagpur 2005-06**
ODI debut	**England v Sri Lanka at Manchester 2006**
T20I debut	**England v West Indies at The Oval 2007**

THE PROFILE Those in the know were saying that the tall, dark and handsome Alastair Cook was destined for great things very early on. A correct and stylish left-hander strong on the pull, Cook was thrown in at the deep end by Essex the year after he left Bedford School with a fistful of batting records, and has barely looked back since. His early England career was full of successes, although a barren spell in 2010 briefly threatened his place before a century against Pakistan at The Oval – a rather more frenetic affair than Cook's usual knocks – saved his skin for a while. He had looked increasingly vulnerable around off stump, with a tendency to play around the front pad proving costly. Cook had already lost his one-day place after a moderate run, not helped by his fielding sometimes being less than scintillating. He captained England in the Under-19 World Cup in 2004, scored his maiden first-class hundred later that year, and added a double-century for Essex against the Australians in 2005. The following spring he was called up by the full England side when injuries struck in India. He had been in the Caribbean with the A team when the SOS came but, unfazed, stroked 60 and a magnificent century to complete a memorable debut in Nagpur. He remained consistent, seemingly at ease with the pressure, and was a shoo-in for the 2006-07 Ashes where, although he was hardly prolific (276 runs), he did manage a century in Perth. Bowlers began to exploit that penchant for hanging on the front foot, but Cook still made his share of runs, with a languid ease reminiscent of David Gower, if slightly more stiff-legged.

THE FACTS Cook was the 16th England batsman to make a century on Test debut ... Cook's stand of 127 with Marcus Trescothick v Sri Lanka at Lord's in 2006 was the second-highest in Tests by unrelated players who share a birthday, behind 163 by Vic Stollmeyer and Kenneth Weekes (both born Jan 24) for West Indies at The Oval in 1939 ... Cook made centuries in both his Tests as England captain (against Bangladesh in 2009-10) ...

THE FIGURES *to 23.9.10*   **ESPN**cricinfo.com

Batting & Fielding	M	Inns	NO	Runs	HS	Avge	S/R	100	50	4s	6s	Ct	St
Tests	60	108	6	4364	173	42.78	48.33	13	22	515	4	52	0
ODIs	26	26	0	858	102	33.00	71.38	1	5	93	1	10	0
T20Is	4	4	0	61	26	15.25	112.96	0	0	10	0	1	0
First-class	133	237	18	9700	195	44.29	53.30	26	52	–	–	127	0

Bowling	M	Balls	Runs	Wkts	BB	Avge	RpO	S/R	5i	10m
Tests	60	6	1	0	–	–	1.00	–	0	0
ODIs	26	0	–	–	–	–	–	–	–	–
T20Is	4	0	–	–	–	–	–	–	–	–
First-class	133	270	205	6	3–13	34.16	4.55	45.00	0	0

DANISH KANERIA

Full name	**Danish Parabha Shanker Kaneria**
Born	**December 16, 1980, Karachi, Sind**
Teams	**Sind, Habib Bank, Essex**
Style	**Right-hand bat, legspinner**
Test debut	**Pakistan v England at Faisalabad 2000-01**
ODI debut	**Pakistan v Zimbabwe at Sharjah 2001-02**
T20I debut	**No T20Is yet**

THE PROFILE A tall, wiry legspinner, Danish Kaneria mastered the dark arts of wrist-spin at an early age. His stock ball drifts in to the right-hander, and he has a googly as cloaked as any. His whirling approach is reminiscent of Abdul Qadir's, and he picked up the baton from Mushtaq Ahmed as Pakistan's premier legspinner. Kaneria was hyped as a secret weapon when England toured in 2000-01, and although his impact in that series was minimal he made his mark afterwards. Initially he did so against Bangladesh, but then turned it on against South Africa too, when his five-for decided the Lahore Test in October 2003. Since then, Kaneria has quietly moved past 250 Test wickets. Two tours in 2004-05 – to Australia and India, the graveyard of legspin – were arduous but satisfying stepping stones to the big league. In each series he out-scalped the opposition's leading legspinner – Shane Warne, then Anil Kumble – and although Pakistan still lost to Australia, Kaneria's 19 wickets were crucial to a morale-boosting draw in India. He ended 2005 with two more matchwinning last-day turns against England at home, but proved expensive when the teams reconvened the following summer in England, where he has had a lot of success with Essex. Back in England in 2010 he bowled indifferently in the first Test, and was summarily axed from the squad. A back number in one-dayers, he had played only one of Pakistan's previous 27 ODIs before being a surprise inclusion for the 2007 World Cup. He did well enough, but lost his place again in the fallout from that disastrous campaign.

THE FACTS Danish Kaneria was only the second Hindu to play for Pakistan – the first, 1980s wicketkeeper Anil Dalpat, is his cousin ... He took 12 for 92 in his third Test, against Bangladesh in August 2001 ... Kaneria averages 16.41 v Bangladesh – but 49.48 v England ... He has conceded more than 100 runs in an innings 39 times in 61 Tests ... He took 0 for 208 for Essex v Lancashire at Manchester in 2005, equalling the most expensive wicketless spell in the County Championship, set by Peter Smith, another Essex legspinner, in 1934 ...

THE FIGURES to 23.9.10

ESPNcricinfo.com

Batting & Fielding	M	Inns	NO	Runs	HS	Avge	S/R	100	50	4s	6s	Ct	St
Tests	61	84	33	360	29	7.05	48.45	0	0	46	3	18	0
ODIs	18	10	8	12	6*	6.00	54.54	0	0	1	0	2	0
T20Is	0	0	–	–	–	–	–	–	–	–	–	–	–
First-class	180	229	81	1515	65	10.23	–	0	1	–	–	60	0

Bowling	M	Balls	Runs	Wkts	BB	Avge	RpO	S/R	5i	10m
Tests	61	17697	9082	261	7–77	34.79	3.07	67.80	15	2
ODIs	18	854	683	15	3–31	45.53	4.79	56.93	0	0
T20Is	0	0	–	–	–	–	–	–	–	–
First-class	180	47825	23489	885	8–59	26.54	2.94	54.03	61	10

STEVE **DAVIES**

ENGLAND

Full name	**Steven Michael Davies**
Born	**June 17, 1986, Bromsgrove, Worcestershire**
Teams	**Surrey**
Style	**Left-hand bat, wicketkeeper**
Test debut	**No Tests yet**
ODI debut	**England v Australia at Centurion 2009-10**
T20I debut	**England v West Indies at Port-of-Spain 2008-09**

THE PROFILE One thing England are rarely short of is quality wicketkeeper-batsmen, and Steve Davies has emerged from a posse of contenders to claim a place at the top table. He has elbowed Craig Kieswetter out of the 50-overs team, and swiped the keeper's gloves from him in Twenty20s too: meanwhile Matt Prior is aware that only continued excellence behind and in front of the stumps will keep him ahead of Davies in the Test reckoning. Alec Stewart, a distinguished predecessor in the role himself for both Surrey and England, thinks it might not come to that: he feels Davies is talented enough to play for England solely as a batsman – he's an uncomplicated left-hander who likes to give the ball a thump. Davies started with Worcestershire, finishing above Graeme Hick in the batting averages in his debut summer of 2005. His batting and keeping continued to attract good reviews, and a fine season with the bat in one-day cricket in 2008 – 689 runs at 49 – won him a spot as the second keeper for England's tour of the West Indies early in 2009. Davies played in the sole Twenty20 international of that trip – and top-scored with 27 in a chastening defeat – but then found himself shoved down the pecking order when the South African-born Kieswetter completed his qualification period and began his England career in fine style. However, Davies's rocket-fuelled start to 2010 after switching counties and joining Surrey, coupled with Kieswetter's disappointing season, helped Davies back to favour, and he cracked 87 from 67 balls in a one-dayer against Pakistan at Chester-le-Street in September 2010.

THE FACTS Davies made 192 for Worcestershire v Gloucestershire at Bristol in June 2006 ... In 2010 Davies scored 477 first-class runs in April, a number exceeded in England only three times (Chris Rogers, with 563 in 2010, has the most) ... He has scored five centuries in List A (senior one-day) matches, all of them at better than a run a ball ...

THE FIGURES to 23.9.10   **cricinfo.com**

Batting & Fielding	M	Inns	NO	Runs	HS	Avge	S/R	100	50	4s	6s	Ct	St
Tests	0	0	–	–	–	–	–	–	–	–	–	–	–
ODIs	6	6	0	202	87	33.66	106.31	0	1	31	0	8	0
T20Is	3	3	0	69	33	23.00	127.77	0	0	9	0	2	1
First-class	91	152	18	5371	192	40.08	63.81	8	28	–	–	275	14

Bowling	M	Balls	Runs	Wkts	BB	Avge	RpO	S/R	5i	10m
Tests	0	0	–	–	–	–	–	–	–	–
ODIs	6	0	–	–	–	–	–	–	–	–
T20Is	3	0	–	–	–	–	–	–	–	–
First-class	91	0	–	–	–	–	–	–	–	–

AB de VILLIERS

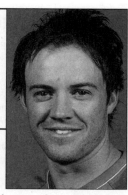

Full name	**Abraham Benjamin de Villiers**
Born	**February 17, 1984, Pretoria**
Teams	**Titans, Delhi Daredevils**
Style	**Right-hand bat, occ. medium-pacer, wicketkeeper**
Test debut	**South Africa v England at Port Elizabeth 2004-05**
ODI debut	**South Africa v England at Bloemfontein 2004-05**
T20I debut	**South Africa v Australia at Johannesburg 2005-06**

THE PROFILE A batsman of breathtaking chutzpah and enterprise, as well as the skills and the temperament required to back up his creative intent. A fielder able to leap tall buildings and still come up with the catch. A wicketkeeper who is perfectly at ease donning pads and gloves. A fine rugby player, golfer, and tennis player. All AB de Villiers needs to show off his abundant gifts is a ball ... just about any ball. Cricket should be pleased to have him. Few drive the ball as sweetly and to the boundary as regularly, and – in South Africa, at any rate – even fewer possess the silkily snappy footwork required to put spinners in their place. He adjusts seamlessly to all formats, averaging in the mid-forties in both Tests and ODIs. His potential was recognised years before he made the leap to senior international level as an opening batsman against England at Port Elizabeth in 2004-05. After a brief slump in form in 2006 and 2007, de Villiers returned to the straight and narrow early in 2008 with a blistering 103 not out off 109 balls against West Indies at Durban. Later that year came his career highlight so far, an undefeated 217 at Ahmedabad, South Africa's first double-century against India. South Africans do not take easily to the precociously talented, but it helps if they do not come across all precocious. Such is the case with de Villiers, whose lazy smile under an every-which-way thatch of blond hair has helped convince the nation that he's worth feeding despite all that talent.

THE FACTS de Villiers made 217 not out at Ahmedabad in April 2008, after India had been bowled out for 76 ... He averages 79.76 in Tests against West Indies – but 17.25 in four matches against Bangladesh ... He scored 151, his maiden first-class century, for Titans v Western Province Boland in October 2004, sharing a stand of 317 with Martin van Jaarsveld ... de Villiers went a Test-record 78 innings before falling for a duck, against Bangladesh at Centurion in November 2008 ... His record includes five ODIs for the Africa XI ...

THE FIGURES to 23.9.10   **ESPncricinfo.com**

Batting & Fielding	M	Inns	NO	Runs	HS	Avge	S/R	100	50	4s	6s	Ct	St
Tests	61	105	12	4232	217*	45.50	52.68	10	23	498	25	86	1
ODIs	101	97	14	3616	146	43.56	89.41	7	22	362	58	63	0
T20Is	30	29	6	579	79*	25.17	125.05	0	4	42	20	32	4
First-class	85	148	17	6081	217*	46.41	55.91	13	37	–	–	132	2

Bowling	M	Balls	Runs	Wkts	BB	Avge	RpO	S/R	5i	10m
Tests	61	198	99	2	2–49	49.50	3.00	99.00	0	0
ODIs	101	12	22	0	–	–	11.00	–	0	0
T20Is	30	0	–	–	–	–	–	–	–	–
First-class	85	228	133	2	2–49	66.50	3.50	114.00	0	0

WEST INDIES

NARSINGH **DEONARINE**

Full name	**Narsingh Deonarine**
Born	**August 16, 1983, Albion, Berbice, Guyana**
Teams	**Guyana**
Style	**Left-hand bat, offspinner**
Test debut	**West Indies v South Africa at Georgetown 2004-05**
ODI debut	**West Indies v India at Dambulla 2005**
T20I debut	**West Indies v Australia at Hobart 2009-10**

THE PROFILE In many respects Narsingh Deonarine is a carbon copy of his distinguished Guyana team-mate Shivnarine Chanderpaul. Both are small, wiry left-handers – although Deonarine is not quite so open and unorthodox at the crease – and both field sharply in the covers. Deonarine also affects the anti-glare patches under the eyes that Chanderpaul borrowed from baseball. Deonarine also started as a handy offspinner, with an easy delivery not unlike Carl Hooper's, although he doesn't bowl so much these days. It was his bowling which first helped him into the regional team in 2005, and he toured Sri Lanka later that year after several leading players dropped out following a contracts dispute. When the seniors returned, however, there was no place for Deonarine – and for four years it looked as if that was his solitary flirtation with the international game. But in 2008-09 he topped 1000 runs for Guyana, finishing as the leading scorer in the regional tournament, and was recalled for the tour of England: although he didn't make the side there, he did make it in Australia, scoring 82 at Perth. Some handy innings followed against South Africa in mid-2010, to suggest that Guyana might be providing much of the West Indian middle-order fibre for a while yet, although there were grumbles about his level of fitness. The feeling persists that Deonarine might not score quickly enough for one-dayers, although he did contribute some handy innings in 2009-10, notably a calm 65 not out to calm the nerves after a wobble against Zimbabwe at Providence in March.

THE FACTS Deonarine scored 198 for Guyana v Combined Campuses and Colleges at Georgetown in March 2009: that season he was the leading run-scorer in the West Indian domestic tournament with 1068 ... Deonarine's maiden first-class century was 100 for West Indies B v India A at Bridgetown in March 2003 ... He took 5 for 94 for Guyana v Leeward Islands in St Maarten in January 2006 ...

THE FIGURES *to 23.9.10*   ESPNcricinfo.com

Batting & Fielding	M	Inns	NO	Runs	HS	Avge	S/R	100	50	4s	6s	Ct	St
Tests	8	13	1	370	82	30.83	40.13	0	2	40	4	5	0
ODIs	20	19	3	510	65*	31.87	69.48	0	4	42	7	6	0
T20Is	7	6	1	49	36*	9.80	98.00	0	0	4	0	0	0
First-class	83	143	18	4724	198	37.79	–	7	30	–	–	52	0

Bowling	M	Balls	Runs	Wkts	BB	Avge	RpO	S/R	5i	10m
Tests	8	503	246	4	2–74	61.50	2.93	125.75	0	0
ODIs	20	321	312	6	2–18	52.00	5.83	53.50	0	0
T20Is	7	36	50	0	–	–	8.33	–	0	0
First-class	83	6235	2945	86	5–94	34.24	2.83	72.50	1	0

MAHENDRA SINGH **DHONI**

Full name	**Mahendra Singh Dhoni**
Born	**July 7, 1981, Ranchi, Bihar**
Teams	**Jharkhand, Chennai Super Kings**
Style	**Right-hand bat, wicketkeeper**
Test debut	**India v Sri Lanka at Chennai 2005-06**
ODI debut	**India v Bangladesh at Chittagong 2004-05**
T20I debut	**India v South Africa at Johannesburg 2006-07**

THE PROFILE The odds against a Virender Sehwag clone emerging from the backwaters of Jharkhand (formerly Bihar) were highly remote – until MS Dhoni arrived (a one-time railway ticket collector, his first love was football). His batting is swashbuckling, and his wicketkeeping secure. It wasn't until 2004 that he became a serious contender: there was a rapid hundred as East Zone clinched the Deodhar Trophy, an audacious 60 in the Duleep Trophy final, and two tons against Pakistan A which established him as a clinical destroyer of bowling attacks. In just his fifth ODI – against Pakistan in April 2005 – Dhoni cracked a dazzling 148, putting even Sehwag in the shade, and followed that with 183 against Sri Lanka in November, beating Adam Gilchrist's highest ODI score by a wicketkeeper. He made an instant impact in Tests, too, pounding 148 at Faisalabad in only his fifth match, when India were struggling to avoid the follow-on. His keeping improved, and he quickly became a key member of a revitalised side. He stepped up to captain the eventual winners in the World Twenty20 in September 2007, then made headlines as the most expensive signing ($1.5million) for the inaugural IPL season in 2008. He took over as full-time Test captain when Anil Kumble retired that November, rubber-stamping victory over Australia then defeating England and New Zealand in short series. He won eight of his first 11 Tests – an unprecedented start for an Indian skipper – and seems happy and secure in the role, although he will want to address his side's patchy performances in 50- and 20-overs global tournaments before he's done.

THE FACTS Dhoni's unbeaten 183 against Sri Lanka at Jaipur in November 2005 is the highest score in ODIs by a wicketkeeper, and included 120 in boundaries (10 sixes and 15 fours) ... Dhoni won eight of his first 11 Tests as captain, and didn't lose any ... The only other Indian to score a century in an ODI in which he kept wicket is Rahul Dravid ... Dhoni's record includes three ODIs for the Asia XI ...

THE FIGURES to 23.9.10   **ᴇsᴘᴨcricinfo.com**

Batting & Fielding	M	Inns	NO	Runs	HS	Avge	S/R	100	50	4s	6s	Ct	St
Tests	46	70	9	2556	148	41.90	60.69	4	18	280	45	119	20
ODIs	171	152	39	5733	183*	50.73	88.36	7	37	442	119	170	55
T20Is	25	24	7	441	46	25.94	112.21	0	0	26	13	11	3
First-class	87	136	12	4718	148	38.04	–	7	32	–	–	227	39

Bowling	M	Balls	Runs	Wkts	BB	Avge	RpO	S/R	5i	10m
Tests	46	12	14	0	–	–	7.00	–	0	0
ODIs	171	12	14	1	1–14	14.00	7.00	12.00	0	0
T20Is	25	0	–	–	–	–	–	–	–	–
First-class	87	42	34	0	–	–	4.85	–	0	0

TILLAKARATNE **DILSHAN**

SRI LANKA

Full name	**Tillakaratne Mudiyanselage Dilshan**
Born	**October 14, 1976, Kalutara**
Teams	**Bloomfield, Basnahira South, Delhi Daredevils**
Style	**Right-hand bat, offspinner**
Test debut	**Sri Lanka v Zimbabwe at Bulawayo 1999-2000**
ODI debut	**Sri Lanka v Zimbabwe at Bulawayo 1999-2000**
T20I debut	**Sri Lanka v England at Southampton 2006**

THE PROFILE Tillakaratne Mudiyanselage Dilshan, who started life as Tuwan Mohamad Dilshan before converting to Buddhism, is a light-footed right-hander who burst onto the international scene with an unbeaten 163 against Zimbabwe in only his second Test in November 1999. Technically sound, comfortable against fast bowling, possessed of quick feet, strong wrists and natural timing, Dilshan has talent in abundance. But that bright start was followed by a frustrating time when he was shovelled up and down the order, and in and out of the side. After a lean series against England in 2001 he didn't play another Test until England toured again, late in 2003. He came back determined to play his own natural aggressive game. This approach was immediately successful, with several good scores against England and Australia. He has continued to be a steady middle-order influence, and was one of four centuries in an innings victory over India in July 2008. He put a lean trot in ODIs behind him just in time for the 2007 World Cup, where he made some useful runs in Sri Lanka's march to the final. Against Bangladesh at Chittagong in January 2009 he hit 162 and 143 then wrapped up the match with four wickets, and later in the year lit up the World Twenty20 in England with some spectacular batting, including his own trademark cheeky scoop over the shoulder. In all, he made ten international centuries during 2009, although the first half of 2010 was rather less spectacular. Dilshan, who started out as a wicketkeeper, is an electric fielder, and once effected four run-outs in an ODI at Adelaide.

THE FACTS Dilshan was the leading runscorer (317) at the World Twenty20 in England in 2009 ... He scored 168 against Bangladesh in Colombo in September 2005: he put on 280 with Thilan Samaraweera, a Sri Lankan fifth-wicket record in Tests ... Dilshan made his first ODI century in the record total of 443 for 9 against the Netherlands at Amstelveen in July 2006 ... He made 200 not out while captaining North Central Province v Central in Colombo in February 2005 ...

THE FIGURES to 23.9.10

ESFNcricinfo.com

Batting & Fielding	M	Inns	NO	Runs	HS	Avge	S/R	100	50	4s	6s	Ct	St
Tests	63	101	11	3906	168	43.40	65.63	11	15	479	18	73	0
ODIs	188	165	29	4860	160	35.73	87.36	8	20	490	30	80	1
T20Is	31	30	5	717	96*	28.68	120.50	0	5	86	12	13	2
First-class	198	320	22	11572	200*	38.83	–	30	48	–	–	337	23

Bowling	M	Balls	Runs	Wkts	BB	Avge	RpO	S/R	5i	10m
Tests	63	1184	590	16	4–10	36.87	2.98	74.00	0	0
ODIs	188	2881	2281	54	4–29	42.24	4.75	53.35	0	0
T20Is	31	120	151	4	2–4	37.75	7.55	30.00	0	0
First-class	198	3796	1841	59	5–49	31.20	2.90	64.33	1	0

RAHUL **DRAVID**

Full name	**Rahul Sharad Dravid**
Born	**January 11, 1973, Indore, Madhya Pradesh**
Teams	**Karnataka, Bangalore Royal Challengers**
Style	**Right-hand bat, occasional wicketkeeper**
Test debut	**India v England at Lord's 1996**
ODI debut	**India v Sri Lanka at Singapore 1995-96**
T20I debut	**No T20Is yet**

THE PROFILE Rahul Dravid has scored more than 10,000 runs in both Tests and ODIs at imposing averages – but impressive as his stats are, they don't show his importance, or the beauty of his batting. When he started, he was pigeonholed as a blocker (an early nickname was "The Wall"), but he grew in stature, finally reaching maturity under Sourav Ganguly's captaincy. As a new India emerged, so did a new Dravid: first, he became an astute one-day finisher, then produced several superb Test performances. His golden phase really began with a supporting act, at Kolkata early in 2001, when his 180 helped VVS Laxman create history against Australia. But after that Dravid became India's most valuable player: at one point he hit four double-centuries in eight months, finishing with an epic 270 to seal the 2004 tour of Pakistan with a victory. In October 2005 he was appointed as one-day captain, began with a 6-1 hammering of Sri Lanka at home, and soon succeeded Ganguly as Test skipper too. He continued to score well, and bounced back from the crushing disappointment of early exit from the 2007 World Cup by leading India to a rare Test-series victory in England, although his own batting lacked sparkle. He relinquished the captaincy after that, but the runs refused to flow: he lost his one-day place, but just as serious questions were being asked about his Test future, Dravid ground out 136 in nearly eight hours against England at Mohali, to ensure a series victory in December 2008. The following year he scored 177, 38, 144 and 74 at home against Sri Lanka, to show that "The Wall" wasn't ready to be demolished just yet.

THE FACTS Dravid hit centuries in four successive Test innings in 2002, three in England and one against West Indies ... He kept wicket in 73 ODIs ... Unusually, Dravid averages more in away Tests (55.53) than at home in India (49.75) ... He averages 97.90 in Tests against Zimbabwe, but only 36.51 v South Africa ... Dravid's record includes one Test and three ODIs for the World XI, and one ODI for the Asia XI ...

THE FIGURES to 23.9.10   **ESP11**cricinfo.com

Batting & Fielding	M	Inns	NO	Runs	HS	Avge	S/R	100	50	4s	6s	Ct	St
Tests	142	245	28	11490	270	52.94	42.34	29	58	1444	18	196	0
ODIs	339	313	40	10765	153	39.43	71.17	12	82	941	42	196	14
T20Is	0	0	–	–	–	–	–	–	–	–	–	–	–
First-class	274	453	63	21873	270	56.08	–	60	112	–	–	337	1

Bowling	M	Balls	Runs	Wkts	BB	Avge	RpO	S/R	5i	10m
Tests	134	120	39	1	1–18	39.00	1.95	120.00	0	0
ODIs	336	186	170	4	2–43	42.50	5.48	46.50	0	0
T20Is	0	0	–	–	–	–	–	–	–	–
First-class	261	617	273	5	2–16	54.60	2.65	123.40	0	0

J-P **DUMINY**

Full name	**Jean-Paul Duminy**
Born	**April 14, 1984, Strandfontein, Cape Town**
Teams	**Cape Cobras, Mumbai Indians**
Style	**Left-hand bat, occasional offspinner**
Test debut	**South Africa v Australia at Perth 2008-09**
ODI debut	**South Africa v Sri Lanka at Colombo 2004-05**
T20I debut	**South Africa v Bangladesh at Cape Town 2007-08**

THE PROFILE A slightly built but stylish left-hander, J-P Duminy had trouble finding a place in South Africa's strong middle order – but when an injury to Ashwell Prince finally let him into the Test side in Australia late in 2008, more than four years after his one-day debut, he certainly made it count. First Duminy stroked a nerveless 50 not out as his side made light of a target of 414 to start with victory at Perth, then he set up a series-winning victory at Melbourne with a superb 166, most of it coming during an eye-popping ninth-wicket stand of 180 with Dale Steyn. A four-hour 73 followed in the return series in a defeat at Durban: Duminy had arrived, a fact confirmed by a big-money IPL contract. He had first featured in a one-day series in Sri Lanka in 2004. He struggled in the one-dayers there, scoring only 29 runs in five attempts, and dropped off the national radar for a couple of years. But he continued to make runs at home, and was given an extended one-day run after the 2007 World Cup, showing signs of developing into a late-innings "finisher": he batted into the final over in three successive victories against West Indies. He finished that series with 227 runs at 113.50, although he was less of a hit in England later in 2008. A horror run in Tests in 2009-10 – only one score above 11 in nine innings – cost him his place, but Duminy seems sure to bounce back. He is also a superb fielder, and his part-time offbreaks occasionally come in handy.

THE FACTS Duminy scored 169 as Cape Cobras followed on against the Eagles at Stellenbosch in February 2007 ... He scored 265 not out for the South African Academy against Pakistan's at Lahore in August 2005 ... Duminy made 111 not out in an ODI against Zimbabwe at Centurion in November 2009 ... He made 116 in an Under-19 Test at Worcester in August 2003, before being caught and bowled by Alastair Cook ...

THE FIGURES to 23.9.10   **ESPNcricinfo.com**

Batting & Fielding	M	Inns	NO	Runs	HS	Avge	S/R	100	50	4s	6s	Ct	St
Tests	12	20	2	518	166	28.77	40.91	1	3	61	3	12	0
ODIs	58	51	12	1391	111*	35.66	80.59	1	7	98	14	23	0
T20Is	25	24	5	456	78	24.00	122.25	0	2	37	13	12	0
First-class	61	102	17	4085	169	48.05	48.61	12	21	–	–	47	0

Bowling	M	Balls	Runs	Wkts	BB	Avge	RpO	S/R	5i	10m
Tests	12	671	408	11	3–89	37.09	3.64	61.0	0	0
ODIs	58	697	581	16	3–31	36.31	5.00	43.5	0	0
T20Is	25	42	52	4	1–3	13.00	7.42	10.5	0	0
First-class	61	2324	1384	35	5–108	39.54	3.57	66.4	1	0

FIDEL **EDWARDS**

Full name	**Fidel Henderson Edwards**
Born	**February 6, 1982, Gays, St Peter, Barbados**
Teams	**Barbados, Deccan Chargers**
Style	**Right-hand bat, right-arm fast bowler**
Test debut	**West Indies v Sri Lanka at Kingston 2002-03**
ODI debut	**West Indies v Zimbabwe at Harare 2003-04**
T20I debut	**West Indies v South Africa at Johannesburg 2007-08**

THE PROFILE Fidel Edwards had an extraordinary start in international cricket, the kind that can either haunt or add lustre to a career. He was spotted in the nets by Brian Lara early in 2003 and called up for his Test debut after only one match for Barbados: he promptly took five wickets against Sri Lanka. He added five in his first overseas Test, and six in his first ODI. Edwards has a slingy round-arm action which leaves him vulnerable to back strains, and indeed he missed most of 2010 after back surgery to correct a slipped disc, which put a question-mark over his international future. When he's fit, though, his unusual action and slippery pace has troubled many a distinguished batsman. Edwards bowls fast, can swing the ball and reverse it too, but insists that he doesn't go for out-and-out pace – which is just as well, because he has learned that pace without control leads straight to the boundary at international level. He showed his increased maturity with a testing spell in Antigua in June 2006 that had India's Virender Sehwag in all kinds of trouble before a hamstring twanged. And he hurried England's batsmen up in 2007, taking nine wickets in two Tests and ten – including 5 for 45 at Lord's – as West Indies won the one-day series 2-1. After that he grabbed eight more, including both openers in both innings, in the first Test against Australia at Kingston in May 2008. He's not much of a batsman, yet twice hung on tenaciously to deny England series-levelling victories in the Caribbean early in 2009.

THE FACTS Edwards had played only one first-class match – taking one wicket – before his Test debut against Sri Lanka at Kingston in June 2003, when he took 5 for 36 ... He later took 6 for 22 on his ODI debut, against Zimbabwe at Harare in November 2003 ... Edwards opened the bowling in Tests several times with his half-brother Pedro Collins ... He averages 21.45 with the ball in Tests against Sri Lanka, but 90.36 in eight matches against South Africa ... Unoriginally, his nickname is "Castro" ...

THE FIGURES *to 23.9.10*   ESPncricinfo.com

Batting & Fielding	M	Inns	NO	Runs	HS	Avge	S/R	100	50	4s	6s	Ct	St
Tests	43	69	21	248	21	5.16	25.59	0	0	32	2	7	0
ODIs	50	22	14	73	13	9.12	45.62	0	0	5	0	4	0
T20Is	12	2	1	3	2*	3.00	75.00	0	0	0	0	2	0
First-class	63	97	34	394	40	6.25	–	0	0	–	–	11	0

Bowling	M	Balls	Runs	Wkts	BB	Avge	RpO	S/R	5i	10m
Tests	43	7259	4811	122	7–87	39.43	3.97	59.50	8	0
ODIs	50	2138	1812	60	6–22	30.20	5.08	35.63	2	0
T20Is	12	219	308	10	3–24	30.80	8.43	21.90	0	0
First-class	63	9992	6634	187	7–87	35.47	3.98	53.43	10	1

GRANT **ELLIOTT**

NEW ZEALAND

Full name	**Grant David Elliott**
Born	**March 21, 1979, Johannesburg, South Africa**
Teams	**Wellington**
Style	**Right-hand bat, right-arm medium-pacer**
Test debut	**New Zealand v England at Napier 2007-08**
ODI debut	**New Zealand v England at Edgbaston 2008**
T20I debut	**New Zealand v Australia at Sydney 2008-09**

THE PROFILE Grant Elliott left his native South Africa for New Zealand in 2001 looking for new horizons, and found them in March 2008 when he was named in New Zealand's Test squad for England's visit less than a year after completing his residency qualification. He won his first cap in the final Test after Jacob Oram was injured, but was not an instant success, with two batting failures and a solitary wicket, although he was included in the squad for the one-dayers in England later in the year. A compact and correct batsman, and a swing bowler of modest pace, albeit from a nice high action, Elliott enjoyed a productive season for Wellington in 2006-07, with 361 runs at 45.12, and backed that up with 565 at 37.66 the following year. In England, he took three wickets in the second ODI, and made 56 in the third, but it was his controversial run-out in the fourth one at The Oval which made all the headlines – after he collided with the bowler while trying a quick single Elliott was lying on the ground clutching his thigh when the bails were removed, and England's captain Paul Collingwood declined to withdraw the appeal. Elliott stomped off, and later the New Zealand dressing-room door was firmly shut in Collingwood's face. Elliott made more of a mark with the bat in Australia in 2008-09, following a matchwinning 61 not out at Melbourne with a superb rearguard 115 at Sydney. Wickets still proved hard to come by, but he looked to have cemented a one-day place for the time being, although a hand injury restricted him in 2009-10.

THE FACTS Elliott scored 196 not out for Wellington v Auckland in April 2008 ... He made 115 in an ODI against Australia at Sydney in February 2009 ... Elliott represented South Africa in the Under-19 World Cup in 1997-98 ... His maiden first-class century came for Griqualand West against Bangladesh at Kimberley in October 2000 ...

THE FIGURES to 23.9.10   ᴇSᴨ cricinfo.com

Batting & Fielding	M	Inns	NO	Runs	HS	Avge	S/R	100	50	4s	6s	Ct	St
Tests	5	9	1	86	25	10.75	26.70	0	0	3	0	2	0
ODIs	31	22	6	628	115	39.25	73.62	1	3	39	4	5	0
T20Is	1	1	1	23	23*	–	76.66	0	0	1	0	0	0
First-class	52	82	4	2288	196*	29.33	–	5	12	–	–	31	0

Bowling	M	Balls	Runs	Wkts	BB	Avge	RpO	S/R	5i	10m
Tests	5	282	140	4	2–8	35.00	2.97	70.50	0	0
ODIs	31	458	376	17	4–31	22.11	4.92	26.94	0	0
T20Is	1	6	11	1	1–11	11.00	11.00	6.00	0	0
First-class	52	5343	2424	65	4–56	37.29	2.72	82.20	0	0

FAISAL HOSSAIN

Full name	**Faisal Hossain**
Born	**October 26, 1978, Chittagong**
Teams	**Chittagong**
Style	**Left-hand bat, slow left-arm orthodox spinner**
Test debut	**Bangladesh v West Indies at Gros Islet 2004**
ODI debut	**Bangladesh v West Indies at St George's 2004**
T20I debut	**No T20Is yet**

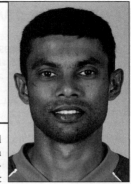

THE PROFILE Faisal Hossain, curiously nicknamed "Dickens", has had an unusual international career. He had a good domestic season in 2003-04, scoring more than 800 first-class runs, and did well enough for the national A team against Zimbabwe early in 2004 to win a place on the full tour of West Indies that followed. He made his Test debut in St Lucia, but managed only two single-figure scores in a match from which Bangladesh emerged with an honourable draw (indeed, they were able to declare for the first time in their history). At this time he was seen solely as a batsman – a left-hander, which Bangladesh were then short of – who was a gifted timer of the ball, relying more on instinct than technique. But after collecting just 18 runs in three innings in the Asia Cup in Sri Lanka later in 2004, Faisal dropped off the national radar. That seemed to be it ... but early in 2010 he followed 96 against Sylhet with 154 against Dhaka, and finished his best season with 880 runs at 58, while his left-arm spin, never previously considered a serious weapon, accounted for 27 wickets. All this earned him a return to national colours – at the advanced age, for a Bangladeshi, of 31 – for the one-day portion of the England tour in mid-2010. He made his ODI comeback at Trent Bridge, where he bowled tidily and took a good boundary catch to dismiss Craig Kieswetter. However, Faisal was on the sidelines again for the next game, when Bangladesh pulled off their historic victory over England at Bristol.

THE FACTS Faisal Hossain scored 180 for Chittagong at Khulna in February 2006 ... He took 5 for 183 for Bangladesh A v South Africa A at Mirpur in April 2010 ... Faisal hit 96, 127, 129, 69 and 102 in successive innings for Chittagong in 2008-09 ... Almost six years elapsed between his fourth ODI and his fifth, in July 2010 ...

THE FIGURES to 23.9.10   **ESPNcricinfo.com**

Batting & Fielding	M	Inns	NO	Runs	HS	Avge	S/R	100	50	4s	6s	Ct	St
Tests	1	2	0	7	5	3.50	25.92	0	0	1	0	0	0
ODIs	6	5	1	43	17	10.75	47.25	0	0	3	1	3	0
T20Is	0	0	–	–	–	–	–	–	–	–	–	–	–
First-class	82	138	11	4992	180	39.30	58.50	10	27	–	–	66	2

Bowling	M	Balls	Runs	Wkts	BB	Avge	RpO	S/R	5i	10m
Tests	1	0	–	–	–	–	–	–	–	–
ODIs	6	73	53	1	1–27	53.00	4.35	73.00	0	0
T20Is	0	0	–	–	–	–	–	–	–	–
First-class	82	3550	1973	48	5–183	41.10	3.33	73.95	1	0

41

FAWAD ALAM

Full name	**Fawad Alam**
Born	**October 8, 1985, Karachi, Sind**
Teams	**Karachi, Sind, National Bank**
Style	**Left-hand bat, slow left-arm orthodox spinner**
Test debut	**Pakistan v Sri Lanka at Colombo 2009**
ODI debut	**Pakistan v Sri Lanka at Abu Dhabi 2006-07**
T20I debut	**Pakistan v Kenya at Nairobi 2007-08**

THE PROFILE Critics scoffed when left-hander Fawad Alam, who had never opened before, went in first in his debut Test, in Colombo in July 2009, after Salman Butt was dropped. Fawad's pronounced shuffle across the crease seemed to open him up to Sri Lanka's swing bowlers, and he duly made an unconvincing 16. But in the second innings he silenced the doubters with a superb 168, working the ball well off his pads when the bowlers targeted that shuffle. He dropped out of the Test side after two less spectacular matches, but remains an important cog in the limited-overs teams: in 12 successive ODI innings between June 2008 and September 2010 he never failed to reach double figures, the highlights 63 against Australia at Perth in a narrow defeat in January 2010, and 64 against England at The Oval in September to start Pakistan's revival in that controversial end-of-season series. Fawad had long been seen as an international prospect: he made his first-class debut at 17, and was part of the side that won the Under-19 World Cup in Dhaka early in 2004. He made 1027 runs at 53.60 in his first full season (2005-06), and averaged around 50 over the following two years as well, just to show that was no fluke. He is also a handy slow left-armer and a lively fielder. A triple-century in a tour match in Kenya late in 2008 was followed by a near-miss in a first-class game at home, then in June 2009 Fawad was part of the side that won the second World Twenty20 in England – and then came that surprising promotion in Sri Lanka.

THE FACTS Fawad Alam made 168 against Sri Lanka in Colombo in July 2009: he was the tenth Pakistani to score a century on Test debut, but the first to do so away from home ... He scored 296 not out for National Bank v Customs in Karachi in January 2009 ... For Pakistan's Academy against Kenya in a non-first-class match in Mombasa in September 2008 Fawad scored 302 not out and shared an unbroken stand of 612 with Raheel Majeed (318 not out) ... His father, Tariq Alam, had a long first-class career in Pakistan ...

THE FIGURES *to 23.9.10*   **ESPMcricinfo.com**

Batting & Fielding	M	Inns	NO	Runs	HS	Avge	S/R	100	50	4s	6s	Ct	St
Tests	3	6	0	250	168	41.66	56.68	1	0	23	1	3	0
ODIs	22	20	8	480	64	40.00	73.05	0	3	26	1	7	0
T20Is	23	16	6	185	28	18.50	117.08	0	0	6	7	7	0
First-class	57	98	19	4423	296*	55.98	–	8	28	–	–	32	0

Bowling	M	Balls	Runs	Wkts	BB	Avge	RpO	S/R	5i	10m
Tests	3	0	–	–	–	–	–	–	–	–
ODIs	22	362	332	4	1–8	83.00	5.50	90.50	0	0
T20Is	23	90	95	8	3–7	11.87	6.33	11.25	0	0
First-class	57	1580	745	22	4–27	33.86	2.82	71.81	0	0

CALLUM **FERGUSON**

Full name	**Callum James Ferguson**
Born	**November 21, 1984, North Adelaide, South Australia**
Teams	**South Australia**
Style	**Right-hand bat, right-arm medium-pacer**
Test debut	**No Tests yet**
ODI debut	**Australia v New Zealand at Melbourne 2008-09**
T20I debut	**Australia v New Zealand at Sydney 2008-09**

THE PROFILE After a few stutters, Callum Ferguson came of age in 2008-09. Easy to watch, more of an accumulator than a big hitter, he had suffered from getting out when set, but came back from a summer of club cricket in England in 2008 more determined to cash in. His 644 first-class runs in the season that followed included two hundreds (his first for nearly four years) and, despite being lightly built, he exhibited some power too, with 401 one-day runs at almost a run a ball. It all earned him a call-up for the Chappell-Hadlee one-dayers against New Zealand in February 2009. He made a rapid 55 not out in the final rain-affected match, and carried on his good start in South Africa before kicking off the one-day series against England in September with 71 not out at The Oval and 55 at Lord's. All this was a welcome return to form: Ferguson had shone in 2004-05, his debut season, with 733 Pura Cup runs – including 93 in his second match and a maiden century in his fourth – while the rest of South Australia's strokemakers struggled. Over the next three seasons he found it hard to replicate that form, before the retirements of Darren Lehmann and Matthew Elliott necessitated more responsibility. There was a setback in October 2009, when Ferguson badly injured his right knee while fielding in the Champions Trophy final victory over New Zealand in October 2009. He needed reconstructive surgery and missed the whole of the following home season, but was still appointed as South Australia's vice-captain – and, after Australia's one-day struggles in England during 2010, a national return is a distinct possibility.

THE FACTS Ferguson made 132 for South Australia v Queensland at Brisbane in November 2008 ... In January 2002 he scored 258 not out for South Australia Under-19s v Queensland ... Ferguson scored 93 (v Queensland) in his second first-class match in 2004-05, and 103 (v New South Wales) in his fourth, in 2004-05 ...

THE FIGURES *to 23.9.10*   **ESPNcricinfo.com**

Batting & Fielding	M	Inns	NO	Runs	HS	Avge	S/R	100	50	4s	6s	Ct	St
Tests	0	0	–	–	–	–	–	–	–	–	–	–	–
ODIs	25	22	9	599	71*	46.07	85.08	0	5	58	0	6	0
T20Is	3	3	0	16	8	5.33	84.21	0	0	1	0	1	0
First-class	47	88	7	2842	132	35.08	56.42	4	19	–	–	21	0

Bowling	M	Balls	Runs	Wkts	BB	Avge	RpO	S/R	5i	10m
Tests	0	0	–	–	–	–	–	–	–	–
ODIs	25	0	–	–	–	–	–	–	–	–
T20Is	3	0	–	–	–	–	–	–	–	–
First-class	47	42	38	0	–	–	5.42	–	0	0

DILHARA **FERNANDO**

Full name	**Congenige Randhi Dilhara Fernando**
Born	**July 19, 1979, Colombo**
Teams	**Sinhalese SC, Kandurata**
Style	**Right-hand bat, right-arm fast-medium bowler**
Test debut	**Sri Lanka v Pakistan at Colombo 2000**
ODI debut	**Sri Lanka v South Africa at Paarl 2000-01**
T20I debut	**Sri Lanka v England at Southampton 2006**

THE PROFILE When Dilhara Fernando burst onto the international scene, young and raw, he was seen as the long-term replacement for Chaminda Vaas as the cutting edge of Sri Lanka's attack. He has natural pace – six months after his debut he was clocked at 91.9mph in Durban – hits the pitch hard, and moves the ball off the seam. He rattled India at Galle in 2001, taking five wickets and sending Javagal Srinath to hospital. At first he paid for an inconsistent line and length, but worked hard with the former Test opening bowler Rumesh Ratnayake and became more reliable. He also learnt the art of reverse swing, and developed a well-disguised slower one. But injuries intervened. Fernando was quick during the 2003 World Cup, but bowled a lot of no-balls, a problem he later blamed on a spinal stress fracture. He returned after six months, only for another fracture to be detected in January 2004. He reclaimed his place in the national squad later that year, and has been there or thereabouts ever since, although latterly he has found Test wickets elusive – in eight matches between August 2007 and August 2010 he took only 12 at 70, double his career average – but the promise of pace ensures he is always in the mix. The no-ball problem does occasionally resurface: he was omitted after the first Test against Pakistan in March 2006 before returning later that year for the one-day series in England, which Sri Lanka swept 5–0: Fernando grabbed three quick wickets in the first match at Lord's, and he remains a one-day regular.

THE FACTS Fernando averages 19.28 with the ball in Tests against Bangladesh – but 49.66 v India, even though his best figures of 5 for 42 came against them ... He took 6 for 27 against England in Colombo in September 2007: overall he averages 20.05 against England in ODIs, but 70.42 in 14 matches v South Africa ... Fernando's record includes one ODI for the Asia XI ...

THE FIGURES *to 23.9.10*　　　ESPncricinfo.com

Batting & Fielding	M	Inns	NO	Runs	HS	Avge	S/R	100	50	4s	6s	Ct	St
Tests	34	40	13	198	36*	7.33	31.68	0	0	22	1	10	0
ODIs	139	56	32	237	20	9.87	62.04	0	0	19	2	26	0
T20Is	15	5	2	24	21	8.00	120.00	0	0	4	0	2	0
First-class	100	98	28	505	42	7.21	–	0	0	–	–	38	0

Bowling	M	Balls	Runs	Wkts	BB	Avge	RpO	S/R	5i	10m
Tests	34	5314	3188	89	5–42	35.82	3.59	59.70	3	0
ODIs	139	6080	5270	176	6–27	29.94	5.20	34.54	1	0
T20Is	15	318	392	16	3–19	24.50	7.39	19.87	0	0
First-class	100	13443	7980	269	6–29	29.66	3.56	49.97	6	0

STEVEN **FINN**

Full name	**Steven Thomas Finn**
Born	**April 4, 1989, Watford, Hertfordshire**
Teams	**Middlesex**
Style	**Right-hand bat, right-arm fast-medium bowler**
Test debut	**England v Bangladesh at Chittagong 2009-10**
ODI debut	**No ODIs yet**
T20I debut	**No T20Is yet**

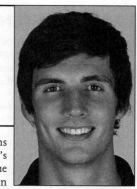

THE PROFILE Steven Finn, who measures up at 6ft 7ins (201cm), is the latest beanpole fast bowler to carry England's hopes, and his impressive arrival sounded the death knell for the international career of the previous one, Steve Harmison. Finn pings the ball down from the clouds with a heady blend of pace and bounce, and can rattle the best players, although he is still inexperienced. He was earmarked as an England prospect from his early days, representing all the age-group teams from under-16 upwards, and became Middlesex's youngest-ever player in 2005, breaking Fred Titmus's record. After he took 53 Championship wickets at 30.64 in 2009, Finn made the England Lions tour of the UAE, where he did well enough, although he still seemed to be well down the pecking order. But when Stuart Broad, Graham Onions and Ryan Sidebottom were all injured at the start of the Bangladesh tour early in 2010, Finn was parachuted in as cover. Barely 24 hours after arriving he was playing in the warm-up game against Bangladesh A, did well, and three days later made his Test debut, displaying good pace and bounce on a docile Chittagong surface. Back in England Finn started the season by taking 14 wickets in a match for Middlesex, then claimed five-fors in both Tests against Bangladesh, collecting the match award for his nine wickets at Lord's. He worried some observers by falling over a lot in his follow-through there, but explained: "I'm like Bambi on ice when I get going sometimes." Pakistan predictably proved tougher nuts to crack later in 2010, but Finn still managed 13 wickets in the four Tests at an average of less than 23.

THE FACTS Finn took 9 for 37 (after 5 for 69 in the first innings) for Middlesex at Worcester in April 2010: his next two five-fors were for England in Tests against Bangladesh ... At 16 in 2005 Finn was the youngest player to appear in a first-class match for Middlesex, beating the record set by Fred Titmus in 1949 ...

THE FIGURES to 23.9.10   **ESPN**cricinfo.com

Batting & Fielding	M	Inns	NO	Runs	HS	Avge	S/R	100	50	4s	6s	Ct	St
Tests	8	9	7	13	9*	6.50	14.77	0	0	2	0	1	0
ODIs	0	0	–	–	–	–	–	–	–	–	–	–	–
T20Is	0	0	–	–	–	–	–	–	–	–	–	–	–
First-class	46	62	21	245	26*	5.97	26.42	0	0	27	1	11	0

Bowling	M	Balls	Runs	Wkts	BB	Avge	RpO	S/R	5i	10m
Tests	8	1182	743	32	5–42	23.21	3.77	36.93	2	0
ODIs	0	0	–	–	–	–	–	–	–	–
T20Is	0	0	–	–	–	–	–	–	–	–
First-class	46	7607	4589	162	9–37	28.32	3.61	46.95	5	1

ANDRE **FLETCHER**

WEST INDIES

Full name	**Andre David Stephon Fletcher**
Born	**November 28, 1987, La Tante, Grenada**
Teams	**Windward Islands**
Style	**Right-hand bat, occasional wicketkeeper**
Test debut	**No Tests yet**
ODI debut	**West Indies v Australia at Kingstown 2007-08**
T20I debut	**West Indies v Australia at Bridgetown 2008**

THE PROFILE   Andre Fletcher is one of several young batsmen West Indies have tested recently by throwing them into international cricket at the deep end without much first-class experience – in his case, just 13 matches. A top-order batsman with a solid technique, Fletcher showed promising signs in his initial international appearances, but a lack of awareness of what was happening in the field around him was a problem, and cost him his wicket more than once – he was run out after a promising 26 in his first one-day international, when he sauntered back to the crease and was run out by Australia's wicketkeeper Brad Haddin, then he was twice stumped later in the series. Fletcher had earned the call for those limited-overs matches against Australia in 2008 after a domestic season in which he posted his maiden first-class century for Windward Islands in an otherwise dismal batting display against Jamaica – Fletcher's unbeaten 103 came out of 187, and he also top-scored in the first innings with 25 out of 61 in a match that lasted less than two days. He also did well in Twenty20 cricket, in which he usually keeps wicket (he is an excellent outfielder, so this is a slight waste). He was one of the instant millionaires created by the now-disgraced tycoon Allen Stanford's brief foray into cricket – Fletcher was at the other end to Chris Gayle as the "Stanford Superstars" completed a ten-wicket victory over a rather embarrassed England side late in 2008 – and regained his West Indian place soon afterwards. However, runs remained elusive, and he needs more consistency if he is to nail down a permanent spot in all formats.

THE FACTS   Fletcher scored 123 for West Indies A against India A at Croydon in June 2010 ... He made 53 from 32 balls in the World Twenty20 match against Australia at The Oval in June 2009 – but his highest score in 13 other T20Is is just 19, and he has bagged five ducks ... Fletcher made 32 not out as the "Stanford Superstars" beat England by ten wickets in Antigua in November 2008 ...

THE FIGURES to 23.9.10   **ESPNcricinfo.com**

Batting & Fielding	M	Inns	NO	Runs	HS	Avge	S/R	100	50	4s	6s	Ct	St
Tests	0	0	–	–	–	–	–	–	–	–	–	–	–
ODIs	15	15	0	256	54	17.06	70.13	0	2	30	5	5	3
T20Is	14	14	2	137	53	11.41	93.83	0	1	15	2	11	1
First-class	30	55	4	1595	123	31.27	–	2	10	–	–	30	1

Bowling	M	Balls	Runs	Wkts	BB	Avge	RpO	S/R	5i	10m
Tests	0	0	–	–	–	–	–	–	–	–
ODIs	15	0	–	–	–	–	–	–	–	–
T20Is	14	0	–	–	–	–	–	–	–	–
First-class	30	121	68	0	–	–	3.37	–	0	0

DANIEL **FLYNN**

Full name	**Daniel Raymond Flynn**
Born	**April 16, 1985, Rotorua**
Teams	**Northern Districts**
Style	**Left-hand bat, occasional left-arm spinner**
Test debut	**England v New Zealand at Lord's 2008**
ODI debut	**New Zealand v England at Christchurch 2007-08**
T20I debut	**New Zealand v England at Christchurch 2007-08**

THE PROFILE   The early days of Daniel Flynn's international career will be remembered for him walking off Old Trafford in May 2008 with fewer teeth than he started with, after being hit by James Anderson. Such an injury could have severely dented the confidence (as well as the gums) of a young batsman, but Flynn is made of sterner stuff. He made his first-class debut for Northern Districts soon after the 2003-04 Under-19 World Cup, in which he captained New Zealand. A stocky, powerful left-hander, he struck his maiden century in December 2005, but two mixed seasons followed, and it wasn't until 2007-08 that he showed his true colours – particularly in one-dayers – and joined the national Twenty20 squad. He didn't get many opportunities at first, but did make the tour of England that followed. He made his Test debut at Lord's, defending coolly for 29 not out from 118 balls in the second innings, leading his captain Daniel Vettori to declare that "He's got the No. 6 spot basically for as long as he wants it". Flynn then suffered that sickening blow in the mouth in the next game. However, he was fit enough to play in the final Test at Trent Bridge, and generally looked a readymade replacement for the just-retired Stephen Fleming (an altogether different type of left-hander). In 2008-09 Flynn just missed a maiden Test century, with 95 against West Indies at Dunedin, then – after being moved up to No. 3 by new coach Andy Moles – made 67 against India at Hamilton. However, he lost his place after a run of low scores, and worryingly lost his central contract too for 2010-11.

THE FACTS   Flynn made his maiden first-class hundred for Northern Districts v Otago at Gisborne in December 2005, then didn't make another one for almost two years ... In 2007-08 he hit 143 (from 117 balls) against Wellington and 149 (from 141 balls, with six sixes) against Canterbury in one-day games for ND ...

THE FIGURES to 23.9.10   **ᴇsᴨ cricinfo.com**

Batting & Fielding	M	Inns	NO	Runs	HS	Avge	S/R	100	50	4s	6s	Ct	St
Tests	16	29	5	689	95	28.70	40.57	0	4	89	3	7	0
ODIs	16	13	2	167	35	15.18	57.19	0	0	14	1	4	0
T20Is	4	4	0	37	23	9.25	115.62	0	0	1	2	2	0
First-class	54	91	10	2528	110	31.20	45.10	5	12	–	–	20	0

Bowling	M	Balls	Runs	Wkts	BB	Avge	RpO	S/R	5i	10m
Tests	16	0	–	–	–	–	–	–	–	–
ODIs	16	6	6	0	–	–	6.00	–	0	0
T20Is	4	6	7	0	–	–	7.00	–	0	0
First-class	54	241	143	1	1–37	143.00	3.56	241.00	0	0

GAUTAM **GAMBHIR**

INDIA

Full name	**Gautam Gambhir**
Born	**October 14, 1981, Delhi**
Teams	**Delhi, Delhi Daredevils**
Style	**Left-hand bat, occasional legspinner**
Test debut	**India v Australia at Mumbai 2004-05**
ODI debut	**India v Bangladesh at Dhaka 2002-03**
T20I debut	**India v Scotland at Durban 2006-07**

THE PROFILE Gautam Gambhir's attacking left-handed strokeplay has set tongues wagging ever since he was a schoolboy. Compact footwork and high bat-speed meant defence was often replaced by the aerial route over point. He pasted successive double-centuries early in 2002, but didn't get the nod from the selectors: he soldiered on, doing well in the Caribbean with India A early in 2003, and joined the one-day squad when several seniors took a rest after that year's World Cup. He finally made the Test side late the following year, hitting 96 against South Africa in his second match and 139 against Bangladesh in his fifth. Leaner times followed, punctuated by cheap runs in Zimbabwe, and although he celebrated his one-day return after 30 months on the sidelines with 103 against Sri Lanka in April 2005, he struggled for big scores and soon found himself out again. After the disasters of the 2007 World Cup Gambhir was given another chance, and this time immediately looked the part. He made two one-day centuries in Australia early in 2008, and carried his good form into the inaugural IPL. He crashed 67, 104 and a superb 206 in successive innings as Australia were beaten in October 2008 then – after a one-match ban for elbowing Shane Watson while running – helped ensure a series victory over England with 179 and 97 in the drawn second Test at Mohali in December. In ODIs he hammered 150 against Sri Lanka in Colombo in February 2009. Gambhir kept up this astonishing run of form with centuries in five successive Tests in 2009-10, although he had a quieter time after that then picked up a knee injury in Sri Lanka.

THE FACTS Gambhir made 206 against Australia at Delhi in October 2008: VVS Laxman also scored a double-century, the first time Australia had ever conceded two in the same innings ... Gambhir scored centuries in five successive Test matches in 2009 and 2010: only Don Bradman (six0 has ever done better ... He made 214 (for Delhi v Railways) and 218 (for the Board President's XI v Zimbabwe) in successive innings early in 2002 ...

THE FIGURES to 23.9.10   **ESP11** cricinfo.com

Batting & Fielding	M	Inns	NO	Runs	HS	Avge	S/R	100	50	4s	6s	Ct	St
Tests	32	57	4	2800	206	52.83	54.64	9	11	342	7	25	0
ODIs	100	96	8	3351	150*	38.07	84.72	7	21	367	16	30	0
T20Is	23	22	0	621	75	28.22	124.20	0	6	74	8	5	0
First-class	115	195	19	9797	233*	55.66	–	32	40	–	–	74	0

Bowling	M	Balls	Runs	Wkts	BB	Avge	RpO	S/R	5i	10m
Tests	32	0	–	–	–	–	–	–	–	–
ODIs	100	6	13	0	–	–	13.00	–	0	0
T20Is	23	0	–	–	–	–	–	–	–	–
First-class	115	385	277	7	3–12	39.57	4.31	55.00	0	0

CHRIS **GAYLE**

Full name	**Christopher Henry Gayle**
Born	**September 21, 1979, Kingston, Jamaica**
Teams	**Jamaica, Kolkata Knight Riders, Western Australia**
Style	**Right-hand bat, offspinner**
Test debut	**West Indies v Zimbabwe at Port-of-Spain 1999-2000**
ODI debut	**West Indies v India at Toronto 1999-2000**
T20I debut	**West Indies v New Zealand at Auckland 2005-06**

THE PROFILE An attacking left-hander, Chris Gayle earned himself a black mark on his first senior tour when the new boys were felt to be insufficiently respectful of their elders. But a lack of respect, for opposition bowlers at least, has served him well since then. Tall and imposing, he loves to carve through the covers off either foot (without moving either of them much), and has the ability to take any opening bowler apart. In a lean era for West Indian cricket in general – and fast bowling in particular – Gayle's pugnacious approach has become an attacking weapon in its own right, in Tests as well as one-dayers. His 79-ball century at Cape Town in January 2004, after South Africa had made 532, was typical of his approach. He came unstuck against England shortly afterwards, when that lack of positive footwork was exposed – but men with little footwork often baffle experts, and in May 2005 he punched 317 against South Africa in Antigua. Gayle also bowls brisk non-turning offspin, which makes him a genuine one-day allrounder. He took over the one-day captaincy after a miserable Test series in England in 2007, and electrified the side with unexpected flair. Later that year he inspired a stunning Test victory in South Africa, although the series was eventually lost. But after a chastening time in England in 2009 he suggested he might not hang around much longer in Test cricket, and two months later he and other senior players boycotted the home series against Bangladesh as a contracts dispute rumbled on. Gayle has lucrative Twenty20 deals in India and Australia, and would be a major loss if he did turn his back on West Indian cricket.

THE FACTS Gayle's 317 against South Africa in Antigua in May 2005 has been exceeded for West Indies only by Brian Lara (twice) and Garry Sobers ... Gayle hit the first century in Twenty20 internationals, 117 v South Africa at Johannesburg in September 2007 ... He made 208 for Jamaica v West Indies B in February 2001, sharing an unbroken opening stand of 425 with Leon Garrick ... His record includes three ODIs for the World XI ...

THE FIGURES *to 23.9.10*   **ᴇꜱᴘⁿcricinfo.com**

Batting & Fielding	M	Inns	NO	Runs	HS	Avge	S/R	100	50	4s	6s	Ct	St
Tests	88	155	6	6007	317	40.31	58.33	12	33	895	66	84	0
ODIs	220	215	15	7885	153*	39.42	83.77	19	42	919	165	95	0
T20Is	20	20	1	617	117	32.47	144.49	1	5	57	34	5	0
First-class	162	288	21	11761	317	44.04	–		28	59	–	–	142	0

Bowling	M	Balls	Runs	Wkts	BB	Avge	RpO	S/R	5i	10m
Tests	88	6851	2992	72	5–34	41.55	2.62	95.15	2	0
ODIs	220	6816	5395	156	5–46	34.58	4.74	43.69	1	0
T20Is	20	209	254	12	2–15	21.16	7.29	17.41	0	0
First-class	162	12127	5012	129	5–34	38.85	2.47	94.00	2	0

HERSCHELLE **GIBBS**

SOUTH AFRICA

Full name	**Herschelle Herman Gibbs**
Born	**February 23, 1974, Green Point, Cape Town**
Teams	**Cape Cobras, Yorkshire, Deccan Chargers**
Style	**Right-hand bat, occasional legspinner**
Test debut	**South Africa v India at Calcutta 1996-97**
ODI debut	**South Africa v Kenya at Nairobi 1996-97**
T20I debut	**South Africa v New Zealand at Johannesburg 2005-06**

THE PROFILE Herschelle Gibbs was summoned from the classroom at 16 to make his first-class debut in 1990: his feet moved beautifully at the crease, but struggled to find the ground in real life. Admitting that a Test debut in front of 70,000 at Eden Gardens wasn't as nerve-wracking as his final exams, as well as the fact that he reads little other than magazines and comics, contributed to a reputation for simplicity: his passion for one-liners and verbal jousting hampered his advancement, and his brush with career death in the match-fixing scandal in 2000 added to the impression of one who had failed to grasp the magnitude of his impact on South Africa's youth. But Gibbs can be a warm and generous person, and at the crease no shot is beyond him, while opening did not temper his desire for explosive entertainment. The speed of his hands is hypnotic, frequently allowing him to hook off the front foot and keep out surprise lifters. His trademark is the lofted extra-cover drive, hit inside-out with the certainty of a square cut. He is stunning at backward point, even in his mid-thirties. Gibbs had two double-centuries among his 14 Test tons, and 21 one-day hundreds too – the best of them in March 2006, when his 111-ball 175 powered South Africa past Australia's 434 with a ball to spare in probably the greatest one-day cracker of them all. He lost his Test place soon after the 2007 World Cup, although he remains in the frame in the shorter formats.

THE FACTS Gibbs and Graeme Smith are the only opening pair to share three stands of 300 or more in Tests ... He hit six sixes in an over from Holland's Daan van Bunge during the 2007 World Cup, winning a million dollars for charity ... He averages 56.42 in Tests against New Zealand, but only 23.30 v Sri Lanka ... He was bowled in 35 (23.8%) of his Test innings ...

THE FIGURES to 23.9.10   ᴇsᴘᴨcricinfo.com

Batting & Fielding	M	Inns	NO	Runs	HS	Avge	S/R	100	50	4s	6s	Ct	St
Tests	90	154	7	6167	228	41.95	50.26	14	26	887	47	94	0
ODIs	248	240	16	8094	175	36.13	83.26	21	37	930	128	108	0
T20Is	23	23	1	400	90*	18.18	125.78	0	3	45	12	8	0
First-class	193	331	13	13425	228	42.21	–		31	60	–	–	176	0

Bowling	M	Balls	Runs	Wkts	BB	Avge	RpO	S/R	5i	10m
Tests	90	6	4	0	–	–	4.00	–	0	0
ODIs	248	0	–	–	–	–	–	–	–	–
T20Is	23	0	–	–	–	–	–	–	–	–
First-class	193	138	78	3	2–14	26.00	3.39	46.00	0	0

MARTIN **GUPTILL**

Full name	**Martin James Guptill**
Born	**September 30, 1986, Auckland**
Teams	**Auckland**
Style	**Right-hand bat, occasional offspinner**
Test debut	**New Zealand v India at Hamilton 2008-09**
ODI debut	**New Zealand v West Indies at Auckland 2008-09**
ODI debut	**New Zealand v Australia at Sydney 2008-09**

THE PROFILE A tall right-hander, Martin Guptill made a bittersweet entry into first-class cricket in March 2006, not long after playing in the Under-19 World Cup, collecting a duck in his first innings against Wellington, then making 99 in the second before tickling a catch behind off his future New Zealand team-mate Jesse Ryder. By 2007-08 Guptill was tickling the selectors, too: he topped the State Shield run-lists that season with 596 as Auckland reached the final. Guptill carried his purple patch into an Emerging Players tournament in Australia, finishing as NZ's highest run-scorer there too with 280. His rise continued with an A-team tour of India and, after a maiden first-class century followed at home, he received the national call for the one-day series against the touring West Indians early in 2009. He lit up his debut in familiar surroundings in Auckland, reaching three figures with a huge six off Chris Gayle and finishing with a superb unbeaten 122 – the second-highest score by anyone in their first ODI, and only the fifth debut century. He was dropped three times before he reached 30, but his running (not one of New Zealand's strengths) was notable. Indeed, Guptill's general speed – between wickets or in the outfield, from a high-stepping run – is particularly remarkable as he has only two toes on his left foot after a forklift accident when he was 13. He consolidated his place in 2009-10, although his stats were boosted by 91 in a one-dayer against Bangladesh, and a massive 189 against them in a Test at Hamilton, where he shared a big stand with Brendon McCullum.

THE FACTS Guptill was only the fifth batsman to score a century in his first one-day international, following Dennis Amiss, Desmond Haynes, Andy Flower and Saleem Elahi ... Guptill made 189 against Bangladesh at Hamilton in February 2010, sharing a sixth-wicket partnership of 339 with Brendon McCullum ... On his first-class debut, against Wellington in Auckland in March 2006, Guptill made 0 and 99 ...

THE FIGURES to 23.9.10   **ESPRIcricinfo.com**

Batting & Fielding	M	Inns	NO	Runs	HS	Avge	S/R	100	50	4s	6s	Ct	St
Tests	11	20	1	672	189	35.36	48.20	1	3	76	9	8	0
ODIs	33	32	3	959	122*	33.06	82.38	1	7	89	21	16	0
T20Is	20	18	2	341	45*	21.31	106.89	0	0	31	11	8	0
First-class	33	57	2	1694	189	30.80	43.20	2	9	221	18	20	0

Bowling	M	Balls	Runs	Wkts	BB	Avge	RpO	S/R	5i	10m
Tests	11	86	47	3	3–37	15.66	3.27	28.66	0	0
ODIs	33	65	53	2	2–7	26.50	4.89	32.50	0	0
T20Is	20	6	11	0	–	–	11.00	–	0	0
First-class	33	206	127	4	3–37	31.75	3.69	51.50	0	0

BRAD **HADDIN**

Full name	**Bradley James Haddin**
Born	**October 23, 1977, Cowra, New South Wales**
Teams	**New South Wales**
Style	**Right-hand bat, wicketkeeper**
Test debut	**Australia v West Indies at Kingston 2007-08**
ODI debut	**Australia v Zimbabwe at Hobart 2000-01**
T20I debut	**Australia v South Africa at Brisbane 2005-06**

THE PROFILE For years Brad Haddin held the most nerve-fraying position in Australian cricket – wicketkeeper-in-waiting, warming the seat whenever Adam Gilchrist needed a rest. Now Haddin is up there to be shot at himself. He became Australia's 400th Test cricketer in the West Indies early in 2008, and did well enough, playing through the series despite breaking a finger early on, which might explain his comparative lack of runs to start with. But he cemented his place with a blazing – almost Gilchristian – 169 against New Zealand at Adelaide in November, pulling and cutting strongly, and added another century in the first Ashes Test in 2009, before a valiant 80 in defeat at Lord's. After that, though, his fortunes waned: he broke another finger just before the start of the third Test, and after a brief return had to surrender the gloves to Tim Paine for the one-dayers that followed. Surgery meant he missed the Champions Trophy in South Africa too, then an elbow-tendon problem forced him out of the internationals in England in 2010: Paine again showed himself to be a capable deputy – and a potential rival. Haddin has long been a consistent scorer at domestic level, making 916 runs at 57.25 in 2004-05. He passed 600 runs in each of the next two seasons, and although his output dipped to 489 in 2007-08, that still included three centuries. A former Australia Under-19 captain who grew up in Gundagai, Haddin began his senior domestic career in 1997-98 with the Australian Capital Territory in their debut season in Australia's one-day competition.

THE FACTS Haddin took up a novel batting position behind the stumps when facing a Shoaib Akhtar "free ball" (after a no-ball) early in 2005: he reasoned that he had more time to sight the ball, and if it hit the stumps it would confuse the fielders (it did hit the stumps, and he managed a bye) ... Haddin was the unwitting "villain" of the 2005 Ashes Test at Edgbaston: he rolled a ball near Glenn McGrath, who stepped on it, badly sprained his ankle, and missed the match, which England eventually won by just two runs: in 2009 Haddin himself missed the Edgbaston Test when he broke a finger minutes before the start ...

THE FIGURES to 23.9.10   **ESPN**cricinfo.com

Batting & Fielding	M	Inns	NO	Runs	HS	Avge	S/R	100	50	4s	6s	Ct	St
Tests	27	45	5	1545	169	38.62	59.72	2	5	178	27	110	2
ODIs	66	61	6	1796	110	32.65	84.27	2	10	150	47	90	7
T20Is	22	20	4	300	47	18.75	111.11	0	0	23	9	11	3
First-class	122	201	23	7209	169	40.50	–	12	37	–	–	384	27

Bowling	M	Balls	Runs	Wkts	BB	Avge	RpO	S/R	5i	10m
Tests	27	0	–	–	–	–	–	–	–	–
ODIs	66	0	–	–	–	–	–	–	–	–
T20Is	22	0	–	–	–	–	–	–	–	–
First-class	122	0	–	–	–	–	–	–	–	–

HARBHAJAN SINGH

Full name	**Harbhajan Singh**
Born	**July 3, 1980, Jullundur, Punjab**
Teams	**Punjab, Mumbai Indians**
Style	**Right-hand bat, offspinner**
Test debut	**India v Australia at Bangalore 1997-98**
ODI debut	**India v New Zealand at Sharjah 1997-98**
T20I debut	**India v South Africa at Johannesburg 2006-07**

THE PROFILE Harbhajan Singh represents the spirit of the new Indian cricketer. His arrogance and cockiness translate into self-belief and passion on the field, and he has the talent to match. An offspinner with a windmilling, whiplash action, remodelled after questions about his action, he exercises great command over the ball, has the ability to vary his length and pace, and bowls a deadly *doosra* too – although his main wicket-taking ball is the one that climbs wickedly from a length. In March 2001 it proved too much for the previously all-conquering Australians, as Harbhajan collected 32 wickets in three Tests while none of his team-mates managed more than three. He has occasionally been bothered by injury, while in Pakistan early in 2006 he went for 0 for 355 in two Tests before bouncing back with five-fors in St Kitts and Jamaica. He still sailed past 350 Test wickets before he turned 30, and in 2010 Muttiah Muralitharan nominated him (somewhat optimistically) as the man most likely to pass his own stratospheric tally of 800. Harbhajan's rivalry with the Aussies – against whom he has taken 79 wickets in 14 Tests – boiled over in Sydney in January 2008 when he was charged with racially abusing Andrew Symonds. He was initially given a three-Test ban before the charge was reduced, on appeal. Then in April Harbhajan slapped his Indian team-mate Sreesanth without any provocation after an IPL game, which cost him an 11-match ban. But when he can control his temper – as in New Zealand early in 2009, when he took 16 wickets in the three Tests – Harbhajan remains a world-beater.

THE FACTS Harbhajan's match figures of 15 for 217 against Australia at Chennai in 2000-01 have been bettered for India only by Narendra Hirwani (16 for 136 in 1987-88, also at Chennai) ... Harbhajan took 32 wickets at 17.03 in that three-match series: his haul at Kolkata included India's first-ever Test hat-trick, when he dismissed Ricky Ponting, Adam Gilchrist and Shane Warne ... He has taken 45 wickets at 21.93 in Tests against West Indies, but 25 at 52.04 v Pakistan ... His record includes two ODIs for the Asia XI ...

THE FIGURES *to 23.9.10*

Batting & Fielding	M	Inns	NO	Runs	HS	Avge	S/R	100	50	4s	6s	Ct	St
Tests	85	117	20	1595	66	16.44	64.39	0	7	215	21	41	0
ODIs	212	112	30	1083	49	13.20	82.10	0	0	86	29	60	0
T20Is	22	9	2	84	21	12.00	112.00	0	0	9	3	6	0
First-class	149	198	37	3003	84	18.65	–	0	11	–	–	74	0

Bowling	M	Balls	Runs	Wkts	BB	Avge	RpO	S/R	5i	10m
Tests	85	23928	11289	357	8–84	31.62	2.83	67.02	24	5
ODIs	212	11075	7949	242	5–31	32.84	4.30	45.76	3	0
T20Is	22	480	516	16	3–30	32.25	6.45	30.00	0	0
First-class	149	37867	17810	634	8–84	28.09	2.82	59.72	38	7

PAUL **HARRIS**

Full name	**Paul Lee Harris**
Born	**Nov 2, 1978, Salisbury (now Harare), Zimbabwe**
Teams	**Titans**
Style	**Right-hand bat, slow left-arm orthodox spinner**
Test debut	**South Africa v India at Cape Town 2006-07**
ODI debut	**South Africa v Bangladesh at Chittagong 2007-08**
T20I debut	**No T20Is yet**

THE PROFILE   Tall and not unlike the former England bowler Phil Tufnell in appearance and style, slow left-armer Paul Harris was a rather surprise inclusion for the 2006-07 series against India as South Africa's selectors continued their usually fruitless quest for quality spin. He made his debut in the New Year Test at Cape Town, and took four wickets in the first innings, including Sachin Tendulkar and Virender Sehwag. He added Rahul Dravid in the second innings: his nagging over-the-wicket line kept the Indians quiet, and helped his side reclaim the initiative. Until then the selectors had ignored Harris, even though he led the 2005-06 SuperSport Series wicket-takers with 49, and it seemed possible that he might be lost to South African cricket altogether after a successful stint for Warwickshire in 2006 as a Kolpak player. But then Nicky Boje retired disenchanted, and the call went out to Harris – a departure from South Africa's usual policy of choosing slow bowlers who can also contribute in the field and with the bat (although he can be a useful blocker). Harris was born in Zimbabwe but grew up in Cape Town, where his rise was originally blocked by Paul Adams and Claude Henderson. More of a roller than a big spinner, he is accurate and can get surprising bounce, from an unprepossessing approach, and he silenced some of his critics by taking nine wickets in victory over Australia at Cape Town in March 2009, before seven wickets in the nailbiting draw against England at Centurion in December set up another consistent season.

THE FACTS   Harris took 7 for 94 (12 for 180 in the match) for Titans v Eagles at Benoni in 2008-09 ... When he took 6 for 127 against Australia at Cape Town in March 2009 Harris became the first South African spinner to take a five-for in a home Test since off-spinner Harry Bromfield, also at Newlands, against England in 1964-65 ... For Warwickshire v Durham at Chester-le-Street in July 2007 Harris reached his maiden fifty in 34 balls ..

THE FIGURES *to 23.9.10*   **ᴇѕᴨcricinfo.com**

Batting & Fielding	M	Inns	NO	Runs	HS	Avge	S/R	100	50	4s	6s	Ct	St
Tests	32	42	5	427	46	11.54	34.94	0	0	45	2	14	0
ODIs	3	0	–	–	–	–	–	–	–	–	–	2	0
T20Is	0	0	–	–	–	–	–	–	–	–	–	–	–
First-class	104	126	18	1568	55	14.51	–	0	3	–	–	39	0

Bowling	M	Balls	Runs	Wkts	BB	Avge	RpO	S/R	5i	10m
Tests	32	7387	3414	92	6–127	37.10	2.77	80.29	3	0
ODIs	3	180	83	3	2–30	27.66	2.76	60.00	0	0
T20Is	0	0	–	–	–	–	–	–	–	–
First-class	104	23527	10793	347	7–94	31.10	2.75	67.80	19	1

RYAN **HARRIS**

Full name	**Ryan James Harris**
Born	**October 11, 1979, Sydney**
Teams	**Queensland, Deccan Chargers**
Style	**Right-hand bat, right-arm fast bowler**
Test debut	**Australia v New Zealand at Wellington 2009-10**
ODI debut	**Australia v South Africa at Hobart 2008-09**
T20I debut	**Australia v West Indies at Sydney 2009-10**

THE PROFILE   Ryan Harris leapt onto the international stage in 2009-10, a season which he initially feared would be a write-off after knee surgery: he narrowly avoided a second operation before benefiting from injuries to Peter Siddle and Ben Hilfenhaus. A stocky, skiddy bowler who is surprisingly fast, Harris quickly became too good to ignore, and remained in the one-day mix until another knee problem impinged in England in 2010. Harris made a dream start to his one-day career: in only his second match, against Pakistan in January 2010, he collected five wickets, and repeated the performance in the next game. All this led to a Test debut in New Zealand, and he did well during both matches there, taking nine wickets in terribly windy conditions in Wellington. Opportunities may be limited if all the fast men are fit, but Harris has proven strike power, hurrying to 41 wickets in his first 17 one-dayers, an Australian record, and is also a handy batsman. However, until his international debut at 29, he almost qualified as a journeyman. In 2007-08 he was South Australia's top wicket-taker with 37 at 29.86, and it was hard to see why they didn't try harder to stop him moving to Queensland. At the same time he joined Sussex on his British passport, but played only once before they realised he had signed with Queensland as a local. In his first season for the Bulls he collected 33 wickets at 26.48 before breaking his foot stopping a drive late in the season. A muscular hitter, an early limited-overs highlight was lofting a six over long-on when the Redbacks needed five to win against Queensland at Adelaide in December 2006.

THE FACTS   Harris took five wickets in both his second and third ODIs, a feat unmatched at that level: only Ajantha Mendis (48) had more wickets after 17 ODIs than Harris (Curtly Ambrose also had 41) ... Harris scored 94 for Surrey at Northampton in June 2009 ... He took 7 for 108 for South Australia v Tasmania at Adelaide in February 2008 ...

THE FIGURES *to 23.9.10*   **ᴇꜱᴘʀɪ cricinfo.com**

Batting & Fielding	M	Inns	NO	Runs	HS	Avge	S/R	100	50	4s	6s	Ct	St
Tests	2	2	1	28	18*	28.00	65.11	0	0	5	0	1	0
ODIs	17	11	6	43	21	8.60	122.85	0	0	3	1	4	0
T20Is	3	1	1	2	2*	–	200.00	0	0	0	0	0	0
First-class	40	66	8	1175	94	20.25	61.45	0	6	–	–	19	0

Bowling	M	Balls	Runs	Wkts	BB	Avge	RpO	S/R	5i	10m
Tests	2	423	207	9	4–77	23.00	2.93	47.0	0	0
ODIs	17	845	661	41	5–19	16.12	4.69	20.6	3	0
T20Is	3	70	95	4	2–27	23.75	8.14	17.5	0	0
First-class	40	7379	3860	118	7–108	32.71	3.13	62.5	2	0

NATHAN **HAURITZ**

AUSTRALIA

Full name	**Nathan Michael Hauritz**
Born	**October 18, 1981, Wondai, Queensland**
Teams	**New South Wales**
Style	**Right-hand bat, offspinner**
Test debut	**Australia v India at Mumbai 2004-05**
ODI debut	**Australia v South Africa at Johannesburg 2001-02**
T20I debut	**Australia v Pakistan at Dubai 2009**

THE PROFILE Nathan Hauritz, a former Australian Under-19 captain, leapfrogged several other spinners to finish the 2008-09 season as the only specialist slow bowler with a national contract. It was a stunning turnaround for a tidy, flighty offspinner who had been largely ignored – and indeed was not a regular choice for his state – since a promising Test debut in November 2004. But after Beau Casson, Jason Krejza, Cameron White and Bryce McGain took turns following Stuart MacGill's retirement early in 2008, Hauritz was suddenly picked for the second Test against New Zealand at Adelaide in November despite being left out by New South Wales the previous week. He took nine wickets in three home Tests, and also played his first ODI for nearly six years. He made the squad for the 2009 Ashes tour as the only specialist spinner and, despite being written off in the English media, did well enough in the three Tests he played, taking ten wickets at 32, which compared favourably with Graeme Swann's 14 at 40 in five matches for England. Back home, Hauritz took five-fors against Pakistan at both Melbourne and Sydney – surprisingly, his first such hauls in first-class cricket – before a foot problem sent him home early from England in 2010. Before all this, Hauritz's five wickets (including Tendulkar and Laxman) on his surprise Test debut in 2004 had become a distant memory when he struggled back in Australia. He was dropped by Queensland before the end of that season, and moved to NSW after another disappointing summer. The four seasons after his return from India produced only ten first-class wickets, although he was a one-day fixture, before his return to the limelight.

THE FACTS Hauritz had never taken five wickets in a first-class innings until he took 5 for 101 against Pakistan in the Boxing Day Test at Melbourne in 2009: he promptly grabbed another five-for in the next Test, at Sydney … Hauritz took a wicket (Anil Kumble) with his third ball in Test cricket, at Mumbai in November 2004 … He scored 94 for Queensland v Western Australia at Perth in January 2004 …

THE FIGURES *to 23.9.10*   ESPNcricinfo.com

Batting & Fielding	M	Inns	NO	Runs	HS	Avge	S/R	100	50	4s	6s	Ct	St
Tests	15	20	6	370	75	26.42	51.46	0	2	45	3	3	0
ODIs	55	30	17	330	53*	25.38	97.34	0	1	21	8	24	0
T20Is	3	2	0	6	4	3.00	60.00	0	0	1	0	1	0
First-class	58	75	19	1053	94	18.80	–	0	4	–	–	28	0

Bowling	M	Balls	Runs	Wkts	BB	Avge	RpO	S/R	5i	10m
Tests	15	3660	1814	57	5–53	31.82	2.97	64.21	2	0
ODIs	55	2562	2014	62	4–29	32.48	4.71	41.32	0	0
T20Is	3	44	47	2	1–20	23.50	6.40	22.00	0	0
First-class	58	11297	5628	133	5–53	42.31	2.98	84.93	2	0

JOSH **HAZLEWOOD**

Full name	**Josh Reginald Hazlewood**
Born	**January 8, 1991, Tamworth, New South Wales**
Teams	**New South Wales**
Style	**Left-hand bat, right-arm fast-medium bowler**
Test debut	**No Tests yet**
ODI debut	**Australia v England at Southampton 2010**
T20I debut	**No T20Is yet**

THE PROFILE Josh Hazlewood is tall (6ft 5ins/196cm), but solidly built, and became the youngest fast bowler ever to be selected by New South Wales when he faced the New Zealanders in November 2008. Then only 17, he took the new ball and picked up two wickets in each innings, but that was his only senior appearance of the summer. However, it helped him pick up the Rising Star Award at the end of the season, to continue a rapid rise for a bowler who had been the youngest member of Australia's squad for the 2008 Under-19 World Cup. Hazlewood, who began playing at the age of seven and whose favourite player is Glenn McGrath, was handed a rookie state contract for 2008-09, despite still being at school in Tamworth, in country New South Wales. In New Zealand early in 2010 he took 13 wickets in Australia's successful run in another Under-19 World Cup, including four – and the match award – in the final as Pakistan were defeated, which put him in the frame for higher honours. Still, Hazlewood was a surprise choice as Mitchell Johnson's replacement for the one-day series in England in mid-2010, and made his international debut in the first match at the Rose Bowl. Australia's youngest-ever one-day international player, Hazlewood let no-one down, with 1 for 41 in his seven overs. Andrew Miller observed on Cricinfo: "His cross-seam cutter to bowl Craig Kieswetter was a peach, and it was notable that Ponting trusted him with a slip in a hunt for mid-innings wickets." Although Hazlewood did not feature again in the series, he remains very much one for the future.

THE FACTS Hazlewood was the youngest Australian ever to play in a one-day international, being 19 years 165 days old when he made his debut in 2010: the previous-youngest was slow left-armer Ray "Candles" Bright (19 years 260 days in 1973-74) ... Hazlewood was named Man of the Match in the Under-19 World Cup final in New Zealand in January 2010, after his 4 for 30 helped Australia beat Pakistan ...

THE FIGURES to 23.9.10   **ESPN**cricinfo.com

Batting & Fielding	M	Inns	NO	Runs	HS	Avge	S/R	100	50	4s	6s	Ct	St
Tests	0	0	–	–	–	–	–	–	–	–	–	–	–
ODIs	1	0	–	–	–	–	–	–	–	–	–	0	0
T20Is	0	0	–	–	–	–	–	–	–	–	–	–	–
First-class	6	5	3	23	9*	11.50	35.38	0	0	2	0	3	0

Bowling	M	Balls	Runs	Wkts	BB	Avge	RpO	S/R	5i	10m
Tests	0	0	–	–	–	–	–	–	–	–
ODIs	1	42	41	1	1–41	41.00	5.85	42.00	0	0
T20Is	0	0	–	–	–	–	–	–	–	–
First-class	6	844	447	17	3–94	26.29	3.17	49.64	0	0

RANGANA **HERATH**

Full name	**Herath Mudiyanselage Rangana Keerthi Bandara Herath**
Born	**March 19, 1978, Kurunegala**
Teams	**Moors, Wayamba, Hampshire**
Style	**Left-hand bat, left-arm orthodox spinner**
Test debut	**Sri Lanka v Australia at Galle 1999-2000**
ODI debut	**Zimbabwe v Sri Lanka at Harare 2003-04**
T20I debut	**No T20Is yet**

THE PROFILE Slow left-armer Rangana Herath first came to prominence late in 1999, when his so-called mystery ball – *Wisden* called it "a wonderful delivery, bowled out of the front of his hand, which turned back into right-handers" – befuddled the touring Australians. He took four wickets on Test debut at Galle, including Steve Waugh and Ricky Ponting, but was soon unceremoniously dumped as other spinners were tried as foils for Muttiah Muralitharan. Herath's unprepossessing body shape – he's rather short with a hint of excess padding around the midriff – may have counted against him, but he continued to be a regular wicket-taker in domestic cricket. He took 17 wickets in four Tests in 2004, including seven in a rare Murali-less Sri Lankan victory, over Pakistan at Faisalabad, flighting the ball well and making it grip and turn. However, he was soon left out again, seemingly for good. But the wickets still kept coming at home: 45 in 2006-07 and 31 the following season, all at an average under 20, and he was eventually recalled in 2008, although he did little at first and might have returned to anonymity but for an injury which forced Murali out of the home series against Pakistan in July 2009. Herath partnered Ajantha Mendis, and did so well – five wickets in each of the three Tests – that when Murali returned it was Mendis who made way, and Herath took eight wickets to Murali's six in the series-clinching victory over New Zealand in August. He took 11 wickets in three Tests in India that winter, but lost his place after an underwhelming bowling performance in Murali's final Test in July 2010, although he did manage a career-best with the bat.

THE FACTS Herath took 8 for 43 (11 for 72 in the match) for Moors v Police in Colombo in 2002–03 ... In January 2002 he took 8 for 47 (and caught one of the others) for Moors v Galle ... Herath took 72 wickets at 13.59 in Sri Lanka in 2000-01 ... He made 80 not out against India in Colombo in July 2010: he had never previously made more than 71 in first-class cricket, although he had reached 70 four times ...

THE FIGURES *to 23.9.10*   **ESPncricinfo.com**

Batting & Fielding	M	Inns	NO	Runs	HS	Avge	S/R	100	50	4s	6s	Ct	St
Tests	22	28	5	287	80*	12.47	44.15	0	1	35	1	4	0
ODIs	9	2	1	2	2	2.00	50.00	0	0	0	0	4	0
T20Is	0	0	–	–	–	–	–	–	–	–	–	–	–
First-class	184	262	60	3304	80*	16.35	–	0	12	–	–	84	0

Bowling	M	Balls	Runs	Wkts	BB	Avge	RpO	S/R	5i	10m
Tests	22	5383	2690	71	5–99	37.88	2.99	75.81	4	0
ODIs	9	336	215	9	3–28	23.88	3.83	37.33	0	0
T20Is	0	0	–	–	–	–	–	–	–	–
First-class	184	36475	16599	668	8–43	24.84	2.73	54.60	38	5

BEN **HILFENHAUS**

Full name	**Benjamin William Hilfenhaus**
Born	**March 15, 1983, Ulverstone, Tasmania**
Teams	**Tasmania**
Style	**Right-hand bat, right-arm fast-medium bowler**
Test debut	**Australia v South Africa at Johannesburg 2008-09**
ODI debut	**Australia v New Zealand at Hobart 2006-07**
T20I debut	**Australia v England at Sydney 2006-07**

THE PROFILE A few years ago Ben Hilfenhaus – Ricky Ponting's second cousin – was working on a building site, but now he has safely laid down his trowel after a series of dramatic performances for Tasmania catapulted him to a national contract. "Hilfy" established himself quickly in 2005-06 – Man of the Match against Victoria in only his second game, ten wickets against NSW, then called up for Australia A after 39 wickets at 30.82 in his first season. "It has been a fast ride," he admitted after picking up the prestigious Bradman Young Cricketer of the Year prize in February 2007. A month earlier he played a Twenty20 international and then his first ODI, on his home ground at Hobart, trapping Brendon McCullum in front in his second over. He had to wait until the South African trip early in 2009 to crack the Test side, but settled in fast, keeping the runs down. He was duly selected for the Ashes tour, but was not assured of a place, even when Brett Lee broke down. He finally got the vote for the first Test ahead of Stuart Clark and Doug Bollinger, and immediately looked at home, shaping the ball away and finding swing with the Duke ball more readily even than England's practised performers. Hilfenhaus finished the series with 22 wickets – at least four in each game – and seemed set for a long run in the side ... but tendinitis in the knee kept him out for much of the home season that followed. However, he was back for the Tests against Pakistan in England in July 2010, taking eight wickets in the two matches.

THE FACTS Hilfenhaus was the leading wicket-taker on either side in the 2009 Ashes series, with 22 ... He took 7 for 58 (and 10 for 87 in the match) for Tasmania v New South Wales at Hobart in March 2006: in December 2006 he took 7 for 70 against South Australia at Hobart ... He took 5 for 14 as Queensland were bowled out for 62 at Brisbane in October 2008 ...

THE FIGURES to 23.9.10   ᴇѕᴘᴨcricinfo.com

Batting & Fielding	M	Inns	NO	Runs	HS	Avge	S/R	100	50	4s	6s	Ct	St
Tests	11	15	6	145	56*	16.11	60.66	0	1	20	1	3	0
ODIs	15	7	4	29	16	9.66	46.03	0	0	2	0	7	0
T20Is	6	2	1	2	2	2.00	22.22	0	0	0	0	0	0
First-class	50	66	22	544	56*	12.36	–	0	2	–	–	17	0

Bowling	M	Balls	Runs	Wkts	BB	Avge	RpO	S/R	5i	10m
Tests	11	2344	1230	42	4–60	29.28	3.14	55.80	0	0
ODIs	15	758	717	18	2–42	39.83	5.67	42.11	0	0
T20Is	6	138	143	8	2–15	17.87	6.21	17.25	0	0
First-class	50	11239	5870	204	7–58	28.77	3.13	55.09	7	1

JAMES **HOPES**

AUSTRALIA

Full name	**James Redfern Hopes**
Born	**October 24, 1978, Townsville, Queensland**
Teams	**Queensland**
Style	**Right-hand bat, right-arm medium-pacer**
Test debut	**No Tests yet**
ODI debut	**Australia v New Zealand at Wellington 2004-05**
T20I debut	**Australia v New Zealand at Auckland 2004-05**

THE PROFILE James Hopes was earmarked for higher honours after some outstanding performances for Australia's youth teams, but he took a few years to settle once he made it to the first-class scene. A brisk medium-pacer whose aggressive batting has been shuffled up and down the Queensland order, Hopes has made three Sheffield Shield centuries (and two for Australia A), and in 2004-05 his average was in the mid-forties. Bowling was his main weapon the following season – 16 first-class wickets and 15 more in the one-day competition – but he was unable to transfer his regular success into the international arena. In nine ODI appearances, he did not manage more than one wicket in a match, although his batting showed some promise, with a top score of 43 against Sri Lanka. He was dropped early in 2006, but when Shane Watson suffered a calf problem in Bangladesh he was replaced by his Queensland team-mate. Despite that, Hopes was briefly cut from the national-contract list and returned to the domestic fray, although he was put on standby when Watson suffered another injury scare during the 2007 World Cup. A regular sweater in the gym, Hopes would love to be a professional golfer, but instead drives powerfully through the covers. He remained a one-day regular, although rather surprisingly for such a robust performer he has not always featured in Australia's Twenty20 side. Evenly balanced as an allrounder – both disciplines still need polish if he is to survive in the international game – his bowling has variety, and tight final overs have regularly picked up wickets and saved runs.

THE FACTS Hopes took 5 for 14 against Ireland at Dublin in June 2010: only five better analyses have been recorded for Australia in ODIs ... He made his highest score of 146 when opening (with Michael Hussey) for Australia A v Pakistan A at Rawalpindi in September 2005 ... He took 6 for 70 for Queensland v Tasmania at Hobart in March 2006 ... In 2008-09 Hopes passed Michael Kasprowicz's previous record of 117 one-day wickets for Queensland ...

THE FIGURES *to 23.9.10*   ᴇsᴘᴨcricinfo.com

Batting & Fielding	M	Inns	NO	Runs	HS	Avge	S/R	100	50	4s	6s	Ct	St
Tests	0	0	–	–	–	–	–	–	–	–	–	–	–
ODIs	83	61	8	1326	63*	25.01	93.71	0	3	123	6	24	0
T20Is	12	7	2	105	30	21.00	107.14	0	0	7	1	3	0
First-class	61	100	1	2970	146	30.00	–	5	14	–	–	26	0

Bowling	M	Balls	Runs	Wkts	BB	Avge	RpO	S/R	5i	10m
Tests	0	0	–	–	–	–	–	–	–	–
ODIs	83	3115	2328	67	5–14	34.74	4.48	46.49	1	0
T20Is	12	222	283	10	2–26	28.30	7.64	22.20	0	0
First-class	61	8995	4112	132	6–70	31.15	2.74	68.14	3	0

GARETH **HOPKINS**

Full name	**Gareth James Hopkins**
Born	**November 24, 1976, Lower Hutt, Wellington**
Teams	**Auckland**
Style	**Right-hand bat, wicketkeeper**
Test debut	**New Zealand v England at Nottingham 2008**
ODI debut	**New Zealand v England at Chester-le-Street 2004**
T20I debut	**New Zealand v South Africa at Johannesburg 2007-08**

THE PROFILE Gareth Hopkins started as a specialist wicketkeeper, but over time his uncompromising batting improved to the point where he was called up for the one-day series in England in 2004 after Brendon McCullum went home to be with his pregnant wife. McCullum's continued excellence with bat and gloves has meant few chances since then, but Hopkins hung in there, and scored 514 runs at 85 for Otago during 2006-07, with three hundreds, which earned him a central contract for 2007-08. McCullum has loomed like an unwanted wedding guest almost throughout Hopkins's career: he was playing for Canterbury when McCullum moved to Christchurch from Otago, which persuaded Hopkins to make the reverse move. Then McCullum decided to return to Otago, so Hopkins upped sticks again and moved to Auckland, where his wife works. He has also turned out for Northern Districts, and played and coached in Holland. Hopkins was selected for the England tour of 2008, and finally got a Test chance when McCullum felt a twinge in his back and couldn't keep wicket in the third Test at Trent Bridge. In a generally disappointing match for New Zealand, Hopkins batted as soundly as anyone, and kept well. However, he was overlooked in favour of the Auckland stumper Reece Young for the Test portion of the Sri Lankan tour late in 2009, but kept his name in the frame with a fine domestic season with the bat in 2009-10 – including a maiden double-century – and then received a boost when McCullum declared that he would no longer keep wicket in Tests.

THE FACTS Hopkins was run out in international cricket before he'd actually faced a ball, against West Indies at Lord's in 2004 ... He made 201 for Auckland v Central Districts in March 2010 ... Hopkins has twice made ten dismissals in a match, equalling the New Zealand record ... He scored 113 and 175 not out for Canterbury at Auckland in February 2003 ...

THE FIGURES to 23.9.10   ▄▄▀▄cricinfo.com

Batting & Fielding	M	Inns	NO	Runs	HS	Avge	S/R	100	50	4s	6s	Ct	St
Tests	1	2	0	27	15	13.50	23.27	0	0	3	0	3	0
ODIs	22	14	0	203	45	14.50	72.75	0	0	15	2	24	1
T20Is	10	8	0	86	36	10.75	121.12	0	0	5	5	4	2
First-class	117	181	28	5336	201	34.87	–	11	23	–	–	304	20

Bowling	M	Balls	Runs	Wkts	BB	Avge	RpO	S/R	5i	10m
Tests	1	0	–	–	–	–	–	–	–	–
ODIs	22	0	–	–	–	–	–	–	–	–
T20Is	10	0	–	–	–	–	–	–	–	–
First-class	117	17	49	0	–	–	17.29	–	0	0

PHILLIP **HUGHES**

Full name	**Phillip Joel Hughes**
Born	**November 30, 1988, Macksville, New South Wales**
Teams	**New South Wales**
Style	**Left-hand bat**
Test debut	**Australia v South Africa at Johannesburg 2008-09**
ODI debut	**No ODIs yet**
T20I debut	**No T20Is yet**

THE PROFILE Phillip Hughes made an unconvincing start in Tests – a four-ball duck at the Wanderers after becoming Australia's youngest player since Craig McDermott 25 years previously – but he made 75 in the second innings, and by the end of the next Test had shown he was a highly accomplished if unconventional batsman. At Durban he became the youngest ever to make two centuries in the same Test, bringing up the first one with two sixes. His 415 runs in the series were followed by centuries in each of his three Championship games for Middlesex, which further irritated England supporters angry he had been given the chance to fine-tune before the 2009 Ashes series. As it happened it didn't do him that much good, as he failed to shine in the first two Tests and was replaced by Shane Watson, a change made public on Hughes's Twitter site before the official announcement, which provoked reactions ranging from rage to raucous laughter. His country-baked technique includes compulsive slicing through point and slashing to cover, as well as stepping away to provide room for tennis-style drives down the ground. The new Test opening pair of Watson and Simon Katich kept Hughes out for much of 2009-10, although he did make 86 not out at Wellington when Watson was injured – but then a dislocated shoulder, suffered while boxing, knocked Hughes himself out, sparing him a return to English pitches to face Pakistan. He remains the likeliest next cab on the batting rank if any of the Test side suffers injury or loss of form.

THE FACTS Hughes made 115 and 160 in only his second Test, against South Africa at Durban in March 2009: at 20 years 98 days he was the youngest to hit twin centuries in a Test, beating George Headley (20 years 271 days for West Indies v England in 1929-30) ... Hughes hit 198 for NSW v South Australia at Adelaide in November 2008 ... He played three Championship matches for Middlesex in 2009 – and scored centuries in each of them ...

THE FIGURES to 23.9.10   ESPncricinfo.com

Batting & Fielding	M	Inns	NO	Runs	HS	Avge	S/R	100	50	4s	6s	Ct	St
Tests	7	13	1	615	160	51.25	61.62	2	2	82	7	3	0
ODIs	0	0	–	–	–	–	–	–	–	–	–	–	–
T20Is	0	0	–	–	–	–	–	–	–	–	–	–	–
First-class	40	71	6	3882	198	59.72	62.63	13	21	520	25	30	0

Bowling	M	Balls	Runs	Wkts	BB	Avge	RpO	S/R	5i	10m
Tests	7	0	–	–	–	–	–	–	–	–
ODIs	0	0	–	–	–	–	–	–	–	–
T20Is	0	0	–	–	–	–	–	–	–	–
First-class	40	18	9	0	–	–	3.00	–	0	0

DAVID **HUSSEY**

Full name	**David John Hussey**
Born	**July 15, 1977, Morley, Western Australia**
Teams	**Victoria, Nottinghamshire, Kolkata Knight Riders**
Style	**Right-hand bat, occasional offspinner**
Test debut	**No Tests yet**
ODI debut	**Australia v West Indies at Basseterre 2007-08**
T20I debut	**Australia v India at Melbourne 2007-08**

THE PROFILE David Hussey copied his older brother Michael's talent for ridiculous scoring in English county cricket. And, like Michael, David was forced to pile up mountains of runs in Australia before gaining the confidence of the national selectors. It took his first thousand-run home season before he was finally chosen for a tour, the one-day series in the West Indies early in 2008, and earned his first national contract. Earlier that season he made his Twenty20 debut against India at the MCG. He made his first ODI century in 2009 – but it was against Scotland, and couldn't get him into the side for the series against England that followed. Hussey was one of the big surprises in the inaugural Indian Premier League auction when Kolkata paid $625,000 for him – far more than his brother fetched. Despite his crash-and-bash style, David is desperate not to be pigeonholed as a Twenty20 player. His first-class record suggests it is a fair request: he boasts an average in the mid-fifties, a shade higher than his brother's. But his one-day exploits include a 60-ball century – the second-fastest in Australia's domestic history – and in 2007-08 he was Victoria's Player of the Year in all three formats. He has also been a run-machine during his time with Nottinghamshire, with more than 5500 first-class runs at an average above 60. An aggressive batsman with a strong bottom-hand technique, Hussey hit a breathtaking breakthrough 212 not out at nearly a run a ball in 2003-04, his first full season, as Victoria chased a record-breaking 455 for victory against NSW: Steve Waugh, the opposing captain, was impressed.

THE FACTS David Hussey hit 275 (27 fours, 14 sixes) for Nottinghamshire v Essex at Trent Bridge in May 2007 ... He reached 50 in only 19 balls – Australia's second-fastest ODI half-century – against West Indies in St Kitts in July 2008 ... Hussey fetched $625,000 at the inaugural IPL auction in February 2008, much more than his brother Michael ($350,000) and Australia's captain Ricky Ponting ($400,000) ...

THE FIGURES to 23.9.10

ᴇsᴘɴcricinfo.com

Batting & Fielding	M	Inns	NO	Runs	HS	Avge	S/R	100	50	4s	6s	Ct	St
Tests	0	0	–	–	–	–	–	–	–	–	–	–	–
ODIs	23	21	0	598	111	28.47	88.46	1	4	39	13	12	0
T20Is	25	23	3	579	88*	28.95	132.79	0	3	34	27	14	0
First-class	144	223	21	11100	275	54.95	71.36	38	50	–	–	177	0

Bowling	M	Balls	Runs	Wkts	BB	Avge	RpO	S/R	5i	10m
Tests	0	0	–	–	–	–	–	–	–	–
ODIs	23	257	230	3	1–6	76.66	5.36	85.66	0	0
T20Is	25	252	267	15	3–25	17.80	6.35	16.80	0	0
First-class	144	2258	1423	21	4–105	67.76	3.78	107.52	0	0

MICHAEL **HUSSEY**

AUSTRALIA

Full name **Michael Edward Killeen Hussey**
Born **May 27, 1975, Morley, Western Australia**
Teams **Western Australia, Channai Super Kings**
Style **Left-hand bat, occasional right-arm medium-pacer**
Test debut **Australia v West Indies at Brisbane 2005-06**
ODI debut **Australia v India at Perth 2003-04**
T20I debut **Australia v New Zealand at Auckland 2004-05**

THE PROFILE English fans couldn't understand why Australia took so long to recognise Michael Hussey's claims. Bradmanesque in county cricket, he was less prolific at home, and seemed destined to remain unfulfilled. Finally, late in 2005 Justin Langer's fractured rib gave Hussey a chance after 15,313 first-class runs, a record for an Australian before wearing baggy green. He made an attractive century in his second Test, then a memorable 122 against South Africa at the MCG, when he and Glenn McGrath added 107 for the last wicket. The fairytale continued in the 2006-07 Ashes, when he topped the batting averages with 91.60, although his one-day form did finally drop off a little. Hussey has a tidy, compact style: skilled off front foot and back, he is attractive to watch once set. He reinvented himself in one-day cricket as an agile fieldsman and an innovative batsman with cool head and loose wrists, and supplanted Michael Bevan as the Aussies' one-day "finisher". His sky-high standards dipped a little in 2008, then a patchy 2009 Ashes series was redeemed slightly by a fighting century (his first for 16 Tests) at The Oval, although that was tinged with regret as he was last out as Australia surrendered the urn again. Still he evolved: a superb 134 not out, and an unlikely ninth-wicket stand of 123 with Peter Siddle, turned the Sydney Test against Pakistan on its head in January 2010; and in the World Twenty20 semi-final in the West Indies later in the year Hussey's astonishing 60 off 24 balls, with 34 off the final two overs, dragged Australia past Pakistan and into the final.

THE FACTS Hussey scored 229 runs in ODIs before he was dismissed, and had an average of 100.22 after 32 matches ... He took only 166 days to reach 1000 runs in Tests, beating the 228-day record established by England's Andrew Strauss in 2005 ... Hussey's 331 not out against Somerset at Taunton in 2003 is the highest individual score for Northamptonshire ... He has captained Australia in four ODIs, and lost the lot ... Hussey averages 62.65 in Tests in Australia, and 40.00 overseas ...

THE FIGURES to 23.9.10   **ESPn**cricinfo.com

Batting & Fielding	M	Inns	NO	Runs	HS	Avge	S/R	100	50	4s	6s	Ct	St
Tests	52	90	12	3981	182	51.03	48.19	11	21	457	19	50	0
ODIs	146	121	38	4287	109*	51.65	88.48	2	31	307	63	82	0
T20Is	27	20	7	457	60*	35.15	150.32	0	2	40	17	18	0
First-class	235	419	43	19906	331*	52.94	–	52	92	–	–	255	0

Bowling	M	Balls	Runs	Wkts	BB	Avge	RpO	S/R	5i	10m
Tests	52	180	103	2	1–3	51.50	3.43	90.00	0	0
ODIs	146	234	227	2	1–22	113.50	5.82	117.00	0	0
T20Is	27	6	5	0	–	–	5.00	–	0	0
First-class	235	1620	875	22	3–34	39.77	3.24	73.63	0	0

IMRUL KAYES

Full name	**Imrul Kayes**
Born	**February 2, 1987, Meherpur, Kushtia**
Teams	**Khulna**
Style	**Left-hand bat, occasional offspinner**
Test debut	**Bangladesh v South Africa at Bloemfontein 2008-09**
ODI debut	**Bangladesh v New Zealand at Chittagong 2008-09**
T20I debut	**Bangladesh v Pakistan at Gros Islet 2010**

THE PROFILE The elevation of left-hand opener Imrul Kayes to Bangladesh colours was hastened by the mass defections to the unauthorised Indian Cricket League late in 2008. With more than a dozen leading players suddenly unavailable, "Sagar" was called up after a fine home season in 2007-08, when he was the leading scorer for Khulna less than a year after making his first-class debut. His haul included two centuries in separate matches against Sylhet, and he finished the season with 600 runs. He also scored consistently on the Bangladesh Academy's tour of Sri Lanka in September 2008, and was given a run in the senior side. Kayes has a solid, compact technique, and likes to hit through the covers off the back foot, but he had the misfortune to make his Test debut against South Africa: he rarely looked settled against their high-quality pacemen, and managed only 25 runs in four attempts in the Tests. On his debut, at Bloemfontein, he was out twice in the space of about three hours on the second day. He fared a little better in two Tests against Sri Lanka, then made 33 (and added a two-hour 24 in the second innings, in an opening stand of 82 with Tamim Iqbal) in Bangladesh's victory over a depleted West Indian side in St Vincent in July 2009. He retained his place, though, and showed he was coming to terms with the international game with an ODI hundred in New Zealand early in 2010, followed by a patient 75 during a record opening stand with Tamim in the Lord's Test.

THE FACTS Imrul Kayes made 101 v New Zealand in an ODI in Christchurch in February 2010 ... At Lord's in 2010 he and Tamim Iqbal put on 185 – a new national Test record – for the first wicket ... Both Kayes's first-class hundreds were scored for Khulna v Sylhet late in 2007 (121 at Fatullah and 138 at Khulna): in between he made 121 against them in a one-day game ...

THE FIGURES to 23.9.10   **ESPN**cricinfo.com

Batting & Fielding	M	Inns	NO	Runs	HS	Avge	S/R	100	50	4s	6s	Ct	St
Tests	13	26	0	453	75	17.42	44.89	0	1	68	0	12	0
ODIs	22	22	0	671	101	30.50	67.03	1	5	63	5	3	0
T20Is	2	2	0	0	0	0.00	0.00	0	0	0	0	0	0
First-class	35	66	1	1667	138	25.64	–		2	6	–	–	22	0

Bowling	M	Balls	Runs	Wkts	BB	Avge	RpO	S/R	5i	10m
Tests	13	6	7	0	0	0	7.00	–	0	0
ODIs	22	0	–	–	–	–	–	–	–	–
T20Is	2	0	–	–	–	–	–	–	–	–
First-class	35	12	11	0	0	0	5.50	–	0	0

RAVINDRA **JADEJA**

Full name	**Ravindrasinh Anirudhsinh Jadeja**
Born	**December 6, 1988, Navagam-Khed, Saurashtra**
Teams	**Saurashtra**
Style	**Left-hand bat, left-arm orthodox spinner**
Test debut	**No Tests yet**
ODI debut	**India v Sri Lanka at Colombo 2008-09**
T20I debut	**India v Sri Lanka at Colombo 2008-09**

THE PROFILE Left-handed allrounder Ravindra Jadeja elbowed his way into national contention with a stellar 2008-09 season, which followed a good showing in the inaugural IPL, during which Shane Warne labelled him "a superstar in the making". He extended his maiden first-class hundred for Saurashtra against Orissa at Rajkot in November 2008 to 232 not out, although even that was overshadowed by his batting partner Cheteshwar Pujara's triple-century. The pair shared an unbroken partnership of 520 for the fifth wicket, a record for all first-class cricket, erasing the 464 of the Waugh twins for New South Wales against Western Australia in 1990-91. Jadeja collected his best bowling figures, and another century, the following month, finishing the Ranji Trophy season with 739 runs and 42 wickets. He leapfrogged Pujara into the national side, making his ODI and Twenty20 debuts in Sri Lanka early in 2009. Jadeja started with a rearguard 60 not out in Colombo, and although his batting and bowling returns were modest after that he remained in the mix for the World Twenty20 in England in June 2009, helped by his fine fielding. There, though, he was criticised for using up 35 balls over 25 in the defeat by England (in truth the blame lay with whoever put him in at No. 4, ahead of hitters like Yuvraj Singh and MS Dhoni). Jadeja blotted his copybook in 2010, being banned from the third IPL for allegedly trying to negotiate terms with another team; he was also involved in an incident in a St Lucia bar after India's early exit from the World Twenty20. He also did little on the field for India, save for a couple of one-day fifties against Zimbabwe.

THE FACTS Jadeja scored 232 not out for Saurashtra v Orissa at Rajkot in November 2008: he shared an unbroken world-record fifth-wicket stand of 520 with Cheteshwar Pujara, who made 302 not out ... Jadeja took 7 for 31 (10 for 88 in the match) for Saurashtra v Hyderabad at Rajkot in December 2008 ... Ravindra is not related to the former Indian batsman Ajay Jadeja ...

THE FIGURES to 23.9.10   **ESPRI**cricinfo.com

Batting & Fielding	M	Inns	NO	Runs	HS	Avge	S/R	100	50	4s	6s	Ct	St
Tests	0	0	–	–	–	–	–	–	–	–	–	–	–
ODIs	34	22	5	535	61*	31.47	76.97	0	4	39	7	11	0
T20Is	9	6	2	65	25	16.25	86.66	0	0	2	1	5	0
First-class	29	44	3	1547	232*	37.73	54.24	3	8	180	12	22	0

Bowling	M	Balls	Runs	Wkts	BB	Avge	RpO	S/R	5i	10m
Tests	0	0	–	–	–	–	–	–	–	–
ODIs	34	1492	1205	29	4–32	41.55	4.84	51.44	0	0
T20Is	9	186	232	5	2–26	46.40	7.48	37.20	0	0
First-class	29	5854	2313	81	7–31	28.55	2.37	72.27	5	1

JAHURUL ISLAM

Full name	**Mohammad Jahurul Islam**
Born	**December 12, 1986, Rajshahi**
Teams	**Rajshahi**
Style	**Right-hand bat, occasional wicketkeeper**
Test debut	**Bangladesh v England at Mirpur 2009-10**
ODI debut	**Bangladesh v Pakistan at Dambulla 2010**
T20I debut	**Bangladesh v Australia at Bridgetown 2010**

THE PROFILE A superb domestic season in 2009-10, during which he was the only man to pass 1000 runs, with 1008 runs at 63 with four centuries, propelled the tall, aggressive Jahurul Islam into national contention, and when Raqibul Hasan fell out with the selectors and announced a short-lived retirement in a fit of pique just before the home Test series against England, "Aumi" got the call. He made a duck in his first Test innings, courtesy of Graeme Swann, but took his revenge in the second innings, getting off the mark with a six off Swann over long-on, and adding another in James Tredwell's next over to become only the second player to open his account in Tests with two sixes. Jahurul had long been earmarked for high honours: a product of the national academy, he made 78 on his first-class debut in 2002-03, although he was into his fifth season before he finally cracked the three-figure barrier. In England in 2010 Jahurul hit 158 against Surrey, and did reasonably well in the first Test at Lord's (20 and 46) before two low scores in the second. He is also a handy stopgap wicketkeeper, and deputised in some of the one-dayers in Britain later in 2010 after Mushfiqur Rahim was injured. It didn't seem to affect his batting: at Bristol Jahurul made 40 – his top score at the time – during an important stand of 83 with Imrul Kayes in a match Bangladesh ended up winning by five runs, their first-ever victory over England.

THE FACTS Jahurul Islam's first two scoring shots in Test cricket were both sixes (against England in March 2010), equalling the feat of his team-mate Shafiul Islam earlier in the year ... Jahurul scored 158 against Surrey at The Oval in May 2010 ... He made 78 on first-class debut for Rajshahi v Sylhet at Fatullah in December 2002 ...

THE FIGURES to 23.9.10

ESPNcricinfo.com

Batting & Fielding	M	Inns	NO	Runs	HS	Avge	S/R	100	50	4s	6s	Ct	St
Tests	3	6	0	114	46	19.00	40.71	0	0	13	2	3	0
ODIs	6	6	1	156	41	31.20	73.58	0	0	13	1	6	0
T20Is	1	1	0	18	18	18.00	150.00	0	0	1	1	1	0
First-class	66	121	12	3953	158	36.26	48.41	8	25	–	–	69	2

Bowling	M	Balls	Runs	Wkts	BB	Avge	RpO	S/R	5i	10m
Tests	3	0	–	–	–	–	–	–	–	–
ODIs	6	0	–	–	–	–	–	–	–	–
T20Is	1	0	–	–	–	–	–	–	–	–
First-class	66	12	7	1	1–0	7.00	3.50	12.00	0	0

MAHELA **JAYAWARDENE**

SRI LANKA

Full name	**Denagamage Proboth Mahela de Silva Jayawardene**
Born	**May 27, 1977, Colombo**
Teams	**Sinhalese Sports Club, Wayamba, Kings XI Punjab**
Style	**Right-hand bat, right-arm medium-pacer**
Test debut	**Sri Lanka v India at Colombo 1997-98**
ODI debut	**Sri Lanka v Zimbabwe at Colombo 1997-98**
T20I debut	**Sri Lanka v England at Southampton 2006**

THE PROFILE A fine technician with an excellent temperament, Mahela Jayawardene's arrival heralded the start of a new era for Sri Lanka's middle order. Perhaps mindful of his first Test, when he went in against India at 790 for 4, he soon developed an appetite for big scores. His 66 then, in the world-record 952 for 6, was followed by a masterful 167 on a Galle minefield against New Zealand in only his fourth Test, and a marathon 242 against India in his seventh. However, Jayawardene lost form, hardly scored a run in the 2003 World Cup, and was dropped. He soon regained his confidence, though, and benefited from a settled spot at No. 4 after Aravinda de Silva retired. A good Test series against England was followed by more runs in 2004. He took over as captain from the injured Marvan Atapattu in England in 2006, producing a stunning double of 61 and 119 to lead the fine rearguard which saved the Lord's Test. Later he put South Africa to the sword in Colombo, hitting a colossal 374 in a world-record stand of 624 with Kumar Sangakkara. In 2007 he inspired his side to the World Cup final with 548 runs at 60, including a century in the semi-final victory over New Zealand, then became Sri Lanka's leading Test runscorer during 2007-08, a period that included three successive centuries, one of them a double against England. He stepped down as captain early in 2009 to concentrate on his batting – not that leadership had affected it much, as he averaged 66.93 in Tests when skipper – and soon added more hundreds to his bulging collection. In 2010 he emerged as a Twenty20 run-machine, too.

THE FACTS Jayawardene made 374 against South Africa in July 2006, the highest by a right-hander in Tests ... He took 77 Test catches off Muttiah Muralitharan, a record for a fielder-bowler combination ... Jayawardene has scored 2646 runs and ten centuries in Tests at the SSC in Colombo, both records for a single ground ... Against New Zealand in August 2009 he was only the fifth batsman to be out twice in the nineties in the same Test ... His record includes five ODIs for the Asia XI ...

THE FIGURES to 23.9.10   **ESPN cricinfo.com**

Batting & Fielding	M	Inns	NO	Runs	HS	Avge	S/R	100	50	4s	6s	Ct	St
Tests	113	187	13	9408	374	54.06	52.69	28	36	1116	42	161	0
ODIs	326	307	32	9003	128	32.73	77.12	12	55	767	54	168	0
T20Is	31	31	4	760	100	28.14	141.52	1	4	78	21	9	0
First-class	195	310	22	15172	374	52.68	–	45	64	–	–	253	0

Bowling	M	Balls	Runs	Wkts	BB	Avge	RpO	S/R	5i	10m
Tests	113	547	292	6	2–32	48.66	3.20	91.16	0	0
ODIs	326	582	558	7	2–56	79.71	5.75	83.14	0	0
T20Is	31	6	8	0	–	–	8.00	–	0	0
First-class	195	2959	1611	52	5–72	30.98	3.26	56.90	1	0

PRASANNA **JAYAWARDENE**

Full name	**Hewasandatchige Asiri Prasanna Wishvanath Jayawardene**
Born	**October 9, 1979, Colombo**
Teams	**Bloomfield, Basnahira South**
Style	**Right-hand bat, wicketkeeper**
Test debut	**Sri Lanka v Pakistan at Kandy 2000**
ODI debut	**Sri Lanka v Pakistan at Sharjah 2002–03**
T20I debut	**No T20Is yet**

THE PROFILE A neat, unflashy wicketkeeper rated by Sri Lanka's captain Kumar Sangakkara as the best in the world, Prasanna Jayawardene looked set for a long international career after touring England at 19, but he became a back number after Sangakkara's own rocket-fuelled arrival in 2000. Waiting on the sidelines had already been a feature of Jayawardene's career: in his first Test, against Pakistan in June 2000, he was confined to the dressing-room throughout, as rain washed out play on the last two days before Sri Lanka fielded. With the selectors worried about overburdening Sangakkara in Tests, Jayawardene was recalled in April 2004. Sangakkara soon got the gloves back that time, but there was something of a sea-change two years later after the England tour, during which Jayawardene showed that his batting had improved. He was recalled for South Africa's visit in July 2006, and this time the decision to lighten Sangakkara's load paid off spectacularly – he hammered 287, and shared a world-record stand of 642 with Mahela Jayawardene in the first Test in Colombo. Prasanna Jayawardene (no relation to Mahela) contented himself with a couple of catches and a stumping as the South Africans went down by an innings, but finally seemed to have booked in for a long run behind the stumps – at least in Tests, with Sangakkara continuing in one-dayers – and cemented his place in June 2007 with a Test ton of his own, against Bangladesh. A finger injury kept him out of the home series against Pakistan in August 2009, but he was back for the New Zealand Tests which followed, and later in the year shared a record sixth-wicket stand of 351 with Mahela against India at Ahmedabad.

THE FACTS Prasanna Jayawardene made 154 not out v India at Ahmedabad in November 2009: he and Mahela Jayawardene (275) put on 351 for the sixth wicket, beating the old Test record of 346 by Don Bradman and Jack Fingleton in 1936-37 ... All Jayawardene's ODIs have been in the United Arab Emirates (in Sharjah in 2003 and Abu Dhabi in 2007) ...

THE FIGURES to 23.9.10   **ESPNcricinfo.com**

Batting & Fielding	M	Inns	NO	Runs	HS	Avge	S/R	100	50	4s	6s	Ct	St
Tests	33	43	6	1080	154*	29.18	48.51	2	2	111	6	66	22
ODIs	6	5	0	27	20	5.40	61.36	0	0	3	0	4	1
T20Is	0	0	–	–	–	–	–	–	–	–	–	–	–
First-class	180	277	31	6679	166*	27.15	–	9	29	–	–	418	81

Bowling	M	Balls	Runs	Wkts	BB	Avge	RpO	S/R	5i	10m
Tests	33	0	–	–	–	–	–	–	–	–
ODIs	6	0	–	–	–	–	–	–	–	–
T20Is	0	0	–	–	–	–	–	–	–	–
First-class	180	18	9	0	–	–	3.00	–	0	0

MITCHELL **JOHNSON**

AUSTRALIA

Full name	**Mitchell Guy Johnson**
Born	**November 2, 1981, Townsville, Queensland**
Teams	**Western Australia**
Style	**Left-hand bat, left-hand fast-medium bowler**
Test debut	**Australia v Sri Lanka at Brisbane 2007-08**
ODI debut	**Australia v New Zealand at Christchurch 2005-06**
T20I debut	**Australia v Zimbabwe at Cape Town 2007-08**

THE PROFILE He's quick, he's tall, he's talented – but most of all, Mitchell Johnson is a left-armer, and only two others before him (Alan Davidson and Bruce Reid) took 100 Test wickets for Australia. Dennis Lillee spotted him at 17, and called him a "once-in-a-generation bowler". Injuries kept intruding, before in December 2005 Johnson was supersubbed into the final match of the one-day series in New Zealand, but the following season was a sobering one. Johnson, who runs up as if carrying a crate of milk bottles in his left hand, started by reducing India to 35 for 5 in a one-dayer in Kuala Lumpur, but narrowly missed out to the steadier Stuart Clark for the 2006-07 Ashes series, then sat out the World Cup as Shaun Tait and Nathan Bracken bowled consistently well. Test rewards finally came in 2007-08, and he was composed in his first two matches against Sri Lanka, then grabbed 16 wickets against India and 10 in the West Indies. In 2008-09 Johnson was superb against South Africa both home and away, adding a wicked in-ducker to his armoury and claiming 33 wickets in six Tests (and also hammering a maiden century), but then he struggled in England, spraying the ball around from an arm seemingly lower than usual. He did take 5 for 69 in an innings victory at Headingley, but overall he was a disappointment given the advance hype; and even though he finished 2009 as the leading Test wicket-taker with 63, the start of 2010 was similarly up-and-down – ten wickets against New Zealand at Hamilton, but only 11 in five other matches.

THE FACTS Johnson took 8 for 61 – the best bowling figures in Tests by any left-arm fast bowler – against South Africa at Perth in 2008-09 ... He was the world's leading Test wicket-taker in 2009, with 63 ... Johnson took 6 for 51 (10 for 106 in the match) for Queensland v Victoria in the Pura Cup final at Brisbane in March 2006 ... He reached his maiden Test (and first-class) century against South Africa at Cape Town in March 2009 with a six ...

THE FIGURES *to 23.9.10*   ᴇsᴘᴨcricinfo.com

Batting & Fielding	M	Inns	NO	Runs	HS	Avge	S/R	100	50	4s	6s	Ct	St
Tests	36	49	8	969	123*	23.63	60.18	1	4	120	18	9	0
ODIs	82	45	16	467	73*	16.10	93.21	0	1	40	11	21	0
T20Is	24	13	4	76	28*	8.44	122.58	0	0	7	2	4	0
First-class	64	87	19	1649	123*	24.25	–	1	8	–	–	16	0

Bowling	M	Balls	Runs	Wkts	BB	Avge	RpO	S/R	5i	10m
Tests	36	8398	4563	158	8–61	28.87	3.26	53.15	5	2
ODIs	82	3997	3292	128	5–26	25.71	4.94	31.22	2	0
T20Is	24	512	586	30	3–15	19.53	6.86	17.06	0	0
First-class	64	13216	7373	244	8–61	30.21	3.34	54.16	7	3

JUNAID SIDDIQUE

Full name	**Mohammad Junaid Siddique**
Born	**October 30, 1987, Rajshahi**
Teams	**Rajshahi**
Style	**Left-hand bat, occasional offspinner**
Test debut	**Bangladesh v New Zealand at Dunedin 2007-08**
ODI debut	**Bangladesh v New Zealand at Auckland 2007-08**
T20I debut	**Bangladesh v Pakistan at Cape Town 2007-08**

THE PROFILE Left-hander Junaid Siddique made a sensational start in Test cricket at 20 when he and fellow debutant Tamim Iqbal flayed the New Zealand attack in an opening stand of 161 to light up the inaugural Test at Dunedin's University Oval at the start of 2008. *Wisden* said the pair "started the second innings with an entrancing display of classical strokes, their timing perfect as the ball was distributed around the short boundaries". Sadly, their fine start came to nothing: the other batsmen made only 83 between them, and Bangladesh lost yet again. "Imrose" also made a stylish 74 against South Africa at Mirpur – no-one else made more than 24 – and added 71 on his Twenty20 international debut. However, the faster bowlers noticed a compulsion to get onto the front foot – bred on slow, low pitches in Bangladesh – and Junaid began to cop a lot of short stuff. But he persevered, making 78 in victory over a depleted West Indian side in St Vincent in July 2009, while his ODI performances improved: after an anaemic start (62 runs in eight innings), he hit 85 against New Zealand in November 2008, then scored consistently against admittedly modest attacks in the West Indies and Zimbabwe. He remained in the mix, and – now settled at No. 3 – made his first Test century against England at Chittagong in March 2010, before adding a maiden one-day international hundred against Ireland a few months later. Typically, though, Bangladesh again lost both matches.

THE FACTS Junaid Siddique scored 74 on his Test debut at Dunedin in January 2008, putting on 161 for the first wicket with Tamim Iqbal, who was also winning his first cap: it was the highest opening stand between debutants in Tests since Billy Ibadulla and Abdul Kadir put on 249 for Pakistan v Australia at Karachi in 1964-65 ... Junaid hit 71 off 49 balls in his first Twenty20 international, against Pakistan at Cape Town in September 2007... He captained Bangladesh A in England in 2008 ...

THE FIGURES to 23.9.10   **ESPNcricinfo.com**

Batting & Fielding	M	Inns	NO	Runs	HS	Avge	S/R	100	50	4s	6s	Ct	St
Tests	18	35	0	942	106	26.91	41.22	1	7	121	1	11	0
ODIs	38	37	0	864	100	23.35	70.64	1	4	94	4	15	0
T20Is	5	5	0	134	71	26.80	159.52	0	1	13	6	0	0
First-class	42	78	1	1943	114*	25.23	–	2	11	–	–	28	0

Bowling	M	Balls	Runs	Wkts	BB	Avge	RpO	S/R	5i	10m
Tests	18	18	11	0	–	–	3.66	–	0	0
ODIs	38	12	13	0	–	–	6.50	–	0	0
T20Is	5	0	–	–	–	–	–	–	–	–
First-class	42	198	119	1	1–30	119.00	3.60	198.00	0	0

JACQUES **KALLIS**

SOUTH AFRICA

Full name	**Jacques Henry Kallis**
Born	**October 16, 1975, Pinelands, Cape Town**
Teams	**Warriors, Bangalore Royal Challengers**
Style	**Right-hand bat, right-arm fast-medium bowler**
Test debut	**South Africa v England at Durban 1995-96**
ODI debut	**South Africa v England at Cape Town 1995-96**
T20I debut	**South Africa v New Zealand at Johannesburg 2005-06**

THE PROFILE In an era of fast scoring and high-octane entertainment, Jacques Kallis is a throwback – an astonishingly effective one – to a more sedate age, when your wicket was to be guarded with your life, and runs were an accidental by-product of crease-occupation. He blossomed after a quiet start into arguably the world's leading batsman, with the adhesive qualities of a Cape Point limpet. In 2005, he was the ICC's first Test Player of the Year, after a run of performances against West Indies and England that marked him out as the modern game's biggest scalp. His batting is not for the romantic: a Kallis century (of which there have now been 52 in international cricket) tends to be a soulless affair, with ruthless efficiency taking precedence over derring-do, and he has never quite dispelled the notion that he is a selfish batsman, something the Aussies played on during the 2007 World Cup. He also had a subdued time in England the following year, amid whispers that he was carrying some extra weight. But he has sailed to the top of South Africa's batting charts, and until Andrew Flintoff's emergence was comfortably the world's leading allrounder, capable of swinging the ball sharply at a surprising pace. Strong, with powerful shoulders and a deep chest, Kallis has the capacity (if not always the inclination) to play a wide array of attacking strokes. He won his 140th Test cap in 2010, and has a batting average in the mid-fifties to go with more than 500 international wickets all told. He's a fine slip fielder too.

THE FACTS Kallis and Shaun Pollock were the first South Africans to play 100 Tests, reaching the mark, appropriately enough, at Centurion in April 2006 ... Kallis averages 169.75 in Tests against Zimbabwe, and scored 388 runs against them in two Tests in 2001-02 without being dismissed ... Including his next innings he batted for a record 1241 minutes in Tests without getting out ... Kallis scored hundreds in five successive Tests in 2003-04 (only Don Bradman, with six, has done better) ... His record includes one Test and three ODIs for the World XI, and two ODIs for the Africa XI ...

THE FIGURES to 23.9.10   **ESPT**cricinfo.com

Batting & Fielding	M	Inns	NO	Runs	HS	Avge	S/R	100	50	4s	6s	Ct	St
Tests	140	237	35	11126	189*	55.07	44.52	35	53	1243	74	159	0
ODIs	303	289	52	10838	139	45.72	72.72	17	78	851	128	115	0
T20Is	16	16	1	512	73	34.13	119.90	0	4	40	17	6	0
First-class	230	377	52	17478	200	53.77	–	52	91	–	–	221	0

Bowling	M	Balls	Runs	Wkts	BB	Avge	RpO	S/R	5i	10m
Tests	140	17887	8403	266	6–54	31.59	2.81	67.24	5	0
ODIs	303	10108	8142	254	5–30	32.05	4.83	39.79	2	0
T20Is	16	186	229	5	2–20	45.80	7.38	37.20	0	0
First-class	230	26622	12367	401	6–54	30.84	2.78	66.38	8	0

KAMRAN AKMAL

Full name	**Kamran Akmal**
Born	**January 13, 1982, Lahore, Punjab**
Teams	**Lahore, National Bank**
Style	**Right-hand bat, wicketkeeper**
Test debut	**Pakistan v Zimbabwe at Harare 2002-03**
ODI debut	**Pakistan v Zimbabwe at Bulawayo 2002-03**
T20I debut	**Pakistan v England at Bristol 2006**

THE PROFILE Kamran Akmal made his first-class debut at the age of 15 as a useful wicketkeeper and a hard-hitting batsman. Several good performances earned him an A-team spot in 2002, and after doing well he was called up for the Zimbabwe tour ahead of the veteran Moin Khan. He was not expected to play in the Tests, but made his debut – and chipped in with a handy 38 – when Rashid Latif suffered a recurrence of a back injury. By October 2004 Akmal was Pakistan's first-choice keeper. He responded with a magnificent showing with the gloves in Australia, then, in 2005, hit five international centuries. Three of them came while opening in one-dayers, and two in Tests, the first saving the match against India at Mohali, while the second, a blistering 154, came in the emphatic series-sealing win over England at Lahore. However, a nightmare series in England in 2006 set him back again. He retained his place throughout 2006-07 without quite regaining his best touch with bat or gloves: he did make an important 119 against India in the Kolkata Test, but continued fumbles behind the stumps eventually led to Sarfraz Ahmed then Zulqarnain Haider briefly taking his place during 2010. Before that Akmal had caned Bangladesh for an 80-ball ODI century at the start of 2008, then started the following year with an unbeaten 158 in a Test against Sri Lanka and a century against Australia before he played his part as Pakistan won the World Twenty20 in England in June. Indeed, Akmal is quite a force in Twenty20 cricket, in which he has effected numerous stumpings off Pakistan's many spinners.

THE FACTS Kamran Akmal scored five international hundreds in December 2005 and January 2006, including 154 in the Lahore Test against England, when he shared a sixth-wicket stand of 269 with Mohammad Yousuf ... Akmal has scored more Test hundreds than any other Pakistan wicketkeeper: Moin Khan made four and Imtiaz Ahmed three ... His brother Umar joined him in the national side in 2009 ...

THE FIGURES to 23.9.10   **ESPn**cricinfo.com

Batting & Fielding	M	Inns	NO	Runs	HS	Avge	S/R	100	50	4s	6s	Ct	St
Tests	53	92	6	2648	158*	30.79	63.10	6	12	372	14	184	22
ODIs	123	108	13	2577	124	27.12	85.58	5	7	301	28	124	21
T20Is	38	33	3	704	73	23.46	124.60	0	5	67	25	17	28
First-class	154	242	27	6713	174	31.22	–	12	31	–	–	519	44

Bowling	M	Balls	Runs	Wkts	BB	Avge	RpO	S/R	5i	10m
Tests	53	0	–	–	–	–	–	–	–	–
ODIs	123	0	–	–	–	–	–	–	–	–
T20Is	38	0	–	–	–	–	–	–	–	–
First-class	154	0	–	–	–	–	–	–	–	–

CHAMARA **KAPUGEDERA**

Full name	**Chamara Kantha Kapugedera**
Born	**February 24, 1987, Kandy**
Teams	**Colombo Cricket Club, Kandurata, Chennai Super Kings**
Style	**Right-hand bat, occasional right-arm medium-pacer**
Test debut	**Sri Lanka v England at Lord's 2006**
ODI debut	**Sri Lanka v Australia at Perth 2005-06**
T20I debut	**Sri Lanka v England at Southampton 2006**

THE PROFILE A naturally aggressive right-hander and a fine fielder, Chamara Kapugedera is one of the few genuinely exciting batsmen the Sri Lankan selectors have unearthed recently from the Under-19s. From his first appearances for Dharmaraja College in Kandy when he was 11, "Kapu" has rarely wasted an opportunity. After a prolific 2003-04 season, when he scored over 1000 runs at schoolboy level, he was picked for the following year's Under-19 tour of Pakistan and made two centuries in the representative matches. The selectors eventually fast-tracked him into the national squad after glowing reports from his youth coaches: Kapugedera was picked to go to India in November 2005, but injured his knee. However, he made his ODI debut, still only 18, against Australia at Perth early in 2006; a maiden fifty followed against Pakistan in March. He won his first Test cap at Lord's that May, but was unlucky enough to receive the perfect inswinging yorker first ball from Sajid Mahmood (another debutant). But Kapugedera put that disappointment behind him with a composed 50 in the third Test, which Sri Lanka won to level the series. He had a quiet time in 2006-07, missing the World Cup after going 12 ODIs without a fifty, then the following season stepped up in one-dayers – he hit 95 against West Indies at Port-of-Spain and 75 against India in the Asia Cup in June 2008 – without cracking the Test side. However, modest form since then – apart from a Test-best 96 against Bangladesh and a matchwinning 67 not out in a one-dayer against Pakistan in August 2009 – meant Kapugedera faced stiff competition to keep his place.

THE FACTS Kapugedera scored 70 on his first-class debut, for Sri Lanka A v New Zealand A in Colombo in October 2005 ... He made his maiden century – 134 not out v Sussex at Hove – the game after collecting a first-ball duck on his Test debut at Lord's ... Kapugedera made 96 in a Test against Bangladesh in January 2009, and 95 in an ODI v West Indies in April 2008 ... He averages 67.50 in ODIs against West Indies – but 1.00 v England ...

THE FIGURES to 23.9.10   **ESFi**cricinfo.com

Batting & Fielding	M	Inns	NO	Runs	HS	Avge	S/R	100	50	4s	6s	Ct	St
Tests	8	15	3	418	96	34.83	53.18	0	4	48	7	6	0
ODIs	82	69	7	1423	95	22.95	72.86	0	7	104	27	26	0
T20Is	19	17	3	276	47	19.71	118.45	0	0	23	10	7	0
First-class	41	65	10	2048	150*	37.23	61.07	3	15	217	28	27	1

Bowling	M	Balls	Runs	Wkts	BB	Avge	RpO	S/R	5i	10m
Tests	8	12	9	0	–	–	4.50	–	0	0
ODIs	82	240	200	2	1–24	100.00	5.00	120.00	0	0
T20Is	19	0	–	–	–	–	–	–	–	–
First-class	41	425	242	4	1–1	60.50	3.41	106.25	0	0

DINESH **KARTHIK**

Full name	**Krishnakumar Dinesh Karthik**
Born	**June 1, 1985, Madras (now Chennai)**
Teams	**Tamil Nadu, Delhi Daredevils**
Style	**Right-hand bat, wicketkeeper**
Test debut	**India v Australia at Mumbai 2004-05**
ODI debut	**India v England at Lord's 2004**
T20I debut	**India v South Africa at Johannesburg 2006-07**

THE PROFILE Dinesh Karthik may be shy off the field, but he has shown his ability to attack under pressure and improvise on it. He gave glimpses of batting talent at 17, but his keeping wasn't up to scratch and he was dropped for the later stages of the Ranji Trophy. However, in 2004 an impressive display in the Under-19 World Cup (including a whirlwind 70 in a must-win game against Sri Lanka), two vital hundreds in the Ranji Trophy, and some improved keeping alerted the national selectors. Karthik replaced Parthiv Patel in the one-day squad in England in September 2004, and pulled off a superb stumping to dispose of Michael Vaughan on debut at Lord's. Then he won his first Test cap against Australia but, after just one fifty in ten matches, he was dropped in favour of the flamboyant MS Dhoni, whose instant success meant Karthik had to rethink. He reinvented himself as a specialist batsman. After India's forgettable 2007 World Cup (for which he was selected but didn't play), he made a maiden Test century in Bangladesh, and forged a successful opening partnership with Wasim Jaffer which continued in England, where Karthik was India's leading scorer in the Tests. Leaner times followed – he was dropped after six single-figure scores in his next ten innings – but he kept his name in the frame with a fine domestic season in 2008-09. His 1026 first-class runs included five centuries (one of them a double), and he also did well in the IPL. With Dhoni occasionally suffering from back trouble, meaning a spare keeper is a necessity, Karthik remains a valuable squad member.

THE FACTS Karthik hit 213 for Tamil Nadu v Uttar Pradesh at Ghaziabad in November 2008 ... He made 153 and 103 for South Zone v Central Zone in the Duleep Trophy at Bangalore in January 2009 ... Karthik averages 49.33 in Tests against South Africa, but only 1.00 in two Tests against Zimbabwe ... He prefers his surname to be spelt with two As ("Kaarthik") as it is more astrologically propitious ...

THE FIGURES to 23.9.10   **ESPN**cricinfo.com

Batting & Fielding	M	Inns	NO	Runs	HS	Avge	S/R	100	50	4s	6s	Ct	St
Tests	23	37	1	1000	129	27.77	50.00	1	7	132	4	51	5
ODIs	52	44	7	1008	79	27.24	74.50	0	5	106	10	31	5
T20Is	9	8	2	100	31*	16.66	113.63	0	0	14	1	5	2
First-class	79	125	6	4660	213	39.15	59.41	13	23	–	–	216	18

Bowling	M	Balls	Runs	Wkts	BB	Avge	RpO	S/R	5i	10m
Tests	23	0	–	–	–	–	–	–	–	–
ODIs	52	0	–	–	–	–	–	–	–	–
T20Is	9	0	–	–	–	–	–	–	–	–
First-class	79	114	125	0	–	–	6.57	–	0	0

SIMON **KATICH**

AUSTRALIA

Full name	**Simon Mathew Katich**
Born	**August 21, 1975, Middle Swan, Western Australia**
Teams	**New South Wales, Kings XI Punjab**
Style	**Left-hand bat, left-arm unorthodox spinner**
Test debut	**Australia v England at Leeds 2001**
ODI debut	**Australia v Zimbabwe at Melbourne 2000-01**
T20I debut	**Australia v New Zealand at Auckland 2004-05**

THE PROFILE Simon Katich resurrected his international career with a stunning season in 2007-08. He broke the record for runs in a Pura Cup season (1506 at 94.12), captained NSW to the title, and regained his Test place. His campaign featured five centuries, including 306 against Queensland, of which 184 came in an extended 150-minute post-lunch session. The Australian selectors, notoriously reluctant to go back to a jettisoned player, just could not ignore all these runs, and after 30 months out of the Test side Katich made a hundred in Antigua and added 157 at Bridgetown in June 2008. He continued his renaissance with centuries against India, New Zealand and South Africa, but tailed off a little in the 2009 Ashes series, after starting with 122 in the first Test at Cardiff, as the bowlers exploited his exaggerated movement across the stumps. After that, though, the run-glut returned: he scored at least one fifty in each of nine successive Tests up to July 2010. During his break from international cricket Katich simply enjoyed batting without the expectation heaped on a Test player. He had also worked on some technical issues that plagued him during 2005, when he was upset by reverse-swing in the Ashes then bamboozled by Muttiah Muralitharan in the Super Series. Ever since Katich was included in Western Australia's state squad in 1994-95, he looked destined for bigger things. He made his Test debut in England in 2001, then enjoyed surprising success with his chinamen against Zimbabwe at Sydney, later his home ground, at the end of 2003.

THE FACTS Katich made 306 for New South Wales v Queensland in October 2007, the highest score at the SCG since Don Bradman's 452 not out, also against Queensland, in 1929-30 ... Katich passed 50 in each of nine successive Tests in 2009-10, equalling Matthew Hayden's Australian record ... Katich made 1506 runs in 2007-08, a Pura Cup/Sheffield Shield record ... He took 6 for 65 against Zimbabwe at Sydney in 2003-04 ...

THE FIGURES to 23.9.10   ESPncricinfo.com

Batting & Fielding	M	Inns	NO	Runs	HS	Avge	S/R	100	50	4s	6s	Ct	St
Tests	52	91	6	3981	157	46.83	49.72	10	24	467	9	38	0
ODIs	45	42	5	1324	107*	35.78	68.74	1	9	138	4	13	0
T20Is	3	2	0	69	39	34.50	146.80	0	0	8	2	2	0
First-class	223	382	47	18134	306	54.13	–	50	97	–	–	204	0

Bowling	M	Balls	Runs	Wkts	BB	Avge	RpO	S/R	5i	10m
Tests	52	1009	617	21	6–65	29.38	3.66	48.0	1	0
ODIs	45	0	–	–	–	–	–	–	–	–
T20Is	3	0	–	–	–	–	–	–	–	–
First-class	223	5769	3462	95	7–130	36.44	3.60	60.7	3	0

ZAHEER **KHAN**

Full name	**Zaheer Khan**
Born	**October 7, 1978, Shrirampur, Maharashtra**
Teams	**Mumbai, Mumbai Indians**
Style	**Right-hand bat, left-arm fast-medium bowler**
Test debut	**India v Bangladesh at Dhaka 2000-01**
ODI debut	**India v Kenya at Nairobi 2000-01**
T20I debut	**India v South Africa at Johannesburg 2006-07**

THE PROFILE Like Waqar Younis a decade before, left-armer Zaheer Khan yorked his way into the cricket world's consciousness: his performances at the Champions Trophy in Kenya in September 2000 announced the arrival of an all-too-rare star in the Indian fast-bowling firmament. Well-built, quick and unfazed by reputations, Zaheer can move the ball both ways off the pitch and swing the old ball at a decent pace. After initially struggling to establish himself, he came of age in the West Indies in 2002, when he led the attack with great heart. His subsequent displays in England and New Zealand – not to mention some eye-catching moments at the 2003 World Cup – established him at the forefront of the new pace generation, but a hamstring injury saw him relegated to bit-part performer as India enjoyed some of their finest moments away in Australia and Pakistan. In a bid to jump the queue of left-arm hopefuls, Zaheer put in the hard yards for Worcestershire in 2006, bowling a lot of overs and, against Essex, taking the first nine wickets to fall before Darren Gough's flailing bat – and a dropped catch – spoilt his figures and his chances of a rare all-ten. It worked: Zaheer reclaimed his Test place, survived the fallout from the World Cup, and led the way in England in 2007, where his nine wickets at Trent Bridge gave India the match and the series: *Wisden* named him as a Cricketer of the Year. An ankle injury restricted him in 2007-08, but he was back in form the following season, and is now closing in on 250 wickets in both Tests and one-dayers.

THE FACTS Zaheer Khan's 75 against Bangladesh at Dhaka in December 2004 is the highest score by a No. 11 in Tests: he dominated a last-wicket stand of 133 with Sachin Tendulkar ... He took 9 for 138 (including a spell of 9 for 28) for Worcestershire v Essex at Chelmsford in June 2006, but a last-wicket stand of 97 cost him the chance of taking all ten wickets ... Zaheer averages 17.46 with the ball in ODIs against Zimbabwe, but 48.52 v Australia ... His record includes six ODIs for the Asia XI ...

THE FIGURES *to 23.9.10*　　　　　　　**ᴇѕᴘⁿ cricinfo.com**

Batting & Fielding	M	Inns	NO	Runs	HS	Avge	S/R	100	50	4s	6s	Ct	St
Tests	72	94	22	969	75	13.45	51.54	0	3	109	19	18	0
ODIs	175	91	35	719	34*	12.83	76.48	0	0	60	24	37	0
T20Is	12	4	2	13	9	6.50	130.00	0	0	0	1	2	0
First-class	136	176	37	2003	75	14.41	–	0	4	–	–	42	0

Bowling	M	Balls	Runs	Wkts	BB	Avge	RpO	S/R	5i	10m
Tests	72	14417	7983	242	7–87	32.98	3.32	59.57	9	1
ODIs	175	8754	7183	241	5–42	29.80	4.92	36.32	1	0
T20Is	12	250	327	13	4–19	25.15	7.84	19.23	0	0
First-class	136	27899	15505	561	9–138	27.63	3.33	49.73	31	8

CRAIG **KIESWETTER**

Full name	**Craig Kieswetter**
Born	**November 28, 1987, Johannesburg, South Africa**
Teams	**Somerset**
Style	**Right-hand bat, wicketkeeper**
Test debut	**No Tests yet**
ODI debut	**England v Bangladesh at Mirpur 2009-10**
T20I debut	**England v West Indies at Providence 2009-10**

THE PROFILE Craig Kieswetter's attractive, uncomplicated front-foot technique pushed him to the brink of an England place before he'd even finished his qualification period, after choosing his adopted country ahead of his native South Africa (despite a late plea from Graeme Smith). The day after he was qualified, he hit 81 for the Lions against the full England side in Abu Dhabi. Fast-tracked into the limited-overs teams, he spanked a classy century in only his third ODI, in Bangladesh, then gave England a series of rapid starts in the World Twenty20 in the West Indies, crowning his campaign with 63 – and the match award – as the final was won. And then it all started to go wrong. Kieswetter, who had scored 1242 first-class runs in 2009, managed less than 500 in 2010. He did make more than 500 in one-dayers for the second year running – but at almost half his 2009 average. He surrendered the England wicketkeeping gloves to Steven Davies, and eventually lost his place. The problem seemed to be twofold: bowlers had got wise to his strengths, and avoided them more; so, in a bid to combat the lack of drivable balls, Kieswetter moved his stance outside leg and was therefore exposing his stumps. By the end of 2010 he had moved back across, and looked better for it, and he is surely too good a player not to enjoy a second coming. However, it was a rude awakening. Kieswetter first came to prominence at Millfield School, and made his Somerset first-team debut in April 2007, scoring 69 not out off 58 balls and taking a catch his coach described as "world class".

THE FACTS Kieswetter made 107 in only his third ODI, against Bangladesh at Chittagong in March 2010 ... All four of his first-class hundreds to date came in England during 2009 ... Kieswetter scored 150 not out for Somerset (sharing an unbroken stand of 318 with James Hildreth) against Warwickshire at Taunton in April 2009, and next day hit 138 not out against them in a 50-over game ...

THE FIGURES to 23.9.10   **ESM** cricinfo.com

Batting & Fielding	M	Inns	NO	Runs	HS	Avge	S/R	100	50	4s	6s	Ct	St
Tests	0	0	–	–	–	–	–	–	–	–	–	–	–
ODIs	12	12	0	320	107	26.66	85.79	1	1	36	8	11	2
T20Is	9	9	0	244	63	27.11	117.87	0	1	23	12	4	1
First-class	59	84	11	2721	153	37.27	61.82	4	16	356	43	171	2

Bowling	M	Balls	Runs	Wkts	BB	Avge	RpO	S/R	5i	10m
Tests	0	0	–	–	–	–	–	–	–	–
ODIs	12	0	–	–	–	–	–	–	–	–
T20Is	9	0	–	–	–	–	–	–	–	–
First-class	59	0	–	–	–	–	–	–	–	–

VIRAT **KOHLI**

Full name	**Virat Kohli**
Born	**November 5, 1988, Delhi**
Teams	**Delhi, Bangalore Royal Challengers**
Style	**Right-hand bat, occasional medium-pacer**
Test debut	**No Tests yet**
ODI debut	**India v Sri Lanka at Dambulla 2008**
T20I debut	**India v Zimbabwe at Harare 2010**

THE PROFILE An attacking player with a cool head and the hint of a swagger that suggests he knows he's pretty good, Virat Kohli has been making big scores from a young age. He made three double-centuries for Delhi's Under-17s, then captained the Indian side that won the Under-19 World Cup in Malaysia in 2008, with a round 100 against West Indies. By then Kohli had already made his Ranji Trophy debut, making 90 (after Delhi had been 14 for 4) against Karnataka in his fourth match. The upward curve continued in 2007-08, his second season, with a maiden century against Rajasthan and a superb 169 against Karnataka. He was consistent in limited-overs cricket without making big scores (that came later, with four one-day hundreds in a fortnight in February 2009), and was called up for a one-day series in Sri Lanka in August 2008. He wasn't expected to play, but an injury to Virender Sehwag gave Kohli a chance: he reached double figures in all five of his innings, with 54 in the fourth game. He kept his name in the selectors' minds with another good domestic season – 613 runs at 55, with a career-best 197 against Pakistan's national champions – then improved his IPL form after a disappointing first campaign. He enjoyed a dream run in ODIs in 2009-10: successive innings against Sri Lanka and Bangladesh produced 54, 107, 9, 91, 71 not out and 102 not out. Kohli couldn't quite keep that up – although he added 68 and 82 against Sri Lanka in Zimbabwe later in 2010 – but it did establish him in the one-day side.

THE FACTS Kohli scored 197 for Delhi against Pakistan's champions Sui Northern Gas in the Mohammad Nissar Trophy match at Delhi in September 2008: he and Aakash Chopra (182) put on 385 for the second wicket ... Kohli made 105 for the Board President's XI against the Australian tourists at Hyderabad in October 2008 ... He hit 251 not out for Delhi Under-17s v Himachal Pradesh at Una in December 2004 ...

THE FIGURES *to 23.9.10*   **ESPn cricinfo.com**

Batting & Fielding	M	Inns	NO	Runs	HS	Avge	S/R	100	50	4s	6s	Ct	St
Tests	0	0	–	–	–	–	–	–	–	–	–	–	–
ODIs	34	31	4	1127	107	41.74	79.64	2	8	112	5	15	0
T20Is	2	1	1	26	26*	–	123.80	0	0	3	1	0	0
First-class	25	36	6	1673	197	55.76	56.90	5	7	239	8	21	0

Bowling	M	Balls	Runs	Wkts	BB	Avge	RpO	S/R	5i	10m
Tests	0	0	–	–	–	–	–	–	–	–
ODIs	34	58	60	0	–	–	6.20	–	0	0
T20Is	2	0	–	–	–	–	–	–	–	–
First-class	25	180	157	1	1–23	157.00	5.23	180.00	0	0

NUWAN **KULASEKARA**

SRI LANKA

Full name	**Kulasekara Mudiyanselage Dinesh Nuwan Kulasekara**
Born	**July 22, 1982, Nittambuwa**
Teams	**Colts, Basnahira North**
Style	**Right-hand bat, right-arm fast-medium bowler**
Test debut	**Sri Lanka v New Zealand at Napier 2004-05**
ODI debut	**Sri Lanka v England at Dambulla 2003-04**
T20I debut	**Sri Lanka v Pakistan at King City 2008-09**

THE PROFILE Nuwan Kulasekara generates a lively pace from a bustling run-up and a whippy open-chested action, and moves the ball off the seam at upwards of 80mph. He can also maintain a tight line and length, and, after adding a yard or two of pace, suddenly emerged as a formidable bowler, especially in one-day internationals. He did so well in 2008 (33 wickets at 20.87 in 21 matches) that by March 2009 he was proudly sitting on top of the ICC's world one-day rankings. He maintained that form in 2009, and finally showed signs of emerging as a Test force too, grabbing four wickets in each innings as Pakistan lost in Colombo in August, and ending that series with 17 victims. After that, though, the old worries about his supposed lack of pace returned and he was in and out of the side in 2010. Prior to this, Kulasekara's biggest mark on Test cricket had been with the bat: at Lord's in May 2006 he hung on for more than three hours for 64, helping Chaminda Vaas ensure that Sri Lanka clung on for a draw after following on 359 behind. It was his second adhesive performance of the match, as he and Vaas had pushed the first-innings total from 131 for 8 to a more respectable 192. Kulasekara also made an instant impression in his first one-dayer, taking 2 for 19 in nine overs as England subsided for 88 at Dambulla in November 2003. That came soon after a fine first season, in which he took 61 wickets at 21.06 for Colts. He started as a softball enthusiast before turning to cricket, first with Negegoda CC and then with Galle.

THE FACTS Playing for North Central Province at Dambulla in March 2005, Kulasekara dismissed all of Central Province's top six, finishing with 6 for 71 ... He took 7 for 27 for Colts against Bloomfield in January 2008 ... In March 2009 Kulasekara went to the top of the ICC world rankings for ODI bowlers ... He made 95 for Galle against Nondescripts in Colombo in October 2003: he and Primal Buddika doubled the score from 174 for 6 ...

THE FIGURES to 23.9.10   ESPNcricinfo.com

Batting & Fielding	M	Inns	NO	Runs	HS	Avge	S/R	100	50	4s	6s	Ct	St
Tests	11	16	1	245	64	16.33	45.28	0	1	34	4	4	0
ODIs	79	50	23	475	57*	17.59	70.78	0	1	30	10	20	0
T20Is	12	9	2	52	19*	7.42	110.63	0	0	1	2	5	0
First-class	73	97	21	1417	95	18.64	–	0	4	–	–	26	0

Bowling	M	Balls	Runs	Wkts	BB	Avge	RpO	S/R	5i	10m
Tests	11	1612	862	25	4–21	34.48	3.20	64.48	0	0
ODIs	79	3605	2719	94	4–40	28.92	4.52	38.35	0	0
T20Is	12	269	373	11	3–4	33.90	8.31	24.45	0	0
First-class	73	10128	5485	242	7–27	22.66	3.24	41.85	9	1

PRAVEEN **KUMAR**

Full name	**Praveenkumar Sakat Singh**
Born	**October 2, 1986, Meerut, Uttar Pradesh**
Teams	**Uttar Pradesh, Bangalore Royal Challengers**
Style	**Right-hand bat, right-arm fast-medium bowler**
Test debut	**No Tests yet**
ODI debut	**India v Pakistan at Jaipur 2007-08**
T20I debut	**India v Australia at Melbourne 2007-08**

THE PROFILE A fast bowler with the ability to toil away on unresponsive Indian pitches, Praveen Kumar can also double up as a carefree hitter down the order and even, sometimes, as a surprise opener. He shone on his debut in November 2005, collecting nine wickets against Haryana, and was a key performer – 41 wickets and 368 runs – as Uttar Pradesh won the Ranji Trophy in his first season (2005-06). He followed that with 49 wickets the following term, which earned him an A-team place for a one-day tri-series in Kenya in August 2007, in which he excelled with both bat and ball. Kumar continued his fine run in the Challenger Trophy (trial games for the full national team), and was called up for the senior one-dayers against Pakistan, although he went wicketless in his only match. But another strong Ranji season – including 8 for 68 in vain in the final against Delhi – earned him a trip to Australia for the one-day series early in 2008. He returned with reputation enhanced after claiming ten wickets in his four games, including a matchwinning 4 for 46 in the second (and conclusive) final at Brisbane: he dismissed Adam Gilchrist and Ricky Ponting for single figures in both finals. After that Kumar toiled manfully in the IPL's inaugural season, then produced another matchwinning four-wicket effort against Pakistan in a one-dayer in Bangladesh. His progress stalled a little after that – only 18 first-class wickets at 37 in 2008-09 – and he missed the World Twenty20 in the West Indies in 2010 with a side strain, but Kumar remains very much in a one-day regular, rarely failing to strike.

THE FACTS Kumar took 8 for 68 for Uttar Pradesh v Delhi in the Ranji Trophy final at Mumbai in January 2008 ... He took 5 for 93 (and 4 for 55 in the second innings) on his first-class debut for UP v Haryana at Kanpur in November 2005 ... Kumar scored 78 and 57, and also took 5 for 73 and 5 for 87, for UP v Andhra at Anantapur in January 2006 ...

THE FIGURES to 23.9.10   **ESPncricinfo.com**

Batting & Fielding	M	Inns	NO	Runs	HS	Avge	S/R	100	50	4s	6s	Ct	St
Tests	0	0	–	–	–	–	–	–	–	–	–	–	–
ODIs	45	24	7	225	54*	13.23	85.22	0	1	21	4	11	0
T20Is	3	1	0	6	6	6.00	60.00	0	0	0	0	0	0
First-class	37	59	4	1387	98	25.21	74.65	0	8	146	47	6	0

Bowling	M	Balls	Runs	Wkts	BB	Avge	RpO	S/R	5i	10m
Tests	0	0	–	–	–	–	–	–	–	–
ODIs	45	2132	1801	56	4–31	32.16	5.06	38.07	0	0
T20Is	3	36	32	3	2–14	10.66	5.33	12.00	0	0
First-class	37	8254	3845	166	8–68	23.16	2.79	49.72	12	1

CHARL **LANGEVELDT**

SOUTH AFRICA

Full name	**Charl Kenneth Langeveldt**
Born	**December 17, 1974, Stellenbosch**
Teams	**Cape Cobras, Derbyshire, Kolkata Knight Riders**
Style	**Right-hand bat, right-arm fast-medium bowler**
Test debut	**South Africa v England at Cape Town 2004-05**
ODI debut	**South Africa v Kenya at Kimberley 2001-02**
T20I debut	**South Africa v New Zealand at Johannesburg 2005-06**

THE PROFILE   For much of the early part of his career, Charl Langeveldt combined cricket with his job as a prison warder at Drakenstein prison, just north of Cape Town. Always able to swing the ball at a decent pace, he made his one-day international debut in 2001-02, taking two top-order wickets in his first match and 4 for 21 in his second. He was included in the squad for South Africa's ill-starred 2003 World Cup campaign, but played only once, against Kenya. He returned to favour in the middle of 2004, and took 3 for 31 in Sri Lanka and 3 for 17 against Bangladesh in the Champions Trophy in England. Langeveldt made his Test debut in style against England in 2004-05, taking 5 for 46 despite having broken his hand while batting. It was enough to win him selection for the West Indian tour that followed, and in the third one-dayer he produced one of the most sensational finales in history, conjuring up a last-over hat-trick to steal a one-run win that clinched the series. Although Test success proved elusive, he retained his one-day place and did well at the 2007 World Cup, failing to strike only once in eight games, and setting up victory over eventual finalists Sri Lanka with 5 for 39. After this he was handed a Test recall, after two years, for a tour of India – but pulled out when it was alleged he was included to satisfy a quota of non-white players. He joined Derbyshire as a Kolpak, and seemed to be lost to South Africa ... but returned after 18 months and remains, even rising 36, a crafty limited-overs practitioner.

THE FACTS   Langeveldt's hat-trick against West Indies at Bridgetown in May 2005 was South Africa's first in ODIs ... He also took a Twenty20 hat-trick for Cape Cobras v Titans at Centurion in April 2008 ... Langeveldt averages 20.81 with the ball in ODIs against Sri Lanka, but 82 v Australia ... He took 5 for 7 when the SA Board President's XI bowled out the touring Bangladeshis for 51 at Pietermaritzburg in October 2000 ...

THE FIGURES *to 23.9.10*　　　　　　　　　　　　　　　　　**ESΠΠ cricinfo.com**

Batting & Fielding	M	Inns	NO	Runs	HS	Avge	S/R	100	50	4s	6s	Ct	St
Tests	6	4	2	16	10	8.00	30.76	0	0	3	0	2	0
ODIs	68	20	9	69	12	6.27	56.55	0	0	7	0	10	0
T20Is	9	3	2	4	2*	4.00	50.00	0	0	0	0	1	0
First-class	93	116	39	1106	56	14.36	–	0	1	–	–	25	0

Bowling	M	Balls	Runs	Wkts	BB	Avge	RpO	S/R	5i	10m
Tests	6	999	593	16	5–46	37.06	3.56	62.43	1	0
ODIs	68	3255	2728	93	5–39	29.33	5.02	35.00	2	0
T20Is	9	198	241	17	4–19	14.17	7.30	11.64	0	0
First-class	93	17595	8669	310	6–48	27.96	2.95	56.75	9	1

VVS **LAXMAN**

Full name	**Vangipurappu Venkata Sai Laxman**
Born	**November 1, 1974, Hyderabad, Andhra Pradesh**
Teams	**Hyderabad, Lancashire, Deccan Chargers**
Style	**Right-hand bat, occasional offspinner**
Test debut	**India v South Africa at Ahmedabad 1996-97**
ODI debut	**India v Zimbabwe at Cuttack 1997-98**
T20I debut	**No T20Is yet**

THE PROFILE At his best, VVS Laxman is a sight for the gods. Wristy and willowy, he can match – sometimes even better – Tendulkar for strokeplay. His on-side game is comparable to his idol Azharuddin's, yet he is decidedly more assured on the off, and has the rare gift of being able to hit the same ball to either side. The Australians, who have suffered more than most, paid him the highest compliment after India's 2003-04 tour by admitting they did not know where to bowl to him. Laxman, a one-time medical student, graduated after a five-year international apprenticeship in March 2001, when he tormented Steve Waugh's thought-to-be-invincible Aussies with a majestic 281 to stand the Kolkata Test on its head. His form dipped after that, until an uncharacteristic grinding century in Antigua in May 2002 marked his second coming: he has been a picture of consistency since, often dazzling, but less prone to collaborating in his own dismissal. Laxman was left out of the 2003 World Cup, but made an emphatic one-day return with a string of hundreds in Australia, followed by a matchwinning 107 in the deciding ODI of India's ice-breaking tour of Pakistan in March 2004. Eventually he was confined to Tests, and sailed past 7000 runs in 2010. Early in 2008 Laxman scored his third Test century at Sydney, and the Aussies conceded another double-century at Delhi in 2008-09, followed by 64 in the next Test – Laxman's 100th – as the series was won. In August 2010 his 16th Test hundred ensured the series in Sri Lanka ended in a draw.

THE FACTS Laxman's 281 against Australia at Kolkata in March 2001 was India's highest Test score at the time (since passed by Virender Sehwag), and included a national-record fifth-wicket stand of 376 with Rahul Dravid ... He averages 55.10 v Australia, and his highest four scores (281, 200 not out, 178, 167) have all come against them ... Laxman has scored two first-class triple-centuries for Hyderabad – 353 v Karnataka at Bangalore in April 2000, and 301 not out v Bihar at Jamshedpur in February 1998 ...

THE FIGURES *to 23.9.10*   **ESPNcricinfo.com**

Batting & Fielding	M	Inns	NO	Runs	HS	Avge	S/R	100	50	4s	6s	Ct	St
Tests	113	186	29	7415	281	47.22	49.35	16	45	980	4	118	0
ODIs	86	83	7	2338	131	30.76	71.23	6	10	222	4	39	0
T20Is	0	0	–	–	–	–	–	–	–	–	–	–	–
First-class	244	394	49	18154	353	52.62	–	53	86	–	–	260	1

Bowling	M	Balls	Runs	Wkts	BB	Avge	RpO	S/R	5i	10m
Tests	113	324	126	2	1–2	63.00	2.33	162.00	0	0
ODIs	86	42	40	0	–	–	5.71	–	0	0
T20Is	0	0	–	–	–	–	–	–	–	–
First-class	244	1835	754	22	3–11	34.27	2.46	83.40	0	0

BRETT **LEE**

AUSTRALIA

Full name	**Brett Lee**
Born	**November 8, 1976, Wollongong, New South Wales**
Teams	**New South Wales, Kings XI Punjab**
Style	**Right-hand bat, right-arm fast bowler**
Test debut	**Australia v India at Melbourne 1999-2000**
ODI debut	**Australia v Pakistan at Brisbane 1999-2000**
T20I debut	**Australia v New Zealand at Auckland 2004-2005**

THE PROFILE Brett Lee excelled as an exponent of extreme speed over a decade without quite achieving the all-conquering success required to earn the tag of a true Test great. For most of his career he operated as brutal support for Glenn McGrath and Jason Gillespie, then in his final two years was a highly dependable attack leader, until his body held him back in Tests. But at his fastest and best he gained outswing with the new ball and reversed the older one, making him even more difficult for batsmen who knew he could nudge 100mph. The flashing smile, charging run-up and leaping celebrations added to the theatre for a bowler who made an instant impact: 42 victims came in his opening seven Tests to gain him an A-list reputation, but he was soon in rehab after an elbow operation. His ankles were a popular site for surgery, and there were also side strains and stress fractures in a familiar cycle of breathtaking pace, painful injury and long-term layoff. He became a smarter operator under Ricky Ponting's captaincy, learning when to deliver a burst of speed or a containing spell. In nine Tests following McGrath's retirement, Lee took 58 wickets at 21.55, but life soon became harder again and after returning from more ankle surgery – his last act in a Test was limping off the MCG with a broken foot – he missed the 2009 Ashes with a side strain. He retired from Tests at the beginning of 2010 with 310 wickets, hoping to prolong his career in the shorter formats, where he could still try to operate at optimum speed while reducing the load on that aching body.

THE FACTS Lee took a World Cup hat-trick against Kenya in 2002-03 ... His older brother Shane played 45 ODIs for Australia between 1995 and 2001 ... Lee averages 21.09 with the ball in Tests against New Zealand, but 40.61 v England ... He was on the winning side in each of his first ten Tests, a sequence ended by England's win at Leeds in 2001 ... Lee took 5 for 47 in his first Test innings, but did not improve on that until his 44th match ...

THE FIGURES to 23.9.10   **ESPncricinfo.com**

Batting & Fielding	M	Inns	NO	Runs	HS	Avge	S/R	100	50	4s	6s	Ct	St
Tests	76	90	18	1451	64	20.15	52.97	0	5	182	18	23	0
ODIs	186	92	37	897	57	16.30	80.44	0	2	47	25	44	0
T20Is	17	9	4	91	43*	18.20	144.44	0	0	8	4	5	0
First-class	116	139	25	2120	97	18.59	–	0	8	–	–	35	0

Bowling	M	Balls	Runs	Wkts	BB	Avge	RpO	S/R	5i	10m
Tests	76	16531	9554	310	5–30	30.81	3.46	53.32	10	0
ODIs	186	9478	7456	324	5–22	23.01	4.71	29.25	9	0
T20Is	17	355	454	17	3–27	26.70	7.67	20.88	0	0
First-class	116	24194	13746	487	7–114	28.22	3.40	49.67	20	2

BRENDON **McCULLUM**

Full name	**Brendon Barrie McCullum**
Born	**September 27, 1981, Dunedin, Otago**
Teams	**Otago, Sussex, Kolkata Knight Riders**
Style	**Right-hand bat, wicketkeeper**
Test debut	**New Zealand v South Africa at Hamilton 2003-04**
ODI debut	**New Zealand v Australia at Sydney 2001-02**
T20I debut	**New Zealand v Australia at Auckland 2004-05**

THE PROFILE Brendon McCullum stepped up to the national side as a wicketkeeper-batsman after an outstanding career in international youth cricket, where he proved capable of dominating opposition attacks. Not surprisingly he found it hard to replicate that at the highest level at first – he started as a batsman in ODIs in Australia in 2001-02 – although there were occasional fireworks in domestic cricket. But he finally made his mark in England in 2004, with an entertaining 96 at Lord's. He finally brought up his maiden century in Bangladesh in October, and added another hundred in the two-day victory over Zimbabwe in August 2005. With some onlookers murmuring the name "Gilchrist", McCullum hammered 86 from 91 balls as New Zealand overhauled Australia's 346 at Hamilton in February 2007 with one wicket to spare. But he really made his mark in April 2008, when he enlivened the opening night of the much-hyped Indian Premier League by smacking 158 not out from 73 balls for Kolkata Knight Riders. After that, he was a marked man in England that summer, and although there were signs he was having trouble tempering his attacking instincts in the longer game, he lit up Lord's again with 97, and also hit 71 at Trent Bridge. Then he walloped ten sixes in 166 in a one-day mismatch against Ireland. Although he was by now considered a limited-overs specialist, McCullum showed he could still hack it in Tests with 84 and 115 against India in March 2009 and 185 – the highest innings by a New Zealand wicketkeeper – against Bangladesh a year later. Shortly afterwards, he announced that he would no longer keep wicket in Tests.

THE FACTS McCullum made 185, the highest score by a New Zealand wicketkeeper in Tests, against Bangladesh at Hamilton in February 2010 ... He was the first man to score 1000 runs in Twenty20 internationals ... McCullum hit 166, and shared an opening stand of 274 with James Marshall, in an ODI against Ireland at Aberdeen in July 2008 ... His brother Nathan has also played for New Zealand ...

THE FIGURES *to 23.9.10*   **ESPN**cricinfo.com

Batting & Fielding	M	Inns	NO	Runs	HS	Avge	S/R	100	50	4s	6s	Ct	St
Tests	52	87	5	2862	185	34.90	61.92	5	16	351	34	162	11
ODIs	171	145	22	3569	166	29.01	87.86	2	17	313	105	189	13
T20Is	40	40	7	1100	116*	33.33	128.35	1	6	112	39	25	4
First-class	95	163	9	5339	185	34.66	–	9	30	–	–	267	19

Bowling	M	Balls	Runs	Wkts	BB	Avge	RpO	S/R	5i	10m
Tests	52	0	–	–	–	–	–	–	–	–
ODIs	171	0	–	–	–	–	–	–	–	–
T20Is	40	0	–	–	–	–	–	–	–	–
First-class	95	0	–	–	–	–	–	–	–	–

NATHAN **McCULLUM**

NEW ZEALAND

Full name	**Nathan Leslie McCullum**
Born	**September 1, 1980, Dunedin, Otago**
Teams	**Otago, Lancashire**
Style	**Right-hand bat, offspinner**
Test debut	**No Tests yet**
ODI debut	**New Zealand v Sri Lanka at Colombo 2009**
T20I debut	**New Zealand v South Africa at Durban 2007-08**

THE PROFILE The older brother of Brendon McCullum, Nathan is an offspinning allrounder from Otago who played for Lancashire in England's Twenty20 Cup in 2010. Less lavishly gifted than his brother, this McCullum had to work patiently at his game to earn his national colours. He was in the 30-man preliminary squad for the Champions Trophy in 2006 but didn't make the cut, and had to wait until the inaugural World Twenty20 in South Africa in September 2007 for the chance to appear alongside Brendon in New Zealand colours. He scored a single in his only match and didn't bowl – and promptly disappeared back into domestic cricket for nearly 18 months. He was back for the World Twenty20 in England in 2009, and this time added more to the cause, particularly with some tight bowling and taut fielding. Three 50-overs outings produced fewer runs and even fewer wickets, but McCullum was back for the third edition of the World Twenty20 in the West Indies in 2010, where he turned the match against Sri Lanka with a four and a six in the last over, after earlier taking a wicket and three catches: for once he overshadowed his brother, who failed to score. He then took 3 for 16 in his four overs in the next match, against Zimbabwe, to ensure New Zealand reached the second phase. It does look as if 20-over cricket is McCullum's forte: he has only one century and a couple of five-fors to show for a first-class career spanning more than a decade. In his younger days, he was also a useful footballer.

THE FACTS McCullum's best bowling figures of 6 for 90 came for New Zealand A against India A at Chennai in September 2008 ... He scored 106 not out for Otago v Northern Districts at Hamilton in March 2008 ... McCullum's brother Brendon has also played for New Zealand, while their father Stu represented Otago ...

THE FIGURES to 23.9.10   **ESPNcricinfo.com**

Batting & Fielding	M	Inns	NO	Runs	HS	Avge	S/R	100	50	4s	6s	Ct	St
Tests	0	0	–	–	–	–	–	–	–	–	–	–	–
ODIs	6	5	0	58	36	11.60	52.72	0	0	1	1	2	0
T20Is	22	14	8	160	36*	26.66	110.34	0	0	9	5	9	0
First-class	48	73	6	1804	106*	26.92	–	1	11	–	–	50	0

Bowling	M	Balls	Runs	Wkts	BB	Avge	RpO	S/R	5i	10m
Tests	0	0	–	–	–	–	–	–	–	–
ODIs	6	244	185	5	3–35	37.00	4.54	48.80	0	0
T20Is	22	344	370	21	3–15	17.61	6.45	16.38	0	0
First-class	48	8850	4175	100	6–90	41.75	2.83	88.50	2	0

ANDY McKAY

Full name	**Andrew John McKay**
Born	**April 17, 1980, Auckland**
Teams	**Wellington**
Style	**Right-hand bat, left-arm fast-medium bowler**
Test debut	**No Tests yet**
ODI debut	**New Zealand v Bangladesh at Napier 2009-10**
T20I debut	**New Zealand v Sri Lanka at Lauderhill 2010**

THE PROFILE A brisk left-arm seamer who played for Auckland for five years before shifting to Wellington in 2009-10, Andy McKay was held back by injuries – he once missed a whole season with a side strain – and did not make the full New Zealand team until he was almost 30. He showed promise in 2007-08 with 24 wickets, and followed that up with 23 next term. In 2009-10, when Shane Bond's brief comeback fizzled out, New Zealand were in the market for a pace spearhead, and the selectors had a close look at McKay, who was having a decent debut season for Wellington. In his first three one-dayers he hurried the Bangladeshis with his pace: his five wickets were all top-five batsmen, and three of them fell for single figures. Hopes of a Test debut soon afterwards were scuppered by a stress fracture in the foot, but he was back for the brief Twenty20 series in America and the one-day triangular later in the year in Sri Lanka, where he struggled to make much impact after dismissing Yuvraj Singh cheaply in the first match. Although he went into 2010-11 still without a first-class five-for to his name, McKay is highly rated within the squad: Daniel Vettori feels his pace is "on a par" with Bond's, while Ross Taylor believes McKay is "our fastest bowler ... he is going to become a big part of our side and our make-up". With his fellow left-armer James Franklin seemingly out of favour, McKay – a physiotherapist when not playing cricket – has a chance to make a place his own.

THE FACTS McKay is yet to take five wickets in a first-class innings – his best figures are 4 for 37 for Auckland against Canterbury at Rangiora in November 2008 ... After moving to Wellington he took 4 for 47 in a one-day game against Central Districts in November 2009, and 4 for 38 in a Twenty20 match for them against Canterbury in January 2010 ... McKay's first two Twenty20 internationals were both in Florida in the United States ...

THE FIGURES *to 23.9.10*   **ᴇsᴘɴcricinfo.com**

Batting & Fielding	M	Inns	NO	Runs	HS	Avge	S/R	100	50	4s	6s	Ct	St
Tests	0	0	–	–	–	–	–	–	–	–	–	–	–
ODIs	6	4	4	10	4*	–	37.03	0	0	0	0	2	0
T20Is	2	1	0	0	0	0.00	0.00	0	0	0	0	0	0
First-class	24	27	12	175	36*	11.66	–	0	0	–	–	2	0

Bowling	M	Balls	Runs	Wkts	BB	Avge	RpO	S/R	5i	10m
Tests	0	0	–	–	–	–	–	–	–	–
ODIs	6	264	173	7	2–17	24.71	3.93	37.71	0	0
T20Is	2	34	31	2	2–20	15.50	5.47	17.00	0	0
First-class	24	4278	2248	69	4–37	32.57	3.15	62.00	0	0

RYAN McLAREN

SOUTH AFRICA

Full name **Ryan McLaren**
Born **February 9, 1983, Kimberley**
Teams **Eagles, Mumbai Indians**
Style **Left-hand bat, right-arm fast-medium bowler**
Test debut **South Africa v England at Johannesburg 2009-10**
ODI debut **South Africa v Zimbabwe at Benoni 2009-2010**
T20I debut **South Africa v England at Johannesburg 2009-2010**

THE PROFILE Ryan McLaren made an eye-catching start to his first-class career: his first four seasons produced more than 1000 forthright middle-order runs, and over 100 wickets with some aggressive seam bowling. But an international call-up seemed far off, with Shaun Pollock and Jacques Kallis entrenched in the South African side and the likes of Andrew Hall and Johan van der Wath in the queue. Like several of his compatriots McLaren opted for county cricket as a Kolpak player, and soon became an integral part of the Kent side, cementing his position with a hat-trick to help win the Twenty20 Cup final in 2007. After signing a three-year contract before another impressive season for Kent in 2008 McLaren was called up to South Africa's one-day squad that October – but Kent refused to release him, and he was forced to return to Canterbury. At the end of the 2009 season, though, they did let him go – and South Africa lost no time in blooding him. McLaren kept things tight in five one-dayers against Zimbabwe and England without taking many wickets, but injuries to others led to a first Test cap as South Africa squared the series with an emphatic victory on a fast-bowler-friendly pitch at Johannesburg: his contribution was a handy 33 not out and the wicket of England's first-innings top-scorer Paul Collingwood. McLaren is accurate and bowls at a nagging pace, factors which helped him pick up 5 for 19 in a Twenty20 international in the West Indies in May 2010. "You can take five wickets one day," he said, "and the next day take a thumping, but I enjoyed it."

THE FACTS McLaren took a hat-trick for Kent against Gloucestershire in the English Twenty20 Cup final at Edgbaston in August 2007 ... He made 140 for Eagles v Warriors at Bloemfontein in March 2006 ... McLaren took 5 for 19 against West Indies in May 2010, the second-best figures in Twenty20 internationals ... He took 8 for 38 for Eagles v Cape Cobras at Stellenbosch in February 2007 ... His father, uncle and cousin all played for Griqualand West ...

THE FIGURES to 23.9.10   ☰cricinfo.com

Batting & Fielding	M	Inns	NO	Runs	HS	Avge	S/R	100	50	4s	6s	Ct	St
Tests	1	1	1	33	33*	–	58.92	0	0	5	0	0	0
ODIs	10	8	2	37	12	6.16	61.66	0	0	4	0	5	0
T20Is	4	3	3	8	6*	–	88.88	0	0	0	0	1	0
First-class	80	115	19	2710	140	28.22	–	2	14	–	–	39	0

Bowling	M	Balls	Runs	Wkts	BB	Avge	RpO	S/R	5i	10m
Tests	1	78	43	1	1–30	43.00	3.30	78.00	0	0
ODIs	10	432	366	8	3–51	45.75	5.08	54.00	0	0
T20Is	4	95	107	9	5–19	11.88	6.75	10.55	1	0
First-class	80	12627	6361	255	8–38	24.94	3.02	49.51	10	1

FARVEEZ **MAHAROOF**

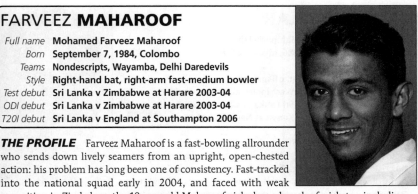

Full name	**Mohamed Farveez Maharoof**
Born	**September 7, 1984, Colombo**
Teams	**Nondescripts, Wayamba, Delhi Daredevils**
Style	**Right-hand bat, right-arm fast-medium bowler**
Test debut	**Sri Lanka v Zimbabwe at Harare 2003-04**
ODI debut	**Sri Lanka v Zimbabwe at Harare 2003-04**
T20I debut	**Sri Lanka v England at Southampton 2006**

THE PROFILE Farveez Maharoof is a fast-bowling allrounder who sends down lively seamers from an upright, open-chested action: his problem has long been one of consistency. Fast-tracked into the national squad early in 2004, and faced with weak opposition in Zimbabwe, the 19-year-old Maharoof picked up a bunch of wickets – including 3 for 3 in his first ODI – but then came up against better players, although his swinging deliveries made an impression when South Africa toured. He had worked his way up through the representative ranks, playing for Sri Lanka's age-group teams, and enjoyed a prolific school career for Wesley College. He has found Test wickets hard to come by, but his occasionally ferocious hitting helped him survive in the one-day side. A mean display during the Champions Trophy in 2004, when he exploited the end-of-summer English pitches expertly, suggested he could be useful when Sri Lanka played in seamer-friendly conditions, although his major contribution to the 5–0 one-day whitewash in England in 2006 was a rapid half-century at Headingley. Maharoof has also shown that he is comfortable under pressure, all too often the Achilles heel of Sri Lanka's fast-bowling allrounders. He was unlucky to miss the 2007 World Cup final after doing well in the lead-up games, although admittedly eight of his nine wickets came against Bermuda and Ireland. But he was back in favour afterwards, grabbing six wickets in three games against Pakistan, before being hampered by side and muscle strains. He returned to the 50-overs side for the Asia Cup in June 2010, and took 5 for 42 against India at Dambulla.

THE FACTS Maharoof had figures of 3-1-3-3 on his ODI debut, as Zimbabwe were bowled out for 35 at Harare in April 2004 ... He took an ODI hat-trick against India at Dambulla during the Asia Cup in June 2010 ... Maharoof claimed 6 for 14 v West Indies at Mumbai during the 2006-07 Champions Trophy, and 7 for 73 for Bloomfield v Ragama in November 2006 ...

THE FIGURES to 23.9.10   **ᴇsᴘᥒcricinfo.com**

Batting & Fielding	M	Inns	NO	Runs	HS	Avge	S/R	100	50	4s	6s	Ct	St
Tests	20	31	4	538	72	19.92	40.00	0	3	66	3	6	0
ODIs	94	64	15	984	69*	20.08	85.19	0	2	83	22	20	0
T20Is	7	4	1	23	13*	7.66	85.18	0	0	0	1	2	0
First-class	49	72	7	1442	115*	22.18	46.08	2	4	–	–	25	0

Bowling	M	Balls	Runs	Wkts	BB	Avge	RpO	S/R	5i	10m
Tests	20	2628	1458	24	4–52	60.75	3.32	109.50	0	0
ODIs	94	3932	3133	121	6–14	25.89	4.78	32.49	2	0
T20Is	7	144	173	7	2–18	24.71	7.20	20.57	0	0
First-class	49	5958	3234	99	7–73	32.66	3.25	60.18	1	0

MAHMUDULLAH

Full name	**Mohammad Mahmudullah**
Born	**February 4, 1986, Mymensingh**
Teams	**Dhaka**
Style	**Right-hand bat, offspinner**
Test debut	**Bangladesh v West Indies at Kingstown 2009**
ODI debut	**Bangladesh v Sri Lanka at Colombo 2007**
T20I debut	**Bangladesh v Kenya at Nairobi 2007-08**

THE PROFILE An offspinning allrounder who is also an assured close-in fielder, Mahmudullah was something of a surprise selection for Bangladesh's chastening tour of Sri Lanka in mid-2007 (all three Tests were lost by an innings, and all three ODIs ended in defeat too). He made his international debut in the second one-dayer, scoring 36 and picking up two wickets in his five overs. As a bowler he does turn the ball, and can also keep the runs down. Mahmudullah spent the summer of 2005 on the groundstaff at Lord's: MCC's head coach, Clive Radley, remembered him bowling "from quite wide of the crease – he spun it a lot and bowled a good *doosra*". Bangladesh have a lot of slow left-armers, but not many offspinners made a mark before "Riyad", although so far he has been needed more for his batting, which has improved as he has got to grips with international cricket. He was stranded on 96 not out against India at Mirpur early in 2010, but made sure of his maiden century in the next Test, with 115 against New Zealand, before making assured fifties in both home Tests against England. Mahmudullah's bowling, after a good start against a depleted West Indian side in July 2009 – 12 wickets in his first two Tests – has proved less incisive, but he looks set to remain a fixture in the side for some time. He came to prominence after a superb domestic season with the bat in 2008-09, making 710 runs at 54.61 to earn a berth on that West Indian tour.

THE FACTS Mahmudullah took 5 for 51 (and 8 for 110 in the match) on his Test debut, against West Indies in St Vincent in July 2009 ... His first four first-class centuries all came within a month at the end of 2008, including 152 for Dhaka at Khulna ... After being stranded on 96 against India at Mirpur in January 2010, Mahmudullah completed his maiden Test century in his next game, against New Zealand at Hamilton ... He spent some time on the MCC groundstaff in 2005, playing alongside World Cup players in Daan van Bunge, Kevin O'Brien and William Porterfield ...

THE FIGURES to 23.9.10   **ESPNcricinfo.com**

Batting & Fielding	M	Inns	NO	Runs	HS	Avge	S/R	100	50	4s	6s	Ct	St
Tests	9	18	2	590	115	36.87	57.67	1	4	85	3	7	0
ODIs	56	47	14	997	64*	30.21	68.90	0	4	65	9	12	0
T20Is	11	11	0	79	21	7.18	63.70	0	0	4	1	6	0
First-class	51	92	11	2859	152	35.29	–	5	13	–	–	48	0

Bowling	M	Balls	Runs	Wkts	BB	Avge	RpO	S/R	5i	10m
Tests	9	1367	799	22	5–51	36.31	3.50	62.13	1	0
ODIs	56	1687	1489	26	3–52	57.26	5.29	64.88	0	0
T20Is	11	85	101	2	1–19	50.50	7.12	42.50	0	0
First-class	51	4534	2430	69	5–51	35.21	3.21	65.71	1	0

LASITH **MALINGA**

Full name	**Separamadu Lasith Malinga Swarnajith**
Born	**August 28, 1983, Galle**
Teams	**Nondescripts, Ruhuna, Mumbai Indians**
Style	**Right-hand bat, right-arm fast bowler**
Test debut	**Sri Lanka v Australia at Darwin 2004**
ODI debut	**Sri Lanka v United Arab Emirates at Dambulla 2004**
T20I debut	**Sri Lanka v England at Southampton 2006**

THE PROFILE A rare Sri Lankan cricketer from the south, whose exotic hairstyles make him stand out on and off the park, Lasith Malinga played hardly any proper cricket until he was 17, preferring the softball version in the coconut groves of Rathgama, a village near Galle. But after he was spotted by the former Test fast bowler Champaka Ramanayake, he was hurried into the Galle team, took 4 for 40 and 4 for 37 on his first-class debut, and has hardly looked back since. He bowls with a distinctive explosive round-arm action, and generates genuine pace, often disconcerting batsmen who struggle to pick up the ball's trajectory. "Slinga" Malinga was a surprise selection for the 2004 tour of Australia, and started with 6 for 90 in a warm-up game. That led to a first Test cap, and he acquitted himself well, with six wickets in his first match and four in the second: he added 5 for 80 (nine in the match) against New Zealand at Napier in April 2005. With a propensity for no-balls he was originally seen as too erratic for one-dayers, but buried that reputation with 13 wickets in the 5–0 whitewash of England in 2006. The following year he collected 18 wickets during the World Cup, including four in four balls against South Africa. Since then, in a reversal of his earlier career pattern, he has been largely overlooked in Tests but a fixture in limited-overs games, where his toe-crushing yorkers have proved hard to get away. He did make a mark at Galle in July 2010 – Murali's final match – when, in his first Test for more than two years, Malinga took 5 for 50 to break India's second-innings resistance.

THE FACTS Malinga is the only bowler to take four wickets in four balls in international cricket, against South Africa at Providence during the 2007 World Cup ... After he took 5 for 80 (9 for 210 in the match) with his low-slung action at Napier in April 2005, New Zealand's captain Stephen Fleming unsuccessfully asked the umpires to change their clothing: "There's a period there where the ball gets lost in their trousers" ... Malinga took 6 for 17 as Galle bowled out the Police for 51 in Colombo in November 2003 ...

THE FIGURES *to 23.9.10*   ESPncricinfo.com

Batting & Fielding	M	Inns	NO	Runs	HS	Avge	S/R	100	50	4s	6s	Ct	St
Tests	30	37	13	275	64	11.45	44.42	0	1	36	6	7	0
ODIs	72	34	12	152	16	6.90	58.91	0	0	10	4	12	0
T20Is	28	12	7	63	27	12.60	100.00	0	0	3	3	12	0
First-class	83	100	41	584	64	9.89	40.58	0	1	–	–	23	0

Bowling	M	Balls	Runs	Wkts	BB	Avge	RpO	S/R	5i	10m
Tests	30	5209	3349	101	5–50	33.15	3.85	51.57	3	0
ODIs	72	3494	2896	106	5–34	27.32	4.97	32.96	1	0
T20Is	28	564	702	34	3–12	20.64	7.46	16.58	0	0
First-class	83	11867	7751	255	6–17	30.39	3.91	46.53	7	0

SHAUN **MARSH**

Full name	**Shaun Edward Marsh**
Born	**July 9, 1983, Narrogin, Western Australia**
Teams	**Western Australia**
Style	**Left-hand bat, occasional left-arm spinner**
Test debut	**No Tests yet**
ODI debut	**Australia v West Indies at Kingstown 2007-08**
T20I debut	**Australia v West Indies at Bridgetown 2008**

THE PROFILE As a child Shaun Marsh spent a lot of time in the Australian set-up travelling with his father Geoff, the former Test opener. That international grounding and a backyard net helped develop him into one of Australia's finest young batsmen. It also gave him a taste of what he could expect when he was picked for the one-dayers in the West Indies in 2008. That came after a fine domestic season: he was also the surprise hit of the inaugural Indian Premier League, finishing as the top runscorer, which helped press his case for an Australian berth. More gifted than his father ("He's got a few more shots than me," Geoff once admitted), Shaun is a left-hander who impressed the Waugh twins during his maiden first-class century in 2003, which he reached with successive sixes over midwicket off Mark's offspin. The second century had to wait until 2004-05 as he struggled with concentration, the finest trait of his father's batting, and he was in and out of the state side for a while. After a subdued 2008-09, the highlights of which were successive ODI scores of 79 and 78 against South Africa in January, Marsh tore a hamstring while fielding against New Zealand, and when he returned to the Australian squad in Dubai he hurt his leg again. That kept him out of the World Twenty20 in England in June 2009, and the one-sided one-dayers that followed the Ashes series. He returned with a century in India then, after a back injury, made a classy 59 (and took two superb boundary-riding catches) as Australia ended the one-day series against England in July 2010 with a victory at Lord's.

THE FACTS Marsh was the leading scorer in the inaugural IPL season, with 616 runs ... He hit 81 on his ODI debut, against West Indies in June 2008, and made 112 v India at Hyderabad in November 2009 ... Marsh made 166 not out for Western Australia v Queensland at Perth in November 2007 ... His father Geoff won 50 Test caps, and his younger brother Mitchell captained Australia to victory in the 2010 Under-19 World Cup ...

THE FIGURES to 23.9.10

ESPAcricinfo.com

Batting & Fielding	M	Inns	NO	Runs	HS	Avge	S/R	100	50	4s	6s	Ct	St
Tests	0	0	–	–	–	–	–	–	–	–	–	–	–
ODIs	27	27	1	1008	112	38.76	76.53	1	7	95	10	6	0
T20Is	3	3	0	53	29	17.66	110.41	0	0	3	3	0	0
First-class	56	104	15	3232	166*	36.31	46.59	5	17	–	–	46	0

Bowling	M	Balls	Runs	Wkts	BB	Avge	RpO	S/R	5i	10m
Tests	0	0	–	–	–	–	–	–	–	–
ODIs	27	0	–	–	–	–	–	–	–	–
T20Is	3	0	–	–	–	–	–	–	–	–
First-class	56	174	131	2	2–20	65.50	4.51	87.00	0	0

CHRIS **MARTIN**

Full name	**Christopher Stewart Martin**
Born	**December 10, 1974, Christchurch, Canterbury**
Teams	**Canterbury, Essex**
Style	**Right-hand bat, right-arm fast-medium bowler**
Test debut	**New Zealand v South Africa at Bloemfontein 2000-01**
ODI debut	**New Zealand v Zimbabwe at Taupo 2000-01**
T20I debut	**New Zealand v Kenya at Durban 2007-08**

THE PROFILE Chris Martin is an angular fast-medium bowler who receives almost as much attention for his inept batting as for his nagging bowling, which has produced nearly 200 Test wickets, including 11 as New Zealand whipped South Africa at Auckland in March 2004. Seven more scalps followed in the next game. It was all the more remarkable as they were his first Tests in almost two years: he had been overlooked since Pakistan piled up 643 at Lahore in May 2002 (Martin 1 for 108). He got his original chance after a crop of injuries, but did not disgrace himself in the first portion of his Test career, taking 34 wickets at 34 in 11 Tests, including six as Pakistan were crushed by an innings at Hamilton in 2000-01. Since his return he has largely maintained that average, happy to bowl long spells *à la* Ewen Chatfield – he took 5 for 152 at Brisbane in November 2004, after a surprisingly unproductive England tour. Back in England in 2008, he again failed to make much impression in the Tests (four wickets at 58.75), but returned to form at home with 14 wickets in three Tests against India, including seven in a high-scoring draw at Wellington. But whatever Martin does with the ball he is likely to be remembered more for his clueless batting: 28 of his 39 Test dismissals have been for ducks, he finally reached double figures against Bangladesh in his 36th match (a Test record) in January 2008, and has bagged six pairs (no-one else has more than four). Mind you, he did once manage 25 for Canterbury, helping Chris Harris put on 75.

THE FACTS Very few players approach Martin's negative ratio of Test runs (89) to wickets (181): two who do are England's Bill Bowes (28 runs, 68 wickets) and David Larter (15, 37) ... Martin is the only man to have bagged six pairs in Tests ... Between March 2001 and October 2007 he played only two ODIs, but took six wickets in them ... In Tests Martin averages 24.59 with the ball against South Africa, but 86.53 v Australia ...

THE FIGURES to 23.9.10   ESPNcricinfo.com

Batting & Fielding	M	Inns	NO	Runs	HS	Avge	S/R	100	50	4s	6s	Ct	St
Tests	56	81	42	89	12*	2.28	19.38	0	0	13	0	12	0
ODIs	20	7	2	8	3	1.60	29.62	0	0	0	0	7	0
T20Is	6	1	1	5	5*	–	83.33	0	0	0	0	1	0
First-class	155	193	96	389	25	4.01	–	0	0	–	–	30	0

Bowling	M	Balls	Runs	Wkts	BB	Avge	RpO	S/R	5i	10m
Tests	56	11069	6341	181	6–54	35.03	3.43	61.15	8	1
ODIs	20	948	804	18	3–62	44.66	5.08	52.66	0	0
T20Is	6	138	193	7	2–14	27.57	8.39	19.71	0	0
First-class	155	29770	15434	477	6–54	32.35	3.11	62.41	18	1

MASHRAFE MORTAZA

Full name	**Mashrafe bin Mortaza**
Born	**October 5, 1983, Norail, Jessore, Khulna**
Teams	**Khulna**
Style	**Right-hand bat, right-arm fast-medium bowler**
Test debut	**Bangladesh v Zimbabwe at Dhaka 2001-02**
ODI debut	**Bangladesh v Zimbabwe at Chittagong 2001-02**
T20I debut	**Bangladesh v Zimbabwe at Khulna 2006-07**

THE PROFILE Quick and aggressive, Mashrafe Mortaza has been the standard-bearer for Bangladesh's pack of young pacemen, although injuries have long been a problem: he got through 2008 unscathed, but injured his right knee after bowling only 6.3 overs in the first Test in West Indies in July 2009, and had to undergo an operation (in fact both knees went under the knife). This was doubly disappointing as it was his first match as captain, and it ended in only Bangladesh's second Test victory – their first overseas, admittedly against a depleted West Indian side. He returned as captain for the mid-season ODIs in Britain in 2010, guiding Bangladesh to their first win over England. Mashrafe won his first Test cap against Zimbabwe in 2001-02, in what was also his first-class debut. Though banging it in is his preferred style, "Koushik" proved adept at reining in his attacking instincts to concentrate on line and length. He excelled in the second Test against England in 2003-04, taking 4 for 60 in the first innings to keep Bangladesh in touch, but suffered a twisted knee that kept him out of Tests for over a year. Mashrafe's 4 for 38 in the 2007 World Cup was key in a famous defeat of India, and the following year he became only the second Bangladeshi – and the first fast bowler – to take 100 wickets in ODIs. He is not a complete mug with the bat: he has a first-class century to his name, and over 20% of his ODI runs have come in sixes.

THE FACTS Mashrafe Mortaza was the first Bangladeshi (Nazmul Hossain in 2004-05 was the second) to make his first-class debut in a Test match: only three others have done this since 1899 – Graham Vivian of New Zealand (1964-65), Zimbabwe's Ujesh Ranchod (1992-93) and Yasir Ali of Pakistan (2003-04) ... Mashrafe started the famous ODI victory over Australia at Cardiff in 2005 by dismissing Adam Gilchrist second ball for 0 ... His 6 for 26 v Kenya in Nairobi in August 2006 are Bangladesh's best bowling figures in ODIs ... His record includes two ODIs for the Asia XI ...

THE FIGURES to 23.9.10   **ESPNcricinfo.com**

Batting & Fielding	M	Inns	NO	Runs	HS	Avge	S/R	100	50	4s	6s	Ct	St
Tests	36	67	5	797	79	12.85	67.20	0	3	95	22	9	0
ODIs	113	89	15	1139	51*	15.39	85.38	0	1	90	39	36	0
T20Is	13	12	3	141	36	15.66	120.51	0	0	6	8	1	0
First-class	51	91	7	1341	132*	15.96	–	1	5	–	–	21	0

Bowling	M	Balls	Runs	Wkts	BB	Avge	RpO	S/R	5i	10m
Tests	36	5990	3239	78	4-60	41.52	3.24	76.79	0	0
ODIs	113	5710	4410	143	6-26	30.83	4.63	39.93	1	0
T20Is	13	297	435	10	2-28	43.50	8.78	29.70	0	0
First-class	51	8391	4371	123	4-27	35.53	3.12	68.21	0	0

ANGELO **MATHEWS**

Full name	**Angelo Davis Mathews**
Born	**June 2, 1987, Colombo**
Teams	**Colts, Basnahira North, Kolkata Knight Riders**
Style	**Right-hand bat, right-arm fast-medium bowler**
Test debut	**Sri Lanka v Pakistan at Galle 2009**
ODI debut	**Sri Lanka v Zimbabwe at Harare 2008-09**
T20I debut	**Sri Lanka v Australia at Nottingham 2009**

THE PROFILE Angelo Mathews first played for Sri Lanka Under-19s when he was just 16, and eventually won 23 one-day caps, many as captain. He was long seen as a potential international, as he is capable of batting anywhere in the top order and also bowls at a lively medium-pace. In first-class cricket he made a quiet start in 2006-07, but made big strides the following season, scoring 696 runs at 58 and earning an A-team trip to South Africa, where he made two centuries. His first internationals were against Zimbabwe – he made 52 not out in his third ODI, in Bangladesh in January 2009 – and shortly after that hammered 270 in a domestic match. He was picked for the World Twenty20 in England in June 2009, and helped Sri Lanka to the final, notably with three wickets against West Indies at The Oval, which effectively settled the semi-final in the first over. There was also handy batting (35 not out in the final) and frenetic fielding, notably a gymnastic juggling effort at Trent Bridge, the legality of which MCC had to confirm: he caught the ball on the field but overbalanced, threw the ball up, patted it back while in mid-air behind the boundary, then picked it up again inside the rope. Mathews made his Test debut at home soon afterwards. He is aiming to sharpen up his pace, as bowling improves his chances of a regular place, but it seems inevitable that it will be batting with which he makes his name in the long run, an impression sharpened by his 99 – he cried when he was narrowly run out – in a Test against India in Mumbai in December 2009.

THE FACTS Mathews was run out for 99 against India in Mumbai in December 2009 ... He made 270 for Basnahira North v Kandurata in Colombo in February 2009 ... Mathews took 6 for 20 in an ODI against India in Colombo in September 2009 ... In the World Twenty20 in England in 2009 his shirt had "Mathew" on the back before he added the final "s" with a marker pen ...

THE FIGURES *to 23.9.10*   **ESPN**cricinfo.com

Batting & Fielding	M	Inns	NO	Runs	HS	Avge	S/R	100	50	4s	6s	Ct	St
Tests	10	14	1	470	99	36.15	59.79	0	2	60	4	2	0
ODIs	29	23	4	563	75	29.63	79.07	0	5	33	7	9	0
T20Is	20	18	8	293	58	29.30	126.29	0	1	19	10	7	0
First-class	40	60	6	2770	270	51.29	54.19	8	11	305	26	24	0

Bowling	M	Balls	Runs	Wkts	BB	Avge	RpO	S/R	5i	10m
Tests	10	696	376	6	1–13	62.66	3.24	116.00	0	0
ODIs	29	1002	765	27	6–20	28.33	4.58	37.11	1	0
T20Is	20	283	346	15	3–16	23.06	7.33	18.86	0	0
First-class	40	3159	1503	36	5–47	41.75	2.85	87.75	1	0

AJANTHA **MENDIS**

SRI LANKA

Full name	**Balapuwaduge Ajantha Winslo Mendis**
Born	**March 11, 1985, Moratuwa**
Teams	**Army, Wayamba, Kolkata KR**
Style	**Right-hand bat, right-arm off- and legspinner**
Test debut	**Sri Lanka v India at Colombo 2008**
ODI debut	**Sri Lanka v West Indies at Port-of-Spain 2007-08**
T20I debut	**Sri Lanka v Zimbabwe at King City 2008-09**

THE PROFILE Those batsmen who thought one Sri Lankan mystery spinner was enough found more on their plate during 2008, when Ajantha Mendis stepped up to join Muttiah Muralitharan in the national side. Mendis sends down a mesmerising mixture of offbreaks, legbreaks, top-spinners, googlies and flippers, plus his very own "carrom ball" – one flicked out using a finger under the ball, in the style of the old Australians Jack Iverson and John Gleeson. He is also very accurate. Mendis was a prolific wicket-taker in 2007-08 for the Army (he received not one but two promotions following his meteoric rise) and was called up for the West Indian tour early in 2008 after taking 46 wickets in six matches. After doing well there he ran rings round the Indians – the supposed masters of spin – in the Asia Cup, rather ruining the final by taking 6 for 13. He was Man of the Series there, and also in his first Test series – against India again – with 26 wickets at 18.38 in three home Tests, including ten in the second Test at Galle and eight in each of the other two. He even achieved the rare feat of outperforming Murali (21 wickets at 22.23). There were signs in 2009, though, that batsmen were beginning to work out Mendis's variations. He was instrumental in Sri Lanka reaching the World Twenty20 final in England with some tight spells, but shortly after that he was dropped for two of the home Tests against Pakistan and New Zealand. He was back the following year, proving effective in one-dayers but less penetrative in Tests, and faces an important challenge after Murali's retirement from Tests.

THE FACTS Mendis took 26 wickets in his first Test series, against India in 2008, the most by anyone in a debut series of three Tests, beating Alec Bedser's 24 for England against India in 1946 ... After taking 33 wickets in his first four Tests, he took only 17 in his next eight ... Mendis took 6 for 13 in the Asia Cup final against India at Karachi in July 2008 ... He took 7 for 37 for Army v Lankan CC at Panagoda in February 2008 ...

THE FIGURES to 23.9.10   **ᴇSᴘᴨcricinfo.com**

Batting & Fielding	M	Inns	NO	Runs	HS	Avge	S/R	100	50	4s	6s	Ct	St
Tests	12	13	4	145	78	16.11	42.77	0	1	17	1	2	0
ODIs	44	21	9	91	15*	7.58	65.94	0	0	6	0	5	0
T20Is	19	4	2	7	4*	3.50	50.00	0	0	1	0	2	0
First-class	35	47	4	572	78	13.30	54.73	0	1	58	4	11	0

Bowling	M	Balls	Runs	Wkts	BB	Avge	RpO	S/R	5i	10m
Tests	12	3228	1644	50	6–117	32.88	3.05	64.56	2	1
ODIs	44	2073	1511	78	6–13	19.37	4.37	26.57	3	0
T20Is	19	432	409	33	4–15	12.39	5.68	13.09	0	0
First-class	35	7545	3597	185	7–37	19.44	2.86	40.78	11	2

DAVID **MILLER**

Full name	**David Andrew Miller**
Born	**June 10, 1989, Pietermaritzburg**
Teams	**Dolphins**
Style	**Left-hand bat, occasional offspinner**
Test debut	**No Tests yet**
ODI debut	**South Africa v West Indies at North Sound 2010**
T20I debut	**South Africa v West Indies at North Sound 2010**

THE PROFILE An explosive left-hander, David Miller was called up to the full South African limited-overs sides at 20 in the wake of the national team's disappointing performance at the World Twenty20 in the Caribbean in 2010. His first assignment was back in the West Indies – and he did as well as could have been expected, smashing his sixth ball in international cricket (from Sulieman Benn) into the stands on the way to 33 in the first Twenty20 match. He made a similarly brisk start in one-day internationals, calmly swinging the pacy Ravi Rampaul over square leg for six more during another cameo knock. Although he had not appeared for the national age-group sides, Miller had a stint at the South African Academy in mid-2009, and then caught the eye during a successful domestic season, in which he was the Dolphins' leading scorer in both 50- and 20-overs cricket. A rapid unbeaten 90 from 52 balls against the Lions in a Pro20 match at Potchefstroom in February 2010 ensured his selection for a triangular A-team tournament in Bangladesh, and it was while he was there that Miller received the call from the national selectors: "We are looking to strengthen our power-hitting in the middle order," explained chairman Andrew Hudson, the former Test opener. Graham Ford, the ex-South African coach who is now in charge of the Dolphins, said: "He is very effective in the powerplays, and we also used him for some big hitting towards the end of the 40-over game. In Twenty20s, I think he will be a real force up front."

THE FACTS Miller hit four sixes en route to his maiden first-class century, 108 not out for Dolphins v Eagles at Kimberley in December 2009 ... He also made a century for South Africa A in a 50-overs match against Bangladesh A at Mirpur in April 2010 ... In his first five international matches Miller hit five sixes but only one four ...

THE FIGURES to 23.9.10   **ESΠ∩cricinfo.com**

Batting & Fielding	M	Inns	NO	Runs	HS	Avge	S/R	100	50	4s	6s	Ct	St
Tests	0	0	–	–	–	–	–	–	–	–	–	–	–
ODIs	4	3	2	54	26*	54.00	122.72	0	0	1	3	1	0
T20Is	1	1	0	33	33	33.00	126.92	0	0	0	2	0	0
First-class	22	34	4	910	108*	30.33	57.12	1	5	134	17	14	0

Bowling	M	Balls	Runs	Wkts	BB	Avge	RpO	S/R	5i	10m
Tests	0	0	–	–	–	–	–	–	–	–
ODIs	4	0	–	–	–	–	–	–	–	–
T20Is	1	0	–	–	–	–	–	–	–	–
First-class	22	8	4	0	–	–	3.00	–	0	0

KYLE **MILLS**

Full name	**Kyle David Mills**
Born	**March 15, 1979, Auckland**
Teams	**Auckland**
Style	**Right-hand bat, right-arm fast-medium bowler**
Test debut	**New Zealand v England at Nottingham 2004**
ODI debut	**New Zealand v Pakistan at Sharjah 2000-01**
T20I debut	**New Zealand v Australia at Auckland 2004-05**

THE PROFILE Injuries at inopportune times have hampered Kyle Mills. They delayed his arrival as an international player, and impinged again in 2009-10, when knee and shoulder problems shortened his season and kept him out of the IPL: he did, however, make it to the World Twenty20 in the West Indies, although he proved expensive in his two matches there in May. A genuine swing bowler of lively pace, Mills yo-yoed in and out of the team after the 2003 World Cup, but he did enough to tour England in 2004, and made his Test debut in the third match at Trent Bridge. But he suffered a side strain there, and missed the one-day series. That was a shame, as one-day cricket is really his forte: he played throughout 2005-06, chipping in with wickets in almost every game, even if his once-promising batting had diminished to the point that he managed double figures only once in 16 matches. A feisty temper remains, though: Stephen Fleming had to pull him away from Graeme Smith during a niggle-strewn one-day series towards the end of 2005. Ankle surgery, then knee trouble – which necessitated another op – sidelined him early in 2007. Mills missed the World Cup, but came back stronger, following up 5 for 25 in a one-dayer in South Africa with a Test-best 4 for 16 against England at Hamilton in March 2008. He lost his Test spot after some anaemic performances the following season, but remained a one-day force, starting the Chappell-Hadlee Series in Australia in February 2009 by taking the match award after claiming four prime scalps.

THE FACTS Mills spanked his only first-class century from No. 9 at Wellington in 2000-01, helping Auckland recover from 109 for 7 to reach 347 ... His 5 for 25 at Durban in November 2007 are NZ's best one-day figures against South Africa ... Mills achieved the first ten-wicket haul of his career, and in the process reached 100 first-class wickets, for Auckland against Canterbury in December 2004 ...

THE FIGURES to 23.9.10   **ESPn cricinfo.com**

Batting & Fielding	M	Inns	NO	Runs	HS	Avge	S/R	100	50	4s	6s	Ct	St
Tests	19	30	5	289	57	11.56	38.58	0	1	37	3	4	0
ODIs	114	65	24	661	54	16.12	77.49	0	2	50	22	32	0
T20Is	19	13	4	119	33*	13.22	120.20	0	0	8	5	4	0
First-class	66	94	23	1840	117*	25.91	–	1	12	–	–	22	0

Bowling	M	Balls	Runs	Wkts	BB	Avge	RpO	S/R	5i	10m
Tests	19	2902	1453	44	4–16	33.02	3.00	65.95	0	0
ODIs	114	5663	4425	170	5–25	26.02	4.68	33.31	1	0
T20Is	19	424	594	21	3–44	28.28	8.40	20.19	0	0
First-class	66	10456	5059	176	5–33	28.74	2.90	59.40	3	1

MISBAH-UL-HAQ

Full name	**Misbah-ul-Haq Khan Niazi**
Born	**May 28, 1974, Mianwali, Punjab**
Teams	**Faisalabad, Baluchistan, Sui Northern Gas**
Style	**Right-hand bat, occasional legspinner**
Test debut	**Pakistan v New Zealand at Auckland 2000-01**
ODI debut	**Pakistan v New Zealand at Lahore 2001-02**
T20I debut	**Pakistan v Bangladesh at Nairobi 2007-08**

THE PROFILE An orthodox right-hander with a tight technique, Misbah-ul-Haq (no relation to Inzamam) caught the eye with his unflappable temperament in a triangular one-day tournament in Nairobi in September 2002, making 50 against Kenya and repeating that in the rain-ruined final against Australia. But then his form slumped: his highest score in three Tests against Australia was 17. Pakistan's abysmal 2003 World Cup campaign – and the wholesale changes to the team that followed – gave him another chance, but he did little of note in his limited opportunities, and seemed to have been forgotten forever afterwards, although he played quite a bit for the A team, often as captain. Misbah remained a consistent domestic performer, making 951 runs at 50 in 2004-05, 882 the following season, and capping that with 1108 at 61 in 2006-07, but it was nonetheless a shock when he was given a national contract for 2007-08 and called up for the inaugural World Twenty20 in South Africa. But he was a surprise hit there, and added 464 runs in three Tests against India, including two important centuries to ensure there was no danger of following on after India had twice totalled more than 600. Suddenly, in his mid-thirties but with a first-class average which remains above 50, Misbah was an automatic choice. He continued to contribute in all forms throughout 2009, and played his part in winning the World Twenty20 in England, although his batting wasn't needed in either the semi or the final. After that, though, he had a poor time in Australia, wasn't required during Pakistan's tour of England in 2010 – but was named as Test captain in October.

THE FACTS Misbah-ul-Haq has made six first-class double-centuries, the highest 284 for Sui Northern Gas v Lahore Shalimar in October 2009 ... He also made 208 not out (in a total of 723 for 4) for Punjab v Baluchistan at Sialkot in March 2008 ... He scored 161 and 133, both not out, in successive Tests against India in 2007-08 ... Misbah hit 87 not out, Pakistan's highest score in Twenty20 internationals, against Bangladesh in April 2008 ...

THE FIGURES to 23.9.10   ᴇsᴘᴎcricinfo.com

Batting & Fielding	M	Inns	NO	Runs	HS	Avge	S/R	100	50	4s	6s	Ct	St
Tests	19	33	3	1008	161*	33.60	38.76	2	4	106	9	24	0
ODIs	56	50	11	1523	79*	39.05	81.22	0	9	112	24	32	0
T20Is	29	25	9	577	87*	36.06	117.51	0	3	32	22	9	0
First-class	155	250	27	11229	284	50.35	–	32	53	–	–	158	0

Bowling	M	Balls	Runs	Wkts	BB	Avge	RpO	S/R	5i	10m
Tests	19	0	–	–	–	–	–	–	–	–
ODIs	56	24	30	0	–	–	7.50	–	0	0
T20Is	29	0	–	–	–	–	–	–	–	–
First-class	155	318	242	3	1–2	80.66	4.56	106.00	0	0

AMIT **MISHRA**

INDIA

Full name	**Amit Mishra**
Born	**November 24, 1982, Delhi**
Teams	**Haryana, Delhi Daredevils**
Style	**Right-hand bat, legspinner**
Test debut	**India v Australia at Mohali 2008-09**
ODI debut	**India v South Africa at Dhaka 2002-03**
T20I debut	**India v Zimbabwe at Harare 2010**

THE PROFILE   Amit Mishra is a confident cricketer, but even he might have thought his international chance had passed when five years went by after he flirted with the one-day team early in 2003. The diminutive Mishra, who bowls big loopy legbreaks and has a fizzing googly, took only two wickets in three matches after several players were rested following the World Cup: pundits thought he was too slow through the air, and back he went to the domestic grind. But Mishra remained a consistent force for Haryana, taking 41 first-class wickets in 2004-05 and 46 in 2007-08, a season which he started by playing for the A team against the touring South Africans. He also did well in the inaugural IPL jamboree, the highlight a hat-trick against Adam Gilchrist's Deccan Chargers. Early the following season Mishra took 6 for 81 (and nine in the match) against New Zealand A, which earned him a Test call-up against Australia a fortnight later at Mohali when Anil Kumble rested a shoulder injury. Mishra grabbed his big chance, becoming the first Indian to take a debut five-for since Narendra Hirwani, one of the selectors who finally chose him. The googly accounted for three of his wickets, but the pick was arguably the legbreak which pinned top-scorer Shane Watson in front. Mishra took 14 Australian wickets in three Tests, then six more against England. Pragyan Ojha's rise meant Mishra was still not an automatic selection, though he had his moments in 2010: seven wickets (and a maiden half-century) against Bangladesh in January, followed by important wickets in victories over South Africa at Kolkata and Sri Lanka in Colombo.

THE FACTS   Mishra took 5 for 71 against Australia at Mohali in October 2008: he was only the sixth Indian to take a five-for on Test debut ... He took a hat-trick in his 5 for 17 for Delhi Daredevils v Deccan Chargers in the first season of the IPL in May 2008 ... Mishra took 6 for 66 for Haryana v Jharkhand in Chandigarh in March 2005 ... He has twice scored 84 for Haryana – against Madhya Pradesh in November 2002 and Saurashtra in January 2007 ...

THE FIGURES to 23.9.10   **ESPNcricinfo.com**

Batting & Fielding	M	Inns	NO	Runs	HS	Avge	S/R	100	50	4s	6s	Ct	St
Tests	10	13	2	205	50	18.63	60.11	0	1	25	1	6	0
ODIs	10	1	0	0	0	0.00	0.00	0	0	0	0	1	0
T20Is	1	0	–	–	–	–	–	–	–	–	–	0	0
First-class	95	127	18	2132	84	19.55	–	0	10	–	–	53	0

Bowling	M	Balls	Runs	Wkts	BB	Avge	RpO	S/R	5i	10m
Tests	10	2850	1429	36	5–71	39.69	3.00	79.16	1	0
ODIs	10	463	376	8	3–40	47.00	4.87	57.87	0	0
T20Is	1	24	21	1	1–21	21.00	5.25	24.00	0	0
First-class	95	20993	10019	371	6–66	27.00	2.86	56.58	19	1

ABHIMANYU **MITHUN**

Full name	**Abhimanyu Mithun**
Born	**October 25, 1989, Bangalore**
Teams	**Karnataka, Bangalore Royal Challengers**
Style	**Right-hand bat, right-arm fast-medium bowler**
Test debut	**India v Sri Lanka at Galle 2010**
ODI debut	**India v South Africa at Ahmedabad 2009-10**
T20I debut	**No T20Is yet**

THE PROFILE Abhimanyu Mithun spent his early teenage years striving for success in athletics – he was a fine discus thrower – and didn't bowl with a leather ball until he was 17. But three years later, after a remarkably successful debut season in 2009-10, he had forced his way into the national squad. Mithun's build, honed at his father's gym in Bangalore, is perfect for a fast bowler: he's 6ft 2ins (188cm) tall, and uses his height to good effect when deploying the bouncer, his favourite weapon. Mithun caught the eye of the Bangalore Royal Challengers' coach Ray Jennings before the second IPL season in 2009 and, although he didn't do much in his only outing there, he certainly made people sit up and take notice when he finally made his Ranji Trophy debut in November: he took 11 Uttar Pradesh wickets in his first match, with a second-innings hat-trick that included two Test players (Piyush Chawla and RP Singh). His pace made batsmen hop about, and he finished with 52 wickets at 23.26 as Karnataka reached the Ranji final for the first time in 12 years. Mithun sat out the home Tests against South Africa, but did play in one of the one-dayers that followed, although he proved expensive. Still, he made the Sri Lankan tour in July, and this time played in all three Tests, starting with the early wicket of Tillakaratne Dilshan in the first at Galle. He took four wickets there, but only one in each of the other two matches, but did reveal unexpected tenacity with the bat, playing long defensive knocks in each Test. Mithun's new-ball partnership with Ishant Sharma could be a formidable prospect.

THE FACTS Mithun took 6 for 86 and 5 for 95 – including a hat-trick – on his first-class debut for Karnataka v Uttar Pradesh at Meerut in November 2009 ... He took 6 for 71 for Karnataka v Mumbai in the Ranji Trophy final at Mysore in January 2010 ... Mithun's first Test, at Galle in July 2010, was only his 12th first-class match ...

THE FIGURES to 23.9.10   **ᴇꜱᴘⁿcricinfo.com**

Batting & Fielding	M	Inns	NO	Runs	HS	Avge	S/R	100	50	4s	6s	Ct	St
Tests	3	4	0	120	46	30.00	49.38	0	0	16	0	0	0
ODIs	2	2	0	28	24	14.00	71.79	0	0	0	2	0	0
T20Is	0	0	–	–	–	–	–	–	–	–	–	–	–
First-class	14	15	4	224	46	20.36	56.70	0	0	29	2	1	0

Bowling	M	Balls	Runs	Wkts	BB	Avge	RpO	S/R	5i	10m
Tests	3	552	372	6	4–105	62.00	4.04	92.00	0	0
ODIs	2	72	87	0	–	–	7.25	–	0	0
T20Is	0	0	–	–	–	–	–	–	–	–
First-class	14	2755	1723	59	6–71	29.20	3.75	46.69	3	1

MOHAMMAD AAMER

PAKISTAN

Full name	**Mohammad Aamer**
Born	**April 13, 1992, Gujjar Khan, Punjab**
Teams	**Rawalpindi, National Bank**
Style	**Left-hand bat, left-arm fast-medium bowler**
Test debut	**Pakistan v Sri Lanka at Galle 2009**
ODI debut	**Pakistan v Sri Lanka at Dambulla 2009**
T20I debut	**Pakistan v England at The Oval 2009**

THE PROFILE Mohammad Aamer, a toothy left-arm pace bowler, reveres Wasim Akram – and like his hero emerged as a genuine prospect at a tender age. Even before he toured England with the Under-19s in 2007 he had been picked out as a special talent – by none other than Akram himself – at a pace camp in Lahore. He did well in England, then helped Pakistan win a triangular tournament in Sri Lanka. Aamer seemed set to be one of the stars of the Under-19 World Cup in Malaysia in 2008, only to go down with dengue fever. However, he was back the following season, and his career really took off. He took 55 wickets for National Bank in his debut season, exhibiting precocious pace and swing, and was a surprise selection for the World Twenty20 squad in England. It turned out to be an inspired choice: he replaced the out-of-sorts Sohail Tanvir and bowled with pace, accuracy and courage as Pakistan stormed to the title after an uncertain start. He bowled several nerveless death overs and one crucial opening one, in the final against Sri Lanka, when he dismissed the tournament's top-scorer Tillakaratne Dilshan for a five-ball duck, peppering him with short, quick balls. A Test debut followed in Sri Lanka, and Aamer started well, taking a wicket in his first over. Nothing but praise came his way on the tours that followed in Australia and England, during which he clocked up 50 Test wickets not long after his 18th birthday ... until his alleged involvement in "spot-fixing" during the Lord's Test against England left him facing an uncertain future.

THE FACTS Mohammad Aamer took 7 for 61 (10 for 97 in the match) for National Bank v Lahore Shalimar in February 2009 ... In his next match he took 6 for 95 against Khan Research Laboratories ... Aamer took a wicket (Sri Lanka's Malinda Warnapura) with his sixth ball in Test cricket in July 2009 ... He claimed 7 for 24 (against Jhelum) and 5 for 7 (v Chakwal) for Rawalpindi in an under-19 tournament in June 2007 ...

THE FIGURES *to 23.9.10*   **ESPN cricinfo.com**

Batting & Fielding	M	Inns	NO	Runs	HS	Avge	S/R	100	50	4s	6s	Ct	St
Tests	14	28	6	278	30*	12.63	27.33	0	0	32	1	0	0
ODIs	15	12	4	167	73*	20.87	78.03	0	1	18	3	6	0
T20Is	18	6	2	39	21*	9.75	108.33	0	0	1	2	3	0
First-class	28	45	9	508	44*	14.11	35.49	0	0	55	7	5	0

Bowling	M	Balls	Runs	Wkts	BB	Avge	RpO	S/R	5i	10m
Tests	14	2867	1484	51	6–84	29.09	3.10	56.21	3	0
ODIs	15	789	600	25	4–28	24.00	4.56	31.56	0	0
T20Is	18	390	457	23	3–23	19.86	7.03	16.95	0	0
First-class	28	4991	2578	120	7–61	21.48	3.09	41.59	7	1

MOHAMMAD ASHRAFUL

Full name	**Mohammad Ashraful**
Born	**July 7, 1984, Dhaka**
Teams	**Dhaka**
Style	**Right-hand bat, legspinner**
Test debut	**Bangladesh v Sri Lanka at Colombo 2001-02**
ODI debut	**Bangladesh v Zimbabwe at Bulawayo 2000-01**
T20I debut	**Bangladesh v Kenya at Nairobi 2007-08**

THE PROFILE On September 8, 2001, at the Sinhalese Sports Club in Colombo, Mohammad Ashraful turned a terrible mismatch into a slice of history by becoming the youngest man – or boy – to make a Test century. Just 17, he broke the long-standing record set by Mushtaq Mohammad (17 years 82 days) in 1960-61. Bangladesh still crashed to heavy defeat, but "Matin" was unbowed, repeatedly dancing down to hit Muttiah Muralitharan and his fellow spinners back over their heads. Inevitably, such a heady early achievement proved hard to live up to, and after a prolonged poor run Ashraful was dropped for England's first visit in October 2003. He returned a better player, but no less flamboyant, as he demonstrated with a glorious unbeaten 158 in defeat against India at Chittagong late in 2004. Still not 21 when Bangladesh made their maiden tour of England the following year, Ashraful confirmed his talent at Cardiff, when his brilliantly paced century set up an astonishing one-day victory over Australia. He continued to fire spasmodically, a superb 87 bringing victory over South Africa in the 2007 World Cup, but that was surrounded by more low scores. When Habibul Bashar stood down in May 2007 Ashraful took on the captaincy – but the results stayed the same and he looked careworn by the time he was replaced after a dismal World Twenty20 campaign in England in 2009. He celebrated his return to the ranks with a couple of fifties in the one-day portion of the successful West Indian tour, and a fine hundred against Zimbabwe at Bulawayo in August 2009, but more indifferent form soon cost him his place again.

THE FACTS Only 11 players have made their Test debuts when younger than Ashraful: three of them are from Bangladesh and seven from Pakistan ... He scored 263, putting on 420 with Marshall Ayub, for Dhaka v Chittagong in November 2006 ... Ashraful averages 42.88 in Tests v India, but only 9.12 v England ... His Test batting average (22.38) is easily the lowest for anyone with five or more centuries: Grant Flower (29.54) is next ... Ashraful's record includes two ODIs for the Asia XI ...

THE FIGURES *to 23.9.10*   **ESPNcricinfo.com**

Batting & Fielding	M	Inns	NO	Runs	HS	Avge	S/R	100	50	4s	6s	Ct	St
Tests	55	107	4	2306	158*	22.38	46.51	5	7	287	21	24	0
ODIs	163	156	13	3354	109	23.45	70.81	3	20	338	29	33	0
T20Is	15	15	0	265	65	17.66	148.04	0	2	27	9	3	0
First-class	104	196	5	5320	263	27.85	–	13	22	–	–	54	0

Bowling	M	Balls	Runs	Wkts	BB	Avge	RpO	S/R	5i	10m
Tests	55	1591	1188	20	2–42	59.40	4.48	79.55	0	0
ODIs	163	570	554	15	3–26	36.93	5.83	38.00	0	0
T20Is	15	138	210	8	3–42	26.25	9.13	17.25	0	0
First-class	104	6448	3942	113	7–99	34.88	3.66	57.06	5	0

MOHAMMAD ASIF

PAKISTAN

Full name **Mohammad Asif**
Born **December 20, 1982, Sheikhupura, Punjab**
Teams **Sialkot, National Bank**
Style **Left-hand bat, right-arm fast-medium bowler**
Test debut **Pakistan v Australia at Sydney 2004-05**
ODI debut **Pakistan v England at Rawalpindi 2005-06**
T20I debut **Pakistan v England at Bristol 2006**

THE PROFILE When Mohammad Asif made his Test debut at Sydney in January 2005, there was little to suggest that Pakistan's long and happy tradition of unearthing fast bowlers out of nowhere was about to continue: he bowled 18 innocuous overs as Australia completed a whitewash. Towards the end that year, though, Asif caught the eye with ten wickets as Pakistan A embarrassed England at the start of their tour. He didn't feature in the Tests, but did make an impressive one-day debut the day after his 23rd birthday, dismissing Marcus Trescothick with his third ball and ending up with 2 for 14. Tall, lean and muscular, he could generate good pace before he eased up a little to protect a suspect back. He grabbed seven plum wickets in a famous victory over India at Karachi early in 2006, and 11 for 71 in a three-day win over Sri Lanka at Kandy. An elbow injury kept him out of the first three Tests in England in 2006, but he looked dangerous when he returned at The Oval, taking four wickets in England's first innings before the ball-tampering row blew up. But then he was embroiled in even worse scandals: he was banned (but subsequently cleared) after failing a drug test, was then arrested at Dubai Airport for allegedly possessing opium, and finally really was suspended after testing positive for nandrolone during the IPL. He was hustled back into national contention as soon as that ban expired in September 2009, but the following year he was again in the newspapers for the wrong reasons, when his alleged involvement in "spot-fixing" during the Lord's Test against England left him facing an uncertain future.

THE FACTS Mohammad Asif took 11 for 71 (6 for 44 and 5 for 27) against Sri Lanka at Kandy in April 2006 ... For Pakistan A v England in Lahore in November 2005 he took 7 for 62 ... At The Oval in 2006 Asif collected his fifth consecutive Test duck, equalling the unwanted record of Australia's Bob Holland and Ajit Agarkar of India ... Asif took 7 for 35 as Sialkot bowled Multan out for 67 in October 2004 ... His record includes three ODIs for the Asia XI ...

THE FIGURES to 23.9.10   **ESPncricinfo.com**

Batting & Fielding	M	Inns	NO	Runs	HS	Avge	S/R	100	50	4s	6s	Ct	St
Tests	23	38	13	141	29	5.64	30.45	0	0	19	0	3	0
ODIs	38	16	7	34	6	3.77	34.00	0	0	2	0	5	0
T20Is	11	3	3	9	5*	–	300.00	0	0	2	0	3	0
First-class	87	120	44	598	42	7.86	–	0	0	–	–	30	0

Bowling	M	Balls	Runs	Wkts	BB	Avge	RpO	S/R	5i	10m
Tests	23	5171	2583	106	6–41	24.36	2.99	48.78	7	1
ODIs	38	1941	1524	46	3–28	33.13	4.71	42.19	0	0
T20Is	11	257	343	13	4–18	26.38	8.00	19.76	0	0
First-class	87	16474	8848	360	7–35	24.57	3.22	45.76	22	5

MOHAMMAD HAFEEZ

Full name	**Mohammad Hafeez**
Born	**October 17, 1980, Sargodha, Punjab**
Teams	**Faisalabad, Sui Northern Gas**
Style	**Right-hand bat, offspinner**
Test debut	**Pakistan v Bangladesh at Karachi 2003**
ODI debut	**Pakistan v Zimbabwe at Sharjah 2002-03**
T20I debut	**Pakistan v England at Bristol 2006**

THE PROFILE Mohammad Hafeez was one of several young players tried after Pakistan's abysmal display in the 2003 World Cup. Some good one-day performances followed, in Sharjah, Sri Lanka and England: he showed good technique and temperament with the bat and bowled his Saqlainish offspinners tidily, but was arguably at his most impressive in the field, where he patrolled the point/cover region with feverish alertness. His organised approach to batting earned him a Test cap when Bangladesh toured shortly afterwards, and he started brightly, scoring a half-century on debut and a maiden hundred in his second Test. However, his form dipped alarmingly in the one-dayers that followed against South Africa – only 33 runs in five innings, and he lost his place. Consistent domestic runs kept him in contention, but he seemed to be a back number after being dropped again early in 2005. Hafeez was not originally chosen for the 2006 England tour, but a superb 180 against Australia A at Darwin in July, while Pakistan struggled to find an opening combination worth the name in England, led to a surprise call-up for the final Test at The Oval. Before the ball-tampering row overshadowed everything, Hafeez contributed a tidy 95, then spanked 46 in the Twenty20 game that followed. From nowhere, a regular place loomed, and he consolidated in 2006-07, scoring another Test century against West Indies before struggling in South Africa, where all six of his Test innings ranged between 10 and 32. Out he went again, for more than two years, before a surprise recall for the World Twenty20 in the West Indies and the one-day portion of the England tour later in 2010.

THE FACTS Mohammad Hafeez scored 50 in his first Test, v Bangladesh at Karachi in August 2003, and added 102 not out in his second, at Peshawar a week later ... He scored 95 in his only Test innings against England (at The Oval in 2006) ... Hafeez scored 180 for Pakistan A v Australia A at Darwin in July 2006 ... He took 8 for 57 (10 for 87 in the match) for Faisalabad v Quetta in December 2004 ...

THE FIGURES to 23.9.10   **ESPncricinfo.com**

Batting & Fielding	M	Inns	NO	Runs	HS	Avge	S/R	100	50	4s	6s	Ct	St
Tests	11	21	1	677	104	33.85	45.43	2	3	89	3	4	0
ODIs	53	53	1	1041	92	20.01	59.21	0	5	120	9	22	0
T20Is	16	14	0	235	46	16.78	107.79	0	0	31	4	8	0
First-class	135	226	7	7476	180	34.13	–	16	37	–	–	119	0

Bowling	M	Balls	Runs	Wkts	BB	Avge	RpO	S/R	5i	10m
Tests	11	750	319	4	1–11	79.75	2.55	187.50	0	0
ODIs	53	1883	1406	39	3–17	36.05	4.48	48.28	0	0
T20Is	16	228	320	9	2–19	35.55	8.42	25.33	0	0
First-class	135	9657	4451	151	8–57	29.47	2.76	63.95	4	1

MOHAMMAD IRFAN

Full name	**Mohammad Irfan**
Born	**June 6, 1982, Gaggu Mandi, Punjab**
Teams	**Multan, Baluchistan, Khan Research Laboratories**
Style	**Right-hand bat, left-arm fast-medium bowler**
Test debut	**No Tests yet**
ODI debut	**Pakistan v England at Chester-le-Street 2010**
T20I debut	**No T20Is yet**

THE PROFILE Few fast bowlers have generated as much advance publicity as Mohammad Irfan, selected at the relatively mature age of 28 as a late replacement for the one-day portion of the 2010 England tour, after the first-choice new-ball bowlers Mohammad Aamer and Mohammad Asif were suspended pending investigations into their alleged involvement in "spot-fixing". But the interest in Irfan was entirely unrelated to that sorry affair; it concerned his height, which had been variously reported as between 6ft 8ins (203cm) and 7ft 1in (216cm). The reality, according to an English journalist with a tape measure, was 6ft 10.5ins (209.6cm), which would still make him the tallest player ever to appear in international cricket. Sadly, his early appearances failed to inspire: he looked nervous and cumbersome when he bowled, and also upset his captain with some amateurish fielding, dropping the century-bound Andrew Strauss when he had 23 at Headingley. "I'm really disappointed with this guy," said Shahid Afridi. "Cricket is not all about just batting and bowling, nowadays fielding is very important." Irfan is from a rural town, and at one stage retired from cricket to work in a pipe factory to support his family. He was hooked out of club cricket to join the national academy, and was soon turning heads on the domestic scene, taking nine wickets in his second first-class match and 11 in his third: he ended 2009-10, his first season, with 43 wickets and a place in the preliminary squad for the World Twenty20 in the West Indies. He missed out there, and might wish he had missed out on that England call-up too after a mixed start to his international career.

THE FACTS Mohammad Irfan is believed to be the tallest international player of all, surpassing Joel Garner and Bruce Reid, who were 6ft 8ins (203cm) ... Irfan took 7 for 113 for Khan Research Laboratories v Habib Bank in only his second first-class match, in October 2009, and added 5 for 27 and 6 for 96 for KRL v Karachi Whites a week later ...

THE FIGURES *to 23.9.10*   **ᴇsᴘncricinfo.com**

Batting & Fielding	M	Inns	NO	Runs	HS	Avge	S/R	100	50	4s	6s	Ct	St
Tests	0	0	–	–	–	–	–	–	–	–	–	–	–
ODIs	2	1	1	3	3*	–	60.00	0	0	0	0	0	0
T20Is	0	0	–	–	–	–	–	–	–	–	–	–	–
First-class	10	10	6	24	8*	6.00	46.15	0	0	2	1	3	0

Bowling	M	Balls	Runs	Wkts	BB	Avge	RpO	S/R	5i	10m
Tests	0	0	–	–	–	–	–	–	–	–
ODIs	2	75	77	0	–	–	6.16	–	0	0
T20Is	0	0	–	–	–	–	–	–	–	–
First-class	10	2056	1237	43	7–113	28.76	3.60	47.81	4	1

MOHAMMAD YOUSUF

Full name	**Mohammad Yousuf Youhana**
Born	**August 27, 1974, Lahore, Punjab**
Teams	**Islamabad, WAPDA**
Style	**Right-hand bat**
Test debut	**Pakistan v South Africa at Durban 1997-98**
ODI debut	**Pakistan v Zimbabwe at Harare 1997-98**
T20I debut	**Pakistan v England at Bristol 2006**

THE PROFILE Until his conversion to Islam in 2005, Mohammad Yousuf (formerly Yousuf Youhana) was one of the rare Christians to play for Pakistan. After a difficult debut, he quickly established himself as a stylish world-class batsman, and a middle-order pillar. After becoming a Muslim, he became a run machine, breaking Viv Richards's 30-year-old record for Test runs in a calendar year during a stellar 2006. Yousuf gathers his runs through composed, orthodox strokeplay: he is particularly strong driving through the covers and flicking wristily off his legs, and has a backlift as decadent and delicious as any, although a tendency to overbalance when playing across his front leg can get him into trouble. He really matured late in 2004. First came a spellbindingly languid century at Melbourne, when he ripped into Shane Warne as few Pakistanis ever did. A century followed in the Kolkata cauldron, and he ended 2005 with 223 against England, eschewing the waftiness that had previously blighted him. His batting (and his beard) burgeoned in 2006, and it was a surprise when he joined the unauthorised Indian Cricket League the following year and was promptly banned. But after an amnesty he returned to the traditional game in 2009, starting with a typically elegant century against Sri Lanka at Galle. A reluctant captain, he oversaw the disastrous tour of Australia in 2009-10. Pakistan's board banned him afterwards for unspecified offences, and Yousuf promptly retired ... but both decisions were overturned when Pakistan needed him in England later in the year: he immediately stiffened a suspect middle order.

THE FACTS Since becoming a Muslim Mohammad Yousuf has averaged 60.33 in 31 Tests: in 59 matches beforehand he averaged 47.46 ... He scored 1788 Test runs in 2006, breaking Viv Richards's old calendar-year record of 1710 in 1976 ... Yousuf has scored four Test double-centuries, but had not made another in first-class cricket until he hit 205 not out for Lancashire v Yorkshire in 2008 ...

THE FIGURES to 23.9.10   **ESPN**cricinfo.com

Batting & Fielding	M	Inns	NO	Runs	HS	Avge	S/R	100	50	4s	6s	Ct	St
Tests	90	156	12	7530	223	52.29	52.39	24	33	957	51	65	0
ODIs	287	272	40	9717	141*	41.88	75.11	15	64	785	90	58	0
T20Is	3	3	0	50	26	16.66	116.27	0	0	5	1	1	0
First-class	134	226	20	10152	223	49.28	–	29	49	–	–	84	0

Bowling	M	Balls	Runs	Wkts	BB	Avge	RpO	S/R	5i	10m
Tests	90	6	3	0	–	–	3.00	–	0	0
ODIs	287	2	1	1	1–0	1.00	3.00	2.00	0	0
T20Is	3	0	–	–	–	–	–	–	–	–
First-class	134	18	24	0	–	–	8.00	–	0	0

EOIN **MORGAN**

Full name	**Eoin Joseph Gerard Morgan**
Born	**September 10, 1986, Dublin, Ireland**
Teams	**Middlesex, Royal Challengers Bangalore**
Style	**Left-hand bat, occasional right-arm medium-pacer**
Test debut	**England v Bangladesh at Lord's 2010**
ODI debut	**Ireland v Scotland at Ayr 2006**
T20I debut	**England v Netherlands at Lord's 2009**

THE PROFILE Eoin Morgan is an impish left-hander with a reputation for inventive and audacious strokeplay. He made his mark for England with two matchwinning innings against South Africa: 67 from 34 balls in the Champions Trophy in September 2009, and an unbeaten 45-ball 85 in the opening Twenty20 of England's tour two months later. With a blend of nous and power, Morgan looks a natural "finisher" – a role England have struggled to fill for a decade. A compact left-hander, he grew up playing hurling, and his trademark change-up sweeps and pulls may well have been helped by his grounding in that Gaelic sport. He gained initial recognition with Ireland, playing 23 ODIs for them, although he was disappointing at the 2007 World Cup, managing only 91 runs in nine games. He joined his fellow Dubliner, Ed Joyce, at Middlesex in 2006, and two years later helped them win the Twenty20 Cup. In 2009 he was called up by England, effectively ending his career with Ireland. After a quiet start in which his fielding was probably more impressive than his batting, Morgan did well as England won the World Twenty20 in the West Indies early in 2010, then, although not widely viewed as a five-day player, he was a surprise inclusion for the first Test of the 2010 summer, against Bangladesh. It was a gentle introduction, and he confidently collected his first boundary with a reverse-sweep. Ian Bell's broken toe kept Morgan in against Pakistan: he responded with a gutsy 130 to set up victory in the first Test at Trent Bridge, and finished the season with a fine century at the Rose Bowl to seal a 3-2 victory in a fractious one-day series.

THE FACTS Morgan is the only player ever to be out (run out, too!) for 99 in his first ODI, against Scotland in August 2006 ... His first 23 ODIs were for Ireland: he made 744 runs at 35.42 for them, including 115 v Canada in Nairobi in February 2007 ... Morgan scored 209 not out – the first double-century for Ireland – against the UAE in Abu Dhabi in February 2007 ... Morgan was the third Irish-born player to score a Test century, after Fred Fane for England in 1905-06 and Australia's Tom Horan (1881-82) ...

THE FIGURES to 23.9.10   **ESFT cricinfo.com**

Batting & Fielding	M	Inns	NO	Runs	HS	Avge	S/R	100	50	4s	6s	Ct	St
Tests	6	8	0	256	130	32.00	52.56	1	0	30	1	4	0
ODIs	55	55	11	1798	115	40.86	81.24	4	10	159	37	24	0
T20Is	14	14	6	416	85*	52.00	140.06	0	3	41	13	8	0
First-class	55	91	12	2930	209*	37.08	50.38	7	13	–	–	47	1

Bowling	M	Balls	Runs	Wkts	BB	Avge	RpO	S/R	5i	10m
Tests	6	0	–	–	–	–	–	–	–	–
ODIs	55	0	–	–	–	–	–	–	–	–
T20Is	14	0	–	–	–	–	–	–	–	–
First-class	55	79	46	2	2–24	23.00	3.49	39.50	0	0

ALBIE **MORKEL**

Full name	**Johannes Albertus Morkel**
Born	**June 10, 1981, Vereeniging, Transvaal**
Teams	**Titans, Durham, Chennai Super Kings**
Style	**Left-hand bat, right-arm fast-medium bowler**
Test debut	**South Africa v Australia at Cape Town 2008-09**
ODI debut	**South Africa v New Zealand at Wellington 2003-04**
T20I debut	**South Africa v New Zealand at Johannesburg 2005-06**

THE PROFILE Albie Morkel, a fast-medium bowler and big-hitting left-handed batsman, was lumbered with the tag of the "new Lance Klusener", and was touted early on by Ray Jennings (his provincial coach, and a former national coach too) as a potential world-class allrounder. It hasn't quite happened so far, although he does average over 40 in first-class cricket, and scored a half-century in his only Test (he was included after his brother Morne lost form). Most notably, Twenty20 seemed to be tailor-made for his style of play. For Easterns (now the Titans) against the touring West Indians at Benoni in 2003-04 Albie defied food poisoning to score a century – putting on 141 for the ninth wicket with his brother – and also took five wickets in the match. He was picked for the senior tour of New Zealand shortly after that, and made his one-day international debut there early in 2004: he performed solidly, if unspectacularly, for a while until the selectors looked elsewhere. Morkel was back for the Afro-Asia Cup in June 2007. In the second match, at Chennai, Albie and Morne opened the bowling together for the African XI, the first instance of brothers sharing the new ball in an ODI since Kenya's Martin and Tony Suji did so during the 1999 World Cup. Shortly after that Albie hit 97 against the outclassed Zimbabweans. His huge sixes were a feature of the inaugural World Twenty20 championship late in 2007, but by 2009-10 the expectation of more rope-clearing every time he came in seemed to be affecting his performances.

THE FACTS Albie Morkel made 204 not out, putting on 264 with Justin Kemp, as Titans drew with Western Province Boland in March 2005 after following on ... He took 6 for 36 for Easterns v Griqualand West in December 1999 ... Morkel's brother Morne has also played for South Africa, while another brother, Malan, played for SA Schools ... His record includes two ODIs for the Africa XI, in one of which he opened the bowling with Morne ...

THE FIGURES to 23.9.10   **ESPncricinfo.com**

Batting & Fielding	M	Inns	NO	Runs	HS	Avge	S/R	100	50	4s	6s	Ct	St
Tests	1	1	0	58	58	58.00	81.69	0	1	10	1	0	0
ODIs	47	34	8	621	97	23.88	101.47	0	2	58	19	12	0
T20Is	29	25	6	443	43	23.31	142.90	0	0	26	29	12	0
First-class	65	94	16	3296	204*	42.25	–	5	20	–	–	27	0

Bowling	M	Balls	Runs	Wkts	BB	Avge	RpO	S/R	5i	10m
Tests	1	192	132	1	1–44	132.00	4.12	192.00	0	0
ODIs	47	1816	1629	48	4–29	33.93	5.38	37.83	0	0
T20Is	29	406	549	16	2–12	34.31	8.11	25.37	0	0
First-class	65	9779	5049	170	6–36	29.70	3.09	57.52	4	0

MORNE **MORKEL**

Full name	**Morne Morkel**
Born	**October 6, 1984, Vereeniging, Transvaal**
Teams	**Titans, Rajasthan Royals**
Style	**Left-hand bat, right-arm fast bowler**
Test debut	**South Africa v India at Durban 2006-07**
ODI debut	**Africa XI v Asia XI at Bangalore 2007**
T20I debut	**South Africa v West Indies at Johannesburg 2007-08**

THE PROFILE Morne Morkel, the taller, faster brother of Easterns allrounder Albie, has been a hot property ever since his first-class debut in 2003-04, when he and Albie put on 141 against the West Indians at Benoni. An out-and-out fast bowler, Morne excelled with 20 wickets at 18.20 apiece in 2004-05, but then sat out most of the following season with injuries. But he had impressed Allan Donald: "He gets serious bounce, and he's got really great pace – genuine pace." Morkel used that to shake up the Indians for the Rest of South Africa in December 2006, bowling Sehwag with his first ball and adding Laxman, Tendulkar and Dhoni as the tourists lurched to 69 for 5. That got him into the national frame, and he played in the second Test when Dale Steyn was ruled out, although three wickets and some handy runs in a crushing victory weren't enough to keep him in when Steyn was fit again. Morkel played his first one-dayers in the Afro-Asia Cup in India in June 2007, taking eight wickets in three games. A stress fracture early in the subsequent Pakistan tour temporarily halted the rapid rise, but he bounced back later in 2008 to lead South Africa's attack in England, without ever quite being at his best as they won the Test series. Early the following year Morne had the unusual experience of being replaced in the Test side by his brother, but he later cemented his place with seven wickets in a crushing victory over England at Johannesburg in January 2010, and six more in another comfortable win over West Indies at Port-of-Spain a few months later.

THE FACTS Morne Morkel took 6 for 43 and 6 for 48 for Titans v Eagles at Bloemfontein in March 2009, a week after being dropped from the Test side ... He took 5 for 50 against Bangladesh at Dhaka in February 2008 ... Morkel's first three ODIs were for the Africa XI: in one he opened the bowling with his brother Albie, the first instance of siblings sharing the new ball in an ODI since Kenya's Martin and Tony Suji did so during the 1999 World Cup ...

THE FIGURES to 23.9.10   **ESP11cricinfo.com**

Batting & Fielding	M	Inns	NO	Runs	HS	Avge	S/R	100	50	4s	6s	Ct	St
Tests	26	31	3	370	40	13.21	42.09	0	0	58	0	7	0
ODIs	28	10	3	102	25	14.57	94.44	0	0	11	2	6	0
T20Is	14	2	1	2	1*	2.00	40.00	0	0	0	0	1	0
First-class	58	72	9	1027	82*	16.30	45.99	0	4	–	–	24	0

Bowling	M	Balls	Runs	Wkts	BB	Avge	RpO	S/R	5i	10m
Tests	26	4855	2831	92	5–50	30.77	3.49	52.77	2	0
ODIs	28	1439	1216	45	4–21	27.02	5.07	31.97	0	0
T20Is	14	317	346	23	4–17	15.04	6.54	13.78	0	0
First-class	58	10134	5778	211	6–43	27.38	3.42	48.02	9	2

MUTTIAH **MURALITHARAN**

Full name	**Muttiah Muralitharan**
Born	**April 17, 1972, Kandy**
Teams	**Tamil Union, Kandurata, Chennai Super Kings**
Style	**Right-hand bat, offspinner**
Test debut	**Sri Lanka v Australia at Colombo 1992-93**
ODI debut	**Sri Lanka v India at Colombo 1993-94**
T20I debut	**Sri Lanka v New Zealand at Wellington 2006-07**

THE PROFILE Muttiah Muralitharan is the most successful bowler the international game has seen, Sri Lanka's greatest player ... and the most controversial cricketer of the modern age. Murali's rise from humble beginnings – the Tamil son of a hill-country confectioner – to the summit of the wicket-taking lists divided opinion because of his weird bent-armed delivery. From a loose-limbed, open-chested action, his chief weapons are the big-turning offbreak and two top-spinners, one of which goes straight on and a *doosra*, which spins from a rubbery wrist in the opposite direction to his stock ball. However, whispers about his action intensified after he was no-balled for throwing in Australia in 1995-96. He was cleared after biomechanical analysis concluded that his action, and a deformed elbow which he can't fully straighten, create the "optical illusion of throwing". But the controversy would not die: Murali was called again in Australia in 1998-99, had more tests, and was cleared again. Then his new *doosra* prompted further suspicion, and he underwent yet more high-tech tests in 2004, which ultimately forced ICC to revise their rules on chucking. On the field, Murali continued to pile up the wickets, overtaking Courtney Walsh's Test-record 519 in May 2004: only shoulder trouble allowed Shane Warne briefly to pass him. Murali returned, potent as ever, flummoxed England with 8 for 70 at Nottingham to square the 2006 series, and four years later signed off his Test career in fairytale fashion by taking the eight wickets he needed to reach 800 in his final match, against India at Galle. He will carry on in one-dayers – in which he's the leading wicket-taker too – until the 2011 World Cup.

THE FACTS Muralitharan was the first to take 1,000 wickets in all international cricket: he reached 800 in Tests with his final delivery, v India at Galle in July 2010... His 67 Test five-fors is easily a record, as is his 22 ten-wicket hauls ... Murali took nine wickets in a Test innings twice, and his 16 for 220 at The Oval in 1998 is the fifth-best haul in all Tests ... His record includes a Test and three ODIs for the World XI, and four ODIs for the Asia XI ...

THE FIGURES to 23.9.10   ** espncricinfo.com**

Batting & Fielding	M	Inns	NO	Runs	HS	Avge	S/R	100	50	4s	6s	Ct	St
Tests	133	164	56	1261	67	11.67	70.28	0	1	146	29	72	0
ODIs	337	159	61	663	33*	6.76	76.82	0	0	49	11	128	0
T20Is	11	2	0	1	1	0.50	20.00	0	0	0	0	0	0
First-class	232	276	83	2192	67	11.35	–	0	1	–	–	123	0

Bowling	M	Balls	Runs	Wkts	BB	Avge	RpO	S/R	5i	10m
Tests	133	44039	18180	800	9–51	22.72	2.47	55.04	67	22
ODIs	337	18169	11885	515	7–30	23.07	3.92	35.27	10	0
T20Is	11	258	266	13	3–29	20.46	6.18	19.84	0	0
First-class	232	66933	26997	1374	9–51	19.64	2.42	48.71	119	34

MUSHFIQUR RAHIM

Full name	**Mohammad Mushfiqur Rahim**
Born	**September 1, 1988, Bogra**
Teams	**Sylhet**
Style	**Right-hand bat, wicketkeeper**
Test debut	**Bangladesh v England at Lord's 2005**
ODI debut	**Bangladesh v Zimbabwe at Harare 2006**
T20I debut	**Bangladesh v Zimbabwe at Khulna 2006-07**

THE PROFILE A wild-card inclusion for Bangladesh's maiden tour of England in 2005, the diminutive Mushfiqur Rahim was just 16 when he was selected for that daunting trip – two Tests in May, followed by six ODIs against England and Australia. He was principally chosen as understudy to long-serving wicketkeeper Khaled Mashud, but he had also exhibited signs of promise with the bat (a century in an A-team Test in Zimbabwe, and 88 against England Under-19s at Taunton). He showed more evidence of grit with the full team, with a maiden first-class half-century to soften the pain of defeat against Sussex, followed by a hundred against Northamptonshire. That earned him a call-up – as a batsman – to become the youngest player to appear in a Test at Lord's. Mushfiqur was one of only three players to reach double figures in a disappointing first innings, but a twisted ankle kept him out of the second Test. Two years later he supplanted Mashud for the 2007 World Cup, anchoring the win over India with 56 not out, and soon established himself as the first-choice keeper, with a short hiatus after a run of low scores (four runs in five ODIs, including three successive ducks). He put that behind him in 2009, and has now become one of Bangladesh's most consistent batsmen: he just missed a one-day hundred against Zimbabwe in August 2009, but made sure in Tests with 101 against India at Chittagong in January 2010. There was a near-miss against England at home (95, again at Chittagong), although he was less prolific in England later the same year.

THE FACTS Mushfiqur Rahim's hundred for Bangladesh v Northants in 2005 made him the youngest century-maker in English first-class cricket: he was 16 years 261 days old, 211 days younger than Sachin Tendulkar in 1990; the youngest Englishman was 17-year-old Stephen Peters for Essex in 1996 ... Mushfiqur was stumped for 98 in an ODI against Zimbabwe at Bulawayo in August 2009 ... He had played two Tests before appearing in a first-class match at home ...

THE FIGURES to 23.9.10   **ESM**cricinfo.com

Batting & Fielding	M	Inns	NO	Runs	HS	Avge	S/R	100	50	4s	6s	Ct	St
Tests	23	45	3	1140	101	27.14	43.86	1	6	156	8	32	7
ODIs	76	68	11	1319	98	23.14	64.94	0	6	100	14	50	17
T20Is	15	13	4	85	24	9.44	86.73	0	0	5	1	7	7
First-class	47	85	10	2190	115*	29.20	–	3	13	–	–	78	11

Bowling	M	Balls	Runs	Wkts	BB	Avge	RpO	S/R	5i	10m
Tests	23	0	–	–	–	–	–	–	–	–
ODIs	76	0	–	–	–	–	–	–	–	–
T20Is	15	0	–	–	–	–	–	–	–	–
First-class	47	0	–	–	–	–	–	–	–	–

NAEEM ISLAM

Full name	**Mohammed Naeem Islam**
Born	**December 31, 1986, Gaibandha**
Teams	**Rajshahi**
Style	**Right-hand bat, offspinner**
Test debut	**Bangladesh v New Zealand at Chittagong 2008-09**
ODI debut	**Bangladesh v New Zealand at Mirpur 2008-09**
T20I debut	**Bangladesh v South Africa at Johannesburg 2008-09**

THE PROFILE A batsman and a handy off-spinner, Naeem Islam was part of the Bangladesh Under-19 side which pulled off a famous triumph against Australia in the 2004 Youth World Cup: eight of his team-mates that day have also made it into the full national team. In Naeem's case the senior call came late in 2008. He had just led – and top-scored for – the Academy side in Sri Lanka, and played his first one-day international against the touring New Zealanders in October, taking 2 for 20 from four overs in his second match and making an adhesive 46 not out – he faced 106 balls in more than two hours as wickets tumbled around him – in the third. He won his first Test cap shortly afterwards, contributing two more solid innings (14 from 46 balls and 19 from 70) in a low-scoring match ultimately decided by a remarkable allround display from Daniel Vettori. Naeem played three adhesive Test innings against England at home early in 2010, but has largely been confined to the one-day arena, where he has sent down some tight spells, although the big haul continued to elude him. An innings of 73 not out against Zimbabwe in November 2009 kick-started a consistent run with the bat: in 13 ODI innings to mid-2010 he was dismissed in single figures only twice. And Naeem provided a rare highlight in Bangladesh's otherwise dismal World Twenty20 campaign in England in 2009 – they lost both their matches, to India and Ireland – by smacking three sixes against India, two of them from successive balls from the pacy Ishant Sharma.

THE FACTS Naeem Islam scored 161 for the Bangladesh Academy against their South African counterparts at Khulna in April 2008: in the previous match, at Jessore, he made 136 ... He took a wicket (Daniel Flynn of New Zealand) with his fifth ball in Test cricket in October 2008 ... Naeem made 110 not out in his sixth first-class match, for Rajshahi v Dhaka at Fatullah in March 2005: his highest score is 126, for Rajshahi v Barisal in December 2006 ...

THE FIGURES to 23.9.10   **ESPncricinfo.com**

Batting & Fielding	M	Inns	NO	Runs	HS	Avge	S/R	100	50	4s	6s	Ct	St
Tests	4	8	1	180	59*	25.71	36.65	0	1	23	3	1	0
ODIs	36	31	13	512	73*	28.44	64.81	0	1	39	12	13	0
T20Is	7	7	1	99	28	16.50	113.79	0	0	4	6	0	0
First-class	52	88	10	2790	126	35.76	43.97	5	18	–	–	35	1

Bowling	M	Balls	Runs	Wkts	BB	Avge	RpO	S/R	5i	10m
Tests	4	276	150	1	1–11	150.00	3.26	276.00	0	0
ODIs	36	1248	1034	27	3–32	38.29	4.97	46.22	0	0
T20Is	7	66	99	2	2–32	49.50	9.00	33.00	0	0
First-class	52	2150	1085	21	3–7	51.66	3.02	102.38	0	0

DIRK **NANNES**

AUSTRALIA

Full name	**Dirk Peter Nannes**
Born	**May 16, 1976, Mount Waverley, Melbourne, Victoria**
Teams	**Victoria, Nottinghamshire, Delhi Daredevils**
Style	**Right-hand bat, left-arm fast bowler**
Test debut	**No Tests yet**
ODI debut	**Australia v Scotland at Edinburgh 2009**
T20I debut	**Netherlands v England at Lord's 2009**

THE PROFILE For most of Dirk Nannes's adult life, cricket was an afterthought. A self-confessed "accidental cricketer", he used to play a couple of games for his Melbourne club Fitzroy at the start of the season, a handful at the end, and in between travel the world pursuing his other passion, skiing. He competed for several years in World Cup events and narrowly missed selection for the Winter Olympics in the late 1990s. But when he started to take his cricket seriously, he quickly grabbed the attention of Victoria's selectors, and made his first-class debut at 29. A genuinely quick left-armer who can swing the ball late, Nannes destroyed Western Australia with 4 for 23 in the Twenty20 final in 2007-08, then headed to England, where an impressive season included helping Middlesex win their domestic 20-over title too. After keeping Glenn McGrath out of Delhi's IPL starting line-up early in 2009 Nannes was an outsider for Australia's World Twenty20 side in England in June, and when he was eventually excluded his Dutch parentage allowed him to turn out for the Netherlands instead: he was a gleeful participant in their defeat of England at Lord's. A couple of months later Nannes was facing England in another Twenty20 game – this time for Australia. He made his ODI debut against Scotland, taking his first wicket the ball after being swiped for six. He retired from first-class cricket in 2010 to concentrate on earning a good living from Twenty20 cricket, in which he has a lucrative IPL contract. Anything but a typical fast bowler, Nannes studied the saxophone at university and runs a successful ski-travel company.

THE FACTS Nannes played for the Netherlands in the World Twenty20 in England in June 2009, dismissing Shahid Afridi at Lord's, and two months later appeared for Australia against England ... Nannes took 7 for 50 (11 for 95 in the match) for Victoria v Queensland at Brisbane in October 2008 ... The previous month he took 6 for 32 for Middlesex v Worcestershire at Kidderminster ...

THE FIGURES to 23.9.10   **ESPncricinfo.com**

Batting & Fielding	M	Inns	NO	Runs	HS	Avge	S/R	100	50	4s	6s	Ct	St
Tests	0	0	–	–	–	–	–	–	–	–	–	–	–
ODIs	1	1	0	1	1	1.00	50.00	0	0	0	0	0	0
T20Is	16	5	3	22	12*	11.00	122.22	0	0	1	1	1	0
First-class	23	24	8	108	31*	6.75	33.12	0	0	14	2	7	0

Bowling	M	Balls	Runs	Wkts	BB	Avge	RpO	S/R	5i	10m
Tests	0	0	–	–	–	–	–	–	–	–
ODIs	1	42	20	1	1–20	20.00	2.85	42.00	0	0
T20Is	16	348	431	27	4–18	15.96	7.43	12.88	0	0
First-class	23	4139	2327	93	7–50	25.02	3.37	44.50	2	1

BRENDAN **NASH**

Full name	**Brendan Paul Nash**
Born	**December 14, 1977, Attadale, Western Australia**
Teams	**Jamaica**
Style	**Left-hand bat, left-arm medium-pacer**
Test debut	**West Indies v New Zealand at Dunedin 2008-09**
ODI debut	**West Indies v Bermuda at King City 2008**
T20I debut	**No T20Is yet**

THE PROFILE A smallish but solid left-hander, Brendan Nash played in three Pura Cup finals for Queensland, scoring 96 in one of them, before losing his state contract after a patchy 2006-07 season. After that he decided to try his luck in Jamaica, where his father Paul was born (he swam for Jamaica in the 1968 Mexico Olympics, but emigrated to Australia while his wife was pregnant with Brendan). Nash had a fine first season, helping Jamaica win the Carib Beer Cup title: after being stranded on 91 against Guyana he made no mistake in the next game, with 102 in Trinidad. Another century in the Carib Beer Challenge final gave him 422 runs in seven first-class matches, and it was no great surprise when he was called up to the West Indian squad, although there were murmurs about an Australian "mercenary" muscling his way in. Nash won his first Test cap in New Zealand in December 2008, then proved a reliable middle-order buttress in the home series against England, with a four-hour 55 in the first Test at Kingston, which West Indies won, and a maiden century (batting for 330 minutes in all) at Port-of-Spain, when a draw clinched the series victory. He added 81 in an otherwise disappointing team display at Lord's a couple of months later, and has proved consistent ever since, adding a second hundred against South Africa in St Kitts in June 2010. He is a handy containing medium-pacer, and remains a fine fielder: earlier in his career he was Australia's substitute fielder in a Test against West Indies (and dropped his future team-mate Denesh Ramdin).

THE FACTS Nash is generally considered to be the first white man to play for West Indies since Geoff Greenidge in 1972-73 ... He hit 176 for Queensland v New South Wales at Brisbane in October 2002 ... Nash averaged 27 with the bat for Queensland, 33 for Jamaica – and 37 for West Indies ... He scored 96 in Australia's Pura Cup final in 2001-02, and 117 in West Indies' Carib Beer Challenge final in April 2008 ...

THE FIGURES to 23.9.10   **ESPricricinfo.com**

Batting & Fielding	M	Inns	NO	Runs	HS	Avge	S/R	100	50	4s	6s	Ct	St
Tests	15	24	0	889	114	37.04	43.42	2	6	113	3	5	0
ODIs	9	7	3	104	39*	26.00	73.75	0	0	11	1	1	0
T20Is	0	0	–	–	–	–	–	–	–	–	–	–	–
First-class	66	113	13	3358	176	33.58	–	7	13	–	–	29	0

Bowling	M	Balls	Runs	Wkts	BB	Avge	RpO	S/R	5i	10m
Tests	15	408	196	1	1–34	196.00	2.88	408.00	0	0
ODIs	9	294	224	5	3–56	44.80	4.57	58.80	0	0
T20Is	0	0	–	–	–	–	–	–	–	–
First-class	66	936	403	10	2–7	40.30	2.58	93.60	0	0

NAZMUL HOSSAIN

Full name	**Mohammad Nazmul Hossain**
Born	**October 5, 1987, Hobigonj**
Teams	**Sylhet**
Style	**Right-hand bat, right-arm fast-medium bowler**
Test debut	**Bangladesh v India at Chittagong 2004-05**
ODI debut	**Bangladesh v South Africa at Edgbaston 2004**
T20I debut	**Bangladesh v West Indies at Basseterre 2009**

THE PROFILE Nazmul Hossain is a hard-working fast bowler with a delivery style not unlike that of Makhaya Ntini, although he is not as quick. He did well at the Youth World Cup early in 2004 – although more fuss was made about his faster team-mate, Shahadat Hossain – and was given a premature Test debut later that year when he was called up to make what was also his first-class debut against India. Only 17, he did not disappoint, claiming the wickets of Gautam Gambhir (for 139) and Harbhajan Singh. After that he has been seen as more of a one-day specialist – although his style of bowling might have been useful on the early-season pitches the Bangladeshis encountered in England in 2010. He spent 30 months out of the side, but returned in August 2008 a cannier bowler. Early in 2009 his 3 for 30 in the tri-series final at home in Mirpur gave Sri Lanka a severe case of the jitters: chasing a modest 153, they were 6 for 5 after Nazmul's initial burst, but regrouped to win by two wickets. Nazmul sticks to an off-stump line, with the natural angle taking the ball in. But the dangerous one is the delivery which straightens or just moves a shade away – batsmen don't expect that from a bowler with his kind of action. He is also a fine fielder, who pulled off a stunning catch at backward point to remove Zimbabwe's Malcolm Waller in an ODI at Chittagong in November 2009.

THE FACTS Nazmul Hossain was the second Bangladeshi (after Mashrafe Mortaza in 2001-02) to make his first-class debut in a Test match: only three others have done this since 1899 – Graham Vivian of New Zealand (1964-65), Zimbabwe's Ujesh Ranchod (1992-93) and Yasir Ali of Pakistan (2003-04) ... He was 17 years 73 days old at the time of his debut (the fifth-youngest for Bangladesh) ... Nazmul took 5 for 30 for Sylhet at Rajshahi in March 2006 ... His father, an army man, was a Bangladesh football international ...

THE FIGURES to 23.9.10   ESFi**cricinfo.com**

Batting & Fielding	M	Inns	NO	Runs	HS	Avge	S/R	100	50	4s	6s	Ct	St
Tests	1	2	1	8	8*	8.00	88.88	0	0	2	0	0	0
ODIs	33	19	11	35	6*	4.37	27.34	0	0	0	0	5	0
T20Is	2	2	2	3	3*	–	20.00	0	0	0	0	0	0
First-class	31	50	12	384	49	10.10	35.65	0	0	–	–	16	0

Bowling	M	Balls	Runs	Wkts	BB	Avge	RpO	S/R	5i	10m
Tests	1	155	114	2	2–114	57.00	4.41	77.50	0	0
ODIs	33	1427	1222	38	4–40	32.15	5.13	37.55	0	0
T20Is	2	24	33	1	1–15	33.00	8.25	24.00	0	0
First-class	31	4141	1992	65	5–30	30.64	2.88	63.70	2	0

ASHISH **NEHRA**

Full name	**Ashish Nehra**
Born	**April 29, 1979, Delhi**
Teams	**Delhi, Delhi Daredevils**
Style	**Right-hand bat, left-arm fast-medium bowler**
Test debut	**India v Sri Lanka at Colombo 1998-99**
ODI debut	**India v Zimbabwe at Harare 2001**
T20I debut	**India v Sri Lanka at Nagpur 2009-10**

THE PROFILE For a short time Ashish Nehra looked the best of India's crop of left-arm pacemen – but injuries, notably several ankle operations after a breakdown late in 2005, seemed to have scuppered his international career. But Nehra sparkled in the IPL, especially in the second season in South Africa early in 2009, when his 19 wickets was exceeded only by RP Singh (another left-armer) and Anil Kumble. That brought Nehra back into national contention, and when Zaheer Khan was rested for the one-day series in the West Indies in June Nehra was recalled after almost four years out. He took three wickets in his comeback at Kingston then three more in the third match, and with Zaheer's shoulder injury still giving cause for concern Nehra looked set for more opportunities. He knew the reason for his renaissance: "The IPL is as good as international cricket. Every team has about eight or nine international cricketers so the standard is really high." Nehra has most of the virtues of a classical left-arm fast bowler: pace (admittedly slightly reduced since his various injuries), accuracy, an ability to move the ball off the pitch, and a devastating late inswinger that can harass the best. On his first full tour – to Zimbabwe in 2000-01 – he took five wickets at Bulawayo to help India win a Test outside the subcontinent for the first time in 15 years. But inconsistency and injuries held him back, although there were occasional signs of a rare talent, notably when he demolished England in the 2003 World Cup, taking six wickets with what *Wisden* called "searing pace and swing".

THE FACTS Nehra took 6 for 23 against England at Durban during the 2003 World Cup: he also took 6 for 59 v Sri Lanka in Colombo in August 2005 ... He took 7 for 14 for North Zone v East Zone at Guwahati in the 2000-01 Duleep Trophy ... Nehra took 19 wickets (18.21) in the second season of the IPL in 2008-09: only RP Singh (23) and Anil Kumble (21) managed more ...

THE FIGURES to 23.9.10   ESFn cricinfo.com

Batting & Fielding	M	Inns	NO	Runs	HS	Avge	S/R	100	50	4s	6s	Ct	St
Tests	17	25	11	77	19	5.50	30.07	0	0	8	3	5	0
ODIs	107	40	20	132	24	6.60	61.39	0	0	11	3	16	0
T20Is	7	3	0	22	22	7.33	137.50	0	0	1	2	2	0
First-class	78	92	30	515	43	8.30	–	0	0	–	–	24	0

Bowling	M	Balls	Runs	Wkts	BB	Avge	RpO	S/R	5i	10m
Tests	17	3447	1866	44	4–72	42.40	3.24	78.34	0	0
ODIs	107	5153	4399	144	6–23	30.54	5.12	35.78	2	0
T20Is	7	162	252	11	3–19	22.90	9.33	14.72	0	0
First-class	78	14829	7677	257	7–14	29.87	3.10	57.70	12	4

MARCUS **NORTH**

AUSTRALIA

Full name	**Marcus James North**
Born	**July 28, 1979, Pakenham, Melbourne, Victoria**
Teams	**Western Australia**
Style	**Left-hand bat, offspinner**
Test debut	**Australia v South Africa at Johannesburg 2009**
ODI debut	**Australia v Pakistan at Abu Dhabi 2008-09**
T20I debut	**Australia v Pakistan at Dubai 2009**

THE PROFILE Marcus North seemed destined to be remembered as a nomad who played for no fewer than five English first-class counties – but finally, after years on the fringe, he was selected at 29 for Australia's tour of South Africa early in 2009. A tall, well-organised left-hander with a peachy cover-drive, North is also a handy containing offspinner, although he surprised even himself by making the Lord's honours board with six wickets against Pakistan in 2010. He made 117 on debut at the Wanderers while the other batsmen struggled, started the Ashes tour which followed with another neat hundred at Cardiff, and added another in the fourth Test after making 96 in the third: when he failed, so did Australia – he managed only 24 runs in the two Tests they lost as the Ashes slipped away. He was less assured at home in 2009-10, although a century and a 90 in New Zealand in March kept him in the side, but questions began to be asked after four low scores against Pakistan in England in 2010. North has long been a key player for Western Australia, latterly as captain (although his first season in charge, 2007-08, was disrupted by knee trouble). He first gained widespread notice in 2003-04, when he made 1074 first-class runs in Australia, although he had made a double-century for WA two years before that (he found it difficult at first to make the transition from star youth player to serious first-class performer). He added another in October 2006, during an Australian-record third-wicket stand of 459 with Chris Rogers against Victoria at the WACA.

THE FACTS North made 239 not out for WA v Victoria at Perth in October 2006, sharing an Australian-record third-wicket stand of 459 with Chris Rogers ... North was the 18th man to score a century on Test debut for Australia ... He took 6 for 55 in a Test against Pakistan at Lord's in 2010 ... North was only the second player, after fast bowler Andrew Harris, to appear in first-class cricket for five English counties (Durham, Lancashire, Derbyshire, Gloucestershire and Hampshire) ...

THE FIGURES *to 23.9.10*   **ESPⁿ cricinfo.com**

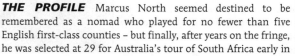

Batting & Fielding	M	Inns	NO	Runs	HS	Avge	S/R	100	50	4s	6s	Ct	St
Tests	17	28	2	981	125*	37.73	48.97	4	4	118	4	14	0
ODIs	2	2	0	6	5	3.00	31.57	0	0	0	0	1	0
T20Is	1	1	0	20	20	20.00	95.23	0	0	1	0	0	0
First-class	153	267	25	10400	239*	42.97	–	28	55	–	–	119	0

Bowling	M	Balls	Runs	Wkts	BB	Avge	RpO	S/R	5i	10m
Tests	17	934	434	12	6–55	36.16	2.78	77.83	1	0
ODIs	2	18	16	0	–	–	5.33	–	0	0
T20Is	1	0	–	–	–	–	–	–	–	–
First-class	153	9762	4953	121	6–55	40.93	3.04	80.67	2	0

PRAGYAN **OJHA**

Full name	**Pragyan Prayash Ojha**
Born	**September 5, 1986, Bhubaneshwar**
Teams	**Hyderabad, Deccan Chargers**
Style	**Left-hand bat, left-arm orthodox spinner**
Test debut	**India v Sri Lanka at Kanpur 2009-10**
ODI debut	**India v Bangladesh at Karachi 2008**
T20I debut	**India v Bangladesh at Nottingham 2009**

THE PROFILE A left-arm spinner of teasing flight and pleasing loop, Pragyan Ojha made a stunning start in first-class cricket: for Hyderabad in the Ranji Trophy semi-final in March 2005 he took the first five wickets to fall in eventual champions Railways' first innings, starting with the Test allrounder Sanjay Bangar. Ojha won an A-team place in 2007, and spun them to an innings victory over South Africa A at Delhi that September. He showed his control with some decent performances for Deccan Chargers in the inaugural Indian Premier League season in 2008: he finished with 11 wickets, added 18 in South Africa in 2009, and took 21 – four more than anyone else – in 2010. He made an immediate impact in his first ODI, in the Asia Cup in Pakistan in June 2008, with three outfield catches and an absolute ripper which foxed Bangladesh's Raqibul Hasan. Still seen by the national selectors as a one-day specialist, Ojha started the 2009 World Twenty20 in England well, taking a wicket with his first ball and finishing with 4 for 21 against Bangladesh, but was omitted later in the tournament, then missed out on the one-day Compaq Cup in Sri Lanka in September as the selectors tried out legspinner Amit Mishra as Harbhajan Singh's partner. But Ojha did win his first Test cap late in 2009, taking a catch off his first ball in the field, and although his strike rate was unspectacular he did take 21 wickets in his first six matches, with seven – including danger men Sangakkara and Jayawardene in both innings – as India squared the series in Sri Lanka in August 2010.

THE FACTS Ojha took a wicket (Bangladesh's Shakib Al Hasan) with his first ball in Twenty20 internationals, at Trent Bridge in June 2009 ... On his first-class debut, v Railways at Delhi in March 2005, Ojha took the first five wickets to fall, finishing with 5 for 55 ... Ojha was the leading wicket-taker of the third IPL, with 21 ... He took 7 for 114 for Hyderabad v Rajasthan in December 2006: the previous week he took 6 for 84 v Maharashtra ...

THE FIGURES to 23.9.10

ESPNcricinfo.com

Batting & Fielding	M	Inns	NO	Runs	HS	Avge	S/R	100	50	4s	6s	Ct	St
Tests	6	7	5	42	18*	21.00	21.76	0	0	3	0	3	0
ODIs	16	9	8	41	16*	41.00	43.61	0	0	3	0	7	0
T20Is	6	1	1	10	10*	–	166.66	0	0	0	1	1	0
First-class	42	56	20	376	35	10.44	31.70	0	0	41	0	17	0

Bowling	M	Balls	Runs	Wkts	BB	Avge	RpO	S/R	5i	10m
Tests	6	1723	899	21	4–115	42.80	3.13	82.04	0	0
ODIs	16	835	601	20	4–38	30.05	4.31	41.75	0	0
T20Is	6	126	132	10	4–21	13.20	6.28	12.60	0	0
First-class	42	9756	4823	165	7–114	29.23	2.96	59.12	10	0

GRAHAM **ONIONS**

ENGLAND

Full name	**Graham Onions**
Born	**September 9, 1982, Gateshead**
Teams	**Durham**
Style	**Right-hand bat, right-arm fast-medium bowler**
Test debut	**England v West Indies at Lord's 2009**
ODI debut	**England v Australia at Chester-le-Street 2009**
T20I debut	**No T20Is yet**

THE PROFILE A brisk seam bowler, with a name that is a headline-writer's dream (especially when Durham's wicketkeeper Phil Mustard does the catching), Graham Onions first took the eye during 2006, taking 54 wickets. He maintained an impressive workload for Durham, and didn't just take wickets on helpful surfaces at Chester-le-Street. He was called up for the late-season ODIs against Pakistan, although he didn't actually play, but he later toured Bangladesh with England A. The following two seasons were more of a struggle – Ottis Gibson sometimes kept him out of the Durham side in 2007, and the following year he had injury problems – but Onions started 2009 in rare form and was called up for the early-season Tests against West Indies. He started in fairytale fashion, mopping up the tail with four wickets in seven balls to finish with 5 for 38 and his name on the Lord's honours board at his first attempt, bowling at a lively pace and swinging the ball away. He played in three of the Ashes Tests without quite recapturing this form, although he did enliven the second morning at Edgbaston by taking wickets with the first two balls of the day. Although he was left out for the final Test he was at The Oval as the Ashes were recaptured, then returned to Durham as they clinched the Championship for the second year running. He then picked up 11 wickets in three Tests in South Africa – although he will be better remembered for his obstinate batting, twice surviving the last over to deny South Africa Test victories. But he also picked up a stress fracture in the back, which ruled him out of the whole of 2010 and cost him an Ashes tour too.

THE FACTS Onions took 8 for 101 for Durham v Warwickshire at Edgbaston in May 2007: two years later he took 7 for 38 in the same fixture ... At Edgbaston in July 2009 Onions took wickets with the first two balls of the second day's play against Australia: this is believed to have happened only once before in Test history, when Australia's "Chuck" Fleetwood-Smith did it against England at Melbourne in 1936-37 ...

THE FIGURES to 23.9.10   **ESPNcricinfo.com**

Batting & Fielding	M	Inns	NO	Runs	HS	Avge	S/R	100	50	4s	6s	Ct	St
Tests	8	10	7	30	17*	10.00	30.92	0	0	4	0	0	0
ODIs	4	1	0	1	1	1.00	50.00	0	0	0	0	1	0
T20Is	0	0	–	–	–	–	–	–	–	–	–	–	–
First-class	71	93	32	758	41	12.42	51.88	0	0	–	–	17	0

Bowling	M	Balls	Runs	Wkts	BB	Avge	RpO	S/R	5i	10m
Tests	8	1429	869	28	5–38	31.03	3.64	51.03	1	0
ODIs	4	204	185	4	2–58	46.25	5.44	51.00	0	0
T20Is	0	0	–	–	–	–	–	–	–	–
First-class	71	11558	6923	230	8–101	30.10	3.59	50.25	9	0

JACOB **ORAM**

Full name	**Jacob David Philip Oram**
Born	**July 28, 1978, Palmerston North, Manawatu**
Teams	**Central Districts**
Style	**Left-hand bat, right-arm fast-medium bowler**
Test debut	**New Zealand v India at Wellington 2002-03**
ODI debut	**New Zealand v Zimbabwe at Wellington 2000-01**
T20I debut	**New Zealand v South Africa at Johannesburg 2005-06**

THE PROFILE It's hard to miss Jacob Oram, and not just because of his height of 6ft 6ins (198cm). He is agile in the field, especially at gully, and complements that with solid fast-medium bowling and aggressive batting. Foot problems cost him a season at a vital stage, but he came back strongly in 2002-03 to seal a regular international place. He narrowly missed a century against Pakistan in the Wellington Boxing Day Test of 2003, but made up for that by carving 119 not out against South Africa, then 90 in the second Test, which earned him an England tour in 2004. By then his bowling was starting to lose its sting, and he went down with back trouble shortly after pounding 126 against Australia at Brisbane in November 2004. After nearly 18 months out Oram showed what New Zealand's middle order had been missing, coming in at 38 for 4 at Centurion and making 133, his highest Test score. He missed the start of the 2006-07 Australian one-day series with a hamstring injury, but bucked the team up with some stirring performances when he did get there, including a 71-ball century – NZ's fastest, and his first in ODIs – against Australia at Perth. He continued to be a regular member of all New Zealand's sides, although a strange diffidence crept into his batting in England in 2008, when many thought he should have been moved up the order in an inexperienced line-up. Shortly after that Oram retired from Tests to preserve himself for limited-overs games – and his lucrative IPL contract with Chennai.

THE FACTS Oram averages 62.00 in Tests against Australia, 52.50 v South Africa – and 10.25 v India ... With the ball in ODIs he averages 16.63 v Bangladesh, but 74.72 v Australia ... Oram scored his maiden century in only his fourth first-class match, for Central Districts v Canterbury at Christchurch in 1998-99, and his 155 remains his highest score ...

THE FIGURES to 23.9.10   ESPNcricInfo.com

Batting & Fielding	M	Inns	NO	Runs	HS	Avge	S/R	100	50	4s	6s	Ct	St
Tests	33	59	10	1780	133	36.32	50.38	5	6	209	21	15	0
ODIs	141	102	13	2203	101*	24.75	84.82	1	12	162	71	42	0
T20Is	27	24	5	396	66*	20.84	138.46	0	2	29	20	10	0
First-class	85	136	18	3992	155	33.83	–	8	18	–	–	36	0

Bowling	M	Balls	Runs	Wkts	BB	Avge	RpO	S/R	5i	10m
Tests	33	4964	1983	60	4–41	33.05	2.39	82.73	0	0
ODIs	141	5999	4334	142	5–26	30.52	4.33	42.24	2	0
T20Is	27	387	564	12	3–33	47.00	8.74	32.25	0	0
First-class	85	10670	4158	155	6–45	26.82	2.33	68.83	3	0

TIM **PAINE**

AUSTRALIA

Full name	**Timothy David Paine**
Born	**December 8, 1984, Hobart, Tasmania**
Teams	**Tasmania**
Style	**Right-hand bat, wicketkeeper**
Test debut	**Australia v Pakistan at Lord's 2010**
ODI debut	**Australia v Scotland at Edinburgh 2009**
T20I debut	**Australia v England at Manchester 2009**

THE PROFILE A talented top-order batsman and wicket-keeper, Tasmania's Tim Paine was earmarked as next in line behind Brad Haddin when he joined the squad for the one-day internationals that followed the Ashes series in England in 2009. In the event Paine ended up playing throughout, as Haddin had to have surgery on the finger he broke before the Edgbaston Test. And he did not disappoint, pulling off some quicksilver stumpings to go with some forthright batting from the top of the order, the highlight a fine century at Trent Bridge which included some whips off the pads – stork-like, with the back foot in the air – which fizzed down to fine leg. When Haddin had elbow-tendon trouble in 2010, Paine deputised again, playing his first two Tests against Pakistan in England and generally performing well enough – behind the stumps and in front of them – to raise doubts about Haddin's future. There were 11 catches in those two matches, plus a neat leg-side stumping to dismiss Salman Butt for 92 at Lord's. Paine's initial call-up came soon after a strong showing for Australia A, including a six-studded 134 against Pakistan A in July 2009, which followed a season in which he finally elbowed his way past the highly rated Sean Clingeleffer as Tasmania's wicketkeeper in all formats. In the Sheffield Shield Paine made 445 runs at a touch under 30, and added 42 dismissals. He had made headlines early on in his career, extending his maiden first-class century against Western Australia at Perth to 215 in only his fifth match in October 2006.

THE FACTS Paine made 215 for Tasmania v Western Australia at Perth in October 2006 ... He scored 111 against England in an ODI at Trent Bridge in September 2009 ... Paine captained Australia at the Under-19 World Cup in Bangladesh in 2003-04, and signed his first contract with Tasmania when he was 16 ...

THE FIGURES to 23.9.10   **ESPNcricinfo.com**

Batting & Fielding	M	Inns	NO	Runs	HS	Avge	S/R	100	50	4s	6s	Ct	St
Tests	2	4	0	104	47	26.00	39.69	0	0	11	0	11	1
ODIs	23	23	1	716	111	32.54	69.44	1	5	85	5	33	4
T20Is	3	2	0	1	1	0.50	16.66	0	0	0	0	2	0
First-class	39	71	5	2024	215	30.66	43.28	1	14	213	6	110	4

Bowling	M	Balls	Runs	Wkts	BB	Avge	RpO	S/R	5i	10m
Tests	2	0	–	–	–	–	–	–	–	–
ODIs	23	0	–	–	–	–	–	–	–	–
T20Is	3	0	–	–	–	–	–	–	–	–
First-class	39	6	3	0	–	–	3.00	–	0	0

MONTY **PANESAR**

Full name	**Mudhsuden Singh Panesar**
Born	**April 25, 1982, Luton, Bedfordshire**
Teams	**Sussex**
Style	**Left-hand bat, slow left-arm orthodox spinner**
Test debut	**England v India at Nagpur 2005-06**
ODI debut	**England v Australia at Melbourne 2006-07**
T20I debut	**England v Australia at Sydney 2006-07**

THE PROFILE Monty Panesar made himself a cult hero to English crowds enchanted by his enthusiastic celebrations and endearingly erratic fielding. That, and equally amateurish batting, had threatened to hold him back, but when Ashley Giles was ruled out of the 2005-06 Indian tour Panesar received a late summons. He's a throwback to an earlier slow left-armer, Bishan Bedi, who also twirled away for Northants in a *patka*, teasing and tempting with flight and guile, although Panesar gives it more of a rip than Bedi did. Panesar's arrival was delayed while he finished university but, finally free from studies, he took 46 Championship wickets at 21.54 in 2005. He made his Test debut at Nagpur that winter, picking up Sachin Tendulkar as his first wicket. At home in 2006 he delivered the ball of the season to bowl Younis Khan and set up victory at Leeds. Next season he claimed 31 wickets in seven home Tests, and remained the crowd's favourite as Montymania showed no sign of stopping. But, lacking variety, he struggled in Sri Lanka at the end of 2007, and laboured a little in England too, while his antics and frequent appealing rubbed some up the wrong way. By the start of 2009 he had lost his place as England's No. 1 spinner to Graeme Swann (ironically, since Panesar's arrival had hastened Swann's departure from Northamptonshire), and his only contribution to the Ashes series was an unlikely match-saving display with the bat in the first Test. Panesar became a back number after that and lost his England contract, but a move to Sussex seemed to pay off, as he took 52 wickets at 25 for his new county in 2010 and persuaded the selectors to give him another Ashes tour.

THE FACTS Panesar took 7 for 181 for Northamptonshire v Essex at Chelmsford in July 2005 ... He was the first Sikh to play Test cricket for anyone other than India: when Panesar opposed Harbhajan Singh during his debut at Nagpur in 2005-06 it was the first instance of Sikh bowling to Sikh in a Test ... He averages 25.00 with the ball in Tests against West Indies – but 53.57 v India ...

THE FIGURES *to 23.9.10*   **ESPncricinfo.com**

Batting & Fielding	M	Inns	NO	Runs	HS	Avge	S/R	100	50	4s	6s	Ct	St
Tests	39	51	17	187	26	5.50	29.44	0	0	20	1	9	0
ODIs	26	8	3	26	13	5.20	28.57	0	0	2	0	3	0
T20Is	1	1	0	1	1	1.00	50.00	0	0	0	0	0	0
First-class	131	168	53	1021	46*	8.87	33.64	0	0	–	–	29	0

Bowling	M	Balls	Runs	Wkts	BB	Avge	RpO	S/R	5i	10m
Tests	39	9042	4331	126	6–37	34.37	2.87	71.76	8	1
ODIs	26	1308	980	24	3–25	40.83	4.49	54.50	0	0
T20Is	1	24	40	2	2–40	20.00	10.00	12.00	0	0
First-class	131	28767	13562	419	7–181	32.36	2.82	68.65	21	3

THARANGA **PARANAVITANA**

Full name	**Nishad Tharanga Paranavitana**
Born	**April 15, 1982, Kegalle**
Teams	**Sinhalese Sports Club, Kandurata**
Style	**Left-hand bat, offspinner**
Test debut	**Sri Lanka v Pakistan at Karachi 2008-09**
ODI debut	**No ODIs yet**
T20I debut	**No T20Is yet**

THE PROFILE Tharanga Paranavitana is a tall, upright left-handed opener who scored consistently on the domestic scene before a stellar 2007-08 season established him as a real Test prospect. Paranavitana was the leading runscorer in the top tier of the Premier League with 893, and his 236 against Colombo CC in the last match helped Sinhalese Sports Club clinch the title. That was his third century of the summer (and the second double of his career), and he added another in the regional competition for Kandurata to finish the first-class season with 1059 runs at 81. All that – and 159 in a representative match against South Africa A – meant he had to be given a Test chance, and he eventually won his first cap at Karachi early in 2009. The disappointment of a first-ball duck was followed by a chest wound in the terrorist attack on the Sri Lankan team bus in Lahore. Thankfully, Paranavitana was back to full fitness in time for the return series in Sri Lanka, and made his mark with 72 and 49 in a narrow victory at Galle, then 73 in the final Test in Colombo. Leaner times followed against New Zealand, and he was also fined for claiming a catch which replays showed had clearly bounced in front of him. But in July 2010 Paranavitana cemented his place with a maiden Test century against India at Galle – Murali's last match – and added another in the next game. In Tests he ambles along at a strike rate of less than 50, the main reason why he is yet to feature in Sri Lanka's limited-overs teams.

THE FACTS Paranavitana scored 236 (and 80 not out) for Sinhalese Sports Club v Colombo CC in March 2008 ... He made 232 not out for Sinhalese v Tamil Union in February 2007 ... Paranavitana started his Test career (against Pakistan at Karachi in February 2009) with a first-ball duck – just like his opening partner that day, Malinda Warnapura (against Bangladesh in June 2007) ...

THE FIGURES to 23.9.10   **ᴇꜱᴘⁿcricinfo.com**

Batting & Fielding	M	Inns	NO	Runs	HS	Avge	S/R	100	50	4s	6s	Ct	St
Tests	13	24	1	822	111	35.73	49.75	2	4	103	1	6	0
ODIs	0	0	–	–	–	–	–	–	–	–	–	–	–
T20Is	0	0	–	–	–	–	–	–	–	–	–	–	–
First-class	103	170	16	6345	236	41.20	51.78	17	26	–	–	103	0

Bowling	M	Balls	Runs	Wkts	BB	Avge	RpO	S/R	5i	10m
Tests	13	90	76	1	1–26	76.00	5.06	90.00	0	0
ODIs	0	0	–	–	–	–	–	–	–	–
T20Is	0	0	–	–	–	–	–	–	–	–
First-class	103	1388	704	20	4–39	35.20	3.04	69.40	0	0

WAYNE **PARNELL**

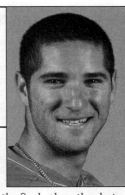

Full name	**Wayne Dillon Parnell**
Born	**July 30, 1989, Port Elizabeth, Cape Province**
Teams	**Warriors**
Style	**Left-hand bat, left-arm fast-medium bowler**
Test debut	**South Africa v England at Johannesburg 2009-10**
ODI debut	**South Africa v Australia at Perth 2008-09**
T20I debut	**South Africa v Australia at Brisbane 2008-09**

THE PROFILE Tall, slim, and waspishly fast, left-armer Wayne Parnell can also bat well, and exhibited strong leadership qualities during a glittering junior career. In the Under-19 World Cup in Malaysia in 2008 he led by example, taking 18 wickets and scoring useful middle-order runs to steer South Africa into the final, where they lost a rain-affected game to India. The national selectors were already on alert, and after Parnell tested out the conditions Down Under during an Emerging Players tournament he was drafted for the one-day series in Australia early in 2009. He played only one ODI there, proving a little expensive in a victory over Australia at the WACA, but began to make his presence felt in the return series back home, taking 4 for 25 as the Aussies were rolled for 131 at Centurion. He was rewarded by becoming the youngest South African to be awarded a national contract. Then, after warming up with some useful spells for Kent, Parnell was one of the stars of the World Twenty20 in England in 2009, derailing England (3 for 16) and West Indies (4 for 13) inside 48 hours. He bowled with pace and accuracy during the powerplays and the final overs, at an economy rate of less than six an over. He was outstanding in the semi-final against eventual champions Pakistan: after conceding 14 runs in his first over, he bounced back strongly to give away only 12 off his next three. He was a big-money ($610,000) signing for Delhi in the IPL for 2010, but injured his groin in practice and never appeared; the injury kept him out of the World Twenty20 and the following West Indian tour too.

THE FACTS In the quarter-final of the 2008 Under-19 World Cup in Kuala Lumpur Parnell top-scored with 57 from No. 7, and then took 6 for 8 as Bangladesh were bowled out for 41 ... He scored 90 for Kent v Glamorgan at Canterbury in May 2009, putting on 151 for the seventh wicket with James Tredwell ... Parnell's best first-class bowling figures of 4 for 7 came in his second match, for Eastern Province v KwaZulu/Natal in November 2006 ...

THE FIGURES to 23.9.10   **ESPn cricinfo.com**

Batting & Fielding	M	Inns	NO	Runs	HS	Avge	S/R	100	50	4s	6s	Ct	St
Tests	3	2	0	34	22	17.00	35.41	0	0	6	0	1	0
ODIs	11	4	1	78	49	26.00	68.42	0	0	5	1	1	0
T20Is	8	0	–	–	–	–	–	–	–	–	–	0	0
First-class	23	28	3	542	90	21.68	51.86	0	3	71	4	6	0

Bowling	M	Balls	Runs	Wkts	BB	Avge	RpO	S/R	5i	10m
Tests	3	306	227	5	2–17	45.40	4.45	61.20	0	0
ODIs	11	591	626	25	5–48	25.04	6.35	23.64	2	0
T20Is	8	173	192	11	4–13	17.45	6.65	15.72	0	0
First-class	23	3605	1992	56	4–7	35.57	3.31	64.37	0	0

NELON **PASCAL**

WEST INDIES

Full name	**Nelon Troy Pascal**
Born	**April 25, 1987, St David's, Grenada**
Teams	**Windward Islands**
Style	**Right-hand bat, right-arm fast bowler**
Test debut	**West Indies v South Africa at Port-of-Spain 2010**
ODI debut	**West Indies v Bangladesh at Roseau 2009**
T20I debut	**No T20Is yet**

THE PROFILE Nelon Pascal from Grenada – an island which had produced only three previous Test cricketers – found a place in the notebooks of the regional selectors early on, after jolting the Barbados top order in his first match for the Windward Islands in St Vincent in January 2008. Pascal grabbed the first four wickets as Barbados slipped to 74 for 4, bowling the future Test opener Dale Richards and trapping another Test batsman, Dwayne Smith, in front of his stumps. Pascal sharpened his skills with a summer of league cricket in Durham, and returned in 2008-09 to take 25 wickets at an impressive pace during the regional competition, including his maiden five-for against Trinidad and Tobago, when his wickets included Adrian Barath and Daren Ganga. Pascal toured England early in 2009, and also featured in the depleted squad for the home series against Bangladesh. He didn't play in the Tests then, although he did make his one-day debut in Dominica without disturbing the wickets column. Pascal didn't set the world alight in 2009-10, but injuries to other fast bowlers – notably long-term setbacks for Fidel Edwards and Jerome Taylor – meant there were vacancies in the attack, and in June 2010 Pascal made his Test debut against South Africa in Trinidad, alongside his Windward Islands team-mate Shane Shillingford. Again, wickets proved elusive, although he nudged the speed-gun over 90mph on a few occasions, suggesting that he might prove a handful when a little more experienced: the prospect of Pascal sharing the new ball with Kemar Roach might not be an appetising one for batsmen in years to come.

THE FACTS Pascal took 5 for 57 for the Windward Islands against Trinidad & Tobago at Kingstown in March 2009 ... He had taken eight wickets in the match against Guyana earlier in the season ... Pascal was the fourth Test cricketer from Grenada, following Junior Murray, Rawl Lewis and Devon Smith ...

THE FIGURES to 23.9.10   **ESPn**cricinfo.com

Batting & Fielding	M	Inns	NO	Runs	HS	Avge	S/R	100	50	4s	6s	Ct	St
Tests	1	2	0	12	10	6.00	44.44	0	0	2	0	1	0
ODIs	1	1	0	0	0	0.00	0.00	0	0	0	0	0	0
T20Is	0	0	–	–	–	–	–	–	–	–	–	–	–
First-class	26	40	13	116	19	4.29	–	0	0	–	–	13	0

Bowling	M	Balls	Runs	Wkts	BB	Avge	RpO	S/R	5i	10m
Tests	1	102	59	0	–	–	3.47	–	0	0
ODIs	1	24	29	0	–	–	7.25	–	0	0
T20Is	0	0	–	–	–	–	–	–	–	–
First-class	26	3495	2264	68	5–57	33.29	3.88	51.39	1	0

JEETAN **PATEL**

Full name	**Jeetan Shashi Patel**
Born	**May 7, 1980, Wellington**
Teams	**Wellington**
Style	**Right-hand bat, offspinner**
Test debut	**New Zealand v South Africa at Cape Town 2005-06**
ODI debut	**New Zealand v Zimbabwe at Harare 2005-06**
T20I debut	**New Zealand v South Africa at Johannesburg 2005-06**

THE PROFILE The son of Indian parents, but born and brought up in Wellington's eastern suburbs, offspinner Jeetan Patel was fast-tracked into New Zealand's one-day side after being identified as the sort of slow bowler who could be effective at the death. Patel first played for Wellington in 1999-2000, bowling 59 overs and taking 5 for 145 against Auckland on debut. Three middling seasons followed, and he seemed to be heading nowhere, with an average in the mid-forties. But then he took 6 for 32 against Otago in 2004-05, propelling Wellington into the final against Auckland, which they lost. Suddenly good judges were noting his ability to make the ball loop and drift, not unlike a right-handed Daniel Vettori. Patel toured Zimbabwe in August 2005, and has been a regular in the one-day squad since. At home his 2 for 23 from ten overs throttled Sri Lanka at Wellington, then three wickets at Christchurch helped subdue West Indies too. All this put him in line for a first Test cap, which came against South Africa in April 2006: he wheeled away for 42 overs and took three good wickets. Since then Patel has often been used as a foil to Vettori on spinning tracks, winkling out six West Indians at Napier in December 2008, and six Sri Lankans in Colombo the following August. After that, though, in early 2010 he featured only in the two Hamilton Tests. He usually succeeds in keeping the runs down, and his batting, initially underwhelming, has improved: he more than doubled his highest score during a county stint with Warwickshire, thwacking 120 from No. 10 against Yorkshire.

THE FACTS Patel won the Man of the Match award for 2 for 23 in ten overs against Sri Lanka at Wellington in 2005-06 after being supersubbed into the game ... He also won the match award in his first Twenty20 international, after taking 3 for 20 v South Africa at Johannesburg in October 2005 ... Patel made 120 for Warwickshire v Yorkshire at Edgbaston in May 2009, sharing a county-record ninth-wicket stand of 233 with Jonathan Trott ...

THE FIGURES to 23.9.10

ESPNcricinfo.com

Batting & Fielding	M	Inns	NO	Runs	HS	Avge	S/R	100	50	4s	6s	Ct	St
Tests	11	15	3	153	27*	12.75	43.96	0	0	16	0	6	0
ODIs	39	13	7	88	34	14.66	58.66	0	0	5	2	12	0
T20Is	11	4	1	9	5	3.00	64.28	0	0	1	0	4	0
First-class	90	110	36	1438	120	19.43	–	1	4	–	–	30	0

Bowling	M	Balls	Runs	Wkts	BB	Avge	RpO	S/R	5i	10m
Tests	11	3024	1587	37	5–110	42.89	3.14	81.72	1	0
ODIs	39	1804	1513	42	3–11	36.02	5.03	42.95	0	0
T20Is	11	199	269	16	3–20	16.81	8.11	12.43	0	0
First-class	90	17035	8237	197	6–32	41.81	2.90	86.47	5	0

MUNAF **PATEL**

Full name **Munaf Musa Patel**
Born **July 12, 1983, Ikhar, Gujarat**
Teams **Baroda, Rajasthan Royals**
Style **Right-hand bat, right-arm fast-medium bowler**
Test debut **India v England at Mohali 2005-06**
ODI debut **India v England at Goa 2005-06**
T20I debut **No T20Is yet**

THE PROFILE Few fast men generated as much hype before bowling a ball in first-class – let alone international – cricket as Munaf Patel, from the little town of Ikhar in Gujarat, did early in 2003. Kiran More spotted him: soon Patel was being hailed as the fastest bowler in India, although at first he spent more time recovering from injuries than actually playing. He's strongly built, though not overly tall, and bustles up to the crease, gathering momentum before releasing in a windmill-whirl of hands. He has a well-directed yorker, and can reverse-swing the ball. In March 2006 he finally received a call from the selectors – now chaired by his old pal More – after taking 10 for 91 in a match for the Board President's XI against the England tourists. He finished his first Test with 7 for 97, and continued to strike consistently in the West Indies later in 2006. Things got harder after that. He picked up an ankle niggle in South Africa, and was criticised when it bothered him in the final Test – but he regained full fitness in time for the World Cup. Then it was a back injury, and Patel returned to the Chennai academy – which he calls his "second home" – to remodel his action. In Australia in 2007-08 he sometimes seemed uninterested, and certainly didn't make the batsmen hop about much. He played his first Test for 16 months in New Zealand in March 2009, taking five wickets in a comfortable victory at Hamilton, although his bowling after that was unspectacular, and lacked the fiery pace that earned him those early rave reviews: Patel runs the risk of being overtaken by younger models, like Abhimanyu Mithun.

THE FACTS Patel's match figures of 7 for 97 were the best on Test debut by an Indian fast bowler, beating Mohammad Nissar's 6 for 135 v England at Lord's in India's inaugural Test 1932 (Abid Ali, more of a medium-pacer, took 7 for 116 on debut against Australia in 1967-68) ... Patel's best first-class figures are 6 for 50, for Maharashtra v Railways at Delhi in January 2006 ..

THE FIGURES to 23.9.10   **ESFT**cricinfo.com

Batting & Fielding	M	Inns	NO	Runs	HS	Avge	S/R	100	50	4s	6s	Ct	St
Tests	12	13	5	56	15*	7.00	40.87	0	0	7	1	6	0
ODIs	45	19	10	61	15	6.77	64.89	0	0	6	1	6	0
T20Is	0	0	–	–	–	–	–	–	–	–	–	–	–
First-class	48	55	17	545	78	14.34	70.32	0	1	-	-	12	0

Bowling	M	Balls	Runs	Wkts	BB	Avge	RpO	S/R	5i	10m
Tests	12	2394	1230	34	4–25	36.17	3.08	70.41	0	0
ODIs	45	1999	1614	52	4–49	31.03	4.84	38.44	0	0
T20Is	0	0	–	–	–	–	–	–	–	–
First-class	48	8557	4124	171	6–50	24.11	2.89	50.00	7	1

YUSUF **PATHAN**

Full name	**Yusuf Khan Pathan**
Born	**November 17, 1982, Baroda, Gujarat**
Teams	**Baroda, Rajasthan Royals**
Style	**Right-hand bat, offspinner**
Test debut	**No Tests yet**
ODI debut	**India v Pakistan at Dhaka 2008**
T20I debut	**India v Pakistan at Johannesburg 2007-08**

THE PROFILE A hard-hitting batsman and handy offspinner, Yusuf Pathan made his Ranji Trophy debut in 2001-02. But it wasn't for another three years – by which time his younger half-brother Irfan was already a Test player – that Yusuf established himself as a regular. Over the next three seasons he scored plenty of runs and took a fair few wickets for Baroda, and eventually his ability to score runs quickly – he had the highest strike rate in the Ranji Trophy in 2006-07 – were rewarded with a place in India's squad for the inaugural World Twenty20 championship in South Africa, alongside his brother. He didn't play in the qualifying matches, but was drafted in for the final, when he opened and smote his second ball into the stands. He followed that with an impressive showing for Rajasthan Royals in the inaugural IPL season early in 2008, finishing with 435 runs at a heady strike rate of 179, boosted by a 21-ball fifty against Deccan Chargers. In the final, he helped Shane Warne's team to the title by following up three important wickets with a 39-ball 56. All this earned Pathan a national call-up, but his early performances were unconvincing, and he eventually lost his place to Ravindra Jadeja. But he got the selectors interested again with a couple of stunning batting performances in 2010. In the Duleep Trophy final he hammered ten sixes in his 210 as West Zone broke the first-class record by scoring 541 to win. Then Pathan hammered an IPL century in 37 balls – Warne called it the best innings he'd ever seen – for Rajasthan against Mumbai Indians. That innings included 11 successive boundary hits (66664464444).

THE FACTS Pathan hit his second ball in international cricket for six – from Mohammad Asif in the final of the first World Twenty20 in South Africa in September 2007 ... Pathan clouted 210 not out – with ten sixes – as West Zone scored a record 541 for 6 to beat South Zone in the 2009-10 Duleep Trophy final at Hyderabad ... He hit 100 from 37 balls for Rajasthan Royals v Mumbai Indians in the third IPL in March 2010 ...

THE FIGURES to 23.9.10   **ESPN**cricinfo.com

Batting & Fielding	M	Inns	NO	Runs	HS	Avge	S/R	100	50	4s	6s	Ct	St
Tests	0	0	–	–	–	–	–	–	–	–	–	–	–
ODIs	37	26	9	376	59*	22.11	103.01	0	2	31	17	9	0
T20Is	18	15	4	205	37*	18.63	151.85	0	0	10	15	8	0
First-class	41	66	8	2315	210*	39.91	90.74	6	10	-	-	43	0

Bowling	M	Balls	Runs	Wkts	BB	Avge	RpO	S/R	5i	10m
Tests	0	0	–	–	–	–	–	–	–	–
ODIs	37	890	854	21	3–56	40.66	5.75	42.38	0	0
T20Is	18	239	351	10	2–23	35.10	8.81	23.90	0	0
First-class	41	7203	3301	96	6–47	34.38	2.74	75.03	7	1

ALVIRO **PETERSEN**

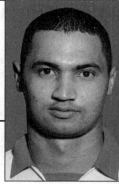

SOUTH AFRICA

Full name	**Alviro Nathan Petersen**
Born	**November 25, 1980, Port Elizabeth**
Teams	**Lions, Khulna**
Style	**Right-hand bat, occasional medium-pacer**
Test debut	**South Africa v India at Kolkata 2009-10**
ODI debut	**South Africa v Zimbabwe at East London 2006-07**
T20I debut	**South Africa v West Indies at North Sound 2009-10**

THE PROFILE Alviro Petersen grew up in the suburbs of Cape Town, honing his cricket skills at the Gelvandale club, which also produced Ashwell Prince. A century in only his second first-class match, for Northerns against a Free State attack containing five international bowlers, kick-started his career in 2001-02, and he was soon playing for South Africa A: but the next step eluded him until 2006, when he hit 80 against Zimbabwe in his second one-day international. However, with Graeme Smith and Herschelle Gibbs seemingly entrenched for good at the top of the order, opportunities were few, and by mid-2008 Petersen had played only three more one-dayers. But then it all changed: in the 2008-09 season he hit 1376 first-class runs, including six centuries, two of which came in the Lions' final game against the Titans. It was a South African record, surpassing H. D. Ackerman (1373) and Barry Richards (1285). With Gibbs out of favour, Petersen was given another chance in the one-day team early the following season, and capitalised with half-centuries in each of his three innings against England. That got him on the plane to India, and Petersen finally made his Test debut at 29 in the second match at Kolkata in February 2010. He opened, with his old pal Prince sliding down the order, and made a round 100, pulling and hooking well. It was a particularly sweet moment for Petersen's father, Isaac, who had driven journalists around Cape Town for years and rarely missed an opportunity to remind them of his son's abilities.

THE FACTS At Kolkata in February 2010 Petersen became only the third batsman to score a century on Test debut for South Africa, following Andrew Hudson (in 1991-92) and Jacques Rudolph (2002-03) ... Petersen made 152 for North West v Northerns at Potchefstroom in February 2009 ... He scored 129 and 105 not out for Lions v Titans at Johannesburg in April 2009, and finished the season with 1376 runs, a South African record ...

THE FIGURES to 23.9.10   **ESETI cricinfo.com**

Batting & Fielding	M	Inns	NO	Runs	HS	Avge	S/R	100	50	4s	6s	Ct	St
Tests	4	8	0	272	100	34.00	47.71	1	1	27	4	4	0
ODIs	14	12	1	377	80	34.27	83.40	0	4	38	2	2	0
T20Is	2	2	0	14	8	7.00	73.68	0	0	1	0	1	0
First-class	97	176	10	6352	152	38.26	–	19	27	–	–	81	0

Bowling	M	Balls	Runs	Wkts	BB	Avge	RpO	S/R	5i	10m
Tests	4	42	21	1	1–2	21.00	3.00	42.00	0	0
ODIs	14	6	7	0	–	–	7.00	–	0	0
T20Is	2	0	–	–	–	–	–	–	–	–
First-class	97	234	125	4	2–7	31.25	3.20	58.50	0	0

KEVIN **PIETERSEN**

Full name	**Kevin Peter Pietersen**
Born	**June 27, 1980, Pietermaritzburg, Natal, South Africa**
Teams	**Hampshire, Bangalore Royal Challengers**
Style	**Right-hand bat, offspinner**
Test debut	**England v Australia at Lord's 2005**
ODI debut	**England v Zimbabwe at Harare 2004-05**
T20I debut	**England v Australia at Southampton 2005**

THE PROFILE Expansive with bat and explosive with bombast, Kevin Pietersen is not one for the quiet life. Bold-minded and big-hitting, he first ruffled feathers by quitting South Africa – he was disenchanted with the race-quota system – in favour of England, his eligibility coming courtesy of an English mother. He never doubted he would play Test cricket: he has self-confidence in spades and, fortunately, sackfuls of talent too. As soon as he was eligible, he was chosen for a one-day series in Zimbabwe, where he averaged 104. Then, in South Africa, and undeterred by hostile crowds, he hammered a robust century in the second match. Test cricket was next on the to-do list. In 2005 he replaced Graham Thorpe, against Australia, at Lord's ... and coolly blasted a couple of fifties in a losing cause, then, with the Ashes at stake, hit 158 on the final day at The Oval. "KP" had arrived – and how. The runs kept coming: 158 at Adelaide and 226 against West Indies at Headingley sandwiched two tons in the 2007 World Cup, where he was the star of England's lame campaign. Late in 2008 he succeeded Michael Vaughan as captain, starting with a hundred as South Africa were beaten in the Oval Test, then inspiring a landslide in the one-day series. But his captaincy ended in tears after a fallout with the coach, then his form dipped as he battled a persistent Achilles injury. That eventually needed an operation, which kept him out of the last three Ashes Tests in 2009, and indifferent form dogged him during 2010 too. But no-one was writing off the man who Ricky Ponting once said could be "the next superstar of world cricket".

THE FACTS Pietersen reached 100 against South Africa at East London in February 2005 in 69 balls, the fastest for England in ODIs ... After 25 Tests he had made 2448 runs, more than anyone else except Don Bradman (3194) ... He averages 71.55 in ODIs v South Africa – but 14.80 v Bangladesh ... Pietersen was out for 158 three times in Tests before going on to 226 against West Indies in May 2007 ... His record includes two ODIs for the World XI ...

THE FIGURES to 23.9.10   ≡ᴦ≡cricinfo.com

Batting & Fielding	M	Inns	NO	Runs	HS	Avge	S/R	100	50	4s	6s	Ct	St
Tests	66	117	6	5306	226	47.80	62.26	16	20	627	53	39	0
ODIs	104	94	15	3332	116	42.17	86.50	7	20	315	60	32	0
T20Is	28	28	4	911	79	37.95	141.67	0	5	90	24	10	0
First-class	154	256	18	11726	254*	49.26	–	38	49	–	–	119	0

Bowling	M	Balls	Runs	Wkts	BB	Avge	RpO	S/R	5i	10m
Tests	66	843	568	4	1–0	142.00	4.04	210.75	0	0
ODIs	104	274	246	6	2–22	41.00	5.38	45.66	0	0
T20Is	28	18	36	1	1–27	36.00	12.00	18.00	0	0
First-class	154	5647	3279	61	4–31	53.75	3.48	92.57	0	0

WEST INDIES

KIERON **POLLARD**

Full name	**Kieron Adrian Pollard**
Born	**May 12, 1987, Cacariqua, Trinidad**
Teams	**Trinidad, Mumbai Indians, Somerset, South Australia**
Style	**Right-hand bat, right-arm medium-pacer**
Test debut	**No Tests yet**
ODI debut	**West Indies v South Africa at St George's 2006-07**
T20I debut	**West Indies v Australia at Bridgetown 2008**

THE PROFILE Kieron Pollard shot to prominence in 2006-07 when still only 19, with his muscular batting doing much to take Trinidad & Tobago to the final of the inaugural Stanford 20/20 competition: in the semi-final, against Nevis, he clobbered 83 in only 38 balls, and then grabbed a couple of wickets with his medium-pacers. That won him a first-class start against Barbados, and it was a memorable one: he got off the mark with a six, and cleared the boundary six more times on his way to 117. Another hundred, and six more sixes, followed in his third match, and in between he hit 87 off 58 balls – seven sixes this time – in a one-dayer against Guyana. That was followed by his inclusion in West Indies' World Cup squad. The cometary rise inevitably tailed off a bit after that: he finished his first Carib Beer season with 420 runs at 42, and played only once in the World Cup itself, as a rather surprise selection in the Super Eight match against South Africa (a must-win encounter which West Indies lost). Pollard spent some time on the sidelines after that, but his big-hitting potential earned him megabucks contracts with the Mumbai Indians (he was signed for a whopping $750,000) and South Australia, for whom he thumped 52 off 22 balls against Victoria at Adelaide early in 2010. But international success proved elusive: after 50 limited-overs matches for West Indies his only half-century came against Australia at Brisbane in February 2010, and he still needs to make the transition from promising – the step that other big hitters, like Andrew Symonds, have taken a long time to negotiate.

THE FACTS Pollard hit 126 on his first-class debut, for Trinidad & Tobago against Barbados at Crab Hill in January 2007: his innings included 11 fours and seven sixes, one of which got him off the mark ... In his second match (against Guyana) he hit 69 in 31 balls, with one four and six sixes, and in his third (against the Leeward Islands) he made 117 from 87 balls with 11 fours and six more sixes ... Pollard was the only player from any country to make his international debut at the 2007 World Cup ...

THE FIGURES to 23.9.10   **ESPncricinfo.com**

Batting & Fielding	M	Inns	NO	Runs	HS	Avge	S/R	100	50	4s	6s	Ct	St
Tests	0	0	–	–	–	–	–	–	–	–	–	–	–
ODIs	30	27	0	538	62	19.92	94.22	0	1	32	22	10	0
T20Is	20	17	2	190	38	12.66	124.18	0	0	17	8	11	0
First-class	20	33	1	1199	174	37.46	–	3	5	–	–	32	0

Bowling	M	Balls	Runs	Wkts	BB	Avge	RpO	S/R	5i	10m
Tests	0	0	–	–	–	–	–	–	–	–
ODIs	30	936	833	30	3–27	27.76	5.33	31.20	0	0
T20Is	20	258	360	11	2–22	32.72	8.37	23.45	0	0
First-class	20	571	313	6	2–29	52.16	3.28	95.16	0	0

RICKY **PONTING**

Full name	**Ricky Thomas Ponting**
Born	**December 19, 1974, Launceston, Tasmania**
Teams	**Tasmania**
Style	**Right-hand bat, right-arm medium-pace bowler**
Test debut	**Australia v Sri Lanka at Perth 1995-96**
ODI debut	**Australia v South Africa at Wellington 1994-95**
T20I debut	**Australia v New Zealand at Auckland 2004-05**

THE PROFILE Ricky Ponting began with Tasmania at 17 and Australia at 20, and was unluckily given out for 96 on his Test debut. He remains the archetypal modern cricketer, playing all the shots with a full flourish – and his dead-eye fielding is another plus. A gambler and a buccaneer, Ponting has had setbacks, against probing seam and high-class finger-spin, which he plays with hard hands when out of form. In the '90s there were off-field indiscretions, but his growing maturity was acknowledged when he succeeded Steve Waugh as one-day captain in 2002. It was a seamless transition: Ponting led the 2003 World Cup campaign from the front, clouting a coruscating century in the final, and took over in Tests too when Waugh finally stepped down early in 2004. But things changed the following year. A humiliating one-day defeat by Bangladesh caused the first ripples of dissent against his leadership style, and more followed as the Ashes series progressed. The loss of the urn hurt, and the pain lingered. Ponting bounced back by winning 11 of 12 Tests in 2005-06, which was just a warm-up for the Ashes rematch. He led that off with 196 at Brisbane – and was furious to miss his double-century – and remained tight-lipped until the 5-0 whitewash was sealed. His batting never wavered and, after retaining the World Cup in 2007, he sailed past 25,000 international runs during 2010. But another Ashes defeat the previous year (Billy Murdoch, in the 1890s, was the last Australian captain to lose two series in England) reopened those old wounds far enough to have Ponting dreaming of a possible return to England in 2013.

THE FACTS The only Australian with a higher Test batting average is Don Bradman (99.94) ... Ponting uniquely scored two hundreds in his 100th Test, v South Africa at Sydney in January 2006 ... His 242 v India at Adelaide in 2003-04 is the highest in a losing cause in a Test (in the next game he made 257, and they won) ... When he was 8, Ponting's grandmother gave him a T-shirt that read "Under this shirt is a Test player" ... His record includes one ODI for the World XI ...

THE FIGURES to 23.9.10   **ESPncricinfo.com**

Batting & Fielding	M	Inns	NO	Runs	HS	Avge	S/R	100	50	4s	6s	Ct	St
Tests	146	247	27	12026	257	54.66	59.48	39	52	1362	70	172	0
ODIs	351	342	37	13072	164	42.85	80.64	29	79	1164	157	152	0
T20Is	17	16	2	401	98*	28.64	132.78	0	2	41	11	8	0
First-class	246	418	54	20873	257	57.34	–		73	90	–	–	261	0

Bowling	M	Balls	Runs	Wkts	BB	Avge	RpO	S/R	5i	10m
Tests	146	539	242	5	1–0	48.40	2.69	107.80	0	0
ODIs	351	150	104	3	1–12	34.66	4.16	50.00	0	0
T20Is	17	–	–	–	–	–	–	–	–	–
First-class	246	1434	768	14	2–10	54.85	3.21	102.42	0	0

ASHWELL **PRINCE**

Full name	**Ashwell Gavin Prince**
Born	**May 28, 1977, Port Elizabeth, Cape Province**
Teams	**Warriors, Lancashire**
Style	**Left-hand bat, occasional left-arm spinner**
Test debut	**South Africa v Australia at Johannesburg 2001-02**
ODI debut	**South Africa v Bangladesh at Kimberley 2002-03**
T20I debut	**South Africa v New Zealand at Johannesburg 2005-06**

SOUTH AFRICA

THE PROFILE A crouching left-hander with a high-batted stance and a Gooch-like grimace, Ashwell Prince was helped into the national team by South Africa's controversial race-quota system, although he quickly justified his selection by top-scoring with a gutsy debut 49 against Australia in 2001-02. That, and a matchwinning 48 in the third Test, seemed to have buried an early reputation as a one-day flasher. But a run of low scores saw him left out for a while, before he bounced back with Test hundreds against outclassed Zimbabwe and almost-outclassed West Indies early in 2005. However, his 119 at Sydney in January 2006 was an altogether better performance after his previous one-sided battles with Shane Warne. Prince did well in the Tests in England in 2008, with centuries at Lord's and Leeds, but by then he was a back number in one-dayers, having been left out after a largely anonymous World Cup. He made a Test-best 162 not out against Bangladesh at Centurion in November 2008, but was then sidelined by a broken thumb. J-P Duminy's stellar arrival meant there was no automatic return for Prince, and he showed what he thought of that by grafting 150 when he was asked to open instead of the injured Graeme Smith against Australia at Cape Town in March 2009. He struggled against Graeme Swann's offspin at the end of the year, but scored consistently in the West Indies in mid-2010. Long rated highly by Ali Bacher, Prince is strong through the off side, and although his throwing has been hampered by a long-term shoulder injury, he remains a fine fielder in the covers.

THE FACTS Prince became South Africa's first black captain when the injured Graeme Smith missed the series in Sri Lanka in 2006 ... Prince averages 77.75 in Tests against West Indies, but 27.57 v Sri Lanka ... In his first 18 Test innings against Australia, Prince was dismissed 11 times by Shane Warne ... Prince made 254 for Warriors v Titans at Centurion in March 2009, a week before being recalled to the Test side against Australia and hitting 150 ... His record includes three ODIs for the Africa XI ...

THE FIGURES to 23.9.10   **ESPncricinfo.com**

Batting & Fielding	M	Inns	NO	Runs	HS	Avge	S/R	100	50	4s	6s	Ct	St
Tests	57	91	14	3355	162*	43.57	43.71	11	10	362	13	36	0
ODIs	52	41	12	1018	89*	35.10	67.77	0	3	77	4	26	0
T20Is	1	1	0	5	5	5.00	83.33	0	0	0	0	0	0
First-class	189	304	41	11418	254	43.41	–		28	55	–	–	126	0

Bowling	M	Balls	Runs	Wkts	BB	Avge	RpO	S/R	5i	10m
Tests	57	96	47	1	1–2	47.00	2.93	96.00	0	0
ODIs	52	12	3	0	–	–	1.50	–	0	0
T20Is	1	0	–	–	–	–	–	–	–	–
First-class	189	276	166	4	2–11	41.50	3.60	69.00	0	0

MATT **PRIOR**

Full name	**Matthew James Prior**
Born	**February 26, 1982, Johannesburg, South Africa**
Teams	**Sussex**
Style	**Right-hand bat, wicketkeeper**
Test debut	**England v West Indies at Lord's 2007**
ODI debut	**England v Zimbabwe at Bulawayo 2004-05**
T20I debut	**England v West Indies at The Oval 2007**

THE PROFILE Matt Prior represented England at several junior levels, and completed his set by making his Test debut in May 2007, against West Indies at Lord's. He started with a cracking century, the first by a wicketkeeper on debut for England. It was full of solid drives and clumping pulls, and seemed to announce a readymade star. He finished that series with 324 runs – but there were already rumbles about his wicketkeeping technique, which didn't seem to matter while England were winning. But then India arrived, and Prior's fumbles were magnified as the visitors stole the series: he dropped Sachin Tendulkar and VVS Laxman as India made 664 at The Oval. The runs dried up, too, and suddenly Prior's talkativeness behind the stumps, and his footwork, were called into question. Eventually he was dropped, in favour of his old Sussex team-mate Tim Ambrose. Prior went back to Hove and sharpened up his technique, and was ready when Ambrose in turn faltered during 2008: Prior returned for the one-dayers against South Africa, and pouched a record-equalling six catches (one a one-handed flying stunner) at Trent Bridge. By 2009 he looked even more the part – and even more like his mentor, Alec Stewart – with several smart catches and some quick runs in the Ashes victory. More runs followed in 2010, including an important century against Pakistan at Trent Bridge: Prior seemed established as England's Test keeper, although others had moved ahead of him in the one-day stakes. Prior was born in South Africa, moved to England at 11 – he says he lost his accent within a week – and first played for Sussex in 2001.

THE FACTS Prior was the 17th man to score a century on Test debut for England: he was the fifth to score a century on Test debut at Lord's, after Australia's Harry Graham, John Hampshire and Andrew Strauss of England, and India's Sourav Ganguly ... Prior equalled the ODI wicketkeeping record with six catches against South Africa at Nottingham in August 2008 ... He made 201 not out for Sussex v Loughborough UCCE at Hove in May 2004 ...

THE FIGURES to 23.9.10

ESPNcricinfo.com

Batting & Fielding	M	Inns	NO	Runs	HS	Avge	S/R	100	50	4s	6s	Ct	St
Tests	35	55	10	1896	131*	42.13	62.49	3	15	221	8	94	4
ODIs	55	50	8	1066	87	25.38	74.80	0	2	116	5	60	4
T20Is	10	8	2	127	32	21.16	127.00	0	0	11	5	6	3
First-class	173	272	29	9651	201*	39.71	66.77	22	55	–	–	416	26

Bowling	M	Balls	Runs	Wkts	BB	Avge	RpO	S/R	5i	10m
Tests	35	0	–	–	–	–	–	–	–	–
ODIs	55	0	–	–	–	–	–	–	–	–
T20Is	10	0	–	–	–	–	–	–	–	–
First-class	173	0	–	–	–	–	–	–	–	–

SURESH **RAINA**

Full name **Suresh Kumar Raina**
Born **November 27, 1986, Ghaziabad, Uttar Pradesh**
Teams **Uttar Pradesh, Chennai Super Kings**
Style **Left-hand bat, occasional offspinner**
Test debut **India v Sri Lanka at Colombo 2010**
ODI debut **India v Sri Lanka at Dambulla 2005**
T20I debut **India v South Africa at Johannesburg 2006-07**

INDIA

THE PROFILE In April 2005 Suresh Raina strolled in to bat in the domestic one-day final, spanked nine fours and a six in 48 from 33 balls as Uttar Pradesh tied with Tamil Nadu and shared the title, then left to catch the flight home for his school exams. The following season his 620 runs in six matches helped UP win the Ranji Trophy for the first time. His electric fielding added zing to India's one-day side, and it came as no surprise when, even before he'd managed a one-day fifty, he was fast-tracked into the Test squad against England in March 2006. However, despite three fifties in five one-day knocks against England, the early promise turned out to be a false dawn – he couldn't manage another in 16 more attempts before being dropped early in 2007. A powerful left-hander, he was back a year later and hit two centuries in the Asia Cup in June 2008, against Hong Kong and Bangladesh, then made 53 and 76 in Sri Lanka as India fought back to win the one-day series there. In New Zealand at the start of 2009 he slammed 61 not out from 43 balls in a Twenty20 international then 66 from 39 in a one-dayer, but was underwhelming in the World Twenty20 in England in June. Test cricket seemed to have passed him by, but after a record 98 one-day internationals – and becoming the first non-Test player to captain India in an ODI, in a tri-series in Zimbabwe in June 2010 – he finally made his debut in Sri Lanka the following month, and made up for lost time with a fine 120, and added 62 and 41 not out in the next match.

THE FACTS Raina played a record 98 ODIs before making his Test debut in July 2010 – then promptly became the 12th Indian to score a century in his first Test ... He made 203 for Uttar Pradesh against Orissa at Cuttack in November 2007 ... Raina made 520 runs in the third IPL in 2010, a number exceeded only by Sachin Tendulkar and Jacques Kallis ...

THE FIGURES to 23.9.10   **ESPNcricinfo.com**

Batting & Fielding	M	Inns	NO	Runs	HS	Avge	S/R	100	50	4s	6s	Ct	St
Tests	2	3	1	223	120	111.50	58.07	1	1	26	3	4	0
ODIs	103	86	17	2444	116*	35.42	89.22	3	15	206	55	45	0
T20Is	18	17	3	468	101	33.42	138.46	1	3	42	18	5	0
First-class	53	89	4	3907	203	45.96	59.90	7	26	–	–	58	0

Bowling	M	Balls	Runs	Wkts	BB	Avge	RpO	S/R	5i	10m
Tests	2	30	21	0	–	–	4.20	–	0	0
ODIs	103	344	309	6	1–13	51.50	5.38	57.33	0	0
T20Is	18	24	39	1	1–6	39.00	9.75	24.00	0	0
First-class	53	960	424	12	3–31	35.33	2.65	80.00	0	0

DENESH **RAMDIN**

Full name	**Denesh Ramdin**
Born	**March 13, 1985, Couva, Trinidad**
Teams	**Trinidad & Tobago**
Style	**Right-hand bat, wicketkeeper**
Test debut	**West Indies v Sri Lanka at Colombo 2005**
ODI debut	**West Indies v India at Dambulla 2005**
T20I debut	**West Indies v New Zealand at Auckland 2005-06**

THE PROFILE Wicketkeeper-batsman Denesh Ramdin has long been viewed in the Caribbean as the solution to the void which has never really been satisfactorily filled since Jeff Dujon retired in 1991. Originally a fast bowler who kept wicket when he had finished with the ball, at 13 Ramdin decided to concentrate on keeping, honing his reflexes and working on his agility. He led both the Trinidad and West Indies Under-19 sides before being selected, still only 19 and with just 13 first-class games behind him, as the first-choice keeper for the senior tour of Sri Lanka in 2005. He impressed everyone with his work behind and in front of the stumps, and continued to do so in Australia later in 2005, especially with a plucky 71 at Hobart, where he shared a fine partnership of 182 with his fellow Trinidadian Dwayne Bravo, just after they'd heard that T&T had qualified for the football World Cup. Carlton Baugh was preferred for some of the home one-dayers early in 2006, and it was something of a surprise when Ramdin returned for the Tests against India. But he justified his selection with some neat keeping on pitches on which the ball often died before it reached him, and a gritty unbeaten 62 that took West Indies frustratingly close to victory in the deciding fourth Test in Jamaica. He started the 2007 series in England with a bright 60 at Lord's, but then struggled with the bat. His keeping was patchy, but he ended his fallow period with the bat by cashing in on a Bridgetown featherbed to make a seven-hour 166 against England early in 2009.

THE FACTS Ramdin's 166 against England at Bridgetown in 2008-09 was the second-highest score by a West Indian wicketkeeper in a Test, after Clyde Walcott's 168 not out at Lord's in 1950 ... Ramdin also made 166 not out for T&T v Barbados in January 2010 ... He played in the West Indies side that won the Under-15 World Challenge in 2000, beating Pakistan in the Lord's final; four years later he captained in the Under-19 World Cup, when WI lost the final at Dhaka – to Pakistan ...

THE FIGURES *to 23.9.10*   **ESPncricinfo.com**

Batting & Fielding	M	Inns	NO	Runs	HS	Avge	S/R	100	50	4s	6s	Ct	St
Tests	42	73	8	1482	166	22.80	47.99	1	8	202	2	119	3
ODIs	81	62	16	899	74*	19.54	77.70	0	2	74	3	109	5
T20Is	22	17	4	219	44	16.84	115.87	0	0	27	2	19	2
First-class	81	137	19	3346	166*	28.35	–	7	14	–	–	214	21

Bowling	M	Balls	Runs	Wkts	BB	Avge	RpO	S/R	5i	10m
Tests	42	0	–	–	–	–	–	–	–	–
ODIs	81	0	–	–	–	–	–	–	–	–
T20Is	22	0	–	–	–	–	–	–	–	–
First-class	81	0	–	–	–	–	–	–	–	–

RAVI **RAMPAUL**

WEST INDIES

Full name	**Ravindranath Rampaul**
Born	**October 15, 1984, Preysal, Trinidad**
Teams	**Trinidad & Tobago**
Style	**Left-hand bat, right-arm fast-medium bowler**
Test debut	**West Indies v Australia at Brisbane 2009-10**
ODI debut	**West Indies v Zimbabwe at Bulawayo 2003-04**
T20I debut	**West Indies v England at The Oval 2007**

THE PROFILE Ravi Rampaul is tall and well-built but his career has been hamstrung by injuries and ill-luck. He made his Trinidad debut in 2002, and 18 wickets in six matches the following year propelled him to the verge of full international selection. It was his aggressive approach that really caught the eye: in a one-dayer against Antigua & Barbuda he unleashed four successive bouncers at the opener, then finished him off with a yorker. Just 19, he made his ODI debut late in 2003: he was rarely collared, but hardly ran through sides either – in 14 matches in Africa and the Caribbean that season he took nine wickets, only once managing more than one, a statistic that was echoed when his Test career eventually started. Nonetheless he was retained for the 2004 England tour, and played three more ODIs before he broke down and returned home ahead of the Tests. Sidelined by shin splints, Rampaul did not play another first-class match until 2006-07, taking 7 for 51 as T&T beat Barbados in the Carib Beer final. That won him another England tour but, restricted by a groin tear, he again missed the Tests, before helping to turn the one-day series around with 4 for 41 in the pivotal second match at Edgbaston. There were still no Tests: he was named to play Bangladesh in July 2009, only for the whole squad to withdraw as a contracts dispute rumbled on. Rampaul finally made his Test debut in Australia late in 2009 – he'd been around so long it was a surprise he was still only 25 – but although he worked up a fair head of steam at times, success proved elusive at first.

THE FACTS Rampaul took 7 for 51 as Trinidad & Tobago beat Barbados in the final of the Carib Beer Challenge at Pointe-à-Pierre in February 2007 ... His highest score of 64 not out was for West Indies A v Sri Lanka A at Basseterre in December 2006 ... In the World Under-15 Challenge in 2000, Rampaul took 7 for 11 against Holland, and opened both the bowling and the batting in the final at Lord's, as West Indies beat Pakistan ... Rampaul played for Ireland in the Friends Provident Trophy in 2008 ...

THE FIGURES to 23.9.10   **ESPN**cricinfo.com

Batting & Fielding	M	Inns	NO	Runs	HS	Avge	S/R	100	50	4s	6s	Ct	St
Tests	5	9	3	114	40*	19.00	60.00	0	0	15	2	1	0
ODIs	50	19	2	165	26*	9.70	75.68	0	0	14	5	6	0
T20Is	8	3	2	11	8	11.00	61.11	0	0	0	0	0	0
First-class	42	59	9	713	64*	14.26	–	0	2	–	–	15	0

Bowling	M	Balls	Runs	Wkts	BB	Avge	RpO	S/R	5i	10m
Tests	5	732	439	4	1–21	109.75	3.59	183.00	0	0
ODIs	50	1990	1673	49	4–37	34.14	5.04	40.61	0	0
T20Is	8	180	274	9	3–17	30.44	9.13	20.00	0	0
First-class	42	6127	3652	118	7–51	30.94	3.57	51.92	6	1

SURAJ **RANDIV**

Full name	**Hewa Kaluhalamullage Suraj Randiv Kaluhalamulla**
Born	**January 30, 1985, Matara**
Teams	**Bloomfield, Kandurata**
Style	**Right-hand bat, offspinner**
Test debut	**Sri Lanka v India at Colombo 2010**
ODI debut	**Sri Lanka v India at Nagpur 2009-10**
T20I debut	**Sri Lanka v Zimbabwe at Providence 2009-10**

THE PROFILE Suraj Randiv – who changed his name from Mohamed Marshuk Mohamed Suraj in 2009, after converting to Buddhism – has the unenviable task of being Sri Lanka's next offspinner in line after Muttiah Muralitharan. A consistent domestic performer for some years, Randiv made his Test debut in July 2010 in the match immediately following Murali's retirement, and matched his predecessor's appetite for hard work by toiling through 73 overs in the first innings and taking 2 for 222 (a record number of runs conceded by a debutant). On a more sporting pitch for the third Test, at the Sara Oval in Colombo, he hinted at a good future with nine wickets, including all five to fall in the second innings as India successfully chased their target of 257. He actually started as a fast bowler, but switched to offspin at school. Randiv started with the Matara club, but Marvan Atapattu and Mahela Jayawardene spotted his potential and enticed him to the Sinhalese Sports Club in 2004 (he later moved on to Bloomfield). Randiv is a tidy bowler – and a better batsman than Murali, with a first-class century as nightwatchman to his name – but doesn't possess the variety of his illustrious predecessor: "I will stick to my offbreaks and top-spinners," he once said when questioned about his plans for perfecting a *doosra*. He took 55 first-class wickets at 15.05 in domestic cricket in 2005-06, including the first of his two nine-wicket hauls, and after a couple of quieter seasons returned to top form with 43 in 2008-09 and 67 (at 20.85) the following season.

THE FACTS Randiv took 2 for 222 in his first Test innings, the most runs ever conceded by a debutant ... He took 9 for 62 for Sinhalese SC v Colombo CC in February 2006 ... Randiv took 9 for 109 (the other wicket was a run-out) for Bloomfield v Army in October 2009: earlier in the match he had scored his maiden century after going in as nightwatchman ...

THE FIGURES *to 23.9.10*   ≡**ᴄʀɪᴄinfo.com**

Batting & Fielding	M	Inns	NO	Runs	HS	Avge	S/R	100	50	4s	6s	Ct	St
Tests	2	2	0	14	8	7.00	20.89	0	0	1	0	0	0
ODIs	18	9	1	139	56	17.37	69.50	0	1	12	0	5	0
T20Is	5	2	0	8	6	4.00	133.33	0	0	1	0	0	0
First-class	68	91	13	1331	112	17.06	48.77	1	5	–	–	50	0

Bowling	M	Balls	Runs	Wkts	BB	Avge	RpO	S/R	5i	10m
Tests	2	763	384	11	5–82	34.90	3.01	69.36	1	0
ODIs	18	842	638	19	3–23	33.57	4.54	44.31	0	0
T20Is	5	78	90	4	3–20	22.50	6.92	19.50	0	0
First-class	68	12270	6875	272	9–62	25.27	3.36	45.11	18	4

RAQIBUL HASAN

BANGLADESH

Full name	**Mohammad Raqibul Hasan**
Born	**October 8, 1987, Jamalpur**
Teams	**Barisal**
Style	**Right-hand bat, legspinner**
Test debut	**Bangladesh v South Africa at Centurion 2008-09**
ODI debut	**Bangladesh v South Africa at Chittagong 2007-08**
T20I debut	**Bangladesh v South Africa at Johannesburg 2008-09**

THE PROFILE Another of Bangladesh's young achievers, Raqibul Hasan toured with Bangladesh A before he had played a first-class match, made a hundred on his first-class debut, and hit a triple-century – the first in Bangladesh domestic cricket – before he was 20 years old. It was clearly only a matter of time until he was given a chance in the full national team, and he duly made his one-day debut in March 2008, scoring 63 in his second match and adding 89 against India and 52 against Sri Lanka shortly afterwards. "Nirala" is a complete batsman, with a fine cover-drive, and although he started as more of an accumulator than a dasher, he showed signs in 2009 of being able to up the tempo to claim a regular spot in one-day international cricket. His best innings in the shorter format have been 63 against South Africa, in only his second ODI, and a patient 89 against India at Mirpur in June 2008. He looks a natural for Tests, though – that triple-century, an innings of 313 not out in a Barisal total of 712 for 7 (another domestic record) against Sylhet, occupied 11 hours. However, he made a slow start in the five-day game, until a well-played double of 44 and 65 in Grenada helped seal a 2-0 series victory over a depleted West Indian side in July 2009. After that he fell out with the selectors after being overlooked for the World Twenty20 early in 2010, and announced his retirement – aged only 22 – just before the home series against England – but wiser counsel prevailed and he was soon back in the fold.

THE FACTS Raqibul Hasan scored 313 not out for Barisal v Sylhet at Fatullah in March 2007: he was 19 years 161 days old, the third-youngest triple-centurion in first-class history after Javed Miandad and Wasim Jaffer ... He was selected for the Bangladesh A tour of Zimbabwe in 2004-05 before he had played first-class cricket: on his debut, against Zimbabwe A at Bulawayo, he scored 100 ...

THE FIGURES to 23.9.10   **ESPncricinfo**.com

Batting & Fielding	M	Inns	NO	Runs	HS	Avge	S/R	100	50	4s	6s	Ct	St
Tests	7	14	0	268	65	19.14	42.27	0	1	34	1	7	0
ODIs	42	41	5	1103	89	30.63	62.74	0	7	89	6	12	0
T20Is	5	5	0	51	18	10.20	82.25	0	0	3	1	1	0
First-class	35	63	2	1932	313*	31.67	–	2	10	–	–	26	0

Bowling	M	Balls	Runs	Wkts	BB	Avge	RpO	S/R	5i	10m
Tests	7	18	5	1	1–0	5.00	1.66	18.00	0	0
ODIs	42	0	–	–	–	–	–	–	–	–
T20Is	5	0	–	–	–	–	–	–	–	–
First-class	35	306	207	5	1–0	41.40	4.05	61.20	0	0

ADIL **RASHID**

Full name	**Adil Usman Rashid**
Born	**February 17, 1988, Bradford, Yorkshire**
Teams	**Yorkshire**
Style	**Right-hand bat, legspinner**
Test debut	**No Tests yet**
ODI debut	**England v Ireland at Belfast 2009**
T20I debut	**England v Netherlands at Lord's 2009**

THE PROFILE Yorkshire have rarely had much truck with legspinners, but a funny thing happened in 2006: they suddenly started playing two of them. The first was Mark Lawson, and he was soon joined by 18-year-old Adil Rashid, a product of the young-spinner programme set up by Terry Jenner, Shane Warne's Australian mentor. Rashid, who bowls with a high action and has all the legspin variations, plus the priceless virtue of accuracy, bowled Yorkshire to victory over Warwickshire in his first match, then had purists licking their lips as he and Lawson shared all ten Middlesex wickets in an innings at Scarborough. The first home-grown player of Asian descent to appear regularly for Yorkshire, Rashid finished his first season with 25 wickets in six matches – plus 14 in three Under-19 Tests against India, traditionally good players of spin – then toured Bangladesh with England A. He consolidated in 2007, after remodelling his action following back trouble, then took 65 more wickets in 2008. Rashid is also a wristy middle-order batsman with four first-class centuries under his belt, the highest an unbeaten 157 against Lancashire in 2009. That was the year he represented England for the first time: after trundling around the Caribbean without playing, he kept things reasonably quiet during England's up-and-down World Twenty20 campaign, then made a promising start in ODIs. He did well with bat and ball against Australia at The Oval before perplexingly being left out for the next two matches. Others moved ahead of him in the reckoning after that, but a return to form with the ball in 2010 – 57 first-class wickets against 31 in 2009 – made sure his name was still very much in the frame.

THE FACTS Rashid took 6 for 67 on his first-class debut, for Yorkshire v Warwickshire at Scarborough in July 2006 ... He scored 114, and then took 8 for 157, for England Under-19s v India at Taunton in August 2006 ... Rashid made 157 not out against Lancashire at Headingley in August 2009 (Yorkshire made 429 after being 144 for 6 when he came in) ... Rashid was the Cricket Writers' Club's Young Cricketer of the Year in 2007 ...

THE FIGURES to 23.9.10   **ESPNcricinfo.com**

Batting & Fielding	M	Inns	NO	Runs	HS	Avge	S/R	100	50	4s	6s	Ct	St
Tests	0	0	–	–	–	–	–	–	–	–	–	–	–
ODIs	5	4	1	60	31*	20.00	111.11	0	0	8	0	2	0
T20Is	5	2	1	10	9*	10.00	52.63	0	0	0	0	0	0
First-class	69	97	21	2937	157*	38.64	52.44	4	19	390	5	37	0

Bowling	M	Balls	Runs	Wkts	BB	Avge	RpO	S/R	5i	10m
Tests	0	0	–	–	–	–	–	–	–	–
ODIs	5	204	191	3	1–16	63.66	5.61	68.00	0	0
T20Is	5	84	120	3	1–11	40.00	8.57	28.00	0	0
First-class	69	12856	7593	228	7–107	33.30	3.54	56.38	10	13

AARON **REDMOND**

Full name	**Aaron James Redmond**
Born	**September 23, 1979, Auckland**
Teams	**Otago, Gloucestershire**
Style	**Right-hand bat, legspinner**
Test debut	**New Zealand v England at Lord's 2008**
ODI debut	**New Zealand v Pakistan at Johannesburg 2009-10**
T20I debut	**New Zealand v Ireland at Nottingham 2009**

THE PROFILE Aaron Redmond learned his cricket on the hard tracks of Western Australia after his father – the ultimate one-cap wonder Rodney, who scored a hundred in his only Test, in 1972-73 – moved the family there when Aaron was a youngster. Back in New Zealand he started with Canterbury, primarily as a legspinner, before establishing himself as a top-order batsman with Otago. He was earmarked as a potential international early on, touring England with New Zealand A in 2000 (and making 92 against Sussex) after only seven first-class matches. But it took him a long time to reach the highest rung of the ladder: his first Test cap came at Lord's in May 2008 after four solid domestic seasons with the bat. But he struggled on the early-season English pitches, especially against the swing of James Anderson, and made only 54 runs in six innings. A 79 followed in Bangladesh, then an attacking 83 at Adelaide in what, oddly, was his last Test to date. With Tim McIntosh and Martin Guptill making their marks at the top of the order, Redmond seemed to have been forgotten – until a clutch of injuries led to an emergency call-up from club cricket in Lancashire to reinforce the side for the World Twenty20 in June 2009. Redmond borrowed a shirt from his Otago opening partner Brendon McCullum, and proceeded to bat like him, belting 13 fours in 63 from 30 balls against Ireland at Trent Bridge. He played a few ODIs later in the year, making 52 against Pakistan in Abu Dhabi, and although injury restricted him at home in 2009-10 he remained in the Twenty20 shake-up.

THE FACTS Redmond made 146 for the touring New Zealanders against England Lions at Southampton in May 2008 ... He rarely bowls his legspin now, but did take 4 for 30 for New Zealand A v India A at Chennai in October 2008 ... Redmond's father, Rodney, played one Test for New Zealand in 1972-73, scoring 107 and 56 v Pakistan but never played again: he had trouble adjusting from glasses to contact lenses and eventually retired ...

THE FIGURES to 23.9.10

ESPYcricinfo.com

Batting & Fielding	M	Inns	NO	Runs	HS	Avge	S/R	100	50	4s	6s	Ct	St
Tests	7	14	1	299	83	23.00	38.08	0	2	42	2	5	0
ODIs	5	5	0	136	52	27.20	59.38	0	1	18	0	2	0
T20Is	7	6	0	126	63	21.00	150.00	0	1	19	2	3	0
First-class	86	147	10	4528	146	33.05	–	8	27	–	–	66	0

Bowling	M	Balls	Runs	Wkts	BB	Avge	RpO	S/R	5i	10m
Tests	7	75	62	3	2–47	20.66	4.96	25.00	0	0
ODIs	5	0	–	–	–	–	–	–	–	–
T20Is	7	17	24	2	2–24	12.00	8.47	8.50	0	0
First-class	86	7862	4283	98	4–30	43.70	3.26	80.22	0	0

KEMAR **ROACH**

Full name	**Kemar Andre Jamal Roach**
Born	**June 30, 1988, St Lucy, Barbados**
Teams	**Barbados, Deccan Chargers**
Style	**Right-hand bat, right-arm fast-medium bowler**
Test debut	**West Indies v Bangladesh at Kingstown 2009**
ODI debut	**West Indies v Bermuda at King City 2008**
T20I debut	**West Indies v Australia at Bridgetown 2008**

THE PROFILE A genuinely fast bowler with a free-flowing action, Kemar Roach had played only four first-class matches when he was called into the squad for the third Test against Australia at Bridgetown in June 2008. He was only 19, and slightly fortunate still to be around: he had agreed to play in the Birmingham League, but was deemed ineligible as he had not played five first-class games, as required of overseas players by the league's rules. Roach didn't play in Barbados – he was mature enough to realise that he was only there for the experience – but he was included for the Twenty20 international shortly afterwards, and took two of the three wickets to fall, dismissing both Australian openers after starting with a nervous beamer. The following year he was one of West Indies' few successes after the senior players withdrew from the series against Bangladesh, taking 13 wickets in the two Tests. Floyd Reifer, the stand-in captain, observed: "He does a lot, especially with the old ball, getting it to move in and out." Roach hit trouble during the ODIs, when he let loose two beamers and was taken off and fined, but he still took ten wickets. When the seniors returned Roach retained his place, winning admirers in Australia in 2009-10 for his hostile pace. He unsettled Ricky Ponting, dismissing him in each of the three Tests, and also smashed him on the elbow at Perth, forcing him to retire hurt. After that eye-catching display Down Under, Roach was one of the star buys at the third IPL auction early in 2010, and was signed by the Deccan Chargers for $720,000.

THE FACTS Roach took 6 for 48 in the second Test against Bangladesh at St George's in July 2009, and followed that with 5 for 44 in the first ODI at Roseau (he had Tamim Iqbal caught behind off the first ball in international cricket in Dominica) ... He took 7 for 23 (five bowled and two lbw) for Barbados v Combined Colleges and Campuses in Nevis in January 2010 ...

THE FIGURES *to 23.9.10*   **ESPNcricinfo.com**

Batting & Fielding	M	Inns	NO	Runs	HS	Avge	S/R	100	50	4s	6s	Ct	St
Tests	7	13	4	57	17	6.33	35.18	0	0	10	0	4	0
ODIs	13	8	4	20	10	5.00	58.82	0	0	1	0	1	0
T20Is	10	1	1	3	3*	–	150.00	0	0	0	0	1	0
First-class	26	35	8	266	52*	9.85	–	0	1	–	–	14	0

Bowling	M	Balls	Runs	Wkts	BB	Avge	RpO	S/R	5i	10m
Tests	7	1472	772	26	6–48	29.69	3.14	56.61	1	0
ODIs	13	677	554	26	5–44	21.30	4.90	26.03	1	0
T20Is	10	210	248	9	2–25	27.55	7.08	23.33	0	0
First-class	26	4007	2365	73	7–23	32.39	3.54	54.89	3	0

RUBEL HOSSAIN

Full name	**Mohammad Rubel Hossain**
Born	**January 1, 1990, Bagerhat**
Teams	**Chittagong**
Style	**Right-hand bat, right-arm fast-medium bowler**
Test debut	**Bangladesh v West Indies at Kingstown 2009**
ODI debut	**Bangladesh v Sri Lanka at Mirpur 2008-09**
T20I debut	**Bangladesh v South Africa at Johannesburg 2008-09**

THE PROFILE A right-arm fast bowler with a slingy action not unlike Lasith Malinga's, Rubel Hossain began by playing tape-ball cricket in his home town of Bagerhat (in Khulna), before he was discovered during a national search for fast bowlers after getting the highest reading on the speed-gun. He made his first-class debut in October 2007 against Khulna, whose side included his hero Mashrafe Mortaza – not that that had stopped him bouncing Mortaza in their previous encounters. He remains raw – his debut Test was only his 11th first-class match – but is pacier than most of his contemporaries. Rubel played in the Under-19 World Cup in Malaysia in February 2008, and later that year was called into the full national squad. In his first ODI, a rain-affected game against Sri Lanka at Mirpur in January 2009, he helped set up a rare Bangladesh victory with 4 for 33. He toured the Caribbean later in the year, playing in both Tests as Bangladesh pulled off a clean sweep against a depleted West Indian side. Rubel again made a decent start, taking three first-innings wickets in St Vincent – his three victims (Ryan Austin, Omar Phillips and Nikita Miller) were, like himself, making their Test debut. He didn't strike again in the Tests, and went for a few in the subsequent one-dayers: he was left out for a while, but was back to take five expensive wickets in a one-off Test against New Zealand early in 2010, before looking the pick of the pacemen in the home-and-away series against England. Rubel's love of speed also runs to a fascination with motor-bikes.

THE FACTS Rubel Hossain took 5 for 60 for Chittagong at Sylhet in December 2008 ... He took 4 for 33 on his ODI debut as Bangladesh beat Sri Lanka at Mirpur in January 2009 ... Rubel took 5 for 166 (in 29 overs) against New Zealand at Hamilton in February 2010 ... He took 4 for 19 against the Netherlands and 5 for 16 against Scotland on successive days in warm-up games for the World Twenty20 in England in May 2009 ...

THE FIGURES to 23.9.10   **ESPNcricinfo.com**

Batting & Fielding	M	Inns	NO	Runs	HS	Avge	S/R	100	50	4s	6s	Ct	St
Tests	8	15	6	43	17	4.77	24.85	0	0	5	0	4	0
ODIs	18	8	5	8	4	2.66	26.66	0	0	0	0	2	0
T20Is	3	1	1	8	8*	–	160.00	0	0	1	0	1	0
First-class	20	31	9	83	17	3.77	–	0	0	–	–	8	0

Bowling	M	Balls	Runs	Wkts	BB	Avge	RpO	S/R	5i	10m
Tests	8	1278	997	12	5–166	83.08	4.68	106.50	1	0
ODIs	18	786	812	19	4–33	42.73	6.19	41.36	0	0
T20Is	3	62	93	2	1–13	46.50	9.00	31.00	0	0
First-class	20	2914	2106	36	5–60	58.50	4.33	80.94	2	0

JESSE **RYDER**

Full name	**Jesse Daniel Ryder**
Born	**August 6, 1984, Masterton, Wellington**
Teams	**Wellington, Bangalore Royal Challengers**
Style	**Left-hand bat, right-arm medium-pacer**
Test debut	**New Zealand v Bangladesh at Chittagong 2008-09**
ODI debut	**New Zealand v England at Wellington 2007-08**
T20I debut	**New Zealand v England at Auckland 2007-08**

THE PROFILE Jesse Ryder had a troubled childhood, and latterly battled with his weight and demons of his own: just after establishing himself in the one-day side after a series of promising performances early in 2008, he injured tendons in his hand when he smashed a window in a bar at 5.30 in the morning after a tight series victory over England. He missed the Tests, and the England tour which followed. But Ryder, who can also bowl useful gentle seamers, is seriously talented: New Zealand's board had already forgiven him for snubbing their A team (he briefly threatened to try to qualify for England), and gave him yet another chance despite continued concerns about his drinking. Ryder gives the ball a good thump: he biffed 79 not out in the second game of that series against England, going run for run with Brendon McCullum in a rollicking opening stand of 165 which won the Hamilton game with half the overs unused. He finally made his Test debut in Bangladesh in November 2008, collecting 91 in his second match then three successive fifties against West Indies at home. In the Tests that followed against India he hit his maiden century at Hamilton, then cracked a superb 201 in the second Test at Napier, setting up a massive total of 619 after entering at 23 for 3. A groin strain ruined his World Twenty20 campaign in England in 2009, but he did well on the Sri Lankan tour that followed. More muscle trouble ruined his 2009-10 home season, but he was back for the next World Twenty20 in the West Indies early in 2010, and remains one of New Zealand's brightest prospects.

THE FACTS Ryder scored 236 for Wellington v Central Districts at Palmerston North in March 2005 ... When he scored 201 against India at Napier in March 2009 it was the second time "J. Ryder" had made 201 in a Test – Jack of Australia made 201 not out v England at Adelaide in 1924-25 ... Ryder played two one-day games for Ireland in 2007 before being dumped after missing the plane to the next match ...

THE FIGURES *to 23.9.10*   **ᴇsᴘⁿcricinfo.com**

Batting & Fielding	M	Inns	NO	Runs	HS	Avge	S/R	100	50	4s	6s	Ct	St
Tests	11	20	2	898	201	49.88	55.50	2	4	103	3	8	0
ODIs	21	19	1	637	105	35.38	93.26	1	3	71	20	5	0
T20Is	14	14	0	324	62	23.14	125.09	0	2	33	14	5	0
First-class	53	85	6	3514	236	44.48	–	8	17	–	–	44	0

Bowling	M	Balls	Runs	Wkts	BB	Avge	RpO	S/R	5i	10m
Tests	11	378	212	4	2–7	53.00	3.36	94.50	0	0
ODIs	21	256	282	8	3–29	35.25	6.60	32.00	0	0
T20Is	14	60	68	2	1–2	34.00	6.80	30.00	0	0
First-class	53	2789	1294	45	4–23	28.75	2.78	61.97	0	0

SAEED AJMAL

Full name	**Saeed Ajmal**
Born	**October 14, 1977, Faisalabad, Punjab**
Teams	**Faisalabad, Zarai Taraqiati Bank**
Style	**Right-hand bat, offspinner**
Test debut	**Pakistan v Sri Lanka at Galle 2009**
ODI debut	**Pakistan v India at Karachi 2008**
T20I debut	**Pakistan v Australia at Dubai 2009**

THE PROFILE Offspinner Saeed Ajmal had been a first-class player for more than ten years when the selectors came calling. Given Pakistan's usual propensity for plucking teenagers from obscurity, he must have thought, at 30, that his chance had gone. However, another impressive domestic season – 38 wickets at 28.63 in 2007-08, plus some decent one-day performances, which followed 62 wickets at 24.29 the previous term – earned him a place at the Asia Cup in Pakistan in mid-2008. He started reasonably well, taking 1 for 47 against India and strangling Bangladesh with two late strikes in his second match. Ajmal is very much a modern offspinner, tossing in a handy *doosra* from a high action. His stock ball remains the offie, although it doesn't turn much, but he has a nice rhythmic delivery, and can get a good loop on the ball. He received a jolting setback when the umpires reported his action during the one-day series against Australia in Abu Dhabi early in 2009 – he was also fined after he complained about being complained about – but tests found any elbow flexion was within the permitted 15-degree limit, and he was cleared to resume bowling. "I was carrying a 50-kilo bag on my head," said Ajmal of the verdict, "but this decision has allowed me to throw that bag off." He showed his delight by bowling with guile and maturity as Pakistan swept to the World Twenty20 title in England in June, taking 12 wickets (only Umar Gul, with 13, took more) and often bottling up the middle overs. He was retained for the Test tour of Sri Lanka that followed, making his mark with 14 wickets in three matches there, and remained in the mix throughout 2010.

THE FACTS Saeed Ajmal took 7 for 63 for Khan Research Laboratories v Zarai Taraqiati Bank in December 2008 ... He took 7 for 220 in 63 overs in only his second first-class match, for Faisalabad v Karachi Whites in November 1996 ... Ajmal had figures of 4.5-3-4-5 for Faisalabad v Karachi Blues in January 1998 ... In 2006-07, his best season, he took 62 wickets at 24.29 in Pakistan ...

THE FIGURES to 23.9.10   **ᴇsᴘᴨcricinfo.com**

Batting & Fielding	M	Inns	NO	Runs	HS	Avge	S/R	100	50	4s	6s	Ct	St
Tests	8	15	7	96	50	12.00	49.23	0	1	12	0	2	0
ODIs	32	21	10	109	33	9.90	64.11	0	0	8	0	5	0
T20Is	24	6	5	24	13*	24.00	126.31	0	0	2	1	4	0
First-class	91	122	42	963	53	12.03	–	0	3	–	–	30	0

Bowling	M	Balls	Runs	Wkts	BB	Avge	RpO	S/R	5i	10m
Tests	8	2375	1114	30	5–82	37.13	2.81	79.16	1	0
ODIs	32	1692	1230	42	4–33	29.28	4.36	40.28	0	0
T20Is	24	539	571	36	4–19	15.86	6.35	14.97	0	0
First-class	91	18103	8354	299	7–63	27.93	2.76	60.54	18	1

SALMAN BUTT

Full name	**Salman Butt**
Born	**October 7, 1984, Lahore, Punjab**
Teams	**Lahore, National Bank**
Style	**Left-hand bat, occasional offspinner**
Test debut	**Pakistan v Bangladesh at Multan 2003-04**
ODI debut	**Pakistan v West Indies at Southampton 2004**
T20I debut	**Pakistan v Bangladesh at Nairobi 2007-08**

THE PROFILE Because he's left-handed, with supple wrists, it's easy to compare Salman Butt with Saeed Anwar. His drives and cuts through extra cover and backward point are flicked or scooped: it is a high-scoring region for him, as it was for Anwar. He doesn't mind pulling, and off his toes he's efficient, rather than whippy as Anwar was. But in attitude and temperament – a confident air and a touch of spikiness – he's more like Anwar's long-time opening partner, Aamer Sohail. Butt's breakthrough came late in 2004. After a maiden one-day century at Eden Gardens, he made 70 at Melbourne and 108 in the New Year Test at Sydney. Then came the fall: he failed to consolidate during 2005, despite another one-day hundred against India, and was dropped as doubts crept in about his defence and his dash. He responded by unveiling startling restraint against England late in the year, grinding out a hundred and two fifties in the Tests, followed by another ton at India's expense. He was in and out of the side for a couple of years – there were three one-day hundreds in the first six months of 2008, but that was followed by a prolonged run of poor form. Recalled for the tour of England in 2010, Butt inherited the captaincy when Shahid Afridi abruptly retired after the first Test against Australia, and immediately oversaw Pakistan's first victory over the Aussies for 15 years ... but the trip ended in controversy when he was implicated in allegations about "spot-fixing" during the Lord's Test against England, and he now faces an uncertain future.

THE FACTS Salman Butt's first four ODI hundreds – and his seventh – all came against India: he averages 52.21 against them, but only 13.33 against West Indies (and 1.00 v Scotland) ... His highest score is 290, for Punjab v Federal Areas at Lahore in February 2008 ... Butt's first Test as captain, in July 2010, resulted in Pakistan's first win over Australia for almost 15 years ...

THE FIGURES to 23.9.10   ESPNcricinfo.com

Batting & Fielding	M	Inns	NO	Runs	HS	Avge	S/R	100	50	4s	6s	Ct	St
Tests	33	62	0	1889	122	30.46	47.20	3	10	276	1	12	0
ODIs	78	78	4	2725	136	36.82	76.28	8	14	343	7	20	0
T20Is	24	23	2	595	74	28.33	107.98	0	3	66	10	3	0
First-class	90	159	7	6232	290	41.00	–	17	24	–	–	33	0

Bowling	M	Balls	Runs	Wkts	BB	Avge	RpO	S/R	5i	10m
Tests	33	137	106	1	1–36	106.00	4.64	137.00	0	0
ODIs	78	69	90	0	–	–	7.82	–	0	0
T20Is	16	0	–	–	–	–	–	–	–	–
First-class	90	938	653	11	4–82	59.36	4.17	85.27	0	0

THILAN **SAMARAWEERA**

Full name	**Thilan Thusara Samaraweera**
Born	**September 22, 1976, Colombo**
Teams	**Sinhalese Sports Club, Kandurata**
Style	**Right-hand bat, offspinner**
Test debut	**Sri Lanka v India at Colombo 2001-02**
ODI debut	**Sri Lanka v India at Sharjah 1998-99**
T20I debut	**No T20Is yet**

THE PROFILE Early in 2009, cricket seemed insignificant for Thilan Samaraweera as he lay in hospital, the most badly injured of the Sri Lankan players subjected to terrorist attack in Pakistan. A bullet was lodged in his left thigh, and a distinguished career hung in the balance – all the more galling as he was in the form of his life, having scored 231 in the first Test at Karachi and 214 in the ongoing one at Lahore. Mercifully, he was soon back to his best, scoring 159 and 143 in successive Tests against New Zealand at home in August before settling a few scores with his first one-day international century, after long being branded too slow for the limited-overs side. In all he made 1234 runs in 11 Tests in 2009 at an average of 72.58, and continued in like vein in 2010: not bad for a man who started out as an offspinner, seemingly destined to play the odd Test in the shadow of Muttiah Muralitharan. Realising he was on a hiding to nothing there, Samaraweera reinvented himself as a specialist batsman, starting with a century on Test debut against India in August 2001, helping Sri Lanka to a 2-1 series win. The retirement of Aravinda de Silva helped him secure a middle-order place, where his patient approach makes him a valuable foil for his more flamboyant colleagues. An adhesive and well-organised player, Samaraweera has a particular liking for his home ground, the Sinhalese Sports Club, where he has now scored five Test centuries and averages 82. His steady offspin is rarely used now, although he has a reputation as a partnership-breaker.

THE FACTS Samaraweera was the third Sri Lankan, after Brendon Kuruppu and Romesh Kaluwitharana, to score a century on Test debut, against India in August 2001 ... Five of his Test centuries have come at the Sinhalese Sports Club, his home ground in Colombo, where he averages 82.60 ... He averages 75.00 in Tests against New Zealand, but 24.66 v South Africa ... Samaraweera's brother Dulip played seven Tests for Sri Lanka in the early 1990s ...

THE FIGURES to 23.9.10   ESPNcricinfo.com

Batting & Fielding	M	Inns	NO	Runs	HS	Avge	S/R	100	50	4s	6s	Ct	St
Tests	60	95	16	4244	231	53.72	47.86	12	23	500	6	36	0
ODIs	41	34	7	748	105*	27.70	68.75	2	0	66	0	11	0
T20Is	0	0	–	–	–	–	–	–	–	–	–	–	–
First-class	219	305	55	12257	231	49.02	–	33	60	–	–	175	0

Bowling	M	Balls	Runs	Wkts	BB	Avge	RpO	S/R	5i	10m
Tests	60	1291	679	14	4–49	48.50	3.15	92.21	1	0
ODIs	41	690	538	10	3–34	53.80	4.67	69.00	0	0
T20Is	0	0	–	–	–	–	–	–	–	–
First-class	219	17458	8132	348	6–55	23.36	2.79	50.16	15	2

DARREN **SAMMY**

Full name	**Darren Julius Garvey Sammy**
Born	**December 20, 1983, Micoud, St Lucia**
Teams	**Windward Islands**
Style	**Right-hand bat, right-arm medium-pacer**
Test debut	**West Indies v England at Manchester 2007**
ODI debut	**West Indies v New Zealand at Southampton 2004**
T20I debut	**West Indies v England at The Oval 2007**

THE PROFILE Darren Julius Garvey Sammy has names invoking images of great leadership. He was the first Test cricketer to emerge from St Lucia, an island rediscovering its cricket culture as the new Beausejour Stadium has captured imaginations, and is also believed to be the only Seventh Day Adventist to have played a Test. Sammy, who spent some time at Lord's with the MCC cricket staff, is a handy batsman and a tall, nagging medium-pacer. He joined the regional one-day squad in 2004, and was a late call-up to the Champions Trophy squad in England that September after Jermaine Lawson pulled out with a stress fracture of the back. In July 2006 Sammy captained St Lucia in the inaugural Stanford 20/20 tournament, and a decent first-class season – 269 runs at 44 in five matches, plus 16 wickets at less than 20 – earned him a recall for the 2007 England tour. He was drafted into the side for the third Test at Old Trafford, and celebrated with seven wickets in the second innings – three of them in one over. His pace is unthreatening, but he brings the ball down from quite a height and wobbles it around. He was overlooked for a while in Tests, perceived to be short of the requisite pace, but when the senior players withdrew from the series against Bangladesh in mid-2009 as a divisive contracts dispute rumbled on Sammy imposed himself with five-fors in both Tests. A virtuoso performance in the second match at St George's nearly brought victory as Bangladesh chased 215: he took five of the six wickets to fall and caught the other one.

THE FACTS Sammy took 7 for 66 in his first Test, against England at Old Trafford in 2007: only Alf Valentine, with 8 for 104 against England at Old Trafford in 1950, has returned better figures on Test debut for West Indies ... Sammy made 121 for Windward Islands v Barbados at Bridgetown in March 2009 ... After top-scoring with 30, he took three wickets and four catches in the World Twenty20 match against Ireland at Providence in April 2010 ...

THE FIGURES to 23.9.10   **ESPITcricinfo.com**

Batting & Fielding	M	Inns	NO	Runs	HS	Avge	S/R	100	50	4s	6s	Ct	St
Tests	8	15	0	291	48	19.40	53.88	0	0	36	2	8	0
ODIs	43	32	11	508	58*	24.19	95.66	0	2	35	19	23	0
T20Is	19	14	5	140	30	15.55	121.73	0	0	8	7	9	0
First-class	61	102	7	2382	121	25.07	–	1	16	–	–	76	0

Bowling	M	Balls	Runs	Wkts	BB	Avge	RpO	S/R	5i	10m
Tests	8	1462	749	27	7–66	27.74	3.07	54.14	3	0
ODIs	43	1790	1335	31	4–26	43.06	4.47	57.74	0	0
T20Is	19	345	359	24	5–26	14.95	6.24	14.37	1	0
First-class	61	8467	3804	147	7–66	25.87	2.69	57.59	9	0

KUMAR **SANGAKKARA**

Full name	**Kumar Chokshanada Sangakkara**
Born	**October 27, 1977, Matale**
Teams	**Nondescripts, Kandurata, Kings XI Punjab**
Style	**Left-hand bat, wicketkeeper**
Test debut	**Sri Lanka v South Africa at Galle 2000**
ODI debut	**Sri Lanka v Pakistan at Galle 2000**
T20I debut	**Sri Lanka v England at Southampton 2006**

THE PROFILE Within months of making the side at 22, Kumar Sangakkara had become one of Sri Lanka's most influential players: a talented left-hand strokemaker, a slick wicketkeeper, and a sharp-eyed strategist. From the start his effortless batting oozed class: he possesses the grace of David Gower, but the attitude of an Aussie. At the outset he was happier on the back foot, but a fierce work ethic and a deep interest in the theory of batsmanship helped him, and he is now as comfortable driving through the covers as cutting behind point. He was briefly relieved of keeping duties after the 2003 World Cup: he made more runs, but soon got the gloves back. The extra burden had no obvious effect on his batting: he made 185 against Pakistan in March 2006, and scored consistently in England too. But there was a change of thinking after that, and Prasanna Jayawardene was given the gloves in Tests. Sangakkara responded with seven centuries, among them three doubles, in his next nine Tests, including 287 as he and Mahela Jayawardene put on a 624 against South Africa, successive double-centuries against Bangladesh, and a magnificent 192 against Australia at Hobart in November 2007. An astute thinker, he took over as captain early in 2009, and reached the final of the World Twenty20 in England. His batting seemed unaffected: he made five centuries in his first ten Tests in charge, including three in successive matches against India in 2009 and 2010. His 219 against them in Colombo in July completed his nap hand of 150s against all nine Test countries, and he sailed past 8000 Test runs in the next match.

THE FACTS Sangakkara scored 287, and put on 624 (the highest stand in first-class cricket) with Mahela Jayawardene against South Africa in Colombo in July 2006 ... He also made 270, adding 438 with Marvan Atapattu, v Zimbabwe at Bulawayo in May 2004 ... Sangakkara averages 76.54 in Tests when he is not the designated wicketkeeper, but 40.48 when lumbered with the gloves ... His record includes three ODIs for the World XI and four for the Asia XI ...

THE FIGURES to 23.9.10   **ESPNcricinfo.com**

Batting & Fielding	M	Inns	NO	Runs	HS	Avge	S/R	100	50	4s	6s	Ct	St
Tests	91	152	11	8016	287	56.85	55.85	23	33	1029	24	163	20
ODIs	276	259	28	8510	138*	36.83	75.29	10	58	847	37	271	69
T20Is	28	27	2	733	78	29.32	120.36	0	6	72	14	12	8
First-class	176	281	21	12400	287	47.69	–	31	57	–	–	324	33

Bowling	M	Balls	Runs	Wkts	BB	Avge	RpO	S/R	5i	10m
Tests	91	66	38	0	–	–	3.45	–	0	0
ODIs	276	0	–	–	–	–	–	–	–	–
T20Is	28	0	–	–	–	–	–	–	–	–
First-class	176	192	108	1	1–13	108.00	3.37	192.00	0	0

RAMNARESH **SARWAN**

Full name	**Ramnaresh Ronnie Sarwan**
Born	**June 23, 1980, Wakenaam Island, Essequibo, Guyana**
Teams	**Guyana**
Style	**Right-hand bat, legspinner**
Test debut	**West Indies v Pakistan at Bridgetown 1999-2000**
ODI debut	**West Indies v England at Nottingham 2000**
T20I debut	**West Indies v South Africa at Johannesburg 2007-08**

THE PROFILE A light-footed right-hander, Ramnaresh Sarwan was brought up in the South American rainforest. After his first Test innings – 84 against Pakistan – the former England captain Ted Dexter was moved to predict a Test average of 50. And on his first tour, to England in 2000, Sarwan lived up to the hype by topping the averages: his footwork was strikingly confident and precise, and it was a surprise when a horror run of three runs in five innings followed in Australia. He soon put that behind him, although his maiden Test century still took 28 matches. He has scored consistently since: 392 runs in four Tests against South Africa in 2003-04 then, after a lean run at home against England, an unbeaten 261 against Bangladesh in June 2004. Then came another England tour: although his form was patchy he did play a big part as West Indies reached the final of the one-day series then won the Champions Trophy, and carried on his good form in Australia. Sarwan took on the captaincy for the 2007 England tour – but that ended in tears with an injured shoulder during the second Test, which seems to have permanently affected his throwing. Chris Gayle took over as captain, but Sarwan was in peerless form in the home series against England in 2009, collecting 626 runs at 104.33, with three centuries – one of them a monumental 291 on a Bridgetown featherbed – plus a 94. Another silky hundred followed at Chester-le-Street in the return series, before a back injury disrupted the early part of 2010.

THE FACTS Sarwan scored 291 at Bridgetown in 2008-09: only Brian Lara (twice) and Lawrence Rowe (302) have made higher Test scores for West Indies against England (Viv Richards also made 291, at The Oval in 1976) ... Sarwan made 107, 94 and 106 in his previous three Test innings against England in the series ... In ODIs Sarwan averages 65.00 v India – but only 22.40 v Sri Lanka ... Sarwan made 100 and 111 for the West Indies Board President's XI against the touring Zimbabweans at Pointe-à-Pierre in March 2000 ...

THE FIGURES to 23.9.10   ᴇꜱᴘⁿcricinfo.com

Batting & Fielding	M	Inns	NO	Runs	HS	Avge	S/R	100	50	4s	6s	Ct	St
Tests	83	146	8	5759	291	41.73	47.01	15	31	738	14	50	0
ODIs	156	146	30	5098	115*	43.94	77.52	4	33	426	51	43	0
T20Is	18	16	3	298	59	22.92	104.19	0	2	19	6	7	0
First-class	187	314	22	11739	291	40.20	–	31	62	–	–	134	0

Bowling	M	Balls	Runs	Wkts	BB	Avge	RpO	S/R	5i	10m
Tests	83	2022	1163	23	4–37	50.56	3.45	87.91	0	0
ODIs	156	581	586	16	3–31	36.62	6.05	36.31	0	0
T20Is	18	12	10	2	2–10	5.00	5.00	6.00	0	0
First-class	187	4193	2224	54	6–62	41.18	3.18	77.64	1	0

VIRENDER **SEHWAG**

Full name	**Virender Sehwag**
Born	**October 20, 1978, Delhi**
Teams	**Delhi, Delhi Daredevils**
Style	**Right-hand bat, offspinner**
Test debut	**India v South Africa at Bloemfontein 2001-02**
ODI debut	**India v Pakistan at Mohali 1998-99**
T20I debut	**India v South Africa at Johannesburg 2006-07**

INDIA

THE PROFILE   Soon after his Test-debut century late in 2001 Virender Sehwag was being compared to Sachin Tendulkar. It is half-true: Sehwag is also short and square, and plays the straight drive, back-foot punch and whip off the hips identically – but he leaves even Sachin standing when it comes to audacity. He also bowls effective, loopy offspin. Asked to open in England in 2002, Sehwag proved an instant hit, and many pivotal innings followed, including India's first triple-century (brought up, characteristically, with a six), in Pakistan early in 2004. Oddly, he struggled in ODIs after an electric start, enduring a run of 60 games from January 2004 in which he averaged below 30. His fitness levels also dropped, but he continued to sparkle in Tests, making 254 – in an opening stand of 410 with Rahul Dravid – at Lahore in January 2006. Then in St Lucia he came excruciatingly close (99 not out) to a century before lunch on the first day, a feat no Indian has yet managed. Dropped after the 2007 World Cup, Sehwag practised hard, lost a stone, and the following March bounced back with another triple-century, against South Africa. Later that year he carried his bat for 201 at Galle, and overall scored 1462 runs in 2008, at a strike-rate (85.84) unprecedented for an opener. His mould-breaking efforts earned him recognition as *Wisden's* Leading Cricketer in the World, a title he retained in 2009 despite injuring his shoulder in the IPL. When fit again, though, he embarked on a run of ten successive Tests with at least a half-century, a sequence that included five hundreds, one of them a superb 293 against Sri Lanka in Mumbai.

THE FACTS   Sehwag's 319 v South Africa at Chennai in March 2008 is India's highest Test score: he reached 300 in 278 balls, the fastest-known Test triple-century (he is third on the list too) ... He made 105 on Test debut, v South Africa in Nov 2001 ... Sehwag carried his bat v Sri Lanka at Galle in 2008 ... His record includes a Test and three ODIs for the World XI, and seven ODIs for the Asia XI ...

THE FIGURES *to 23.9.10*   **ESPncricinfo.com**

Batting & Fielding	M	Inns	NO	Runs	HS	Avge	S/R	100	50	4s	6s	Ct	St
Tests	79	135	5	7039	319	54.14	81.56	21	22	1007	79	61	0
ODIs	228	222	9	7380	146	34.64	103.27	13	36	1019	121	84	0
T20Is	14	13	0	313	68	24.07	153.43	0	2	34	14	1	0
First-class	143	236	9	11544	319	50.85	–	35	40	–	–	120	0

Bowling	M	Balls	Runs	Wkts	BB	Avge	RpO	S/R	5i	10m
Tests	79	3139	1598	39	5–104	40.97	3.05	80.48	1	0
ODIs	228	4230	3716	92	4–6	40.39	5.27	45.97	0	0
T20Is	14	6	20	0	–	–	20.00	–	0	0
First-class	143	7878	4098	104	5–104	39.40	3.12	75.75	1	0

SHAFIUL ISLAM

Full name	**Shafiul Islam**
Born	**October 6, 1989, Bogra**
Teams	**Rajshahi**
Style	**Right-hand bat, right-arm fast-medium bowler**
Test debut	**Bangladesh v India at Chittagong 2009-10**
ODI debut	**Bangladesh v Sri Lanka at Dhaka 2009-10**
T20I debut	**Bangladesh v New Zealand at Hamilton 2009-10**

THE PROFILE An enthusiastic medium-pacer who maintains a decent economy rate in first-class cricket, if not yet in limited-overs games, rather oddly Shafiul Islam initially made more of a name for himself in international cricket with the bat. Against India in January 2010 his first two scoring shots were big sixes smeared off the legspin of Amit Mishra (his next runs came when he was dropped on the boundary): Shafiul was the first to achieve this feat in Tests, although his team-mate Jahurul Islam followed suit against England at Mirpur two months later. During that match, "Suhas" again starred with the bat, making a forthright 53 (from 51 balls, with 11 fours) from No. 10 and sharing a ninth-wicket partnership of 74 with Naeem Islam that helped push Bangladesh's total to 419. But it is as a brisk medium-pacer that he is likely to make his mark in the long term. In 2008-09, his first full season, Shafiul took 23 wickets at 22.30 on Bangladesh's usually benign pitches, and was rewarded with a call-up to the national squad when several senior bowlers went down injured. He made his one-day debut in the Asia Cup at the start of 2010, and managed a decent start, although he proved expensive later on, going for 95 in ten overs against Pakistan (with Shahid Afridi in full flow) at Dambulla in June 2010 and 97 off nine against England a month later. He needs to tighten up his control, although the suspicion lingers that he might just be too hittable in the shorter formats.

THE FACTS Shafiul Islam's first two scoring shots in Test cricket were sixes, off Amit Mishra in two innings at Chittagong in January 2010: he was the first to achieve this in Tests ... Shafiul took 4 for 59 in an ODI against Ireland at Belfast in July 2010, while his best first-class figures of 4 for 38 came for Rajshahi at Khulna in November 2008 ...

THE FIGURES *to 23.9.10*   **ESPncricinfo.com**

Batting & Fielding	M	Inns	NO	Runs	HS	Avge	S/R	100	50	4s	6s	Ct	St
Tests	5	10	1	137	53	15.22	62.55	0	1	24	2	0	0
ODIs	16	8	3	43	16	8.60	69.35	0	0	5	1	2	0
T20Is	3	2	0	17	16	8.50	77.27	0	0	1	1	1	0
First-class	18	28	7	298	53	14.19	65.63	0	1	43	7	5	0

Bowling	M	Balls	Runs	Wkts	BB	Avge	RpO	S/R	5i	10m
Tests	5	798	502	7	3–86	71.71	3.77	114.00	0	0
ODIs	16	715	824	24	4–59	34.33	6.91	29.75	0	0
T20Is	3	54	66	1	1–25	66.00	7.33	54.00	0	0
First-class	18	2653	1361	39	4–38	34.89	3.07	68.02	0	0

SHAHADAT HOSSAIN

BANGLADESH

Full name	**Kazi Shahadat Hossain**
Born	**August 7, 1986, Dhaka**
Teams	**Dhaka**
Style	**Right-hand bat, right-arm fast-medium bowler**
Test debut	**Bangladesh v England at Lord's 2005**
ODI debut	**Bangladesh v Kenya at Bogra 2005-06**
T20I debut	**Bangladesh v Zimbabwe at Khulna 2006-07**

THE PROFILE Shahadat Hossain was discovered during a talent-spotting camp in Narayanganj, and whisked away to the Institute of Sports for refinement. In the 2004 Under-19 World Cup he stood out in a tournament which generally lacked firepower, and made rapid progress after that. "Rajib" has all the necessary attributes for a genuine fast bowler: he is tall and strong, and doesn't put unnecessary pressure on his body with a slightly open-chested delivery position after a smooth run-up. He is naturally aggressive and has raw pace. But his Test debut at Lord's in 2005 was a chastening experience, as his 12 overs disappeared for 101. He was just 18 then: after that he did well against Sri Lanka, taking four wickets in an innings twice before going one better in Bogra's inaugural Test in March 2006 with 5 for 86. Early in 2008 his 6 for 27 at Mirpur gave his side a rare first-innings lead over South Africa – and an even rarer (if illusory) sniff of victory. In one-day internationals, despite a hat-trick against Zimbabwe, he was in and out of the side: he played only once in the 2007 World Cup (and was hit around in the sobering defeat by Ireland), and after that has generally been viewed as too expensive for the shorter formats. In Tests, however, he was part of the side which won an overseas series for the first time, when a severely depleted West Indies were walloped 2-0 in the Caribbean, and in May 2010 he erased some of the memories of that painful Test debut by taking 5 for 98 at Lord's – although England still made 505 and won comfortably.

THE FACTS Shahadat Hossain's 6 for 27 against South Africa at Mirpur in February 2008 are the best by a Bangladesh fast bowler in Tests ... He took Bangladesh's first hat-trick in ODIs, against Zimbabwe at Harare in August 2006 ... Shahadat averages 26.75 in Tests against India – but 258.00 v Australia ... He took only two wickets – both against Kenya – in his first six ODIs ...

THE FIGURES to 23.9.10   **ESPNcricinfo.com**

Batting & Fielding	M	Inns	NO	Runs	HS	Avge	S/R	100	50	4s	6s	Ct	St
Tests	29	55	15	394	40	9.85	45.54	0	0	56	3	7	0
ODIs	46	25	15	79	16*	7.90	55.24	0	0	7	1	5	0
T20Is	5	5	3	8	4*	4.00	66.66	0	0	0	0	0	0
First-class	52	89	28	731	40	11.98	–	0	0	–	–	11	0

Bowling	M	Balls	Runs	Wkts	BB	Avge	RpO	S/R	5i	10m
Tests	29	4334	2992	66	6–27	45.33	4.14	65.66	4	0
ODIs	46	1928	1824	42	3–34	43.42	5.67	45.90	0	0
T20Is	5	96	144	4	2–22	36.00	9.00	24.00	0	0
First-class	52	7662	5162	134	6–27	38.52	4.04	57.17	7	0

SHAHID AFRIDI

Full name	**Sahibzada Mohammad Shahid Khan Afridi**
Born	**March 1, 1980, Khyber Agency**
Teams	**Karachi, Habib Bank, South Australia**
Style	**Right-hand bat, legspinner**
Test debut	**Pakistan v Australia at Karachi 1998-99**
ODI debut	**Pakistan v Kenya at Nairobi 1996-97**
T20I debut	**Pakistan v England at Bristol 2006**

THE PROFILE A flamboyant allrounder introduced to international cricket as a 16-year-old legspinner, Shahid Afridi astonished everyone except himself by pinch-hitting the fastest one-day hundred, from 37 balls in his maiden innings. He's a compulsive shotmaker, and although initially that was too often his undoing, he eventually blossomed. A string of incisive contributions culminated in a violent century against India in April 2005: the only faster ODI hundred was Afridi's own. A few weeks before he had smashed 58 in 34 balls, and also grabbed three crucial wickets, as Pakistan memorably squared the Test series at Bangalore. And so it continued: a Test ton against West Indies, important runs against England, then, early in 2006, he went berserk on some flat tracks against India. An Afridi assault is laced with lofted drives and short-arm jabs over midwicket. He's at his best when forcing straight, and at his weakest pushing just outside off. His legspin is often under-rated: when conditions suit, he gets turn as well as lazy drift, but variety is the key – there's a vicious faster ball and an offbreak too. After an uncertain start in 20-overs cricket – a format which might have been invented with Afridi in mind – he roared back to form in the World Twenty20 in England in 2009 with important runs and wickets, including a ferocious 51 as Pakistan romped to victory in the final. He retired from Test cricket in 2006 – a surprise after finally establishing himself in the five-day team – but returned as captain in 2010, only to quit dramatically after just one match (and two irresponsible shots in a big defeat by Australia at Lord's), saying "With my temperament I can't play Test cricket".

THE FACTS In his second match (he hadn't batted in the first) Shahid Afridi hit the fastest hundred in ODIs, from only 37 balls, v Sri Lanka in Nairobi in October 1996 ... Afridi has the highest strike rate – 113.29 runs per 100 balls – of anyone with more than 20 innings in ODIs ... Afridi has hit more sixes in ODIs than anyone else ... Afridi's record includes three ODIs for the Asia XI and two for the World XI ...

THE FIGURES *to 23.9.10*   **ESPNcricinfo.com**

Batting & Fielding	M	Inns	NO	Runs	HS	Avge	S/R	100	50	4s	6s	Ct	St
Tests	27	48	1	1716	156	36.51	86.97	5	8	220	52	10	0
ODIs	301	283	18	6321	124	23.85	113.29	6	30	583	276	100	0
T20Is	37	35	3	602	54*	18.81	140.32	0	3	52	19	11	0
First-class	111	183	4	5631	164	31.45	–	12	30	–	–	75	0

Bowling	M	Balls	Runs	Wkts	BB	Avge	RpO	S/R	5i	10m
Tests	27	3194	1709	48	5–52	35.60	3.21	66.54	1	0
ODIs	301	12810	9885	282	6–38	35.05	4.62	45.42	3	0
T20Is	37	858	884	47	4–11	18.80	6.18	18.25	0	0
First-class	111	13493	7023	258	6–101	27.22	3.12	52.29	8	0

AJMAL **SHAHZAD**

Full name	**Ajmal Shahzad**
Born	**July 27, 1985, Huddersfield, Yorkshire**
Teams	**Yorkshire**
Style	**Right-hand bat, right-arm fast-medium bowler**
Test debut	**England v Bangladesh at Manchester 2010**
ODI debut	**England v Bangladesh at Chittagong 2009-10**
T20I debut	**England v Pakistan at Dubai 2009-10**

THE PROFILE Ajmal Shahzad made history in May 2004 when he became the first British-born Asian to play for Yorkshire. Born in Huddersfield and raised in Bradford, Shahzad is a nippy fast bowler and a useful late-order batsman, who excelled at schoolboy level and for Yorkshire's academy sides. Graham Roope, his coach there, said he was "far too mature for most schoolboy opponents of his age". Shahzad endured a couple of sluggish seasons as injuries restricted his development, and he managed only a solitary appearance in 2006 – but he finally allied consistency to his undoubted talent and, given a first-team chance following Tim Bresnan's promotion to the national squad, Shahzad claimed 40 wickets and scored 445 runs for Yorkshire in the Championship in 2009. This was enough to earn him a place on England's Test tour of Bangladesh, much to his own surprise: the decisive factor seems to have been an impressive stint with the England Performance Programme in South Africa a few months earlier, when he caught the eye of the senior management, including Andy Flower, with his pace, control and desire to succeed. "He looks like an impressive young man," said Flower, "and how well he does will be determined by himself." After displaying a happy knack for early strikes – wickets in his first over in both ODIs and Twenty20s – Shahzad made his Test debut against Bangladesh at Old Trafford in June 2010 when Stuart Broad was rested. There were no early breakthroughs this time, but he did take four wickets overall. Broad soon returned, and Shahzad returned to county duty.

THE FACTS Shahzad took two wickets in his first over in Twenty20 internationals, dismissing Imran Nazir third ball and Imran Farhat fifth against Pakistan at Dubai in February 2010 … The following month he struck with his third ball in ODIs, dismissing Tamim Iqbal of Bangladesh at Chittagong … Shahzad took his maiden five-for (5 for 51, all bowled or lbw) for Yorkshire v Durham at Chester-le-Street in August 2010 …

THE FIGURES *to 23.9.10*

Batting & Fielding	M	Inns	NO	Runs	HS	Avge	S/R	100	50	4s	6s	Ct	St
Tests	1	1	0	5	5	5.00	41.66	0	0	1	0	2	0
ODIs	4	1	0	5	5	5.00	55.55	0	0	0	0	1	0
T20Is	1	–	–	–	–	–	–	–	–	–	–	0	0
First-class	32	40	12	796	88	28.42	40.77	0	2	96	10	7	0

Bowling	M	Balls	Runs	Wkts	BB	Avge	RpO	S/R	5i	10m
Tests	1	102	63	4	3–45	15.75	3.70	25.50	0	0
ODIs	4	197	151	8	3–41	18.87	4.59	24.62	0	0
T20Is	1	24	38	2	2–38	19.00	9.50	12.00	0	0
First-class	32	5165	2933	91	5–51	32.23	3.40	56.75	1	0

SHAKIB AL HASAN

Full name	**Shakib Al Hasan**
Born	**March 24, 1987, Magura, Khulna**
Teams	**Khulna, Worcestershire**
Style	**Left-hand bat, slow left-arm orthodox spinner**
Test debut	**Bangladesh v India at Chittagong 2006-07**
ODI debut	**Bangladesh v Zimbabwe at Harare 2006**
T20I debut	**Bangladesh v Zimbabwe at Khulna 2006-07**

THE PROFILE Shakib Al Hasan was earmarked for international honours after starring for the Under-19s in 2005, with 83 in victory over England and an 82-ball century against Sri Lanka, after taking three wickets. His full debut duly arrived against Zimbabwe in August 2006: he took a wicket and then strolled in at No. 4 to make 30 not out in the matchwinning partnership. A stylish left-hander, Shakib proved remarkably consistent at first, being dismissed in single figures only once in 18 one-dayers leading up to the 2007 World Cup: that run included 134 not out against Canada. The heady start continued in the Caribbean with a half-century in the famous win over India, and another against England. After the World Cup came the inevitable dip – 17 runs in three innings in Sri Lanka – but he soon returned to form. Shakib sealed Bangladesh's 2-0 triumph over a depleted West Indies side in July 2009, finishing just short of a maiden Test century in Grenada: by then he had taken over from the injured Mashrafe Mortaza as captain. He looked a natural there, too, and it was a surprise when Mortaza was restored for the one-dayers in England in 2010. Shakib's flattish left-arm spin – always effective and economical in ODIs – blossomed almost overnight in Tests. After only three wickets in his first six matches, he took 7 for 36 against New Zealand in October 2008, and rubber-stamped his arrival as an international-class allrounder with 13 wickets in those two Tests in the West Indies. He also sailed past 100 ODI wickets in mid-2010, just before becoming the first Bangladeshi to play county cricket during a brief stint as Worcestershire's overseas player.

THE FACTS Shakib Al Hasan took 7 for 36, Bangladesh's best bowling figures in Tests, against New Zealand at Chittagong in October 2008 ... He made 100 against New Zealand at Hamilton in February 2010 – and additionally has scored 96 in Tests three times ... Shakib hit 134 not out v Canada in an ODI in Antigua in February 2007 ... He averages 59.66 with the bat in Tests against New Zealand – and 15.12 v South Africa ...

THE FIGURES *to 23.9.10*

ESPNcricinfo.com

Batting & Fielding	M	Inns	NO	Runs	HS	Avge	S/R	100	50	4s	6s	Ct	St
Tests	21	40	2	1179	100	31.02	55.53	1	5	158	6	8	0
ODIs	94	90	15	2465	134*	32.86	75.75	4	14	219	18	24	0
T20Is	14	14	0	207	47	14.78	111.89	0	0	17	4	4	0
First-class	46	85	8	2633	129	34.19	–	4	13	–	–	25	0

Bowling	M	Balls	Runs	Wkts	BB	Avge	RpO	S/R	5i	10m
Tests	21	5083	2410	75	7–36	32.13	2.84	67.77	7	0
ODIs	94	4790	3350	109	4–33	30.73	4.19	43.94	0	0
T20Is	14	294	328	17	4–34	19.29	6.69	17.29	0	0
First-class	46	9152	4115	129	7–36	31.89	2.69	70.94	9	0

ISHANT **SHARMA**

INDIA

Full name	**Ishant Sharma**
Born	**September 2, 1988, Delhi**
Teams	**Delhi, Kolkata Knight Riders**
Style	**Right-hand bat, right-arm fast-medium bowler**
Test debut	**India v Bangladesh at Dhaka 2006-07**
ODI debut	**India v South Africa at Belfast 2007**
T20I debut	**India v Australia at Melbourne 2007-08**

THE PROFILE Tall fast bowlers have always been a much-prized rarity in Indian cricket. Their earliest Tests featured Mohammad Nissar, a few years ago Abey Kuruvilla flitted across the international scene ... and now there's Ishant Sharma, a lofty 6ft 4ins (193cm). He's regularly above 80mph, and possesses a sharp and deceptive bouncer, delivered from a high arm action. He started to play seriously at 14, rose quickly, and played one-dayers for Delhi in 2005-06 when only 17. The following season he took 4 for 65 from 34 overs on his first-class debut and finished his first term with 29 wickets at 20.10. Early in 2007 he was on the verge of reinforcing the national team in South Africa – flights had been booked and visa arrangements made – but in the end he was left to concentrate on domestic cricket and a youth tour. However, when Munaf Patel was injured again in Bangladesh in May, Sharma finally did get on the plane, and took a wicket in a landslide victory at Dhaka. In Australia at the end of 2007 he looked the real deal, especially in the Perth Test, when he dismissed Ricky Ponting during a sensational spell, and again in the one-dayers as India surprised the hosts to snaffle the series. His returns since then have been a little disappointing: he hasn't managed a five-for since his second Test ... but he's still only 22. He has been one of the faces of the IPL, if not one of its greatest successes, and – if a worryingly frail-looking physique holds up – he is set for a long and successful career.

THE FACTS Sharma took 7 for 24 (11 for 51 in the match) for Delhi v Orissa at Delhi in November 2008 ... He has taken 24 of his 56 ODI wickets against Sri Lanka ... His bowling average in ODIs against Australia is 25.13, but 64.00 v Pakistan ... In 2006-07, his first season of first-class cricket, Sharma took 29 wickets at 20.10 for Delhi, then made his Test debut in only his seventh match ...

THE FIGURES to 23.9.10   ESPNcricinfo.com

Batting & Fielding	M	Inns	NO	Runs	HS	Avge	S/R	100	50	4s	6s	Ct	St
Tests	26	35	17	238	31*	13.22	28.70	0	0	24	0	8	0
ODIs	45	14	6	47	13	5.87	35.33	0	0	4	0	11	0
T20Is	11	2	2	8	5*	–	100.00	0	0	1	0	2	0
First-class	47	54	27	293	31*	10.85	28.86	0	0	31	0	13	0

Bowling	M	Balls	Runs	Wkts	BB	Avge	RpO	S/R	5i	10m
Tests	26	4818	2738	73	5–118	37.50	3.40	66.00	1	0
ODIs	45	2035	1947	63	4–38	30.90	5.74	32.30	0	0
T20Is	11	206	291	6	2–34	48.50	8.47	34.33	0	0
First-class	47	8755	4634	155	7–24	29.89	3.17	56.48	3	1

ROHIT **SHARMA**

Full name	**Rohit Gurunathan Sharma**
Born	**April 30, 1987, Bansod, Nagpur, Maharashtra**
Teams	**Mumbai, Deccan Chargers**
Style	**Right-hand bat, offspinner**
Test debut	**No Tests yet**
ODI debut	**India v Ireland at Belfast 2007**
T20I debut	**India v England at Durban 2007-08**

THE PROFILE Rohit Sharma made a great start to his first-class career, hitting 205 against Gujarat in only his fourth match for Mumbai, after a near-miss (95) in his previous game. Earlier in 2006 he had made his first-class debut for India A, and also exuded class in the Under-19 World Cup. Sharma was at No. 3 then, probably his best position as he is an adaptable batsman, strong off the back foot, equally happy as accumulator or aggressor. He finished 2006-07 with 600 runs at 40, plus 356 in one-dayers and a 49-ball Twenty20 century against Gujarat, which all earned him a national call as the dust settled on India's disastrous World Cup campaign. He made his ODI debut in Ireland, retained his place for the one-day leg of the tour of England that followed, then had a couple of useful innings in the inaugural World Twenty20 in South Africa. Then, during the second edition of the IPL in 2009, Sharma's Deccan Chargers entered the last over against Kolkata needing 21 to win – and Sharma hit 26, including a six off the final ball, off Bangladesh's Mashrafe Mortaza. A few matches previously Sharma's seldom-seen offspin had claimed an unlikely hat-trick to derail the Mumbai Indians. In 2009-10 he followed a triple-century for Mumbai with successive ODI hundreds against Zimbabwe and Sri Lanka, and remains an automatic one-day pick. He would have had a Test cap, too, except he twisted his ankle during the warm-up before the first match against South Africa at Nagpur in February 2010, and had to miss out.

THE FACTS Sharma extended his maiden first-class century to 205, for Mumbai v Gujarat in December 2006 ... He scored 309 not out for Mumbai v Gujarat in December 2009: in his next innings he was out for a duck ... Sharma took a hat-trick (and four wickets in five balls) as Deccan Chargers beat Mumbai Indians in the IPL in May 2009 ... He hit 101 not out, off only 45 balls, against Gujarat in a Twenty20 match in April 2007 ...

THE FIGURES *to 23.9.10* ░ESPncricinfo.com

Batting & Fielding	M	Inns	NO	Runs	HS	Avge	S/R	100	50	4s	6s	Ct	St
Tests	0	0	–	–	–	–	–	–	–	–	–	–	–
ODIs	54	51	11	1155	114	28.87	77.00	2	5	81	11	21	0
T20Is	19	16	6	335	79*	33.50	125.46	0	3	28	14	6	0
First-class	36	52	4	2641	309*	55.02	–	8	11	–	–	23	0

Bowling	M	Balls	Runs	Wkts	BB	Avge	RpO	S/R	5i	10m
Tests	0	0	–	–	–	–	–	–	–	–
ODIs	54	221	179	3	2–27	59.66	4.85	73.66	0	0
T20Is	19	30	37	1	1–22	37.00	7.40	30.00	0	0
First-class	36	648	328	5	1–1	65.60	3.03	129.60	0	0

SHANE **SHILLINGFORD**

Full name	**Shane Shillingford**
Born	**February 22, 1983, Dominica**
Teams	**Windward Islands**
Style	**Right-hand bat, offspinner**
Test debut	**West Indies v South Africa at Port-of-Spain 2010**
ODI debut	**No ODIs yet**
T20I debut	**No T20Is yet**

THE PROFILE Off-spinner Shane Shillingford started his first-class career with a bang in January 2001, taking 7 for 66 in the first innings of his debut, for the Windward Islands against Jamaica at Kingston: his victims included a former West Indian Test batsman in Robert Samuels, and a future one in Brenton Parchment. It was always going to be difficult to live up to such a start, and his career received what might have been a terminal setback later the same month when he was called for throwing three times by leading umpire Steve Bucknor during the match against the Leeward Islands. Shillingford carried on, but when he played only two matches in 2005-06 and none at all the following season it seemed that his career was over. But the new rules which permitted a 15-degree elbow-bend quietened the talk about his action, and Shillingford returned with 31 wickets at 20.64 in 2007-08, and went even better with 56 at 19.05 in 2008-09. The regional selectors could ignore him no longer, and in 2010, not long after taking nine wickets in the match against Barbados and some good performances for the A team in Bangladesh, Shillingford became only the fifth player from Dominica to play Test cricket, and bowled tidily in harness with slow left-armer Sulieman Benn to take nine wickets in the three matches against South Africa. Two of his predecessors share his surname, but they are not related: "Shillingford is a very common name in Dominica," says the veteran West Indian journalist Tony Cozier. "The original Mr Shillingford must have been quite a man."

THE FACTS Shillingford took 7 for 66 on his first-class debut, for the Windward Islands against Jamaica at Kingston in January 2001 ... He took 56 wickets at 19.05 in the 2008-09 West Indian season ... He was the fifth Dominican to play a Test for West indies, after Grayson and Irvine Shillingford (no relations), Norbert Phillip and Adam Sanford ...

THE FIGURES *to 23.9.10*   **ESPncricinfo.com**

Batting & Fielding	M	Inns	NO	Runs	HS	Avge	S/R	100	50	4s	6s	Ct	St
Tests	3	5	0	59	27	11.80	37.82	0	0	7	2	1	0
ODIs	0	0	–	–	–	–	–	–	–	–	–	–	–
T20Is	0	0	–	–	–	–	–	–	–	–	–	–	–
First-class	61	102	18	1136	63	13.52	–	0	4	–	–	31	0

Bowling	M	Balls	Runs	Wkts	BB	Avge	RpO	S/R	5i	10m
Tests	3	978	520	9	3–96	57.77	3.19	108.66	0	0
ODIs	0	0	–	–	–	–	–	–	–	–
T20Is	0	0	–	–	–	–	–	–	–	–
First-class	61	13703	5966	225	7–66	26.51	2.61	60.90	8	0

SHOAIB AKHTAR

Full name	**Shoaib Akhtar**
Born	**August 13, 1975, Rawalpindi, Punjab**
Teams	**Islamabad, Federal Areas, Khan Research Laboratories**
Style	**Right-hand bat, right-arm fast bowler**
Test debut	**Pakistan v West Indies at Rawalpindi 1997-98**
ODI debut	**Pakistan v Zimbabwe at Harare 1997-98**
t20I debut	**Pakistan v England at Bristol 2006**

THE PROFILE Shoaib Akhtar electrified the 1999 World Cup with his spectacular run-up and blistering speed. But it was too much, too young, for the "Rawalpindi Express": breaking the 100mph barrier seemed more important than cementing his place. He was twice sidelined after throwing allegations, and although his action was cleared – tests showed a hyper-extensible elbow – injuries often impinged. He shook up the Aussies in 2002, and promised much in the following year's World Cup, but came a cropper, especially in a needle encounter with Sachin Tendulkar. Then Pakistan lost a series to India, and Shoaib felt the heat as his commitment was questioned. He blew hot and cold in Australia in 2004-05, by turns Pakistan's most incisive threat and their most disinterested player. He bounced back at the end of 2005 with 17 England wickets, mixing yorkers and bouncers with lethal slower balls. But there were further whispers about his action, ankle trouble kept him out of most of the 2006 England tour, then he was banned for two years after a positive drug test. The ban was lifted on appeal, but it and various injuries kept him out of the 2007 World Cup. He was back later that year – briefly, being sent home from the World Twenty20 championship after a dressing-room spat left Mohammad Asif with a bat-bruised thigh – then copped a five-year ban early in 2008 for criticising the board. The end? No ... it was later reduced to 18 months, then suspended. Shoaib was still around in England late in 2010, hurling down 94mph toe-crushers in the one-dayers to show that he wasn't quite finished yet.

THE FACTS Shoaib was clocked at 100.04mph by an unofficial speed-gun during a one-dayer v New Zealand in April 2002: he also recorded 100.23mph (161.3kph) at the 2003 World Cup ... His best figures in Tests and ODIs both came against New Zealand ... Against England in the 2003 World Cup Shoaib was the fifth No. 11 to top-score in an ODI innings, with 43 ... His record includes three ODIs for the Asia XI and two for the World XI ...

THE FIGURES to 23.9.10

ESPNcricinfo.com

Batting & Fielding	M	Inns	NO	Runs	HS	Avge	S/R	100	50	4s	6s	Ct	St
Tests	46	67	13	544	47	10.07	41.43	0	0	53	22	12	0
ODIs	152	76	35	383	43	9.34	74.51	0	0	27	11	18	0
T20Is	11	3	1	5	4	2.50	71.42	0	0	1	0	2	0
First-class	133	186	50	1670	59*	12.27	–	0	1	–	–	41	0

Bowling	M	Balls	Runs	Wkts	BB	Avge	RpO	S/R	5i	10m
Tests	46	8143	4574	178	6–11	25.69	3.37	45.74	12	2
ODIs	152	7242	5660	235	6–16	24.08	4.68	30.81	4	0
T20Is	11	222	287	12	2–11	23.91	7.75	18.50	0	0
First-class	133	20460	12265	467	6–11	26.26	3.59	43.81	28	2

SHOAIB MALIK

Full name	**Shoaib Malik**
Born	**February 1, 1982, Sialkot, Punjab**
Teams	**Sialkot, Pakistan International Airlines**
Style	**Right-hand bat, offspinner**
Test debut	**Pakistan v Bangladesh at Multan 2001-02**
ODI debut	**Pakistan v West Indies at Sharjah 1999-2000**
T20I debut	**Pakistan v England at Bristol 2006**

THE PROFILE Short of wicketkeeping, there are few roles Shoaib Malik hasn't tried. He has batted everywhere from 1 to 10 in one-dayers, eventually settling at 3 or 4. He began in Tests in the lower order, then tried opening. He is an uncomplicated batsman, free with checked drives and cuts, or slogging when needed. Probably his finest performance in Tests came when he defied Murali with an unbeaten eight-hour 148 to earn a draw in Colombo in March 2006. As an offspinner, everything about his bowling, from the short-stepping run-up to the *doosra*, bears a striking similarity to Saqlain Mushtaq. But his action was reported twice, and he now bowls less after two bouts of elbow surgery. Finally, in the wake of the disasters of the 2007 World Cup, came his biggest challenge ... captaincy. He had a poor start in Tests, and although the results looked better in one-dayers he was flattered by a national-record run of 11 consecutive victories early in 2008, since ten of them came against Zimbabwe and Bangladesh. Heavy defeat to Sri Lanka in a one-day series in January 2009 spelt the end of his spell as captain: seemingly relieved to be back in the ranks, he contributed to victory in the World Twenty20 in England in June, then hit another important century in the drawn third Test in Colombo the following month. But he was rather a peripheral figure in Australia at the turn of 2010 and later in the year in England, making more headlines for his marriage to the Indian tennis star Sania Mirza than on the field for his cricket.

THE FACTS Shoaib Malik extended his first Test century, against Sri Lanka in Colombo in March 2006, to 148 not out in 448 minutes as Pakistan forced a draw ... He made 90, 95 and 106 in successive one-day innings against India in February 2006 ... Shoaib has batted in every position except No. 11 in ODIs, averaging 52.80 from No. 2, 44.61 from No. 4, and 39.68 at No. 3 (and 7.50 at No. 10) ... He took 7 for 81 for PIA v WAPDA in Feb 2001 ...

THE FIGURES to 23.9.10   **ESPN**cricinfo.com

Batting & Fielding	M	Inns	NO	Runs	HS	Avge	S/R	100	50	4s	6s	Ct	St
Tests	32	54	6	1606	148*	33.45	44.40	2	8	209	13	16	0
ODIs	192	172	21	5188	143	34.35	78.82	7	31	432	59	68	0
T20Is	32	31	6	636	57	25.44	113.77	0	2	53	13	14	0
First-class	95	147	17	3856	148*	29.66	–	8	17	–	–	44	0

Bowling	M	Balls	Runs	Wkts	BB	Avge	RpO	S/R	5i	10m
Tests	32	2245	1291	21	4–42	61.47	3.45	106.90	0	0
ODIs	192	6384	4864	134	4–19	36.29	4.57	47.64	0	0
T20Is	32	258	286	14	2–14	20.42	6.65	18.42	0	0
First-class	95	11144	5559	179	7–81	31.05	2.99	62.25	5	1

PETER **SIDDLE**

Full name	**Peter Matthew Siddle**
Born	**November 25, 1984, Traralgon, Victoria**
Teams	**Victoria**
Style	**Right-hand bat, right-arm fast bowler**
Test debut	**Australia v India at Mohali 2008-09**
ODI debut	**Australia v New Zealand at Brisbane 2008-09**
T20I debut	**Australia v New Zealand at Sydney 2008-09**

THE PROFILE Peter Siddle was long considered one of the most dangerous fast bowlers in Australia – but also one of the most fragile. A shoulder reconstruction sidelined him for most of 2006-07, then he dislocated the joint at the start of the following season, and aggravated it again later on. He still finished 2007-08 with 33 wickets in just five matches. He emerged from reconstructive surgery fitter than ever, and was a surprise inclusion for the Test tour of India in October 2008, after visiting there with the A team the previous month. His first Test wicket was the plum one of Sachin Tendulkar. The burly Siddle has elements of two illustrious predecessors in his run-up and general attitude: the approach is reminiscent of Craig McDermott's, while the bustling delivery reminds some of Merv Hughes – and he has a touch of the old Hughes banter, too. In England in 2009 he fought off the challenges of other pacemen to play throughout the series, moving the ball at pace, and finishing up with 20 wickets. That included a decisive first-day spell of 5 for 21 to put England on the ropes in the fourth Test at Headingley, which Australia won easily. He looked to have booked a spot – but then a stress fracture ruled him out for most of 2010, with an Ashes return a cherished hope. Siddle grew up in Morwell in rural Victoria, and was a promising competitive wood-chopper before concentrating on cricket at 14. "I did it between the ages of 11 and 13 but thought if I was going to play competitive sport I should give it away because I didn't want to chop any toes off!"

THE FACTS Siddle took 5 for 21 in the Ashes Test against England at Headingley in 2009 ... He took 9 for 167 in the match in the Pura Cup final against New South Wales at Sydney in March 2008, although Victoria still lost ... Siddle took a wicket (New Zealand's Kyle Mills) with his sixth ball in one-day internationals, at Brisbane in February 2009 ...

THE FIGURES to 23.9.10   ESPncricinfo.com

Batting & Fielding	M	Inns	NO	Runs	HS	Avge	S/R	100	50	4s	6s	Ct	St
Tests	17	22	6	256	38	16.00	48.30	0	0	30	1	10	0
ODIs	15	3	1	12	8*	6.00	92.30	0	0	1	0	1	0
T20Is	1	1	1	1	1*	–	100.00	0	0	0	0	0	0
First-class	32	40	11	433	38	14.93	43.04	0	0	47	2	15	0

Bowling	M	Balls	Runs	Wkts	BB	Avge	RpO	S/R	5i	10m
Tests	17	3763	1892	60	5–21	31.53	3.01	62.71	2	0
ODIs	15	660	499	14	3–55	35.64	4.53	47.14	0	0
T20Is	1	24	24	2	2–24	12.00	6.00	12.00	0	0
First-class	32	6062	3136	109	6–57	28.77	3.10	55.61	6	0

DEVON **SMITH**

WEST INDIES

Full name	**Devon Sheldon Smith**
Born	**Oct 21, 1981, Hermitage, Sauteurs, St Patrick, Grenada**
Teams	**Windward Islands**
Style	**Left-hand bat, occasional offspinner**
Test debut	**West Indies v Australia at Georgetown 2002-03**
ODI debut	**West Indies v Australia at Kingston 2002-03**
T20I debut	**West Indies v England at The Oval 2007**

THE PROFILE A belligerent left-handed opener whose eye makes up for a lack of footwork, Grenada's Devon Smith made 750 runs in the 2001-02 Busta Cup, and made his Test debut against Australia in Guyana the following year. Smith blazed 62 in his first Test, but bagged a pair in the next. Early in 2004 he dragged West Indies out of a hole with a stroke-filled century against England on the first day of the series at Kingston – but then fractured his thumb in the nets and missed the next two Tests, then was dropped after three failures in the return series in England. It became a similar refrain: he started the 2005-06 Australian tour well, making a hundred against Queensland then 88 in the first Test at Brisbane, but five single-figure scores followed, and the axe fell again. In one-dayers he was originally overshadowed by another Smith, the unrelated Dwayne, but both played in the 2007 World Cup, Devon making 61 in West Indies' last match, the thriller against England, which ensured him another English tour. He made several starts in the Tests there, crunching some classy cover-drives, but got out too often when set, making five scores between 16 and 42 before a double failure at The Oval. A maiden double-century for the Windward Islands early in 2009 ensured his selection for the Tests against England that followed, but his best score in seven matches was just 55. He kept his name in the frame during 2010 as captain of West Indies A, but at international level he remains another underachiever in a side rather too full of them.

THE FACTS Smith scored 61 (in 34 balls) in his first Twenty20 international, against England at The Oval in June 2007 ... His highest first-class score is 212 for Windward Islands v Guyana at St George's in January 2009 ... Smith made 181 for West Indies A against Lancashire at Liverpool in July 2002 ... His 31 Tests include 15 against England ...

THE FIGURES to 23.9.10   ᴇsᴘᴨ cricinfo.com

Batting & Fielding	M	Inns	NO	Runs	HS	Avge	S/R	100	50	4s	6s	Ct	St
Tests	31	55	2	1315	108	24.81	47.18	1	4	188	0	27	0
ODIs	32	30	2	681	91	24.32	69.63	0	3	69	5	10	0
T20Is	6	6	0	203	61	33.83	126.08	0	2	22	5	1	0
First-class	129	229	9	8134	212	36.97	–	18	36	–	–	122	0

Bowling	M	Balls	Runs	Wkts	BB	Avge	RpO	S/R	5i	10m
Tests	31	6	3	0	–	–	3.00	–	0	0
ODIs	32	0	–	–	–	–	–	–	–	–
T20Is	6	0	–	–	–	–	–	–	–	–
First-class	129	444	218	2	1–2	109.00	2.94	222.00	0	0

GRAEME **SMITH**

Full name	**Graeme Craig Smith**
Born	**February 1, 1981, Johannesburg, Transvaal**
Teams	**Cape Cobras, Rajasthan Royals**
Style	**Left-hand bat, occasional offspinner**
Test debut	**South Africa v Australia at Cape Town 2001-02**
ODI debut	**South Africa v Australia at Bloemfontein 2001-02**
T20I debut	**South Africa v New Zealand at Johannesburg 2005-06**

THE PROFILE In March 2003, Graeme Smith became South Africa's youngest captain at 22, when Shaun Pollock was dumped after a disastrous World Cup. A tall, aggressive left-hand opener, Smith had few leadership credentials – and only a handful of caps – but the selectors' faith was instantly justified: in England in 2003 he collected back-to-back double-centuries. Reality bit back the following year, with Test-series defeats in Sri Lanka and India. There was also a run of 11 losses in 12 ODIs, a mixed time in New Zealand, and the start of an ultimately fruitless series against England. Yet Smith continued to crunch runs aplenty: his 125 to square the New Zealand series was a minor epic. He yields to no-one physically, but can be subdued by more insidious means: by the end of 2004, as Matthew Hoggard's inswinger had him frequently fumbling around his front pad, even the runs started to dry up. But he roared back in the Caribbean in 2005, with hundreds in three successive Tests. Smith did well at the 2007 World Cup, except when it really mattered – a wild stroke gifted Nathan Bracken his wicket as South Africa subsided in the semi. A baton-charge to 85 squared the home Test series against West Indies at the start of 2008, and later that year Smith achieved what he narrowly missed in 2003 – winning a Test series in England, his unbeaten 154 in a stiff run-chase at Edgbaston being one of the great captain's innings. In 2008-09 he presided over South Africa's first Test-series victory in Australia, although his own contribution to that and the return rubber was hampered by two hand fractures courtesy of Mitchell Johnson.

THE FACTS In the first Test against England in 2003 Smith scored 277 at Birmingham, the highest score by a South African in Tests: in the second he made 259, the highest Test score by a visiting player at Lord's, beating Don Bradman's 254 in 1930 ... He averages 69.26 in Tests against West Indies, but only 32.73 against Australia ... Smith played four matches for Somerset in 2005, scoring 311 against Leicestershire in one of them ... His record includes one Test for the World XI (as captain) and one ODI for the Africa XI ...

THE FIGURES *to 23.9.10*   **ᴇsᴘncricinfo.com**

Batting & Fielding	M	Inns	NO	Runs	HS	Avge	S/R	100	50	4s	6s	Ct	St
Tests	86	151	9	7170	277	50.49	60.06	21	28	917	22	114	0
ODIs	154	152	9	5732	141	40.08	82.88	8	41	667	36	81	0
T20Is	27	27	2	803	89*	32.12	127.46	0	4	99	22	15	0
First-class	123	213	14	10121	311	50.85	–	29	38	–	–	169	0

Bowling	M	Balls	Runs	Wkts	BB	Avge	RpO	S/R	5i	10m
Tests	86	1322	805	8	2–145	100.62	3.65	165.25	0	0
ODIs	154	1026	951	18	3–30	52.83	5.56	57.00	0	0
T20Is	27	24	57	0	–	–	14.25	–	0	0
First-class	123	1690	1052	11	2–145	95.63	3.73	153.63	0	0

STEVEN **SMITH**

AUSTRALIA

Full name	**Steven Peter Devereux Smith**
Born	**June 2, 1989, Sydney**
Teams	**New South Wales, Worcestershire**
Style	**Right-hand bat, legspinner**
Test debut	**Australia v Pakistan at Lord's 2010**
ODI debut	**Australia v West Indies at Melbourne 2009-10**
T20I debut	**Australia v Pakistan at Melbourne 2009-10**

THE PROFILE Steven Smith is the most promising Australian spinner since Shane Warne emerged – but he is even more than that. He carries the extra advantage of being an outstanding batsman who could eventually slot in to the top six, whether his legspin (unsurprisingly less threatening than Warne's at the moment) trains on or not. By the time he was 21 Smith was in all of Australia's senior squads, picked on promise and quickly showing the composure of a seasoned professional. There were words of caution about his early elevation, but there was no hiding the excitement about a player who gives the ball air, hits it hard, catches it at will, and seems unbothered by pressure. Smith became an international player in 2009-10 after starring with New South Wales, striking four Sheffield Shield centuries and finishing the season with career-best figures of 7 for 64. After only 13 first-class matches he was picked for the Test tour of New Zealand, but didn't get to play. He had already been trialled in the limited-overs sides, impressing with his attitude, and was used more as a legspinner than a batsman. Two for 78 in his first one-dayer against West Indies doesn't sound very special, but he convinced Ricky Ponting to keep the field up to build pressure: not many 20-year-olds – Smith looks even younger – win arguments like that. His maiden Test series, against Pakistan in England in 2010, was encouraging: there were three wickets in the two games, and a muscular 77 at Headingley. Smith started his state career in 2007-08, making his biggest impact in the Twenty20 Big Bash, in which he took nine wickets at the remarkable average of 5.33.

THE FACTS Smith's first four first-class hundreds – including his highest of 177 for NSW v Tasmania at Hobart – came during the 2009-10 Australian season ... He took 7 for 64 for NSW v South Australia at Adelaide in March 2010, after scoring 100 in the first innings ... Smith played in the Under-19 World Cup in Malaysia in 2007-08, alongside Phillip Hughes and Josh Hazlewood ...

THE FIGURES to 23.9.10   **ESPncricinfo.com**

Batting & Fielding	M	Inns	NO	Runs	HS	Avge	S/R	100	50	4s	6s	Ct	St
Tests	2	4	0	100	77	25.00	75.75	0	1	12	2	1	0
ODIs	5	4	1	94	41	31.33	98.94	0	0	9	0	2	0
T20Is	13	8	2	62	27	10.33	131.91	0	0	6	2	12	0
First-class	15	26	4	1112	177	50.54	64.65	4	3	139	16	22	0

Bowling	M	Balls	Runs	Wkts	BB	Avge	RpO	S/R	5i	10m
Tests	2	186	82	3	3–51	27.33	2.64	62.00	0	0
ODIs	5	275	260	9	2–34	28.88	5.67	30.55	0	0
T20Is	13	240	300	15	3–20	20.00	7.50	16.00	0	0
First-class	15	2085	1352	29	7–64	46.62	3.89	71.89	1	0

TIM **SOUTHEE**

Full name	**Timothy Grant Southee**
Born	**December 11, 1988, Whangarei**
Teams	**Northern Districts**
Style	**Right-hand bat, right-arm fast-medium bowler**
Test debut	**New Zealand v England at Napier 2007-08**
ODI debut	**New Zealand v England at Chester-le-Street 2008**
T20I debut	**New Zealand v England at Auckland 2007-08**

THE PROFILE Few players have made such a remarkable Test debut as 19-year-old Tim Southee in March 2008. First, swinging the ball at a healthy pace, he took 5 for 55 as England were restricted to 253, his victims including Andrew Strauss for 0 and Kevin Pietersen for 129. Later, with New Zealand in a hopeless position, he strolled in and smashed 77 not out from just 40 balls, with nine sixes, five of them off an unamused Monty Panesar. His second Test, at Lord's in May 2008, was rather more mundane – one run, no wickets – then he fell ill. Later that year he shook up the Aussies with three wickets in his first four overs at Brisbane, but leaner times almost inevitably followed, and he was sidelined after ten expensive overs in a one-dayer against India in March 2009. But Southee remained very much one for the future, and looked set for a long run in all formats after four more wickets in a one-dayer against Australia at Wellington, followed by six wickets in the Test against them at Hamilton in March 2010. Southee made his first-class debut for Northern Districts at 18 in February 2007, and the following season claimed 6 for 68 in a particularly impressive effort against Auckland. He was chosen for the Under-19 World Cup, but had to interrupt his preparations when he was drafted into the senior set-up for the Twenty20 games against England in early 2008. He ended the Under-19 World Cup as the second-highest wicket-taker, with 17, and was named Player of the Tournament. After that he barely had time to unpack before that Test call came.

THE FACTS Southee hit nine sixes in his first Test innings, a number only ever exceeded by four players, none of whom was making his debut: he had earlier become only the sixth New Zealander to take a five-for on Test debut ... He conceded 105 runs in ten overs against India at Christchurch in March 2009, a number exceeded in ODIs only by Australia's Mick Lewis, with 113 v South Africa at Johannesburg in 2005-06 ... Southee took 8 for 27 from 25 overs for Northern Districts v Wellington at Hamilton in November 2009 ...

THE FIGURES to 23.9.10   **ESPncricinfo.com**

Batting & Fielding	M	Inns	NO	Runs	HS	Avge	S/R	100	50	4s	6s	Ct	St
Tests	9	14	3	199	77*	18.09	92.99	0	1	18	14	3	0
ODIs	33	19	5	132	32	9.42	92.30	0	0	8	6	6	0
T20Is	16	6	2	25	12*	6.25	92.59	0	0	2	1	6	0
First-class	31	39	6	476	77*	14.42	72.12	0	2	43	22	7	0

Bowling	M	Balls	Runs	Wkts	BB	Avge	RpO	S/R	5i	10m
Tests	9	1743	1022	25	5–55	40.88	3.51	69.72	1	0
ODIs	33	1645	1469	44	4–36	33.38	5.35	37.38	0	0
T20Is	16	330	473	14	3–28	33.78	8.60	23.57	0	0
First-class	31	6199	3103	106	8–27	29.27	3.00	58.48	5	0

SREESANTH

Full name	**Shanthakumaran Sreesanth**
Born	**February 6, 1983, Kothamangalam, Kerala**
Teams	**Kerala, Kings XI Punjab**
Style	**Right-hand bat, right-arm fast-medium bowler**
Test debut	**India v England at Nagpur 2005-06**
ODI debut	**India v Sri Lanka at Nagpur 2005-06**
T20I debut	**India v South Africa at Johannesburg 2006-07**

THE PROFILE For three seasons, Sreesanth was little more than a quiz question, as the only Kerala bowler to take a Ranji Trophy hat-trick. He started as a legspinner, idolising Anil Kumble, then once he turned to pace his rise was rapid if, since he played for a weak side, almost unnoticed. Not many bowlers play in the Duleep Trophy in their first season, but Sreesanth did, after taking 22 wickets in his first seven games in 2002-03. A couple of years later, now equipped with a more side-on action and increased pace, a superb display at the Challenger Trophy (trial matches for the national squad) propelled him into the side for the Sri Lanka series. Later he snapped up 6 for 55 against England, still the best one-day figures by an Indian fast bowler at home. Idiosyncratic, with an aggressive approach – to the stumps and the game – he can be expensive, but is also a wicket-taking bowler: in Antigua in June 2006 he fired out Ramnaresh Sarwan and Brian Lara (both for 0) in successive overs. He sometimes rubs opponents up the wrong way, but there is talent among the tantrums: Sreesanth took 19 wickets in the inaugural IPL season in 2007-08, although his international form tailed off a little. A back injury in the second IPL didn't help, although a stint with Warwickshire – during which he took 5 for 93 against Yorkshire – formed part of his rehabilitation. More injuries – thigh and knee this time – disrupted the first half of 2010, and the emergence of the tall Abhimanyu Mithun as an imposing new-ball partner for Ishant Sharma further threatened Sreesanth's national place.

THE FACTS Sreesanth took a hat-trick for Kerala v Himachal Pradesh in the Ranji Trophy in November 2004 ... He is only the second Indian Test player from Kerala, after Tinu Yohannan, another fast-medium bowler ... Sreesanth did not score a run in ODIs until his 16th match, although that was only his fourth innings ... He took 19 wickets in the first IPL season in 2008, the same as Shane Warne and exceeded only by Sohail Tanvir (22) ...

THE FIGURES to 23.9.10   **ESPNcricinfo.com**

Batting & Fielding	M	Inns	NO	Runs	HS	Avge	S/R	100	50	4s	6s	Ct	St
Tests	17	24	7	226	35	13.29	62.43	0	0	30	4	2	0
ODIs	49	20	10	40	10*	4.00	34.78	0	0	1	0	7	0
T20Is	10	3	2	20	19*	20.00	142.85	0	0	4	0	2	0
First-class	56	74	22	524	35	10.07	47.29	0	0	–	–	11	0

Bowling	M	Balls	Runs	Wkts	BB	Avge	RpO	S/R	5i	10m
Tests	17	3385	1921	60	5–40	32.01	3.40	56.41	2	0
ODIs	49	2312	2326	68	6–55	34.20	6.03	34.00	1	0
T20Is	10	204	288	7	2–12	41.14	8.47	29.14	0	0
First-class	56	9840	5565	170	5–40	32.73	3.39	57.88	5	0

DALE **STEYN**

Full name	**Dale Willem Steyn**
Born	**June 27, 1983, Phalaborwa, Limpopo Province**
Teams	**Cape Cobras, Bangalore Royal Challengers**
Style	**Right-hand bat, right-arm fast bowler**
Test debut	**South Africa v England at Port Elizabeth 2004-05**
ODI debut	**Africa XI v Asia XI at Centurion 2005-06**
T20I debut	**South Africa v New Zealand at Johannesburg 2007-08**

THE PROFILE Dale Steyn's rise to the South African side was as rapid as his bowling: he was picked for his first Test little more than a year after his first-class debut. A rare first-class cricketer from the Limpopo province close to the Kruger National Park and the Zimbabwe border, Steyn is genuinely fast, and moves the ball away. He took eight wickets in three Tests against England in 2004-05 before returning to domestic cricket, but was recalled in April 2006 and claimed 5 for 47 as New Zealand were routed at Centurion. He had half a season of county cricket with Essex in 2005, and also rattled a few helmets for Warwickshire in 2007. But Steyn really came of age in 2007-08, taking 40 wickets in five home Tests against New Zealand and West Indies, then 14 on Bangladesh's traditionally slow tracks. Finally he blew India away with 5 for 23 as they subsided to 76 all out and defeat at Ahmedabad. After a subdued time in England in 2008 – he broke his thumb and missed the last two Tests – Steyn confirmed his rise to world class with 34 victims in the home-and-away series against Australia, including ten wickets – and a rollicking 76 during a match-turning stand of 180 with J-P Duminy – in the win at Melbourne that sealed South Africa's first-ever series win Down Under. He had a middling 2009, but all that changed the following year: after Steyn took 13 wickets in the last two Tests against England in January, his 7 for 51 helped sink India at Nagpur, then 15 wickets in the Caribbean helped seal a 2-0 series win.

THE FACTS Steyn took 8 for 41 (14 for 110 in the match) for Titans v Eagles at Bloemfontein in December 2007 ... He took 10 for 93 and 10 for 91 in successive home Tests against New Zealand in November 2007 ... Of Steyn's 211 Test wickets, 47 (22.27%) have been out for ducks: no-one inflicting more zeroes has had a higher percentage ... Steyn made his ODI debut for the Africa XI, and his record includes two matches for them ...

THE FIGURES to 23.9.10   ᴇsᴘⁿcricinfo.com

Batting & Fielding	M	Inns	NO	Runs	HS	Avge	S/R	100	50	4s	6s	Ct	St
Tests	41	52	12	540	76	13.50	42.89	0	1	54	12	11	0
ODIs	41	14	5	86	35	9.55	90.52	0	0	4	4	7	0
T20Is	21	4	2	8	5	4.00	80.00	0	0	0	0	8	0
First-class	82	98	24	1044	82	14.10	49.61	0	3	–	–	17	0

Bowling	M	Balls	Runs	Wkts	BB	Avge	RpO	S/R	5i	10m
Tests	41	8273	4881	211	7–51	23.13	3.53	39.20	14	4
ODIs	41	2012	1778	58	4–16	30.65	5.30	34.68	0	0
T20Is	21	468	531	29	4–9	18.31	6.80	16.13	0	0
First-class	82	15723	8875	365	8–41	24.31	3.38	43.07	22	6

ANDREW **STRAUSS**

Full name	**Andrew John Strauss**
Born	**March 2, 1977, Johannesburg, South Africa**
Teams	**Middlesex**
Style	**Left-hand bat**
Test debut	**England v New Zealand at Lord's 2004**
ODI debut	**England v Sri Lanka at Dambulla 2003-04**
T20I debut	**England v Australia at Southampton 2005**

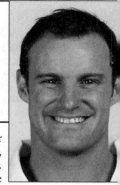

THE PROFILE A compact left-hander with a preference for pummelling the ball square off the back foot with a crunching cut, Andrew Strauss has worked out a superb technique for Test cricket. He put early problems against Shane Warne behind him to make two hundreds in the epic 2005 Ashes series, and added 161 in 2009 to set up England's first victory over Australia at Lord's since 1934. Calm and urbane, Strauss put the disappointment of being passed over as England's captain for the 2006-07 Ashes series to bounce back in 2009 and orchestrate the recapture of the urn. His early cricket with Middlesex did not exactly suggest a star in the making, but a 2003 century against Lancashire, with Andrew Flintoff charging in, got the selectors sniffing. After a few one-day caps that winter Strauss was called up against New Zealand in 2004 after Michael Vaughan twisted his knee in the Lord's nets. He responded with a confident century, and was unlucky to miss another in the second innings when Nasser Hussain ran him out. But Hussain had seen enough: with Vaughan set to return, he announced his retirement, confident that Strauss was the real deal. Strauss has been emphasising that almost ever since, responding to being dropped from the one-day team by upping his strike rate, and probably saving his Test career after a poor run with an eight-hour 177 against New Zealand early in 2008. After an early flirtation with captaincy in 2006, when Vaughan and Flintoff were injured, Strauss inherited the armband again early in 2009, after the messy sacking of Kevin Pietersen. It was not a good way to start – but Strauss has hardly put a foot wrong since.

THE FACTS Strauss was the 15th England player to score a century on Test debut, with 112 v New Zealand at Lord's in May 2004 ... In July 2006 he became only the third man to make a century on debut as England captain, following Archie MacLaren (1897-98) and Allan Lamb (1989-90); Kevin Pietersen followed suit in 2008 ... England never lost a Test in which Strauss scored a century, until he made two at Chennai in December 2008 (his 15th and 16th hundreds) but India won by six wickets ...

THE FIGURES *to 23.9.10*

ESPNcricinfo.com

Batting & Fielding	M	Inns	NO	Runs	HS	Avge	S/R	100	50	4s	6s	Ct	St
Tests	77	140	6	5777	177	43.11	50.13	18	21	714	9	86	0
ODIs	113	112	8	3692	154	35.50	79.89	5	24	403	22	49	0
T20Is	4	4	0	73	33	18.25	114.06	0	0	9	0	1	0
First-class	199	353	17	14061	177	41.84	–	35	63	–	–	175	0

Bowling	M	Balls	Runs	Wkts	BB	Avge	RpO	S/R	5i	10m
Tests	77	0	–	–	–	–	–	–	–	–
ODIs	113	6	3	0	–	–	3.00	–	0	0
T20Is	4	0	–	–	–	–	–	–	–	–
First-class	199	102	89	2	1–16	44.50	5.23	51.00	0	0

SCOTT **STYRIS**

Full name	**Scott Bernard Styris**
Born	**July 10, 1975, Brisbane, Queensland, Australia**
Teams	**Auckland, Essex**
Style	**Right-hand bat, right-arm fmedium-pace bowler**
Test debut	**New Zealand v West Indies at St George's 2002**
ODI debut	**New Zealand v India at Rajkot 1999-2000**
T20I debut	**New Zealand v Australia at Auckland 2004-05**

THE PROFILE   Scott Styris, who was born in Australia but moved to New Zealand when he was six, had a long apprenticeship in domestic cricket, playing almost ten years for Northern Districts before finally making the Test side. By the time of his debut, in Grenada in June 2002, he had been a one-day regular for three years, and had done nothing to suggest that he was a Test batsman: he had 418 runs at 16 in 40 ODIs, and was regarded more as a containing medium-pacer. But he thumped an uncomplicated 107 in his first Test innings, added 69 not out in the second, and sealed a place, eventually adding solidity at the giddy heights of No. 4 – from where, in March 2004, his 170 set up a winning total against South Africa at Auckland. On that 2002 tour of the Caribbean Styris took 6 for 25 at Port-of-Spain, New Zealand's best ODI bowling analysis at the time (since beaten by Shane Bond, twice). Styris continued to score consistently – in a county stint for Middlesex, for his new province Auckland, and for New Zealand. After recovering from a back injury he never failed to reach double figures in nine visits to the crease during the 2007 World Cup, including 87 against England, 80 v West Indies and 111 v Sri Lanka – all not out – and finished with 499 runs at 83.16. Soon after that he announced his retirement from Test cricket, in order to concentrate on one-dayers (and a lucrative IPL contract), but has remained an important part of New Zealand's limited-overs sides.

THE FACTS   Styris was the seventh New Zealander to score a century on Test debut, following Jackie Mills, Bruce Taylor, Rodney Redmond, Mark Greatbatch, Mathew Sinclair and Lou Vincent ... He averages only 24 in ODIs against Australia, despite making 101 against them at Christchurch in 2005-06 ... He has made two centuries in the World Cup, but finished on the losing side both times ... Styris was actually awarded his first cap on the eve of the Karachi Test against Pakistan in May 2002, only for it to be taken back when the match was cancelled after a bomb blast ...

THE FIGURES to 23.9.10   ᴇꜱᴘⁿcricinfo.com

Batting & Fielding	M	Inns	NO	Runs	HS	Avge	S/R	100	50	4s	6s	Ct	St
Tests	29	48	4	1586	170	36.04	51.34	5	6	205	13	23	0
ODIs	169	146	22	4056	141	32.70	79.07	4	25	318	63	67	0
T20Is	28	26	2	492	66	20.50	115.22	0	1	31	20	7	0
First-class	126	210	19	5964	212*	31.22	–	10	29	–	–	99	0

Bowling	M	Balls	Runs	Wkts	BB	Avge	RpO	S/R	5i	10m
Tests	29	1960	1015	20	3–28	50.75	3.10	98.00	0	0
ODIs	169	5642	4464	128	6–25	34.87	4.74	44.07	1	0
T20Is	28	279	327	17	3–5	19.23	7.03	16.41	0	0
First-class	126	12664	6359	203	6–32	31.32	3.01	62.38	9	1

GRAEME **SWANN**

ENGLAND

Full name	**Graeme Peter Swann**
Born	**March 24, 1979, Northampton**
Teams	**Nottinghamshire**
Style	**Right-hand bat, offspinner**
Test debut	**England v India at Chennai 2008-09**
ODI debut	**England v South Africa at Bloemfontein 1999-2000**
T20I debut	**England v New Zealand at Auckland 2007-08**

THE PROFILE Self-confident and gregarious, Graeme Swann is an aggressive offspinner, not afraid to give the ball a real tweak, and a hard-hitting lower-order batsman. He claimed a place in the revamped England squad which toured South Africa in 1999-2000 under new coach Duncan Fletcher, but Swann found life outside the Test side frustrating, although he did play an ODI, in which he bravely continued to give the ball a rip. However, he was less impressive off the field – what some saw as confidence, others interpreted as arrogance or cheek – and slid out of the international reckoning. After marking time with Northamptonshire for a while, not helped by Monty Panesar's arrival, Swann moved to Trent Bridge in 2005 – a decision immediately justified when he helped Nottinghamshire win the Championship. He was recalled for the Sri Lankan tour late in 2007, and took 4 for 34 in a one-day win at Dambulla, but more modest performances followed against New Zealand, home and away, and he was soon on the outer again. However, with Panesar in something of a slump, Swann finally won his first Test cap in India in December 2008, making up for lost time by dismissing Gautam Gambhir and Rahul Dravid in his first over. He soon developed a reputation for troubling left-handers: 33 of his first 50 Test wickets were lefties, an unprecedented number (the next-best is 26). He also continued his enviable knack of taking wickets in the first over of a spell. Swann played throughout the 2009 Ashes, with middling results, but after that he blossomed, in South Africa and at home, and by September 2010 was ranked second in the world among Test bowlers.

THE FACTS Swann took two wickets in his first over in Test cricket: the only other bowler ever to do this was England's Richard Johnson (v Zimbabwe at Chester-le-Street in 2003) ... Swann took 7 for 33 (after not bowling in the first innings) for Northamptonshire v Derbyshire in June 2003 ... He made 183 for Northants v Gloucestershire at Bristol in August 2002, helping Michael Hussey (310 not out) put on 318 for the sixth wicket ...

THE FIGURES *to 23.9.10*   **ESPN**cricinfo.com

Batting & Fielding	M	Inns	NO	Runs	HS	Avge	S/R	100	50	4s	6s	Ct	St
Tests	24	31	5	653	85	25.11	81.62	0	4	82	9	19	0
ODIs	43	27	4	295	34	12.82	80.60	0	0	25	1	19	0
T20Is	20	8	6	42	15*	21.00	116.66	0	0	2	0	2	0
First-class	200	276	22	6740	183	26.53	–	4	35	–	–	146	0

Bowling	M	Balls	Runs	Wkts	BB	Avge	RpO	S/R	5i	10m
Tests	24	6116	3001	113	6–65	26.55	2.94	54.12	9	1
ODIs	43	1902	1436	59	5–28	24.33	4.52	32.23	1	0
T20Is	20	402	435	30	3–14	14.50	6.49	13.40	0	0
First-class	200	35333	17608	553	7–33	31.84	2.99	63.89	24	4

SYED RASEL

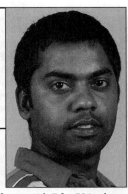

Full name	**Syed Rasel**
Born	**July 3, 1984, Jessore, Khulna**
Teams	**Khulna**
Style	**Left-hand bat, left-arm medium-pacer**
Test debut	**Bangladesh v Sri Lanka at Colombo 2005-06**
ODI debut	**Bangladesh v Sri Lanka at Colombo 2005-06**
T20I debut	**Bangladesh v Kenya at Nairobi 2007-08**

THE PROFILE A sensational spell of swing bowling for Bangladesh A at Canterbury in August 2005 propelled Syed Rasel into the international reckoning at the age of 21. He had missed the senior tour earlier in the season, but, having steadily developed his trade on a difficult five-week trip, Rasel tore through Kent's defences with 7 for 50 in the first innings, and finished with 10 for 91 in the match. It wasn't enough to win the game, but he was immediately drafted into the senior squad for the tour of Sri Lanka that followed in September, and he made his Test and one-day debuts there. With shades of Chaminda Vaas in his left-arm approach, Rasel took six wickets in his first two matches, including 4 for 129 in the second Test, which Bangladesh lost by an innings. Nevertheless, he soon had his revenge on home soil, taking 2 for 28 at Bogra the following February as Sri Lanka slumped to their first-ever one-day defeat at Bangladesh's hands. Rasel rose through the ranks from divisional cricket in his home province of Khulna, and his ability to swing the ball at a modest pace sets him apart from many of his rivals. He injured his foot in a motorbike accident shortly before the Champions Trophy in India in October 2006, but recovered to play, and did enough over the season to claim a World Cup place. He troubled many batsmen in the Caribbean with his left-arm approach, only once failing to take a wicket in seven starts, but took a step backwards in 2008, not helped when he dislocated his collarbone while fielding in New Zealand then injured his back in South Africa. He remained in the one-day mix throughout 2010, but hasn't played a Test since July 2007.

THE FACTS Fourteen of Syed Rasel's ODI wickets have come against Kenya (at 15.21), and 16 (at 34.37) against Sri Lanka ... He took 7 for 55 (11 for 109 in the match) for Khulna in Dhaka, and 8 for 67 at Barisal, both in 2003-04 ... Rasel's first four Tests – and his sixth – were all against Sri Lanka ... He was Muttiah Muralitharan's 700th Test wicket, at Kandy in July 2007 ...

THE FIGURES *to 23.9.10* ▄▄▄▄cricinfo.com

Batting & Fielding	M	Inns	NO	Runs	HS	Avge	S/R	100	50	4s	6s	Ct	St
Tests	6	12	4	37	19	4.62	38.94	0	0	6	0	0	0
ODIs	52	27	11	81	15	5.06	43.78	0	0	7	0	8	0
T20Is	8	3	1	7	6	3.50	77.77	0	0	1	0	1	0
First-class	49	76	23	691	54	13.03	47.68	0	1	–	–	11	0

Bowling	M	Balls	Runs	Wkts	BB	Avge	RpO	S/R	5i	10m
Tests	6	879	573	12	4–129	47.75	3.91	73.25	0	0
ODIs	52	2657	2051	61	4–22	33.62	4.63	43.55	0	0
T20Is	8	174	202	4	1–10	50.50	6.96	43.50	0	0
First-class	49	8241	4053	151	8–67	26.84	2.95	54.57	5	2

SHAUN **TAIT**

AUSTRALIA

Full name	**Shaun William Tait**
Born	**Feb 22, 1983, Bedford Park, Adelaide, South Australia**
Teams	**South Australia, Glamorgan, Rajasthan Royals**
Style	**Right-hand bat, right-arm fast bowler**
Test debut	**Australia v England at Nottingham 2005**
ODI debut	**Australia v England at Sydney 2006-07**
T20I debut	**Australia v New Zealand at Perth 2007-08**

THE PROFILE Shaun Tait's shoulder-strong action slung him on to the 2005 Ashes tour, where he played in two of the Tests, but it soon disrupted his quest for further impact. With a muscular but unrefined method that seems to invite pain, Tait returned from England only to hurt himself in a grade match. Shoulder surgery forced him out for the rest of the year, but there seemed to be no reduction in his frightening pace: an abbreviated 2005-06 included 6 for 41 in the domestic one-day final, an amazing combination of spot-on speed and 14 wides. His old-fashioned approach of yorkers and bumpers, mixed with a modern dose of reverse-swing, produced 65 wickets in 2004-05, earning him that Ashes trip. A hamstring twang delayed Tait's one-day entry, but despite mixed results at first (much speed, less accuracy) he was bravely taken to the 2007 World Cup, and was one of the stars in the Caribbean, blowing away 23 batsmen, more than anyone except Glenn McGrath. Again there was a cost: he needed elbow surgery later in 2007, and eventually withdrew from cricket altogether, citing physical and emotional exhaustion. He did not bowl a ball for six months, but remained determined to rediscover his mojo. By 2010 he was back, in limited-overs matches at least. He shook up the one-day series in England after being called up late, breaking the 100mph barrier and prompting calls for a recall for the Ashes series Down Under (his last first-class game had been late in 2008). Tait's first reaction was to say no. But it might be more tempting once the Poms reach Brisbane ...

THE FACTS Tait took 8 for 43 for South Australia v Tasmania at Adelaide in January 2004, the best figures in Australian domestic one-day cricket ... He played for Durham in 2004, bowling 21 no-balls in his first match, against Somerset, in figures of 12-0-113-0: in his second (and last) game the damage was 6-0-63-0 ... Tait took 23 wickets in the 2007 World Cup, equal with Muttiah Muralitharan and behind only Glenn McGrath (26) ... Tait took 7 for 29 (10 for 98 in the match) for South Australia v Queensland at Brisbane in December 2007 ...

THE FIGURES to 23.9.10   **ESPNcricinfo.com**

Batting & Fielding	M	Inns	NO	Runs	HS	Avge	S/R	100	50	4s	6s	Ct	St
Tests	3	5	2	20	8	6.66	43.47	0	0	4	0	1	0
ODIs	25	5	3	25	11	12.50	89.28	0	0	3	1	3	0
T20Is	17	5	1	10	6	2.50	83.33	0	0	0	1	3	0
First-class	50	70	29	509	68	12.41	51.36	0	2	–	–	15	0

Bowling	M	Balls	Runs	Wkts	BB	Avge	RpO	S/R	5i	10m
Tests	3	414	302	5	3–97	60.40	4.37	82.80	0	0
ODIs	25	1233	1060	46	4–39	23.04	5.15	26.80	0	0
T20Is	17	382	419	26	3–13	16.11	6.58	14.69	0	0
First-class	50	9263	5661	198	7–29	28.59	3.66	46.78	7	1

TAMIM IQBAL

Full name **Tamim Iqbal Khan**
Born **March 20, 1989, Chittagong**
Teams **Chittagong**
Style **Left-hand bat**
Test debut **Bangladesh v New Zealand at Dunedin 2007-08**
ODI debut **Bangladesh v Zimbabwe at Harare 2006-07**
T20I debut **Bangladesh v Kenya at Nairobi 2007-08**

THE PROFILE A flamboyant left-hander, Tamim Iqbal is one of Bangladesh's most assured young batsmen, and one of their hardest hitters. He is particularly strong square of the wicket, and has a good flick shot. Selected for the 2007 World Cup after just four ODIs Tamim lit up the start of the competition with 51 off 53 balls to ensure Bangladesh's successful pursuit of India's modest 191 got off to a flying start. Shrugging off a blow on the neck when he missed a hook at Zaheer Khan, Tamim jumped down the wicket and smashed him over midwicket for six. All this came three days before his 18th birthday. He struggled to reproduce this form afterwards: it wasn't until his 18th ODI, in July 2007, that he reached 50 again. But the following year he made a hundred against Ireland, then in August 2009 rounded off a consistent run by hammering 154 – a Bangladesh one-day record – against Zimbabwe. It was a similar story in Tests: great start (53 and 84 against New Zealand), quieter phase (17 innings with a best of 47), exciting flowering (128 as West Indies were beaten in St Vincent in July 2009). And by 2010 Tamim was clearly Bangladesh's star batsman: a superb 151 forced India to bat again despite amassing 554 at Mirpur, then twin eighties at home against England were followed by centuries in both Tests of the return series, at Lord's and Old Trafford. In ODIs he sometimes struggled to live up to his billing, although a coruscating 125 against England at Mirpur briefly threatened an upset, and the opposition's celebrations whenever he departed cheaply spoke volumes.

THE FACTS Tamim Iqbal hit 154, Bangladesh's highest score in ODIs, v Zimbabwe at Bulawayo in August 2009 ... He scored 53 and 84 on his Test debut, v New Zealand in Dunedin in January 2008 ... Only Sachin Tendulkar and Mohammad Ashraful reached 1000 Test runs at a younger age than Tamim (a week short of his 21st birthday in 2010) ... His brother, Nafees Iqbal, played 11 Tests and 16 ODIs for Bangladesh, while their uncle, Akram Khan, played eight Tests and 44 ODIs, and captained them in pre-Test days ...

THE FIGURES to 23.9.10   **ESPncricinfo.com**

Batting & Fielding	M	Inns	NO	Runs	HS	Avge	S/R	100	50	4s	6s	Ct	St
Tests	19	36	0	1445	151	40.13	61.43	4	8	200	10	8	0
ODIs	85	85	0	2478	154	29.15	78.66	3	15	290	32	25	0
T20Is	14	14	0	193	32	13.78	93.68	0	0	29	0	2	0
First-class	40	73	1	2928	151	40.66	–	6	20	–	–	20	0

Bowling	M	Balls	Runs	Wkts	BB	Avge	RpO	S/R	5i	10m
Tests	19	24	10	0	–	–	2.50	–	0	0
ODIs	85	6	13	0	–	–	13.00	–	0	0
T20Is	14	0	–	–	–	–	–	–	–	–
First-class	40	132	77	0	–	–	3.50	–	0	0

JEROME **TAYLOR**

WEST INDIES

Full name	**Jerome Everton Taylor**
Born	**June 22, 1984, St Elizabeth, Jamaica**
Teams	**Jamaica**
Style	**Right-hand bat, right-arm fast bowler**
Test debut	**West Indies v Sri Lanka at Gros Islet 2002-03**
ODI debut	**West Indies v Sri Lanka at Kingstown 2002-03**
T20I debut	**West Indies v South Africa at North Sound 2010**

THE PROFILE Jerome Taylor was just 18, with a solitary limited-overs game for Jamaica to his name, when he was chosen for the final one-dayer of the home series against Sri Lanka in June 2003. It was the culmination of an explosive first season: 21 wickets at 20.14 included 8 for 59 (and ten in the match) in Jamaica's five-wicket victory in Trinidad. After a back injury, he returned with 26 wickets at 16.61 in 2004-05. The inexperienced Zimbabweans found Taylor too hot to handle in the Caribbean early in 2006, and he continued his good form when the Indians arrived, taking three wickets in a consolation victory at the end of the one-day series, then collecting nine – including his first five-wicket haul – in vain in the deciding Test at Kingston. He took 13 wickets in the 2006-07 Champions Trophy, including a hat-trick against Australia, and showed occasional signs of fire in England the following summer, without much success, but did grab 19 wickets in four home Tests in 2008. He also blasted a maiden Test century in New Zealand later that year (rather a surprise, given his previous-best first-class score was just 40). By the time England arrived early in 2009 Taylor was the most menacing of the bowlers, starting with 5 for 11 as England crashed for 51 at Kingston, gifting West Indies the victory which ultimately won them the series. But various problems with his back and hip sent him home from Australia late in 2009 after bowling only nine overs in the first Test, and he made a tentative comeback six months later against South Africa. Fingers are crossed for a full recovery.

THE FACTS Taylor was 18 years 363 days old when he made his Test debut in June 2003 ... He scored his maiden first-class century in a Test, against New Zealand in Dunedin in December 2008: 34 people had previously done this, but only one other (New Zealander Bruce Taylor in 1964-65) had never even passed 50 before ... Taylor took an ODI hat-trick against Australia in the Champions Trophy in Mumbai in October 2006 ... He took 8 for 59 in only his third first-class game, for Jamaica v Trinidad & Tobago at Port-of-Spain in March 2003 ...

THE FIGURES to 23.9.10   ESPNcricinfo.com

Batting & Fielding	M	Inns	NO	Runs	HS	Avge	S/R	100	50	4s	6s	Ct	St
Tests	29	46	6	629	106	15.72	58.07	1	1	88	12	5	0
ODIs	66	30	7	204	43*	8.86	89.86	0	0	21	4	17	0
T20Is	17	9	5	47	16*	11.75	123.68	0	0	3	2	5	0
First-class	64	97	17	1085	106	13.56	–	1	1	–	–	15	0

Bowling	M	Balls	Runs	Wkts	BB	Avge	RpO	S/R	5i	10m
Tests	29	4935	2923	82	5–11	35.64	3.55	60.18	3	0
ODIs	66	3280	2629	98	5–48	26.82	4.80	33.46	1	0
T20Is	17	360	473	23	3–6	20.56	7.88	15.65	0	0
First-class	64	9995	5421	203	8–59	26.70	3.25	49.23	11	2

ROSS **TAYLOR**

Full name	**Luteru Ross Poutoa Lote Taylor**
Born	**March 8, 1984, Lower Hutt, Wellington**
Teams	**Central Districts, Durham, Bangalore Royal Challengers**
Style	**Right-hand bat, offspinner**
Test debut	**New Zealand v South Africa at Johannesburg 2007-08**
ODI debut	**New Zealand v West Indies at Napier 2005-06**
T20I debut	**New Zealand v Sri Lanka at Wellington 2006-07**

THE PROFILE Ross Taylor was singled out for attention from an early age – he captained New Zealand in the 2001-02 Under-19 World Cup – but it was some time before he made the big breakthrough. In March 2005 he extended his maiden first-class century to 184, then began the following season with a bang: five sixes in a century in a warm-up game against Otago were followed by 107 in a one-dayer, also against Otago, in January 2006. He then cracked 121 against Wellington, 114 off long-suffering Otago in the semi, then 50 in the final against Canterbury. Taylor rounded off a fine season with 106 as CD won the State Championship final at Wellington. It all led to a call-up for the final two ODIs of West Indies' tour early in 2006, and a regular place the following season. He flogged Sri Lanka – Murali and all – for an unbeaten 128 in only his third match, and showed that was no fluke with an equally muscular 117 against Australia at Auckland in February 2007. A belated Test debut followed against South Africa in November, and he hit 120 against England in his third match, before entrancing Old Trafford with an unbeaten 154 in the return series in 2008, during which he also took some fine catches in the slips. Taylor has been consistent ever since: he showed his Test pedigree with a fine 151 against India at Napier in March 2009, followed by 107 in the next Test at Wellington, before a defiant 138 against Australia at Hamilton a year later. He has also entertained the IPL's crowds with his big hitting.

THE FACTS Only two New Zealanders – Martin Donnelly and Bevan Congdon (twice) – have made higher Test scores in England than Taylor's 154 not out at Manchester in 2008 ... He and Jesse Ryder put on 271, a record for New Zealand's fourth wicket, against India at Napier in March 2009 ... Taylor made 217 for Central Districts v Otago at Napier in December 2006 ... He hit 66 from 22 balls in a Twenty20 match against Otago in January 2006 ...

THE FIGURES *to 23.9.10*   **ᴇsᴘɴcricinfo.com**

Batting & Fielding	M	Inns	NO	Runs	HS	Avge	S/R	100	50	4s	6s	Ct	St
Tests	25	46	1	1941	154*	43.13	62.55	5	9	270	21	45	0
ODIs	84	77	11	2376	128*	36.00	81.84	3	16	210	55	62	0
T20Is	34	31	2	590	63	20.34	115.91	0	3	36	26	22	0
First-class	71	120	3	4774	217	40.80	–	10	26	–	–	88	0

Bowling	M	Balls	Runs	Wkts	BB	Avge	RpO	S/R	5i	10m
Tests	25	32	14	0	–	–	2.62	–	0	0
ODIs	84	30	32	0	–	–	6.40	–	0	0
T20Is	34	0	–	–	–	–	–	–	–	–
First-class	71	602	330	4	2–34	82.50	3.28	150.50	0	0

SACHIN **TENDULKAR**

Full name	**Sachin Ramesh Tendulkar**
Born	**April 24, 1973, Bombay (now Mumbai)**
Teams	**Mumbai, Mumbai Indians**
Style	**Right-hand bat, occasional medium-pace/legspin**
Test debut	**India v Pakistan at Karachi 1989-90**
ODI debut	**India v Pakistan at Gujranwala 1989-90**
T20I debut	**India v South Africa at Johannesburg 2006-07**

THE PROFILE You only have to attend a one-dayer at the Wankhede Stadium, and watch the lights flicker and the floor tremble as the massive wave of applause echoes around the ground when he comes in, to realise what Sachin Tendulkar means to Mumbai ... and India. Age, and niggling injuries, may have dimmed the light a little – he's now more of an accumulator than an artist – but he is still light-footed with bat in hand, the nearest thing to Bradman, as The Don himself recognised before his death. Sachin seems to have been around for ever: that's because he made his Test debut at 16, shrugging off a blow on the head against Pakistan; captivated England in 1990, with a maiden Test century; and similarly enchanted Australia in 1991-92. Two more big hundreds lit up the 2007-08 series Down Under, and Tendulkar now has ten Test tons against the Aussies. He leads the list of ODI runscorers by a country mile, and owns the records for most runs, centuries and appearances in Tests too. Early in 2010 he stroked the first double-century in ODIs, against South Africa at Gwalior, and is closing in on 100 international centuries all told. Until he throttled back in his thirties, Tendulkar usually looked to attack, but his wicket still remains the one the opposition wants most. Small, steady at the crease before a decisive move forward or back, he remains a master, and his whipped flick to fine leg is an object of wonder. He could have starred as a bowler, as he can do offbreaks, legbreaks, or dobbly medium-pacers, and remains a handy option, especially in one-dayers.

THE FACTS Tendulkar passed his childhood idol Sunil Gavaskar's record of 34 Test centuries in December 2005: in seven Tests afterwards his highest score was 34 ... No-one is close to his 94 international centuries (Ricky Ponting is next with 68) ... Tendulkar has hit ten Test centuries against Australia, and nine in ODIs ... His first mention in *Wisden* came when he was 14, after a stand of 664 in a school game with another future Test batsman, Vinod Kambli ...

THE FIGURES *to 23.9.10* ᴇSᴘ̄ɴcricinfo.com

Batting & Fielding	M	Inns	NO	Runs	HS	Avge	S/R	100	50	4s	6s	Ct	St
Tests	169	276	29	13837	248*	56.02	–	48	56	–	57	106	0
ODIs	442	431	41	17598	200*	45.12	86.26	46	93	1927	185	134	0
T20Is	1	1	0	10	10	10.00	83.33	0	0	2	0	1	0
First-class	272	428	45	22730	248*	59.34	–	75	102	–	–	174	0

Bowling	M	Balls	Runs	Wkts	BB	Avge	RpO	S/R	5i	10m
Tests	169	3994	2299	44	3–10	52.25	3.45	90.77	0	0
ODIs	442	8020	6817	154	5–32	44.26	5.10	52.07	2	0
T20Is	1	15	12	1	1–12	12.00	4.80	15.00	0	0
First-class	272	7359	4191	69	3–10	60.73	3.41	106.65	0	0

UPUL **THARANGA**

Full name	**Warushavithana Upul Tharanga**
Born	**February 2, 1985, Balapitiya**
Teams	**Nondescripts, Ruhuna**
Style	**Left-hand bat, occasional wicketkeeper**
Test debut	**Sri Lanka v India at Ahmedabad 2005-06**
ODI debut	**Sri Lanka v West Indies at Dambulla 2005-06**
T20I debut	**Sri Lanka v England at Southampton 2006**

THE PROFILE   Upul Tharanga's call-up to Sri Lanka's one-day squad in July 2005 brightened a year marred by the Indian Ocean tsunami, which washed away his family home in Ambalangoda, a fishing town on the west coast. Tharanga, a wispy left-hander blessed with natural timing, had long been tipped for the big time, playing premier-league cricket at 15 and passing seamlessly through the national age-group squads. He first caught the eye during the Under-19 World Cup in 2004, with 117 against South Africa and 61 in 42 balls against India. He won his first one-day cap in August 2005, and hit 105 against Bangladesh in only his fifth match – he celebrated modestly, aware that stiffer challenges lay ahead – then pummelled 165 against them in his third Test. During 2006 he lit up Lord's with 120 in the first of what became five successive defeats of England: he added 109 in the fifth of those, at Headingley, sharing a record opening stand with Sanath Jayasuriya. The feature of those innings was the way he made room to drive through the off side. A bright future beckoned for Tharanga, and he scored consistently during 2006-07, playing throughout the World Cup and scoring 73 in the semi-final against New Zealand, before struggling the following season and losing his place. He emerged from the doldrums in 2008-09, passing 150 twice for the A team in South Africa then making his maiden double-century in a domestic match. In August 2009 he scored 76 in a one-dayer against New Zealand – his first international fifty for more than two years – celebrated with 80 in the next game, and has been just about an automatic 50-over choice ever since.

THE FACTS   Tharanga and Sanath Jayasuriya put on 286 in 31.5 overs against England at Leeds in July 2006, a first-wicket record for all ODIs ... He averages 47.60 in ODIs against England, but 11 v Australia (and 0 v Ireland) ... Tharanga carried his bat for 265 for Ruhuna v Basnahira South in March 2009 ... He scored 165 and 71 not out in the ten-wicket defeat of Bangladesh at Bogra in March 2006 ... His record includes one ODI for the Asia XI ...

THE FIGURES *to 23.9.10*
ESPNcricinfo.com

Batting & Fielding	M	Inns	NO	Runs	HS	Avge	S/R	100	50	4s	6s	Ct	St
Tests	15	26	1	713	165	28.52	49.51	1	3	99	5	11	0
ODIs	106	102	3	3246	120	32.78	73.30	8	17	382	16	19	0
T20Is	8	8	0	114	37	14.25	116.32	0	0	10	3	1	0
First-class	82	137	4	4720	265*	35.48	–	10	19	–	–	61	1

Bowling	M	Balls	Runs	Wkts	BB	Avge	RpO	S/R	5i	10m
Tests	15	0	–	–	–	–	–	–	–	–
ODIs	106	0	–	–	–	–	–	–	–	–
T20Is	8	0	–	–	–	–	–	–	–	–
First-class	82	18	4	0	–	–	1.33	–	0	0

GAVIN **TONGE**

Full name	**Gavin Courtney Tonge**
Born	**January 13, 1983, Antigua**
Teams	**Leeward Islands**
Style	**Right-hand bat, right-arm fast-medium bowler**
Test debut	**West Indies v Australia at Perth 2009-10**
ODI debut	**West Indies v Bangladesh at Roseau 2009**
T20I debut	**West Indies v Bangladesh at Basseterre 2009**

THE PROFILE Gavin Tonge, an enthusiastic fast-medium bowler from Antigua, was called up in mid-2009 when most of West Indies' senior players pulled out of the home series against Bangladesh during a contracts dispute. Tonge didn't play in the Tests, but was given a run in the one-dayers, without taking a wicket. He did rather better in the Champions Trophy that September, pitching the ball up intelligently and taking four wickets to reduce Pakistan to 61 for 4 at Johannesburg – he hit Mohammad Yousuf in the ribs then had him dropped at slip before finally getting him caught behind – but the patched-up West Indian side had made only 133, and the Pakistanis skated home in the end. Still, Tonge had done enough to make the tour of Australia at the end of the year when the seniors returned to the fold, and after injuries to other bowlers he won his first Test cap in the final match at Perth ... and made much more of a mark with bat than ball. He proved expensive in the first innings, and claimed the solitary wicket of Shane Watson in the second – but hung on for 39 exciting balls at No. 11 as West Indies inched towards an unlikely target of 359. He shared a last-wicket stand of 44 before Kemar Roach was controversially given out caught behind with his side still 36 short. Tonge had made his first-class debut at 19 in 2002-03, but his breakthrough season came in 2008-09, when his 44 wickets included a sparkling 7 for 58 in Jamaica.

THE FACTS Tonge took 7 for 58 (9 for 89 in the match) for Leeward Islands against Jamaica at Kingston in 2008-09 ... His four first-class five-fors all came in the space of two months early in 2009 – he finished the 2008-09 regional tournament with 44 wickets at 25.09 ... Tonge played in the 2001-02 Youth World Cup in a West Indies Under-19 side captained by Narsingh Deonarine and including Dwayne Bravo and Ravi Rampaul ...

THE FIGURES to 23.9.10   **ESPNcricinfo.com**

Batting & Fielding	M	Inns	NO	Runs	HS	Avge	S/R	100	50	4s	6s	Ct	St
Tests	1	2	1	25	23*	25.00	96.15	0	0	2	0	0	0
ODIs	5	4	2	10	5	5.00	62.50	0	0	1	0	0	0
T20Is	1	0	–	–	–	–	–	–	–	–	–	1	0
First-class	34	54	9	541	57	12.02	–	0	2	–	–	17	0

Bowling	M	Balls	Runs	Wkts	BB	Avge	RpO	S/R	5i	10m
Tests	1	168	113	1	1–28	113.00	4.03	168.00	0	0
ODIs	5	300	224	5	4–25	44.80	4.48	60.00	0	0
T20Is	1	24	25	1	1–25	25.00	6.25	24.00	0	0
First-class	34	4728	2794	95	7–58	29.41	3.54	49.76	4	0

THILAN **THUSHARA**

Full name	**Magina Thilan Thushara Mirando**
Born	**March 1, 1981, Balapitiya**
Teams	**Sinhalese Sports Club, Kandurata, Chennai Super Kings**
Style	**Left-hand bat, left-arm fast-medium bowler**
Test debut	**Sri Lanka v West Indies at Kingston 2003**
ODI debut	**Sri Lanka v West Indies at Gros Islet 2007-08**
T20I debut	**Sri Lanka v Zimbabwe at King City 2008-09**

THE PROFILE A left-arm seam bowler who bats a bit, Thilan Thushara Mirando served a long international apprenticeship behind the evergreen Chaminda Vaas. And in 2009, with Vaas finally creaking into well-earned retirement, Thushara seemed to have sealed a regular Test place at last. He took 12 wickets in the home series against Pakistan in July 2009, including 5 for 83 – his first five-for – in the third Test in Colombo (Vaas's farewell game). Six more wickets followed in the defeat of New Zealand at Galle in August. However, a shoulder injury hindered him in 2009-10, although he returned for the one-day tri-series in Zimbabwe in June. He hasn't yet matched Vaas's tenacity with the bat, although he does have a first-class century to his name and can give the ball a thump. Thushara hails from the coastal town of Balapitiya, and made his first-class debut as long ago as August 1999. After a few years of steady improvement, including a spell with the Sri Lankan Board's Fast Bowling Unit, he made his Test debut against West Indies in June 2003, but failed to take a wicket and dropped off the international radar for five years. In 2007-08 he was the leading wicket-taker as Kandurata shared the inter-provincial one-day title, and won a recall for another West Indian tour. This time he took five wickets in the Test victory in Guyana, and three more (including Chris Gayle in both innings) as West Indies squared the series in Trinidad. He also made his ODI debut there, and formed an incisive new-ball pairing with Nuwan Kulasekara in 50-overs matches. Thushara took 5 for 47 in vain against India in Colombo in August 2008.

THE FACTS Thushara took 6 for 50 (10 for 86 in the match) for Sinhalese Sports Club v Chilaw Marians in Colombo in March 2008 ... He scored 103 not out (from 81 balls, after coming in at 98 for 7) for Nondescripts v Burgher RC in Colombo in January 2003 ... Thushara took his first Test wicket almost five years after his debut ...

THE FIGURES to 23.9.10   ᴇꜱᴘⁿcricinfo.com

Batting & Fielding	M	Inns	NO	Runs	HS	Avge	S/R	100	50	4s	6s	Ct	St
Tests	9	13	2	90	15*	8.18	45.68	0	0	12	0	3	0
ODIs	38	27	6	392	54*	18.66	92.45	0	1	32	9	4	0
T20Is	6	2	0	4	3	2.00	50.00	0	0	0	0	2	0
First-class	99	146	15	2032	103*	15.51	–	1	6	–	–	38	0

Bowling	M	Balls	Runs	Wkts	BB	Avge	RpO	S/R	5i	10m
Tests	9	1542	961	28	5–83	34.32	3.73	55.07	1	0
ODIs	38	1676	1393	50	5–47	27.86	4.98	33.52	1	0
T20Is	6	132	179	7	2–37	25.57	8.13	18.85	0	0
First-class	99	12698	7536	256	6–50	29.43	3.56	49.60	8	1

ENGLAND

JAMES **TREDWELL**

Full name	**James Cullum Tredwell**
Born	**February 27, 1982, Ashford, Kent**
Teams	**Kent**
Style	**Left-hand bat, offspinner**
Test debut	**England v Bangladesh at Mirpur 2009-10**
ODI debut	**England v Bangladesh at Mirpur 2009-10**
T20I debut	**No T20Is yet**

THE PROFILE James "Pingu" Tredwell has made steady progress since making his debut for Kent in 2001. Initially seen as a containing off-spinner in one-day cricket, it took him a while to establish himself in the Championship side. When he did that, in 2007, he was soon making his way steadily up the batting order: pushed up to No. 4 he made his maiden century against Yorkshire at Tunbridge Wells. He made another hundred against the New Zealand tourists from first drop the following year, and, now settled around No. 7 in the order, reminded the selectors of his batting prowess with 115 against eventual champions Nottinghamshire in June 2010. Tredwell had a place at the ECB National Academy in 2003-04, and made the England Performance Squad in the winter of 2007. The following year he was part of England's one-day squad in New Zealand, although he didn't get a game, but 69 Championship wickets in 2009 kept him in the frame. He was called up as cover for Graeme Swann during England's tour of South Africa that winter, and although he again did not feature in the internationals, his consistent performances booked him a place for the tour of Bangladesh which followed. Finally he won an England cap: after a quiet one-day debut he played in the second Test at Mirpur, dismissed the danger men Tamim Iqbal and Shakib Al Hasan in the first innings, and followed that with four more in the second. However, with Swann having an excellent year, chances were limited after that, although Tredwell looks set to feature in England's one-day plans.

THE FACTS Tredwell took 8 for 66 for Kent v Glamorgan at Canterbury in May 2009 ... He scored 123 not out for Kent against the New Zealanders at Canterbury in April 2008, sharing an unbroken stand of 299 with Robert Key ... Tredwell took 7 for 22, including a hattrick, as Kent beat Yorkshire at Leeds in September 2010 ...

THE FIGURES to 23.9.10   **ESPN cricinfo.com**

Batting & Fielding	M	Inns	NO	Runs	HS	Avge	S/R	100	50	4s	6s	Ct	St
Tests	1	1	0	37	37	37.00	58.73	0	0	6	0	1	0
ODIs	2	1	1	2	2*	–	28.57	0	0	0	0	0	0
T20Is	0	0	–	–	–	–	–	–	–	–	v	–	–
First-class	101	145	19	3005	123*	23.84	42.83	3	13	–	–	106	0

Bowling	M	Balls	Runs	Wkts	BB	Avge	RpO	S/R	5i	10m
Tests	1	390	181	6	4–82	30.16	2.78	65.00	0	0
ODIs	2	78	70	0	–	–	5.38	–	0	0
T20Is	0	0	–	–	–	–	–	–	–	–
First-class	101	18033	9534	267	8–66	35.70	3.17	67.53	9	3

CHRIS **TREMLETT**

Full name	**Christopher Timothy Tremlett**
Born	**September 2, 1981, Southampton, Hampshire**
Teams	**Surrey**
Style	**Right-hand bat, right-arm fast-medium bowler**
Test debut	**England v India at Lord's 2007**
ODI debut	**England v Bangladesh at Nottingham 2005**
T20I debut	**England v India at Durban 2006-07**

THE PROFILE Chris Tremlett has the silent, simmering looks – and impressive sideburns – of a baddie in a spaghetti western, and bangs the ball down from an impressive height at an impressive speed. He has a fine cricket pedigree: his grandfather captained Somerset and played for England, while his father also played for Hampshire. But this Tremlett needed no nepotism: he took 4 for 16 on his first-class debut in 2000, and has rarely looked back since, halted only occasionally by niggling injuries (growing pains, perhaps – he's now 6ft 7ins/201cm). As he matured he was one of the first chosen for the England Academy, and narrowly missed selection for the 2004 Champions Trophy. The following year he almost marked his ODI debut at Trent Bridge with a hat-trick – the vital ball fell on the stumps without dislodging a bail – then was 12th man in the first four Tests of the epic Ashes series before loss of rhythm led to loss of form. As England's pacemen hit the treatment table in 2007 Tremlett finally got the call. He used his height well, and collected 13 wickets in three Tests against India, including Laxman three times, Dravid and Tendulkar. A side strain forced him home early from New Zealand that winter, after which, amid whispers about his temperament, Tremlett became something of a back number. A move to Surrey in 2010 seemed to revitalise him: he immediately looked more threatening, and finished the season with 48 wickets at 20, a vast improvement on 2009 (14 at 40). "I've never bowled as well as I have this season," said Tremlett – and the selectors agreed, naming him in the squad for the Ashes tour.

THE FACTS Tremlett's grandfather, Maurice, played three Tests for England in 1948: his father, Tim, played for Hampshire ... Chris took two wickets in successive balls on his ODI debut, against Bangladesh in June 2005: the hat-trick ball bounced on top of the stumps but didn't dislodge the bails ... He bagged a pair on his Test debut in July 2007, the first person ever to do this at Lord's ... Tremlett took 6 for 44 for Hampshire v Sussex at Hove in April 2005 ...

THE FIGURES *to 23.9.10*   **ESPncricinfo.com**

Batting & Fielding	M	Inns	NO	Runs	HS	Avge	S/R	100	50	4s	6s	Ct	St
Tests	3	5	1	50	25*	12.50	43.85	0	0	5	0	1	0
ODIs	9	6	2	38	19*	9.50	58.46	0	0	2	1	2	0
T20Is	1	0	–	–	–	–	–	–	–	–	–	–	–
First-class	104	139	37	1868	64	18.31	–	0	7	–	–	28	0

Bowling	M	Balls	Runs	Wkts	BB	Avge	RpO	S/R	5i	10m
Tests	3	859	386	13	3–12	29.69	2.69	66.07	0	0
ODIs	9	479	419	9	4–32	46.55	5.24	53.22	0	0
T20Is	1	24	45	2	2–45	22.50	11.25	12.00	0	0
First-class	104	17552	9252	337	6–44	27.45	3.16	52.08	7	0

JONATHAN **TROTT**

ENGLAND

Full name **Ian Jonathan Leonard Trott**
Born **April 22, 1981, Cape Town, South Africa**
Teams **Warwickshire**
Style **Right-hand bat, right-arm medium-pacer**
Test debut **England v Australia at The Oval 2009**
ODI debut **England v Ireland at Belfast 2009**
T20I debut **England v West Indies at The Oval 2007**

THE PROFILE The story sounds familiar: aggressive right-hander, born in South Africa, reputation for cockiness on the county circuit. But no, we're not talking Kevin Pietersen here, rather Jonathan Trott, who moved to England (after playing for South Africa in the Under-19 World Cup) in 2003. His grandparents were British, which meant he could play as a non-overseas player for Warwickshire, although he didn't actually become eligible for England until 2006. He was consistent from the start, following up 763 runs from ten matches in 2003 by passing 1000 in each of the next three seasons. His form dipped in 2007 – only 473 runs at 22 – although, contrarily, he was a left-field pick for England's two Twenty20 games against West Indies that summer. Trott managed only 9 and 2, and returned post haste to county cricket. But he was back to form in 2008 (1240 runs at 62), and when he continued to make runs in 2009, in an eye-catchingly forthright manner, he was named in the squad for the fourth Ashes Test. He didn't play there, but retained his place for the vital final Test at The Oval after Ravi Bopara was dropped. The selectors' bravery in sticking with Trott (the first to make his debut for England in an Ashes decider since 1896) was repaid in spades with a nerveless century. After a quiet time in South Africa, where he was possibly unsettled by jibes about his nationality and his deliberate preparations before facing each ball, Trott returned to form with 226 against Bangladesh in May 2010, and when Pakistan visited he added 184, sharing a Test-record eighth-wicket stand of 332 with Stuart Broad.

THE FACTS Trott was the 18th batsman to score a century on Test debut for England: the previous three (Alastair Cook, Matt Prior and Andrew Strauss) were also playing against Australia at The Oval in 2009 ... In two Tests at Lord's in 2010 Trott scored 226 v Bangladesh and 184 v Pakistan, when he shared a Test-record eighth-wicket stand of 332 with Stuart Broad ... Trott took 7 for 39 for Warwickshire v Kent in September 2003 ...

THE FIGURES to 23.9.10   **ESPN**cricinfo.com

Batting & Fielding	M	Inns	NO	Runs	HS	Avge	S/R	100	50	4s	6s	Ct	St
Tests	13	23	2	1155	226	55.00	47.39	3	4	125	0	8	0
ODIs	11	11	1	483	110	48.30	74.65	1	5	42	0	3	0
T20Is	7	7	1	138	51	23.00	95.83	0	1	9	3	0	0
First-class	153	257	31	10183	226	45.05	–	23	51	–	–	148	0

Bowling	M	Balls	Runs	Wkts	BB	Avge	RpO	S/R	5i	10m
Tests	13	114	86	1	1–16	86.00	4.52	114.00	0	0
ODIs	11	66	47	0	–	–	4.27	–	0	0
T20Is	7	0	–	–	–	–	–	–	–	–
First-class	153	4358	2471	56	7–39	44.12	3.40	77.82	1	0

LONWABO **TSOTSOBE**

Full name	**Lonwabo Lopsy Tsotsobe**
Born	**March 7, 1984, Port Elizabeth**
Teams	**Warriors**
Style	**Right-hand bat, left-arm fast-medium**
Test debut	**South Africa v West Indies at Port-of-Spain 2010**
ODI debut	**South Africa v Australia at Perth 2008-09**
T20I debut	**South Africa v Australia at Melbourne 2008-09**

THE PROFILE A tall left-arm swing bowler, Lonwabo Tsotsobe had a dream start to his one-day international career in Australia in January 2009, when he had Shaun Marsh caught at midwicket, and a couple of overs later removed Ricky Ponting caught behind. Later on he nabbed Mike Hussey and Mitchell Johnson as well, to finish with debut figures of 4 for 50 as South Africa romped to a 4-1 series victory which helped them pinch the No. 1 one-day ranking from the Aussies. This put him in the frame for a Test cap when the Australians visited South Africa shortly afterwards, but after being named in the 12 for the second Test Tsotsobe was forced to withdraw with knee-cartilage damage, which kept him on the sidelines for the rest of the season. In his absence his Warriors team-mate Wayne Parnell, who is a bit quicker through the air and a better batsman, took the chance to claim a one-day place, and he could well prove a formidable obstacle to a regular spot. But in the West Indies early in 2010, with Parnell injured, Tsotsobe did well in the one-dayers and played two of the Tests, although without making much impact. He had made his first-class debut for Eastern Province in 2004-05, taking 7 for 44 in his first match. He moved up a notch to play for the Warriors in 2006-07, and again did well, following a solid debut season for them with 49 wickets at 23.59 the following summer, before 12 wickets in two matches against Sri Lanka A in September 2008 earned him that trip to Australia.

THE FACTS Tsotsobe took 7 for 44 (9 for 96 in the match) on his first-class debut for Eastern Province against Boland at Paarl in November 2004, and took 10 for 72 in the match for EP v South Western Districts in Port Elizabeth in October 2006 ... He took 7 for 39 for Warriors v Lions at Johannesburg in October 2007 ... Tsotsobe's first victim in both Twenty20 internationals and ODIs was the Australian batsman Shaun Marsh ...

THE FIGURES to 23.9.10   **ESPNcricinfo.com**

Batting & Fielding	M	Inns	NO	Runs	HS	Avge	S/R	100	50	4s	6s	Ct	St
Tests	2	1	1	3	3*	–	16.66	0	0	0	0	0	0
ODIs	8	1	1	4	4*	–	200.00	0	0	1	0	4	0
T20Is	2	1	0	1	1	1.00	14.28	0	0	0	0	0	0
First-class	48	62	26	225	27*	6.25	29.72	0	0	28	3	11	0

Bowling	M	Balls	Runs	Wkts	BB	Avge	RpO	S/R	5i	10m
Tests	2	294	106	2	1–20	53.00	2.16	147.00	0	0
ODIs	8	382	338	15	4–50	22.53	5.30	25.46	0	0
T20Is	2	36	44	1	1–16	44.00	7.33	36.00	0	0
First-class	48	8021	4056	165	7–39	24.58	3.03	48.61	5	1

DARYL **TUFFEY**

Full name	**Daryl Raymond Tuffey**
Born	**June 11, 1978, Milton, Otago**
Teams	**Auckland**
Style	**Right-hand bat, right-arm fast-medium bowler**
Test debut	**New Zealand v Australia at Hamilton 1999-2000**
ODI debut	**New Zealand v Zimbabwe at Harare 2000-01**
T20I debut	**New Zealand v Australia at Auckland 2004-05**

THE PROFILE Big Daryl Tuffey has made a surprising comeback to New Zealand colours, resurrecting an international career that looked over after the 2007 World Cup. Tuffey seemed to have burned his bridges by joining the unauthorised Indian Cricket League soon after that, but when an amnesty was declared in mid-2009 he was suddenly back in the national reckoning, after taking 27 wickets in the 2008-09 domestic season for Auckland, his best return since 34 in 2000-01. He was chosen for the tour of Sri Lanka in September, and although he sat out the Tests (despite taking 5 for 53 against Sri Lanka A in a warm-up game), he played in some of the one-dayers – taking a wicket in the first over on his return, continuing a happy knack he had established earlier his career – and, back home, resumed his Test career after a gap of five and a half years in decent style, taking 11 wickets in his first three matches, against Pakistan and Bangladesh. In the first part of his international career Tuffey, a strapping fast-medium bowler in the style of Richard Hadlee's long-time partner Ewen Chatfield, had proved an admirable foil for Shane Bond – slower, but more durable. His best Test performance remains a probing 6 for 54 at Auckland to help New Zealand square the home series against England in 2001-02. After that Tuffey was a regular member of both the Test and one-day sides for a while, before injuries started to impinge, notably a serious shoulder problem which kept him out for almost two years.

THE FACTS Tuffey took 7 for 12 (11 for 66 in the match) for Northern Districts against Wellington at Hamilton in February 2001: he took the first six wickets as Wellington stumbled to 29 for 6 ... His best Test figures are 6 for 54, against England at Auckland in March 2002: the previous week he took 7 for 60 for ND against Canterbury at Christchurch ...

THE FIGURES *to 23.9.10*   **ESPNcricinfo.com**

Batting & Fielding	M	Inns	NO	Runs	HS	Avge	S/R	100	50	4s	6s	Ct	St
Tests	26	36	10	427	80*	16.42	42.52	0	1	46	4	15	0
ODIs	92	50	21	291	36	10.03	79.50	0	0	23	7	20	0
T20Is	3	2	1	5	5*	5.00	100.00	0	0	1	0	0	0
First-class	84	100	25	1232	89*	16.42	–	0	6	–	–	37	0

Bowling	M	Balls	Runs	Wkts	BB	Avge	RpO	S/R	5i	10m
Tests	26	4877	2445	77	6–54	31.75	3.00	63.33	2	0
ODIs	92	4248	3447	106	4–24	32.51	4.86	40.07	0	0
T20Is	3	60	93	3	2–16	31.00	9.30	20.00	0	0
First-class	84	15664	7282	280	7–12	26.00	2.78	55.94	10	1

UMAR AKMAL

Full name	**Mohammad Umar Akmal**
Born	**May 26, 1990, Lahore, Punjab**
Teams	**Lahore, Sui Northern Gas**
Style	**Right-hand batsman**
Test debut	**Pakistan v New Zealand at Dunedin 2009-10**
ODI debut	**Pakistan v Sri Lanka at Dambulla 2009**
T20I debut	**Pakistan v Sri Lanka at Colombo 2009**

THE PROFILE Umar Akmal, the youngest brother of wicketkeeper Kamran Akmal, started his international career with a flourish in 2009. Only 19, he hit a run-a-ball 66 in only his second one-dayer, against Sri Lanka at Dambulla, and bettered that with a superb maiden century to earn a consolation victory in the fourth match in Colombo. An attacking right-hander, he entered in that innings with Pakistan a wobbly 130 for 4 in the 26th over, and hurtled to his hundred from just 70 balls. He outscored Younis Khan in a stand of 176, appearing comfortable from the start. He refused to be tied down, swinging his seventh delivery – from Ajantha Mendis – over long-on for the first of four sixes. Intikhab Alam, Pakistan's then coach, observed: "He accepts challenges, and to hit Lasith Malinga over his head for a six is not a joke. You've got to have a lot of ability to do that." In November 2009 he marked his Test debut, against New Zealand at Dunedin, with 129 and 75, and he continued to look the part throughout 2010, scoring consistently in all three formats, although impetuosity often got the better of him and big scores were elusive. Akmal's international start mirrored his domestic one. In a triumphant 2007-08 season, he amassed 855 runs at 77.72 in nine Quaid-e-Azam Trophy matches, at an impressive strike-rate of 90.18. He extended his maiden century – in his sixth match – to 248 (off 225 balls) against Karachi Blues, and two matches later clattered 186 not out from 170 balls against Quetta. Three centuries followed for Pakistan A in Australia before he joined Kamran in the Pakistan line-up.

THE FACTS Umar Akmal made 129 and 75 on his Test debut, against New Zealand at Dunedin in November 2009: only KS Ranjitsinhji, with 216 for England v Australia in 1896, scored more runs in his debut Test yet finished on the losing side ... Umar made 248 for Sui Northern Gas v Karachi Blues in December 2007, and later that month hit 186 not out against Quetta at Lahore ... He hit a century, from only 70 balls, in his fourth one-day international, against Sri Lanka in Colombo in August 2009 ...

THE FIGURES to 23.9.10   ESPNcricinfo.com

Batting & Fielding	M	Inns	NO	Runs	HS	Avge	S/R	100	50	4s	6s	Ct	St
Tests	12	24	2	818	129	37.18	68.97	1	5	103	14	7	0
ODIs	23	23	3	724	102*	36.20	82.93	1	5	54	8	7	0
T20Is	16	15	3	455	64	37.91	127.80	0	4	32	16	11	0
First-class	42	72	7	3061	248	47.09	72.93	7	18	382	48	34	0

Bowling	M	Balls	Runs	Wkts	BB	Avge	RpO	S/R	5i	10m
Tests	12	0	–	–	–	–	–	–	–	–
ODIs	23	0	–	–	–	–	–	–	–	–
T20Is	16	0	–	–	–	–	–	–	–	–
First-class	42	6	10	0	–	–	10.00	–	0	0

UMAR GUL

Full name	**Umar Gul**
Born	**April 14, 1984, Peshawar, North-Western Frontier Province**
Teams	**Peshawar, Habib Bank**
Style	**Right-hand bat, right-arm fast-medium bowler**
Test debut	**Pakistan v Bangladesh at Karachi 2003-04**
ODI debut	**Pakistan v Zimbabwe at Sharjah 2002-03**
T20I debut	**Pakistan v Kenya at Nairobi 2007-08**

THE PROFILE Umar Gul was called up by Pakistan at 19, after their miserable 2003 World Cup campaign. He usually keeps a good line, and obtains appreciable outswing with the new ball, while he can also nip the ball back in. He had a gentle introduction to Test cricket against Bangladesh before starring against India at Lahore in April 2004. Disparaged by some as the "Peshawar Rickshaw" to Shoaib Akhtar's "Rawalpindi Express", Gul tore through India's imposing top order, moving the ball both ways off the seam at a sharp pace. His 5 for 31 gave Pakistan the early initiative, and they went on to level the series. Stress fractures in the back kept him out for two years after that, but he stepped up in the absence of several senior seamers in England in 2006, particularly enjoying the conditions at Headingley, with five first-innings wickets. He maintained his progress in 2006-07, taking nine wickets against West Indies at Lahore before missing the South African tour with a knee injury. He was back for the World Cup, and was one of the few to return with reputation intact, but more injuries restricted him before he started 2009 in fine fettle with a six-for against Sri Lanka on a batting paradise at Lahore. He has proved a Twenty20 star, usually coming on after the initial overs and firing in yorkers on demand. He was the leading wicket-taker at both the 2007 and 2009 World Twenty20s, and it was a blow when a shoulder injury ruled him out of the 2010 version. But he was back in England later in the year, revealing unexpected talent with the bat and bowling with his old fire.

THE FACTS Umar Gul was the first bowler to take five wickets in a Twenty20 international, with 5 for 6 v New Zealand at The Oval in June 2009: he also took 4 for 8 v Australia in Dubai in May 2009 ... He took 8 for 78 for Peshawar v Karachi Urban at Peshawar in October 2005 ... Gul claimed 5 for 46 on his first-class debut, for Pakistan International Airlines v ADBP at Karachi in his only match in 2000-01, then took 45 wickets at 18.62 in 2001-02, his first full season of domestic cricket ...

THE FIGURES *to 23.9.10* ᴇssɴ**cricinfo**.com

Batting & Fielding	M	Inns	NO	Runs	HS	Avge	S/R	100	50	4s	6s	Ct	St
Tests	30	44	6	421	65*	11.07	50.23	0	1	46	16	7	0
ODIs	74	36	10	241	33	9.26	61.79	0	0	21	5	9	0
T20Is	30	11	6	56	16	11.20	127.27	0	0	2	4	10	0
First-class	61	78	12	864	65*	13.09	–	0	1	–	–	15	0

Bowling	M	Balls	Runs	Wkts	BB	Avge	RpO	S/R	5i	10m
Tests	30	6144	3639	108	6–135	33.69	3.55	56.88	4	0
ODIs	74	3578	3056	115	6–42	26.57	5.12	31.11	2	0
T20Is	30	625	640	47	5–6	13.61	6.14	13.29	1	0
First-class	61	11783	6844	249	8–78	27.48	3.48	47.32	14	1

ROELOF **VAN DER MERWE**

Full name	**Roelof Erasmus van der Merwe**
Born	**December 31, 1984, Johannesburg, Transvaal**
Teams	**Titans, Bangalore Royal Challengers**
Style	**Right-hand bat, slow left-arm orthodox spinner**
Test debut	**No Tests yet**
ODI debut	**South Africa v Australia at Centurion 2008-09**
20I debut	**South Africa v Australia at Centurion 2008-09**

THE PROFILE Roelof van der Merwe is that modern phenomenon, a limited-overs specialist – and his particular speciality is Twenty20 cricket. He is a curious mix: a blacksmith of a batsman, whose main idea is to smash the ball as far as possible, but a tidy left-arm spinner who keeps it tight. He played in the Under-19 World Cup in 2004 before starting a modest first-class career with Northerns (he started with a duck, and still hasn't managed a hundred or a five-for). But he soon made his presence felt in one-day cricket, leading the wicket-takers in the domestic 45-over championship after moving to the Titans for 2007-08. Titans won that and the Standard Bank Pro20 series, and van der Merwe was named player of the year, among a clutch of other awards. The following season he took 30 wickets – 14 more than anyone else – as Titans retained their 45-over title, and was called up for the two Twenty20 games against Australia at home in March 2009. In the first one, at Centurion, he picked up the match award after biffing 48 from 30 balls, with four sixes (oddly, he's hardly batted since), and taking a wicket. He then played a big part in South Africa's march to the semi-finals of the World Twenty20 in England, keeping his economy rate below six an over, although his big hitting was more hit-and-miss. Before that he had helped Bangalore Royal Challengers to the final of the second IPL tournament, held in South Africa. He played only once in the 2010 competition, though, amid signs that his novelty value might be wearing off.

THE FACTS van der Merwe scored 48, took a wicket and effected a run-out to clinch the match award on his Twenty20 international debut against Australia at Centurion in March 2009 ... He made 81 for Northerns v North West in February 2009 ... In a Twenty20 game for Titans v Zimbabwe at Centurion in April 2008 van der Merwe took 3 for 18 then scored 70 not out ... He took 5 for 31, and then made 64 not out from 42 balls, as Titans beat Cape Cobras in a 45-over semi-final at Centurion in January 2009 ...

THE FIGURES to 23.9.10   **ᴇsᴨ cricinfo.com**

Batting & Fielding	M	Inns	NO	Runs	HS	Avge	S/R	100	50	4s	6s	Ct	St
Tests	0	0	–	–	–	–	–	–	–	–	–	–	–
ODIs	13	7	3	39	12	9.75	95.12	0	0	3	2	3	0
20Is	13	6	3	57	48	19.00	114.00	0	0	2	4	6	0
First-class	16	23	5	569	81	31.61	65.02	0	3	62	7	9	0

Bowling	M	Balls	Runs	Wkts	BB	Avge	RpO	S/R	5i	10m
Tests	0	0	–	–	–	–	–	–	–	–
ODIs	13	705	561	17	3–27	33.00	4.77	41.47	0	0
20Is	13	264	305	14	2–14	21.78	6.93	18.85	0	0
First-class	16	2273	1168	30	4–59	38.93	3.08	75.76	2	0

DANIEL **VETTORI**

Full name	**Daniel Luca Vettori**
Born	**January 27, 1979, Auckland**
Teams	**Northern Districts, Delhi Daredevils**
Style	**Left-hand bat, left-arm orthodox spinner**
Test debut	**New Zealand v England at Wellington 1996-97**
ODI debut	**New Zealand v Sri Lanka at Christchurch 1996-97**
T20I debut	**New Zealand v Kenya at Durban 2007-08**

THE PROFILE Daniel Vettori is probably the best left-arm spinner around – an assessment reinforced by his selection for the World XI in Australia late in 2005 – and the only cloud on his horizon is a susceptibility to injury, particularly in the bowler's danger area of the back. He seemed to have recovered from one stress fracture, which led to a dip in form in 2003, but after a couple of matches for Warwickshire in 2006 he was on the plane home nursing another one. Vettori has usually been fit since, though, which is just as well for New Zealand as he carries a huge burden these days as their captain, key batsman and senior bowler who, late in 2009, became the first slow left-armer to reach 300 Test wickets. His early Tests in charge were notable for some superb personal performances – two fifties and nine wickets to stave off an embarrassing defeat by Bangladesh in October 2008, and two similar allround efforts which could not prevent defeat in Sri Lanka the following August. Vettori still has the enticing flight and guile that made him New Zealand's youngest Test player at 18 in 1996-97, and he remains economical in 50- and 20-over games. After his mini-slump he returned to form in England in 2004, then butchered Bangladesh with 20 wickets in two Tests. He has improved his batting – after starting at No. 11, blinking nervously through his glasses – to the point that his five centuries include New Zealand's fastest in Tests, an 82-ball effort against the admittedly hopeless Zimbabweans at Harare in August 2005.

THE FACTS Vettori made his first-class debut in 1996-97, for Northern Districts against the England tourists: his maiden first-class victim was Nasser Hussain ... Three weeks later Vettori became NZ's youngest-ever Test player, at 18 years 10 days: his first wicket was Hussain again ... Vettori averages 23.62 with the ball in Tests against Sri Lanka, but 54.64 v Pakistan and 54.80 v India ... His record includes a Test and four ODIs for the World XI ...

THE FIGURES to 23.9.10   ESᴘᴨcricinfo.com

Batting & Fielding	M	Inns	NO	Runs	HS	Avge	S/R	100	50	4s	6s	Ct	St
Tests	100	152	23	3962	140	30.71	57.91	5	22	492	13	55	0
ODIs	255	160	49	1895	83	17.07	82.57	0	4	142	13	71	0
T20Is	28	20	6	187	38	13.35	109.35	0	0	13	2	8	0
First-class	152	220	31	5809	140	30.73	–	8	32	–	–	79	0

Bowling	M	Balls	Runs	Wkts	BB	Avge	RpO	S/R	5i	10m
Tests	100	24997	11007	325	7–87	33.86	2.64	76.91	18	3
ODIs	255	12111	8367	268	5–7	31.22	4.14	45.19	2	0
T20Is	28	649	580	35	4–20	16.57	5.36	18.54	0	0
First-class	152	35722	15920	499	7–87	31.90	2.67	71.58	28	3

MURALI **VIJAY**

Full name	**Murali Vijay Krishna**
Born	**April 1, 1984, Chennai**
Teams	**Tamil Nadu, Chennai Super Kings**
Style	**Right-hand bat, occasional offspinner**
Test debut	**India v Australia at Nagpur 2008-09**
ODI debut	**No ODIs yet**
T20I debut	**India v Afghanistan at Gros Islet 2008-09**

THE PROFILE All batsmen want to go into their first Test in good form, and Murali Vijay was in better nick than most: when Gautam Gambhir was banned against Australia in November 2008, Vijay was hoicked out of Tamil Nadu's Ranji Trophy game against Maharashtra after making 243. While the Ranji game went on without him, Vijay made a very sound debut at Nagpur, sharing useful opening stands of 98 and 116 with Virender Sehwag as India set about what became a series-clinching 172-run victory. Vijay helped in the field too, running out Matthew Hayden (an IPL team-mate) and Michael Hussey, and also taking a catch at short leg. Once Gambhir returned Vijay sat out the Tests in New Zealand early in 2009, but later that year made 87 in an opening stand of 221 with Sehwag against Sri Lanka in Mumbai. His next five Tests did not produce anything special, but he remained a consistent runscorer for Tamil Nadu – and upped his game in the 2010 IPL, hammering a 46-ball hundred against Rajasthan Royals, and 458 runs overall as Chennai Super Kings lifted the title for the first time. Tall and solid, Vijay was an instant success in first-class cricket, despite being a late starter (he only switched to "proper" cricket from the soft-ball variety at 17, so missed the usual age-group progression): he hit 179 against Andhra in his second match, and finished his first season (2006-07) with 628 runs at 52 – only two others made more. An indication of his class came when there was no second-season dip: 2007-08 brought him 667 runs, including a double-century against Saurashtra.

THE FACTS Vijay made 243 for Tamil Nadu v Maharashtra in November 2008, sharing an opening stand of 462 with Abhinav Mukund, who made 300 ... Vijay also scored 230 not out for Tamil Nadu v Saurashtra in December 2007: this time the opening stand with Mukund was worth 256 ... He hit a 46-ball century against Rajasthan Royals in the 2010 IPL ... Vijay made 179 against Andhra in his second first-class match, in December 2006 ...

THE FIGURES to 23.9.10 · ESPNcricinfo.com

Batting & Fielding	M	Inns	NO	Runs	HS	Avge	S/R	100	50	4s	6s	Ct	St
Tests	7	10	0	333	87	33.30	52.52	0	2	39	1	6	0
ODIs	4	4	0	71	25	17.75	61.20	0	0	7	0	3	0
T20Is	6	6	0	108	48	18.00	96.42	0	0	5	6	3	0
First-class	38	61	2	3033	243	51.40	49.56	7	14	357	43	40	0

Bowling	M	Balls	Runs	Wkts	BB	Avge	RpO	S/R	5i	10m
Tests	7	0	–	–	–	–	–	–	–	–
ODIs	4	0	–	–	–	–	–	–	–	–
T20Is	6	0	–	–	–	–	–	–	–	–
First-class	38	186	118	1	1–16	118.00	3.80	186.00	0	0

ADAM **VOGES**

AUSTRALIA

Full name	**Adam Charles Voges**
Born	**October 4, 1979, Subiaco, Perth, Western Australia**
Teams	**Western Australia, Rajasthan Royals**
Style	**Right-hand bat, left-arm unorthodox spinner**
Test debut	**No Tests yet**
ODI debut	**Australia v New Zealand at Hamilton 2006-07**
T20I debut	**Australia v New Zealand at Perth 2007-08**

THE PROFILE   Part of Western Australia's big-hitting middle order, Adam Voges (it's pronounced Vo-jes) is most famous for his maiden one-day century, against New South Wales in October 2004 – batting at No. 3, he didn't enter until the 30th over, but reached three figures in 62 balls, the fastest in Australian domestic history at the time. He also clattered a sponsor's sign with one of his seven sixes. Voges collected many plaudits for that innings, and a $50,000 bonus for his superb aim ... but was left out for the next Pura Cup match. He returned later that season, and produced his first hundred. Next summer he passed 600 first-class runs and, after Damien Martyn's sudden retirement, Voges was called into Australia's squad for the third Ashes Test of 2006-07 on his home turf at the WACA. He didn't play – Andrew Symonds got the place instead, and made it his own for a while – but Voges kept his name in the frame by ending the season with 630 runs at 57. He made his one-day international debut in New Zealand shortly afterwards, but didn't quite do enough to win a World Cup spot. He is a fine fielder, one of the first to manage the catch that involves leaping around on both sides of the boundary parrying the ball up in the air – Voges did it to remove the dangerous Brendon McCullum in a Twenty20 international at the SCG in February 2009 – but his left-arm wrist-spin hasn't had much chance yet. He remains on the fringes of the one-day sides but, rising 31, he may soon be struggling to stay ahead of younger blood.

THE FACTS   Voges's 100 not out in 62 balls for Western Australia v NSW in October 2004 was the fastest century in Australian domestic one-day cricket at the time ... He made 180 for WA v Tasmania at Hobart in December 2007 ... Voges learnt of his call-up to the Australian Test squad in 2006-07 while playing for a Cricket Australia XI against the England tourists: he was tapped on the shoulder and asked to leave the field, and admitted "I thought I was in trouble" ...

THE FIGURES *to 23.9.10*   ᴇѕᴘⁿ cricinfo.com

Batting & Fielding	M	Inns	NO	Runs	HS	Avge	S/R	100	50	4s	6s	Ct	St
Tests	0	0	–	–	–	–	–	–	–	–	–	–	–
ODIs	14	13	4	312	72	34.66	87.15	0	1	20	7	2	0
T20Is	4	3	1	63	26	31.50	121.15	0	0	6	0	2	0
First-class	79	133	18	4613	180	40.11	50.35	9	26	–	–	100	0

Bowling	M	Balls	Runs	Wkts	BB	Avge	RpO	S/R	5i	10m
Tests	0	0	–	–	–	–	–	–	–	–
ODIs	14	150	159	1	1–22	159.00	6.36	150.00	0	0
T20Is	4	12	5	2	2–5	2.50	2.50	6.00	0	0
First-class	79	2512	1368	40	4–92	34.20	3.26	62.80	0	0

WAHAB RIAZ

Full name	**Wahab Riaz**
Born	**June 28, 1985, Lahore**
Teams	**Lahore, National Bank**
Style	**Right-hand bat, left-arm fast-medium bowler**
Test debut	**Pakistan v England at The Oval 2010**
ODI debut	**Pakistan v Zimbabwe at Sheikhupura 2007-08**
T20I debut	**Pakistan v Bangladesh at Karachi 2007-08**

THE PROFILE Wahab Riaz initially benefited from Pakistan's chronic luck with fast bowlers. With Shoaib Akhtar and Mohammad Asif missing more often than not, for various weird and wonderful reasons, and with Umar Gul prone to injury, Riaz made it into the national squad quicker than he might have expected. He made a good start early in 2008, taking two good wickets (Tatenda Taibu and Sean Williams of Zimbabwe) in his first one-day international, and adding five more scalps in two outings against Bangladesh, including 3 for 22 in the Kitply Cup at Mirpur. But then reality intruded, in the shape of India's batsmen: two days after he'd beaten up the Banglas, Riaz was knocked about himself, conceding 86 runs in 9.2 overs before being removed from the attack for sending down two beamers. He did have the satisfaction of dismissing both openers, though. He faded from the scene before returning to the limelight in England in 2010, taking four wickets at The Oval in his first nine overs in Tests, and finishing with 5 for 63. He also hung around for a while as nightwatchman. But he was less incisive in the next Test, and didn't feature in the one-dayers that followed. He is a bustling bowler whose stock ball is the one angled away from the right-hander, and he is a bit sharper than he looks: at The Oval the speedo was often nudging 90mph. He is a keen learner, and regularly seeks out Wasim Akram for tips and advice, showing that he is a good judge too.

THE FACTS Wahab Riaz took a wicket (Tatenda Taibu of Zimbabwe) with his third ball in international cricket, in an ODI at Sheikhupura in February 2008 ... He was the ninth Pakistani to take a five-for on Test debut, with 5 for 63 against England at The Oval in 2010 ... Against India at Dhaka in June 2008 Riaz conceded 86 runs in 9.2 overs, the fourth-most expensive analysis for Pakistan in ODIs ... Riaz took 6 for 76 (11 for 190 in the match) for Hyderabad at Sialkot in April 2004 ...

THE FIGURES to 23.9.10   **ESPNcricinfo.com**

Batting & Fielding	M	Inns	NO	Runs	HS	Avge	S/R	100	50	4s	6s	Ct	St
Tests	2	3	0	29	27	9.66	29.89	0	0	3	0	0	0
ODIs	5	4	1	4	3	1.33	28.57	0	0	0	0	1	0
T20Is	2	0	–	–	–	–	–	–	–	–	–	0	0
First-class	67	92	15	1156	68	15.01	–	0	3	–	–	22	0

Bowling	M	Balls	Runs	Wkts	BB	Avge	RpO	S/R	5i	10m
Tests	2	320	195	7	5–63	27.85	3.65	45.71	1	0
ODIs	5	241	202	10	3–22	20.20	5.02	24.10	0	0
T20Is	2	24	18	1	1–7	18.00	4.50	24.00	0	0
First-class	67	11663	6579	228	6–64	28.85	3.38	51.15	10	2

DAVID **WARNER**

AUSTRALIA

Full name   **David Andrew Warner**
Born   **October 27, 1986, Paddington, Sydney**
Teams   **New South Wales, Middlesex, Delhi Daredevils**
Style   **Left-hand bat, occasional legspinner**
Test debut   **No Tests yet**
ODI debut   **Australia v South Africa at Hobart 2008-09**
T20I debut   **Australia v South Africa at Melbourne 2008-09**

THE PROFILE   A diminutive and dangerous opener, David Warner exploded onto the international scene in January 2009. His astonishing 89 from 43 balls, wielding the bat more like a baseball one, on his Twenty20 debut against South Africa at the MCG was all the more remarkable as he was the first man to play for the full Australian side before playing first-class cricket since 1877. His surprise call-up capped an eventful couple of months in which he also earned an IPL contract and a deal to use a two-sided bat. The rewards had come after he began the season by smashing nine sixes in 165 not out – a NSW one-day record – against Tasmania in Sydney, and showed it was no fluke with 97 from 54 balls against the luckless islanders the following week. He finished with 390 FR Cup runs at a strike-rate of 129, and did eventually make his first-class debut for NSW. In one-day internationals, Warner has struggled since a muscular 69 in his second game, and hasn't played since a duck against Scotland in August 2009. Since then he has been pigeonholed as a Twenty20 blaster, with predictably volatile results: highlights have included 67 from 29 balls against West Indies at Sydney in February 2010, and 72 from 42 balls (both these innings included seven sixes) against India at Bridgetown in the World Twenty20 three months later. An excellent fieldsman, Warner was used as a substitute in the Perth Test against South Africa in 2005-06. That same season he was the leading run-scorer on the Under-19 tour of India, and went on to play at the Under-19 World Cup. A keen surfer, he was sent home from the Australian academy in 2007 for general untidiness.

THE FACTS   Warner was the first man since John Hodges and Tom Kendall in the first Test of all in 1876-77 to represent Australia in a full international without previously having played a first-class match ... He finally made his first-class debut for New South Wales in March 2009 ... Warner won the match award for his 89 from 43 balls (seven fours and six sixes) on Twenty20 international debut against South Africa in January 2009 ...

THE FIGURES to 23.9.10   ꞔꞔꞔ cricinfo.com

Batting & Fielding	M	Inns	NO	Runs	HS	Avge	S/R	100	50	4s	6s	Ct	St
Tests	0	0	–	–	–	–	–	–	–	–	–	–	–
ODIs	7	7	0	106	69	15.14	77.37	0	1	8	3	1	0
T20Is	22	22	0	644	89	29.27	151.17	0	4	62	31	13	0
First-class	4	6	1	131	48*	26.20	81.87	0	0	16	5	3	0

Bowling	M	Balls	Runs	Wkts	BB	Avge	RpO	S/R	5i	10m
Tests	0	0	–	–	–	–	–	–	–	–
ODIs	7	0	–	–	–	–	–	–	–	–
T20Is	22	0	–	–	–	–	–	–	–	–
First-class	4	25	19	1	1–0	19.00	4.56	25.00	0	0

B-J **WATLING**

Full name	**Bradley-John Watling**
Born	**July 9, 1985, Durban, South Africa**
Teams	**Northern Districts**
Style	**Right-hand bat, occasional wicketkeeper**
Test debut	**New Zealand v Pakistan at Napier 2009-10**
ODI debut	**No ODIs yet**
T20I debut	**New Zealand v Pakistan at Dubai 2009-10**

THE PROFILE A right-hand opening batsman who can also keep wicket, Bradley-John (usually known just by his initials) Watling spent his early years in Durban in South Africa before his family moved to New Zealand when he was ten. He was part of the squad for the Under-19 World Cup in Bangladesh in 2003-04 before making it to the Northern Districts team, but in 2006-07 – his third season – he made 564 runs at 37.60, and passed 500 again in 2009-10. He also did well in one-dayers, and was rewarded with a place in New Zealand's squad for a one-day series against Pakistan in the United Arab Emirates in November 2009. He made his debut in the Twenty20 games there – a slight surprise, since he is not regarded at home as a terribly fast scorer (his overall one-day strike rate is a modest 70.24). However, that doesn't bother Daniel Vettori: "He plays pace well, lets the ball come to him," he said, "and in the middle overs he is very adept at turning the strike over against spin. I've actually opened with him a few times ... but that's not why he has made the team!" When Pakistan toured New Zealand later in 2009 Watling made his debut in the third Test at Napier, making an undefeated 60 in the second innings, and after a couple of quiet matches he resisted the Australian attack for more than two hours in making 46 at Hamilton. He is a reliable stand-in keeper, although Peter McGlashan (who has also played for New Zealand's Twenty20 side) usually takes the gloves for Northern Districts. Away from cricket, Watling also plays hockey.

THE FACTS Watling scored 153 for Northern Districts against Otago at Dunedin in February 2007: his next two first-class hundreds also came at Otago's expense ... He made 145 not out in the final of the NZC one-day competition for Northern Districts v Auckland in February 2010 ... Watling took six catches in an innings for ND v Central Districts at Gisborne in 2006-07 ...

THE FIGURES to 23.9.10   ᴇsᴨ cricinfo.com

Batting & Fielding	M	Inns	NO	Runs	HS	Avge	S/R	100	50	4s	6s	Ct	St
Tests	4	8	1	195	60*	27.85	44.52	0	1	25	1	5	0
ODIs	3	2	0	57	55	28.50	72.15	0	1	8	0	2	0
T20Is	2	2	0	29	22	14.50	64.44	0	0	2	0	2	0
First-class	47	86	4	2460	153	30.00	38.27	5	11	–	–	56	0

Bowling	M	Balls	Runs	Wkts	BB	Avge	RpO	S/R	5i	10m
Tests	4	0	–	–	–	–	–	–	–	–
ODIs	3	0	–	–	–	–	–	–	–	–
T20Is	2	0	–	–	–	–	–	–	–	–
First-class	47	47	39	2	2–31	19.50	4.97	23.50	0	0

SHANE **WATSON**

Full name	**Shane Robert Watson**
Born	**June 17, 1981, Ipswich, Queensland**
Teams	**Queensland, Rajasthan Royals**
Style	**Right-hand bat, right-arm fast-medium bowler**
Test debut	**Australia v Pakistan at Sydney 2004-05**
ODI debut	**Australia v South Africa at Centurion 2001-02**
T20I debut	**Australia v South Africa at Johannesburg 2005-06**

THE PROFILE To conquer international cricket, Shane Watson first had to beat his fragile body. Despite an athletic figure made for photoshoots, Watson's frame was so brittle it threatened to break him. He refused to give up, despite back stress fractures, hamstring strains, calf problems, hip trouble, a dislocated shoulder and a suspected heart attack that turned out to be food poisoning. He changed his training, and gave up alcohol, but not his dream. It finally paid off in 2009, when he was promoted to open in the middle of the Ashes series. Many batsmen would have been uncomfortable with the elevation from the middle order, especially after failing when given the job with Queensland, but Watson was used to reinventing himself. In his first eight Tests in the new role he scored seven fifties and a 120. His first Test century was a long time coming, but after two nineties (and an 89), he finally reached three figures against Pakistan at the MCG in December 2009 ... thanks to a single from a dropped catch. He had earned some luck. At the crease he is an aggressive brute with a broad chest, a right-handed disciple of Matthew Hayden, and someone who often doesn't need to follow through to gain a boundary. As a bowler he is willing and speedy, if not quite as good as he thinks he is: he is prone to verbal exchanges with batsmen, but he does pick up handy wickets – 11 of them in two Tests against Pakistan in England in 2010. But finally, after years of doubt, he has developed into a very modern, complete and enviable package.

THE FACTS Watson hit 201 in the 2005-06 Pura Cup final demolition of Victoria before retiring hurt: uniquely, four batsmen passed 150 in Queensland's 900 for 6 ... He averaged 145 at the 2007 World Cup, thanks to five not-outs, and scored at a rollicking 170.58 runs per 100 balls ... Watson played for Hampshire, alongside Shane Warne: in 2005 he scored 203 not out for them against Warwickshire at the Rose Bowl ...

THE FIGURES to 23.9.10   **ESPNcricinfo.com**

Batting & Fielding	M	Inns	NO	Runs	HS	Avge	S/R	100	50	4s	6s	Ct	St
Tests	20	35	1	1247	120*	36.67	51.23	1	9	173	8	15	0
ODIs	114	96	22	2982	136*	40.29	84.35	4	17	302	50	33	0
T20Is	19	18	2	375	81	23.43	145.34	0	3	28	21	7	0
First-class	84	146	16	5940	203*	45.69	–	14	32	–	–	69	0

Bowling	M	Balls	Runs	Wkts	BB	Avge	RpO	S/R	5i	10m
Tests	20	1995	1048	38	6–33	27.57	3.15	52.50	2	0
ODIs	114	4051	3296	118	4–36	27.93	4.88	34.33	0	0
T20Is	19	249	347	10	2–23	34.70	8.36	24.90	0	0
First-class	84	7872	4478	159	7–69	28.16	3.41	49.50	5	1

CHANAKA **WELAGEDARA**

Full name	**Uda Walawwe Mahim Bandaralage Chanaka Asanga Welagedara**
Born	**March 20, 1981, Matale**
Teams	**Moors, Wayamba**
Style	**Right-hand bat, left-arm fast-medium bowler**
Test debut	**Sri Lanka v England at Galle 2007-08**
ODI debut	**Sri Lanka v India at Rajkot 2009-10**
T20I debut	**Sri Lanka v New Zealand at Providence 2009-10**

THE PROFILE Chanaka Welagedara is a fastish bowler with a sturdy action, who is in competition with Thilan Thushara, another left-armer, to establish himself as the long-term replacement for Chaminda Vaas. Welagedara, whose array of initials outdoes even Vaas's, swings the ball in nicely, and traps a lot of batsmen lbw. He is a little quicker than Thushara, but needs to work on his consistency – against India at home in mid-2010 he sprayed the ball around and proved expensive in his two Tests. A few months earlier, also against India, he was more impressive, reducing them to 31 for 3 at Ahmedabad without the aid of a fielder. He dismissed Rahul Dravid too – but not before he had rescued India with 177. Shortly afterwards he took 5 for 66 against India in a one-dayer in Bangladesh, again removing the top three before proving costly later on. Welagedara was a late starter to cricket, not playing seriously until he was 17 – but he then made rapid progress in provincial matches. When he came to Colombo from Matale (a hill-country town not far from Kandy) in 2000 he was soon chosen for the Sri Lanka Pace Academy, headed by the former Test fast bowler Rumesh Ratnayake. Welagedara bowled Moors to the Premier League title in 2002-03, with 34 wickets at 24.14. An ankle injury, which needed an operation, kept him out for 18 months until the end of 2006, but he made his Test debut against England the following December and took four wickets, three of them top-five batsmen.

THE FACTS Welagedara took 5 for 34 (10 for 95 in the match) for a Sri Lanka Cricket XI against Tamil Nadu in the Gopalan Trophy match in Colombo in September 2007 ... He took 5 for 66 in an ODI against India at Mirpur in January 2010 ... Welagedara scored 76 for Moors v Sinhalese SC in Colombo in October 2009 ...

THE FIGURES to 23.9.10   **ESrn cricinfo.com**

Batting & Fielding	M	Inns	NO	Runs	HS	Avge	S/R	100	50	4s	6s	Ct	St
Tests	6	6	2	27	8	6.75	54.00	0	0	5	0	2	0
ODIs	10	3	2	4	2*	4.00	44.44	0	0	0	0	2	0
T20Is	2	1	1	2	2*	–	66.66	0	0	0	0	0	0
First-class	69	86	30	552	76	9.85	41.69	0	1	–	–	15	0

Bowling	M	Balls	Runs	Wkts	BB	Avge	RpO	S/R	5i	10m
Tests	6	993	707	12	4–87	58.91	4.27	82.75	0	0
ODIs	10	457	433	15	5–66	28.86	5.68	30.46	1	0
T20Is	2	36	61	1	1–21	61.00	10.16	36.00	0	0
First-class	69	9465	5586	189	5–34	29.55	3.54	50.07	6	1

CAMERON **WHITE**

AUSTRALIA

Full name	**Cameron Leon White**
Born	**August 18, 1983, Bairnsdale, Victoria**
Teams	**Victoria, Bangalore Royal Challengers**
Style	**Right-hand bat, legspinner**
Test debut	**Australia v India at Bangalore 2008-09**
ODI debut	**Australia v World XI at Melbourne 2005-06**
T20I debut	**Australia v England at Sydney 2006-07**

THE PROFILE Cameron "Bear" White long seemed destined to play a significant role for Australia. Only the precise nature of that role baffled admirers. Nagging legspinner? Solid middle-order bat? Intuitive skipper? Or a bit of all three? The over-eager Shane Warne comparisons that accompanied his arrival have long since died away. Indeed, White is a peculiarly unAustralian leggie – tall and robust, relying on changes of pace and a handy wrong'un rather than prodigious turn or flight. "There's no flippers or anything exciting like that," he once admitted with a self-deprecating smile. Victoria's youngest-ever captain at 20, he won rave reviews for his handling of more experienced colleagues. White played his first ODIs against the World XI late in 2005. He made little impact, and lost his national contract after a mediocre season. But he batted wonderfully for Somerset in 2006 (David Hookes, the late Victorian coach, always felt White's best chance of representing Australia was to earn a top-six spot), feasting on county bowlers and smashing a Twenty20 ton in 55 balls. That preceded a better home season, and he was recalled for the one-day series at the start of 2007: his bowling lacked control, and batting opportunities were limited. He missed the World Cup, but toured India at the end of 2008. He did little in four Tests there, and returned even more firmly pigeonholed as a one-day player. But back in England late in 2009 he followed mature one-day innings of 53 and 42 with a fine maiden century at the Rose Bowl, and added another century against Pakistan at Brisbane early in 2010 to make his place safe for a while.

THE FACTS White made 260 not out for Somerset v Derbyshire in August 2006, the highest individual score in the fourth innings of any first-class match, beating a record formerly held by Hansie Cronje and Denis Compton ... White took 6 for 66 (10 for 136 in the match) for Victoria v Western Australia at Melbourne in March 2003 ... Ten of his 15 first-class centuries were scored in 24 matches for Somerset ...

THE FIGURES to 23.9.10   ᴇsᴘⁿcricinfo.com

Batting & Fielding	M	Inns	NO	Runs	HS	Avge	S/R	100	50	4s	6s	Ct	St
Tests	4	7	2	146	46	29.20	44.24	0	0	15	1	1	0
ODIs	68	56	11	1642	105	36.48	81.89	2	10	120	37	32	0
T20Is	22	21	8	505	85*	38.84	146.37	0	3	28	31	11	0
First-class	108	181	23	6680	260*	42.27	–	15	31	–	–	101	0

Bowling	M	Balls	Runs	Wkts	BB	Avge	RpO	S/R	5i	10m
Tests	4	558	342	5	2–71	68.40	3.67	111.60	0	0
ODIs	68	325	345	12	3–5	28.75	6.36	27.08	0	0
T20Is	22	24	25	1	1–11	25.00	6.25	24.00	0	0
First-class	108	11730	6901	172	6–66	40.12	3.52	68.19	2	1

KANE **WILLIAMSON**

Full name	**Kane Stuart Williamson**
Born	**August 8, 1990, Tauranga**
Teams	**Northern Districts**
Style	**Right-hand bat, offspinner**
Test debut	**No Tests yet**
ODI debut	**New Zealand v India at Dambulla 2010**
T20I debut	**No T20Is yet**

THE PROFILE Probably the most exciting batting talent New Zealand have unearthed since Martin Crowe in the early 1980s, Kane Williamson had a smooth ride through age-group cricket and made his first-class debut at 17 in December 2007. A slow start (2 and 0) was followed next season by innings of 82, 73 and 98 in his next four matches, and the seemingly inevitable maiden century came up in his tenth. He finished 2008-09 with 812 runs at 50.75, and collected 614 more the following season – at a slightly lower average (47.23) but with two eye-catching big scores, 170 against Wellington and 192 against Auckland. All this propelled him into the squad for the second Test against Australia at Hamilton in March 2010, and although he didn't play in the end it was a clear sign that his entry would not be long delayed. Well balanced, with an enviably perpendicular bat in defence, Williamson was similarly prolific in one-day cricket, collecting 621 runs at 77 in domestic games in 2009-10. He followed that with a good allround performance – 88 and three wickets with his offspin – against the Indian state Maharashtra in Darwin, to justify the recent award of a national contract, and earn a spot in the senior one-day squad for the one-day triangular series in Sri Lanka in August 2010. There, he made his debut against India ... and collected a ninth-ball duck, courtesy of a peach from Praveen Kumar, and another blob in his next game before finally getting off the mark in the third. There was another disappointment for Williamson: he didn't get to meet his cricketing hero, Sachin Tendulkar, who was rested for the series.

THE FACTS Williamson scored 192 for Northern Districts against Auckland at Whangarei in March 2010: in the previous match (at Wellington) he had made 170 ... He hit 75 and 151 against England in an Under-19 Test at Worcester in August 2008 ... Williamson scored more first-class runs before he had turned 20 than Martin Crowe (1428 to 1127) ...

THE FIGURES to 23.9.10   ESPncricinfo.com

Batting & Fielding	M	Inns	NO	Runs	HS	Avge	S/R	100	50	4s	6s	Ct	St
Tests	0	0	–	–	–	–	–	–	–	–	–	–	–
ODIs	4	3	0	13	13	4.33	34.21	0	0	1	0	1	0
T20Is	0	0	–	–	–	–	–	–	–	–	–	–	–
First-class	20	33	2	1428	192	46.06	56.22	4	6	173	12	24	0

Bowling	M	Balls	Runs	Wkts	BB	Avge	RpO	S/R	5i	10m
Tests	0	0	–	–	–	–	–	–	–	–
ODIs	4	84	48	1	1–2	48.00	3.42	84.00	0	0
T20Is	0	0	–	–	–	–	–	–	–	–
First-class	20	2290	1282	30	5–75	42.73	3.35	76.33	1	0

LUKE **WRIGHT**

Full name	**Luke James Wright**
Born	**March 7, 1985, Grantham, Lincolnshire**
Teams	**Sussex**
Style	**Right-hand bat, right-arm fast-medium bowler**
Test debut	**No Tests yet**
ODI debut	**England v India at The Oval 2007**
ODI debut	**England v Zimbabwe at Cape Town 2007-08**

THE PROFILE He's an attacking batsman who can bowl reasonably fast, so it's no great surprise that Luke Wright admires Andrew Flintoff, or that he hoped to follow him into the England side. That ambition was realised when Flintoff, among others, was injured, and Wright was called up against India in September 2007. Like Freddie, Wright marked his ODI debut by scoring 50, an exciting innings which started with a four and a six. But he made little impression after that, although his strike-rate was impressive. He continued in the one-day mix – at least until a ball from a bowling machine broke his toe during the miserable one-day series against Australia in September 2009 – although he hadn't done anything terribly spectacular beyond a rapid 71 in the World Twenty20 opener against the Netherlands at Lord's, and even that ended in embarrassment when England lost off the last ball. Eventually he lost his one-day place late in 2010 after going seven matches without taking a wicket. Wright made his first-class debut for Leicestershire against Sussex in 2003, and although Mushtaq Ahmed nabbed him for a duck Sussex signed him up for the following season. Wright repaid them with a debut century, and had played only ten first-class games when he went to the Caribbean with England A early in 2006. His career really took off the following year, when he was the leading Twenty20 Cup runscorer with 346, including a pyrotechnic 103 in just 45 balls against Kent. That earned him his county cap – and that England call, which he celebrated by hammering 125 in 73 balls in a 40-over game against Gloucestershire.

THE FACTS Wright made 103 from 45 balls (11 fours, six sixes) in a Twenty20 Cup match against Kent at Canterbury in June 2007 … He hit 155 not out for Sussex v MCC at Lord's in the first match of the 2008 season … Wright scored 100 on his debut for Sussex (his second first-class match), v Loughborough UCCE in May 2004 … He took a hat-trick for England Under-19s v South Africa in a one-day game at Hove in August 2003 …

THE FIGURES to 23.9.10   ᴇꜱᴘⁿcricinfo.com

Batting & Fielding	M	Inns	NO	Runs	HS	Avge	S/R	100	50	4s	6s	Ct	St
Tests	0	0	–	–	–	–	–	–	–	–	–	–	–
ODIs	42	31	3	600	52	21.42	90.90	0	2	52	18	16	0
T20Is	27	22	2	328	71	16.40	129.13	0	1	32	11	10	0
First-class	66	93	15	2867	155*	36.75	66.09	8	15	–	–	29	0

Bowling	M	Balls	Runs	Wkts	BB	Avge	RpO	S/R	5i	10m
Tests	0	0	–	–	–	–	–	–	–	–
ODIs	42	906	769	15	2–34	51.26	5.09	60.40	0	0
T20Is	27	156	219	6	1–5	36.50	8.42	26.00	0	0
First-class	66	6671	3924	101	5–65	38.85	3.52	66.04	3	0

MICHAEL **YARDY**

Full name	**Michael Howard Yardy**
Born	**November 27, 1980, Pembury, Kent**
Teams	**Sussex**
Style	**Right-hand bat, slow left-arm orthodox spinner**
Test debut	**No Tests yet**
ODI debut	**England v Pakistan at Nottingham 2006**
T20I debut	**England v Zimbabwe at Cape Town 2007-08**

THE PROFILE A compact, organised left-hander with a technique not unlike Andrew Strauss's – although involving a wide-open stance before a shuffle across to a more orthodox position as the ball is delivered – Michael Yardy was a Sussex stand-in until his maiden first-class century against Surrey in the final match of 2004. He began 2005 in identical fashion, with another hundred against Surrey, to trigger a run of form that carried him to the top of the domestic batting charts. He finished that season with 1520 runs and an England A tour. With Monty Panesar considered too one-dimensional for England's one-day team Yardy got a chance at the end of 2006. He did well against Pakistan, doing well on his Twenty20 debut then, in the 50-over side, obtaining surprising turn to grab three wickets in his first match, and collecting the winning runs in the second. However, things unravelled in the Champions Trophy in India in October: the bowling was fine, but England's strange insistence that he bat at No. 4 meant the overall image suffered, and he was quietly jettisoned. Back at Hove he took over as captain in 2009, leading Sussex to two one-day trophies (but also Championship relegation). His steely approach in one-day cricket kept the selectors interested, and when Andy Flower pinpointed the need for a left-handed allrounder Yardy was recalled for the World Twenty20 in the West Indies in 2010. Darting the ball in sharply, he helped England win their first global tournament. Batting at No. 6 or 7 suited him better, and as he relaxed Yardy looked much more like an authentic England player than before.

THE FACTS Yardy made 257 against Bangladesh at Hove in 2005, the highest score for Sussex against any touring team, beating George Cox's 234 against India in 1946 ... He also took 5 for 83 in the same match, which remain his best figures ... Yardy was at school with the England footballer Gareth Barry ...

THE FIGURES to 23.9.10   ESPn cricinfo.com

Batting & Fielding	M	Inns	NO	Runs	HS	Avge	S/R	100	50	4s	6s	Ct	St
Tests	0	0	–	–	–	–	–	–	–	–	–	–	–
ODIs	19	16	6	170	57	17.00	61.59	0	1	9	0	3	0
T20Is	12	7	5	96	35*	48.00	135.21	0	0	9	1	8	0
First-class	129	217	21	7606	257	38.80	–	15	38	–	–	99	0

Bowling	M	Balls	Runs	Wkts	BB	Avge	RpO	S/R	5i	10m
Tests	0	0	–	–	–	–	–	–	–	–
ODIs	19	852	615	14	3–24	43.92	4.33	60.85	0	0
T20Is	12	228	252	7	2–19	36.00	6.63	32.57	0	0
First-class	129	3441	2003	26	5–83	77.03	3.49	132.34	1	0

YASIR HAMEED

PAKISTAN

Full name	**Yasir Hameed Qureshi**
Born	**February 28, 1978, Peshawar**
Teams	**Abbottabad, Pakistan International Airlines**
Style	**Right-hand bat, occasional offspinner**
Test debut	**Pakistan v Bangladesh at Karachi 2003**
ODI debut	**Pakistan v New Zealand at Dambulla 2002-03**
T20I debut	**No T20Is yet**

THE PROFILE Yasir Hameed announced himself with two centuries on Test debut, against Bangladesh in May 2003. He may look frail, but his game is built on timing and an easy elegance, and a solid technique. His early one-day exploits were equally impressive, and he forged a superb combination with Imran Farhat: against New Zealand at home late in 2003 they put together a record four consecutive three-figure opening stands. But after this promising beginning Yasir developed a worrying tendency to waste his starts, making pretty twenties and then throwing it away, often flailing at wide ones outside off. Selectorial inconsistencies didn't help: he made 58 and 63 against McGrath and Warne at Sydney in January 2005, but was dropped for the next Test (against India) a couple of months later. For a while opportunities were limited to occasional one-dayers, in most of which he made a contribution. However, domestic persistence paid off, and he returned to the one-day squad against West Indies at the end of 2006. He made 71 and 41, but still missed out on a World Cup spot (possibly a blessing in disguise). He was recalled for the post-Cup one-dayers against Sri Lanka in Abu Dhabi, but a series of middling scores – and a triple-century in a domestic first-class game early in 2008 – were still not enough to persuade the selectors that he deserved a regular place. He was eventually recalled for the 2010 England tour, but didn't cover himself with glory: after finally collecting a Test duck, in his 47th innings, he made two single-figure scores at Lord's then got caught up in the "spot-fixing" scandal after apparently shooting his mouth off to an undercover reporter.

THE FACTS Yasir Hameed made 170 and 105 on Test debut against Bangladesh in August 2003: the only other man to make twin centuries on Test debut is Lawrence Rowe (214 and 100* for West Indies v New Zealand in 1971-72) ... Yasir made 300 (49 fours) for NWFP v Baluchistan at Peshawar in March 2008 ... In 2003-04 Yasir and Imran Farhat shared successive opening stands of 115, 142, 134 and 197 in ODIs against New Zealand ...

THE FIGURES to 23.9.10   ESPNcricinfo.com

Batting & Fielding	M	Inns	NO	Runs	HS	Avge	S/R	100	50	4s	6s	Ct	St
Tests	25	49	3	1491	170	32.41	57.61	2	8	223	4	20	0
ODIs	56	56	1	2028	127*	36.87	66.95	3	12	219	6	14	0
T20Is	0	0	–	–	–	–	–	–	–	–	–	–	–
First-class	137	227	14	7733	300	36.30	–	16	35	–	–	108	0

Bowling	M	Balls	Runs	Wkts	BB	Avge	RpO	S/R	5i	10m
Tests	25	78	72	0	–	–	5.53	–	0	0
ODIs	56	18	26	0	–	–	8.66	–	0	0
T20Is	0	0	–	–	–	–	–	–	–	–
First-class	137	921	735	7	2–46	105.00	4.78	131.57	0	0

YOUNIS KHAN

Full name	**Mohammad Younis Khan**
Born	**Nov 29, 1977, Mardan, North-West Frontier Province**
Teams	**NWFP, Peshawar, Habib Bank, Surrey**
Style	**Right-hand bat, occasional legspinner**
Test debut	**Pakistan v Sri Lanka at Rawalpindi 1999-2000**
ODI debut	**Pakistan v Sri Lanka at Karachi 1999-2000**
T20I debut	**Pakistan v England at Bristol 2006**

THE PROFILE Younis Khan is a fearless middle-order batsman, as befits his Pathan ancestry. He plays with a flourish, and is especially strong in the arc from backward point to extra cover; he is prone to getting down on one knee and driving extravagantly. But this flamboyance is coupled with grit. He started with a century on Test debut, against Sri Lanka early in 2000, and scored well in bursts after that, with 153 against West Indies in Sharjah the highlight. Younis was one of the few batsmen who retained his place after Pakistan's disastrous 2003 World Cup, but he lost it soon afterwards after a string of low scores. Another century against Sri Lanka finally cemented that Test place, and he was a heavy runmaker after that, especially against India: in March 2005 he made 147 and 267 in successive Tests against them, and continued in that vein early in 2006, with 199, 83, 194, 0 and 77, before scoring consistently in England too, making 173 at Leeds, his home ground the following year during a successful spell with Yorkshire. He flirted with the captaincy – theatrically resigning more than once – and started his reign as fulltime skipper with 313 in 760 minutes against Sri Lanka on a Karachi featherbed early in 2009. Later in the year he led Pakistan to victory in the World Twenty20 in England, overcoming a lackadaisical start ... but immediately afterwards retired from 20-over cricket. He resigned as Test captain too shortly afterwards, then was banned for unspecified offences during the disastrous Australian tour which followed. Younis remained on the outer and missed the England tour in 2010.

THE FACTS Younis Khan scored 313, Pakistan's third triple-century in Tests, against Sri Lanka at Karachi in February 2009 ... He averages 88.06 in Tests against India – and more than 31 against everyone else ... Younis was the seventh Pakistani to score a century on Test debut, with 107 v Sri Lanka in February 2000 ... Against India at home early in 2006 he shared successive stands of 319, 142, 242, 0 and 158 with Mohammad Yousuf ...

THE FIGURES *to 2.9.10*

Batting & Fielding	M	Inns	NO	Runs	HS	Avge	S/R	100	50	4s	6s	Ct	St
Tests	63	112	7	5260	313	50.09	53.73	16	21	638	24	67	0
ODIs	202	196	19	5765	144	32.57	75.52	6	37	465	50	107	0
T20Is	22	20	3	432	51	25.41	124.85	0	2	31	12	11	0
First-class	150	244	28	10873	313	50.33	–	34	44	–	–	158	0

Bowling	M	Balls	Runs	Wkts	BB	Avge	RpO	S/R	5i	10m
Tests	63	540	341	7	2–23	48.71	3.78	77.14	0	0
ODIs	202	224	224	2	1–3	112.00	6.00	112.00	0	0
T20Is	22	22	18	3	3–18	6.00	4.90	7.33	0	0
First-class	150	2677	1560	35	4–52	44.57	3.49	76.48	0	0

YUVRAJ SINGH

Full name	**Yuvraj Singh**
Born	**December 12, 1981, Chandigarh**
Teams	**Punjab, Kings XI Punjab**
Style	**Left-hand bat, left-arm orthodox spinner**
Test debut	**India v New Zealand at Mohali 2003-04**
ODI debut	**India v Kenya at Nairobi 2000-01**
T20I debut	**India v Scotland at Durban 2007-08**

INDIA

THE PROFILE Yuvraj Singh made a lordly entry into international cricket when still only 18, toppling Australia in the ICC Knockout of October 2000 with a blistering 84 in his first innings and some scintillating fielding. He supplements those skills with some loopy left-arm spin, with which he took two hat-tricks in the second season of the IPL in 2009. While his ability to hit the ball long and clean was instantly recognised, at first he was troubled by quality spin, and temporarily lost his place. But in 2002 he swung the series against Zimbabwe India's way with two matchwinning innings, then went to England and played key roles in three one-day run-chases, culminating at Lord's where his stand of 121 with Mohammad Kaif set up a memorable victory over England. It still took another 15 months, and an injury to Sourav Ganguly, for Yuvraj to get a Test look-in. But in his third match, against Pakistan on a Lahore greentop, he stroked a stunning first-day century off 110 balls. A troublesome knee injury briefly threatened to keep him out of the 2007 World Cup, but later that year he smashed Stuart Broad for six sixes in an over during the inaugural World Twenty20 in South Africa. A scintillating 169 against Pakistan at Bangalore in December 2007 seemed to have nailed down a Test place at last – but a string of modest scores followed, and he was out again by the middle of 2008. Although he remains a one-day regular – and a fearsome sight (for bowlers, at least) in Twenty20 games – Yuvraj was less imposing in 2010, both in international cricket and the IPL, amid whispers about his weight and his attitude.

THE FACTS Yuvraj hit England's Stuart Broad for six sixes in an over during the World Twenty20 at Durban in September 2007 ... He played 73 ODIs before his first Test cap ... He averages 63.55 in Tests against Pakistan, but 9.14 v Australia ... Yuvraj has the highest strike rate in T20Is of anyone with more than 350 runs ... His father, fast bowler Yograj Singh, played one Test in 1980-81 ... Yuvraj's record includes three ODIs for the Asia XI ...

THE FIGURES to 23.9.10

ᴇЅᴨcricinfo.com

Batting & Fielding	M	Inns	NO	Runs	HS	Avge	S/R	100	50	4s	6s	Ct	St
Tests	34	52	6	1639	169	35.63	58.91	3	9	227	17	30	0
ODIs	254	234	32	7420	139	36.73	88.30	12	43	759	136	72	0
T20Is	22	21	4	555	70	32.64	153.73	0	5	33	38	6	0
First-class	91	144	17	5523	209	43.48	–	17	26	–	–	88	0

Bowling	M	Balls	Runs	Wkts	BB	Avge	RpO	S/R	5i	10m
Tests	34	751	431	8	2–9	53.87	3.44	93.87	0	0
ODIs	254	4004	3374	84	4–6	40.16	5.05	47.66	0	0
T20Is	22	120	174	7	3–23	24.85	8.70	17.14	0	0
First-class	91	1813	987	19	3–25	51.94	3.26	95.42	0	0

ZULQARNAIN HAIDER

Full name	**Zulqarnain Haider**
Born	**April 23, 1986, Lahore**
Teams	**Punjab, Zarai Taraqiati Bank**
Style	**Right-hand bat, wicketkeeper**
Test debut	**Pakistan v England at Birmingham 2010**
ODI debut	**No ODIs yet**
T20I debut	**Pakistan v South Africa at Johannesburg 2006-07**

THE PROFILE For three years it seemed likely that Zulqarnain Haider's only tilt at international cricket would be a solitary Twenty20 defeat against South Africa at The Wanderers in February 2007. But after some good work in domestic cricket the lean and lanky Haider was named for the 2010 tour of England as Kamran Akmal's deputy, and when the senior keeper's lapses became too frequent to ignore Haider won his first Test cap against England at Edgbaston. He was out to his first ball, feathering a catch behind off Stuart Broad, but his characterful and determined 88 in the second innings – after being given out lbw first ball but reprieved on review – formed the basis of Pakistan's fightback, and was testament to his fighting spirit. Haider took part in the Under-15 World Cup in England in 2000 at the age of 13, only six months after his mother's death from cancer. Four years later, at the Under-19 World Cup in Dhaka, he scored a vital 23 not out from 18 balls, and claimed three catches, as Pakistan took the title in the final against West Indies. But further tragedy struck as Haider prepared for his Test debut: three days before the match his father was hospitalised with hepatitis C, and soon lapsed into a coma. When Haider stepped onto the field he wasn't sure if his father could see him – but in the event he recovered enough to watch that sterling second-innings effort on television. Sadly that was Haider's only Test of the tour – an injured finger turned out to be a hairline fracture, and he was forced to return home.

THE FACTS Zulqarnain Haider collected a golden duck in his first Test innings – but resisted for 276 minutes in the second, scoring 88 ... He made 161 for Zarai Taraqiati Bank against Customs in Islamabad in November 2009 ... Zulqarnain took five catches in an innings for Zarai Taraqiati Bank v Sui Southern Gas at Lahore in November 2009 – then opened the batting and scored 75 ...

THE FIGURES to 23.9.10

Batting & Fielding	M	Inns	NO	Runs	HS	Avge	S/R	100	50	4s	6s	Ct	St
Tests	1	2	0	88	88	44.00	43.78	0	1	15	0	2	0
ODIs	0	0	–	–	–	–	–	–	–	–	–	–	–
T20Is	1	1	0	5	5	5.00	55.55	0	0	0	0	0	0
First-class	71	109	18	3166	161	34.79	–	3	18	–	–	217	8

Bowling	M	Balls	Runs	Wkts	BB	Avge	RpO	S/R	5i	10m
Tests	1	0	–	–	–	–	–	–	–	–
ODIs	0	0	–	–	–	–	–	–	–	–
T20Is	1	0	–	–	–	–	–	–	–	–
First-class	71	24	26	0	–	–	6.50	–	0	0

AFGHANISTAN

Shapoor Zadran

Samiullah Shenwari

Hamid Hassan

The improbable rise of war-torn Afghanistan as a cricket power was one of the great feelgood stories of 2008 and 2009. Starting in the lowly backwaters of world cricket's fifth division in May 2008, they won in Jersey to progress up the ladder a notch. They topped Division Four, too, in Tanzania, then emerged from Division Three, in Argentina at the end of January 2009. That put them into the World Cup qualifying series in South Africa, where they finished just one win short of a fairytale appearance in the main event itself in 2011. The decision to reduce the number of associate nations in the World Cup from six in 2007 to four next time ultimately cost Afghanistan a place, as they finished sixth – but that did bring the considerable consolation (and considerable funding) of official one-day international status for the next four years. They celebrated by walloping Scotland in their first ODI, and later in the year shared a short series in the unfamiliar surroundings of the Netherlands. They were also holding their own in the ICC's first-class Intercontinental Cup competition: also in Holland, Noor Ali became only the fourth man – after Test players in Arthur Morris of Australia, India's Nari Contractor and Aamer Malik of Pakistan – to score two centuries on his first-class debut. They qualified for the World Twenty20 in the West Indies early in 2010, and did not look out of place despite losing to India and South Africa. Some more impressive Intercontinental Cup performances followed, and by the end of the year the players were starting to bemoan their lack of opportunities against the senior Test nations in 50-overs matches. Afghanistan's cricketers still have hurdles to overcome – it's difficult to imagine many teams wanting to tour there in the current climate, so home matches will be difficult – but they have coped admirably with everything that has been thrown at them so far.

Afghanistan's ODI records as at 23.9.10

Highest total	295-8	v Scotland at Benoni 2008-09
Lowest total	120	v Scotland at Ayr 2010
Most runs	605	Mohammad Shahzad (avge. 55.00)
Highest score	118	Moh'd Shahzad v Canada at Sharjah 2009-10
Most wickets	18	Hamid Hassan (avge. 24.05)
Best bowling	4-24	Shapoor Zadran v Netherlands at Amstelveen 2009
Most matches	13	(four different players)
World Cup record	Have not qualified yet	
Overall ODI record	Played 13: Won 8, Lost 5	

AFGHANISTAN

ASGHAR STANIKZAI, Mohammad February 22, 1987, Kabul
RHB, RFM: 13 ODIs, 289 runs at 26.27, HS 64; 2 wickets at 27.50, BB 1-22.
Middle-order batsman who made 102 against Bahrain in July 2008.

DAWLAT AHMADZAI, Khan September 5, 1984, Loger
RHB, RFM: 3 ODIs, did not bat; 1 wicket at 121.00, BB 1-40.
Long-serving fast bowler, and former captain, who first played for Afghanistan in 2001.

HAMID HASSAN June 1, 1987, Bati Kot, Nangrahar
RHB, RFM: 11 ODIs, 33 runs at 8.25, HS 17; 18 wickets at 24.05, BB 3-32.
Took 5-23 against Ireland in World Cup qualifier in South Africa in April 2009.

JAVED AHMADI January 2, 1992, Kunduz
RHB, OB: 4 ODIs, 31 runs at 10.33, HS 25.
Batsman who appeared in the Under-19 World Cup in New Zealand in 2010.

KARIM SADIQ Khan February 18, 1984, Nangrahar
RHB, OB, WK: 11 ODIs, 212 runs at 26.50, HS 114*, 1x100: 2 wickets at 41.00, BB 2-28.
Scored 114 against Scotland at Ayr in August 2010.*

KHALIQ DAD Noori January 1, 1984, Baghlan
RHB, RFM: 6 ODIs, 40 runs at 13.33, HS 20; 9 wickets at 16.66, BB 3-30.
Medium-pacer whose brother, Allah Dad, has also played for Afghanistan.

MIRWAIS ASHRAF June 30, 1988, Kunduz
RHB, RFM: 4 ODIs, 24 runs at 12.00, HS 17; 4 wickets at 23.50, BB 2-20.
Medium-pacer who took 4-24 v Netherlands in Intercontinental Cup match in August 2009.

MOHAMMAD NABI Eisakhil March 7, 1985, Loger
RHB, OB: 13 ODIs, 241 runs at 30.12, HS 62; 8 wickets at 52.62, BB 2-23.
Hard-hitting batsman who spent some time on the MCC cricket staff at Lord's.

MOHAMMAD SHAHZAD Mohammadi July 15, 1991, Nangrahar
RHB, WK: 12 ODIs, 605 runs at 55.00, HS 118, 3x100; 12 ct, 4 st.
Scored Afghanistan's first ODI hundred. against the Netherlands at Amstelveen in his second match.

NOOR ALI Zadran July 10, 1988, Khost
RHB, RM: 10 ODIs, 315 runs at 31.50, HS 114, 1x100.
Made 130 and 100 on first-class debut, for Afghanistan v Zimbabwe A in August 2009.*

NAWROZ MANGAL, Khan November 28, 1984, Kabul
RHB, OB: 13 ODIs, 324 runs at 36.00, HS 70*; 6 wickets at 28.00, BB 3-35.
Afghanistan's captain during their astonishing rise. Took 5-24 v Malaysia in 2008.

RAEES AHMADZAI, Khan September 3, 1984, Loger
RHB, OB: 5 ODIs, 88 runs at 29.33, HS 39; 0 wicket for 16.
Scored 78 v Uganda in January 2009: has also played for Sebastianites in Sri Lanka.

SAMIULLAH SHENWARI December 31, 1987, Nangrahar
RHB, LBG: 13 ODIs, 265 runs at 37.85, HS 82; 17 wickets at 27.35, BB 4-31.
Improving legspinner who took 4-28 v Bermuda in World Cup qualifier in 2009.

SHABIR NOORI February 23, 1992, Nangrahar
RHB, OB: 6 ODIs, 74 runs at 12.33, HS 38.
Solid batsman who scored 85 in 331 minutes on first-class debut v Ireland in 2009-10.

SHAPOOR ZADRAN January 1, 1985, Loger
LHB, LFM: 10 ODIs, 1 run at 0.33, HS 1; 17 wickets at 23.52, BB 4-24.
Left-armer who took 4-24 – including 3 for 1 in 8 balls – on ODI debut v Netherlands in Aug 2009.

CANADA

Rizwan Cheema

Ashish Bagai

Sunil Dhaniram

Cricket has long been played in Canada: the first-ever international match was not England v Australia but Canada v the United States, in New York in 1844. But although the series continued fitfully over the years, cricket never quite took hold in north America – although the States had several handy teams around the turn of the 20th century, and the Canadians have long hosted visits by strong touring sides. Don Bradman made one such trip in the 1930s, and nominated the Brockton Point ground in Vancouver as the most beautiful he'd ever seen. In 1954 a Canadian side toured England, playing several first-class matches. In a portent of things to come, that team included several players who had moved to Canada from the West Indies for better job prospects. After a quiet period, Canadian cricket received a shot in the arm when they qualified for the 1979 World Cup in England, although the inexperienced team was embarrassed by the hosts, being hustled out for 45 at Old Trafford. Canada missed out on World Cup qualification until 2002-03, when a side largely made up of expats – and a few journeymen who happened to have been born in Canada – gave a decent account of themselves. John Davison, who had hovered on the fringes of the Victoria and South Australia sides, returned for the land of his birth and shocked everyone by hammering a century in 67 balls – the fastest in the World Cup at the time – against West Indies. Sri Lanka proved rather more ruthless, bowling them out for 36. Canada qualified again in 2007, without causing any upsets, and again in 2011. Their administration has been striving hard to become more professional, and in 2009 the first central contracts were introduced. Whether to accept them was simple for some, like the hard-hitting batsman Rizwan Cheema, who was serving behind the counter in a fast-food joint – and harder for others, like the wicketkeeper/batsman Ashish Bagai, was had been carving out a career in banking. The Canadians deserve some success, although the paucity of home-grown talent remains a worry.

Canada's ODI records *as at 23.9.10*

Highest total	312-4	v Ireland at Nairobi 2006-07
Lowest total	36	v Sri Lanka at Paarl 2002-03
Most runs	1736	A Bagai (avge. 37.73)
Highest score	137*	A Bagai v Scotland at Nairobi 2006-07
Most wickets	41	S Dhaniram (avge. 30.24)
Best bowling	5-27	A Codrington v Bangladesh at Durban 2002-03
Most matches	54	A Bagai (2003–2010)
World Cup record	First phase 1979, 2002-03, 2006-07	
Overall ODI record	Played 60: Won 16, Lost 43, No result 1	

CANADA

BAGAI, Ashish January 26, 1982, Delhi, India
RHB, WK: 54 ODIs, 1736 runs at 37.73, HS 137*, 2x100; 50 ct 9 st.
Tidy wicketkeeper/batsman who is usually captain too: hundreds v Scotland and Ireland.

BAIDWAN, Harvir Singh July 31, 1987, Chandigarh, India
RHB, RM: 19 ODIs, 147 runs at 24.50, HS 33; 24 wickets at 31.62, BB 3-24.
Tidy medium-pacer who has a good economy rate (4.83) in ODIs.

BARNETT, Geoffery Edward Fulton February 3, 1984, Nelson, New Zealand
LHB, RM: 22 ODIs, 455 runs at 20.68, HS 77.
Opened for Central Districts in New Zealand: 77 v Bangladesh in Antigua in 2007.

BASTIAMPILLAI, Trevin Callistus October 26, 1985, Sri Lanka
RHB, OB: 11 ODIs, 163 runs at 14.81, HS 49; 0 wickets.
Maturing batsman who passed 50 twice in a match against Afghanistan in 2010.

BHATTI, Umar January 4, 1984, Lahore, Pakistan
LHB, LM: 36 ODIs, 378 runs at 17.18, HS 46; 33 wickets at 34.81, BB 4-45.
Left-armer who took a hat-trick against Ireland in 2007 Intercontinental Cup final.

BILLCLIFF, Ian Shaw October 26, 1972, William's Lake, British Columbia
RHB: 19 ODIs, 529 runs at 27.84, HS 93.
Otago regular who made 93 against Bangladesh in Antigua in 2007.

DAVISON, John Michael May 9, 1970, Vancouver Island, British Columbia
RHB, OB: 27 ODIs, 766 runs at 29.46, HS 111, 1x100; 31 wickets at 28.06, BB 3-15.
Big hitter who reached a World Cup century against West Indies in only 67 balls.

DHANIRAM, Sunil October 17, 1968, Port Mourant, Berbice, Guyana
LHB, SLA: 44 ODIs, 915 runs at 24.72, HS 92; 41 wickets at 30.24, BB 5-32.
Former Guyana allrounder whose brother Sudesh now plays for the United States.

JYOTI, Sandeep December 14, 1973, Shimla, India
RHB, OB: 14 ODIs, 264 runs at 22.00, HS 117; 1 wicket at 90.00, BB 1-26.
Entertaining batsman who scored 117 against Scotland at Aberdeen in 2009.

KHURRAM CHOHAN February 22, 1980, Lahore, Pakistan
RHB, RFM: 15 ODIs, 92 runs at 15.33, HS 35*; 22 wickets at 27.00, BB 4-26.
Medium-pacer who took eight wickets in successive matches against Afghanistan in 2010.

MULLA, Ashif Abdulhai May 5, 1980, Gujarat, India
RHB, WK: 24 ODIs, 482 runs at 20.08, HS 58; 47 ct, 13 st.
Long-serving batsman who made 58 against England in the 2006-07 World Cup.

OSINDE, Henry October 17, 1978, Uganda
RHB, RFM: 34 Odis, 54 runs at 4.50, HS 21*; 35 wickets at 32.37, BB 4-33.
Experienced opening bowler who took 4-33 against Kenya in Nairobi in 2007.

RIZWAN CHEEMA August 15, 1978, Pakistan
RHB, RM: 21 ODIs, 523 runs at 27.52, HS 94; 19 wickets at 32.78, BB 3-31.
Big-hitting batsman with an ODI strike-rate of 119.40 – and 24 sixes.

SAMAD, Abdool Mudassar May 3, 1979, Guyana
RHB, OB: 27 ODIs, 740 runs at 29.60, HS 130, 1x100; 7 wickets at 40.14, BB 1-8.
Stylish batsman who made 130 against Bermuda in July 2008.

SURKARI, Zubin Eruch February 26, 1980, Toronto, Ontario
RHB: 15 ODIs, 210 runs at 19.09, HS 49.
Captained Canada on his ODI debut, against Bermuda in 2008.

IRELAND

William Porterfield

Gary Wilson

George Dockrell

Cricket in Ireland was once so popular that Oliver Cromwell banned it in 1656. Since then, it has been something of a minority sport, although there have been occasional big days, as in 1969 when the West Indians were skittled for 25 on a boggy pitch at Sion Mills in County Tyrone (rumours that the visitors enjoyed lavish hospitality at a nearby Guinness brewery the night before are thought to be unfounded). Cricket continued as an amateur pastime until the 1990s, when the Irish board left the auspices of the English one and attained independent ICC membership. Ireland became eligible to play in the World Cup, and narrowly missed out on the 1999 tournament, when they lost a playoff to Scotland. They made no mistake for 2007, though, winning the ICC Trophy (handily, it was played in Ireland) to ensure qualification. A change of captain to the Australian-born Trent Johnston ushered in a new, more professional set-up, and Ireland travelled to the Caribbean hopeful of making a mark. No-one, though, was quite prepared for what happened – except maybe Johnston himself, who packed enough for a seven-week stay when most were expecting a quiet return home in a week or two. In their first World Cup match, Ireland tied with Zimbabwe, then went one better on a Sabina Park greentop on St Patrick's Day, hanging on to beat Pakistan and eliminate one of the pre-tournament favourites. Ireland sailed on to the Super Eights, where they beat Bangladesh too. They also did well in the World Twenty20 in England in 2009, and soon after that almost capsized England in a one-dayer. But the better Irish players are already with English counties (Ed Joyce and Eoin Morgan have already played for England, and others are trying to follow suit), and the others struggle to fit in ever-increasing international commitments around a steady job. Irish cricket needs a more professional domestic structure – and is trying nobly to create it – if the impression made by Johnston's merry men is to be anything more than a footnote in cricket history.

Ireland's ODI records *as at 23.9.10*

Highest total	325-8	v Canada at Toronto 2010
Lowest total	77	v Sri Lanka at St George's 2006-07
Most runs	1313	WTS Porterfield (avge. 34.55)
Highest score	177	PR Stirling v Canada at Toronto 2010
Most wickets	43	DT Johnston (avge. 30.04)
Best bowling	5-14	DT Johnston v Canada at Centurion 2008-09
Most matches	49	KJ O'Brien (2006-2010)
World Cup record		Reached Super Eight stage in only appearance, 2006-07
Overall ODI record		Played 55: Won 27, Lost 24, Tied 1, No result 3

BOTHA, Andre Cornelius September 12, 1975, Johannesburg, South Africa
LHB, RM: 38 ODIs, 624 runs at 20.80, HS 56; 37 wickets at 26.94, BB 4-19.
Former South African provincial player: made 186 for Ireland v Scotland in August 2007.

CONNELL, Peter August 13, 1981, Dannevirke, New Zealand
RHB, RFM: 13 ODIs, 40 runs at 20.00, HS 22*; 13 wickets at 39.84, BB 3-68.
North Down seamer who took 10 for 69 v Holland in Intercontinental Cup at Rotterdam in July 2008.

CUSACK, Alex Richard October 29, 1980, Brisbane, Australia
RHB, RFM: 31 ODIs, 441 runs at 25.94, HS 59*; 34 wickets at 20.32, BB 5-20.
Man of the Match on ODI debut for 36 and 3-15 v South Africa at Belfast in June 2007.*

DOCKRELL, George Henry July 22, 1992, Dublin
RHB, SLA: 13 ODIs, 7 runs at 3.50, HS 5*; 13 wickets at 32.07, BB 4-35.
Precocious slow left-armer coveted by several English counties.

JOHNSTON, David <u>Trent</u> April 29, 1974, Wollongong, NSW, Australia
RHB, RFM: 44 ODIs, 483 runs at 20.12, HS 45*; 43 wickets at 30.04, BB 5-14.
Inspirational captain (and innovative chicken dancer) during Ireland's 2007 World Cup run.

JONES, Nigel Geoffrey April 22, 1982, Timaru, New Zealand
RHB, RM: 10 ODIs, 62 runs at 20.66, HS 25*; 8 wickets at 18.50, BB 2-19.
Former New Zealander who appears to bowl off the wrong foot.

MOONEY, John Francis February 10, 1982, Dublin
LHB, RM: 26 ODIs, 457 runs at 32.64, HS 54; 11 wickets at 39.36, BB 3-79.
Left-hander with a mean reverse-sweep; his brother Paul played for Ireland too.

O'BRIEN, Kevin Joseph March 4, 1984, Dublin
RHB, RFM: 49 ODIs, 1227 runs at 33.16, HS 142, 1×100; 37 wickets at 31.83, BB 3-18.
Allrounder with Dublin's Railway Union club: hit 142 (11 fours, six sixes) v Kenya in Feb 2007.

O'BRIEN, Niall John November 8, 1981, Dublin
LHB, WK: 37 ODIs, 911 runs at 26.79, HS 72; 28 ct, 6 st.
Feisty keeper who has played for Kent and Northants: made 72 in World Cup win over Pakistan.

PORTERFIELD, William Thomas Stuart September 6, 1984, Londonderry
RHB: 41 ODIs, 1313 runs at 34.55, HS 112*, 5×100.
Solid opener: made two ODI hundreds in three days early in 2007; took over as captain in 2008.

POYNTER, Andrew David April 25, 1987, Hammersmith, London
RHB, OB: 14 ODIs, 149 runs at 18.62, HS 78.
Clontarf batsman who played once for Middlesex in 2005: 78 v Afghanistan in 2010.

RANKIN, William <u>Boyd</u> July 5, 1984, Derry
LHB, RFM: 23 ODIs, 25 runs at 12.50, HS 7*; 33 wickets at 24.69, BB 3-32.
Tall (6ft 8ins) fast bowler who did well at the World Cup and later joined Warwickshire.

STIRLING, Paul Robert September 3, 1990, Belfast
RHB: 20 ODIs, 817 runs at 43.00, HS 177, 1×100; 10 wickets at 26.00, BB 4-11.
Batsman on Middlesex's books who slammed 177 against Canada in September 2010.

WHITE, Andrew Roland July 3, 1980, Newtownards, Co. Down
RHB, OB: 46 ODIs, 620 runs at 18.78, HS 79; 25 wickets at 22.92, BB 4-44.
Offspinner, formerly with Northants, who hit 152 on first-class debut, for Ireland v Holland in 2004.*

WILSON, Gary Craig February 5, 1986, Dundonald, Northern Ireland
RHB, WK: 22 ODIs, 519 runs at 27.31, HS 113, 1×100; 16 ct, 6 st.
Handy keeper-batsman who is on the Surrey staff; scored 113 v Holland in Dublin in 2010.

KENYA

Maurice Ouma   Thomas Odoyo   Hiren Varaiya

The British Empire spread cricket to Kenya: the first notable match was played there in 1899, and English-style country clubs still flourish in Nairobi, which can claim one cricket record – six different grounds there have staged official one-day internationals, more than any other city. Strong MCC teams have made several visits to East Africa – one of them, in the early 1960s, unearthed Basharat Hassan, who went on to enjoy a long career with Nottinghamshire. Kenyan players formed the backbone of the East African side in the first World Cup, in 1975, but soon after that they struck out on their own, joining the ICC in their own right in 1981. Kenyan cricket continued to improve quietly until they qualified for the World Cup in 1995-96, where they amazed everyone by upsetting West Indies in a group game. Players reared on hard pitches struggled in early-season England at the 1999 Cup, but the 2003 version was different: it was held in Africa, and some of the matches were played in Kenya. Helped by outside events (England refused to go to Zimbabwe, while New Zealand boycotted Nairobi for security reasons), the Kenyans progressed to the semi-finals. It seemed like the start of a golden era: instead it ushered in a depressing time, marked by player strikes and arguments about administration. Peace broke out in time for the 2007 World Cup, but with several players approaching the veteran stage – many of them come from the same Luo tribe, which is why so many of their surnames begin with O – the results were poor, and by then Ireland had comfortably usurped them as the leading non-Test nation. More haggling over money intruded in 2010, before a resolution in time for the following year's World Cup. Still, Kenya boast arguably the best batsman outside the Test arena, in the veteran Steve Tikolo, while the solidly built allrounder Thomas Odoyo (who played in the 1996 World Cup at 17) was the first bowler from a non-Test nation to take 100 wickets in one-day internationals.

Kenya's ODI records *as at 23.9.10*

Highest total	347-3	v Bangladesh at Nairobi 1997-98
Lowest total	84	v Australia at Nairobi 2002-03
Most runs	3245	SO Tikolo (avge. 30.32)
Highest score	144	KO Otieno v Bangladesh at Nairobi 1997-98
Most wickets	129	TM Odoyo (avge. 29.91)
Best bowling	5-24	CO Obuya v Sri Lanka at Nairobi 2002-03
Most matches	122	SO Tikolo (1996-2009)
World Cup record		Semi-finalists in 2002-03; first phase 1995-96, 1999, 2006-07
Overall ODI record		Played 133: Won 36, Lost 92, No result 5

KAMANDE, James Kabatha December 12, 1978, Muranga
RHB, OB: 78 ODIs, 997 runs at 18.12, HS 74; 44 wickets at 44.31, BB 4-36.
Former medium-pacer who now bowls offspin, after his action was reported to the ICC.

LUSENO, Alfred Sorongo December 20, 1981, Kakemaga
RHB, RFM: 10 ODIs, 34 runs at 17.00, HS 16*; 9 wickets at 35.11, BB 4-32.
Fast bowler whose brother, Josephat Ababu, has also played for Kenya.

OBANDA, Alex Ouma December 25, 1987, Nairobi
RHB: 36 ODIs, 1017 runs at 32.80, HS 96*.
Strokeplaying batsman who was stranded four short of a century against Zimbabwe in Feb 2009.

OBUYA, Collins Omondi July 27, 1981, Nairobi
RHB, LB: 83 ODIs, 1382 runs at 22.65, HS 78*; 29 wickets at 50.75, BB 5-24.
Tall legspinner who played a few matches for Warwickshire after doing well at the 2003 World Cup.

OBUYA, David Oluoch August 14, 1979, Nairobi
RHB, WK: 64 ODIs, 1183 runs at 19.71, HS 93; 32 ct, 5 st.
Opener, wicketkeeper, and brother of Collins Obuya and Kennedy Otieno.

ODHIAMBO, Nehemiah Ngoche August 7, 1983, Nairobi, Kenya
RHB, RFM: 50 ODIs, 424 runs at 12.84, HS 66; 51 wickets at 36.66, BB 4-61.
Fast bowler who took 5-20 in T20 v Scotland in Feb 2010; three brothers have played for Kenya.

ODOYO, Thomas Migai May 12, 1978, Nairobi
RHB, RFM: ODIs 126 (5 for Africa), 2307 runs (24.54), HS 111*; 133 wkts (30.19), BB 4-25.
Hard-hitting allrounder: the first bowler from a non-Test nation to take 100 wickets in ODIs.

ONGONDO, Peter Jimmy Carter February 10, 1977, Nairobi
RHB, RFM: 77 ODIs (1 for Africa), 385 runs at 9.39, HS 36; 77 wkts at 29.46, BB 5-51.
Handy seamer and useful tailender who once top-scored against West Indies with 36 from No. 11.

OTIENO, Elijah Asoyo January 3, 1988, Nairobi
RHB, RFM: 13 ODIs, 23 runs at 5.75, HS 11; 10 wickets at 42.00, BB 3-39.
Promising young seamer – but with the bat collected five ducks in his first seven first-class innings.

OTIENO, Kennedy Obuya March 11, 1972, Nairobi
RHB, WK: 90 ODIs, 2016 runs at 23.44, HS 144, 2×100; 43 ct, 14 st.
Veteran of the 1996 World Cup win over West Indies: has made two ODI centuries v Bangladesh.

OUMA, Maurice Akumu November 8, 1982, Kiambli
RHB, WK: 64 ODIs, 1237 runs at 20.96, HS 61; 42 ct, 8 st.
Handy striker who often opens: took over as captain in 2009.

PATEL, Rakep Rajendra July 12, 1989, Nairobi
RHB, OB: 21 ODIs, 320 runs at 17.77, HS 92; 0 wicket for 61.
Promising batsman who hit 92 against the Netherlands in February 2010.

TIKOLO, Stephen Ogonji June 25, 1971, Nairobi
RHB, OB: 122 ODIs (4 for Africa), 3230 runs at 30.18, HS 111, 3×100; 88 wkts at 32.30, BB 4-41.
Probably the best batsman outside the Test arena: 28 hundreds for Kenya, including two doubles.

VARAIYA, Hiren Ashok April 9, 1984, Nairobi
RHB, SLA: 51 ODIs, 219 runs at 14.60, HS 34; 57 wickets at 27.91, BB 4-25.
Slow left-armer who flights the ball well: took a wicket with 1st ball in an ODI, v Canada in 2006.

WATERS, Seren Robert April 11, 1990, Nairobi
RHB: 12 ODIs, 261 runs at 21.75, HS 74.
Precocious batsman who scored 74 v South Africa in November 2008 while still a schoolboy.

THE NETHERLANDS

Peter Borren

Tom Cooper

Bas Zuiderent

Cricket was brought to The Netherlands by British soldiers during the Napoleonic War: by 1881 there was a Dutch team, and two years later a national board, comprising 18 clubs, four of which still exist. A league system has long flourished, and there has been a tradition of foreign players coming over to coach. Dutch cricket received a boost in 1964 when Australia visited after an Ashes tour and lost by three wickets, and more noses were tweaked in 1989, with a win over England A. West Indies (1991) and South Africa (1994) also succumbed – it's safe to say they were more relaxed than they might have been for an official international – and another strongish England side was beaten in 1993. The Netherlands qualified for their first World Cup three years later, and weren't disgraced, and they were there again in 2003, when they beat Namibia. They just scraped in to the 2007 tournament, winning a playoff against the UAE, but again managed a consolation win, this time over Scotland, which made up for being pummelled by South Africa and Australia. Perhaps their biggest moment, though, came in the first match of the World Twenty20 in 2009, when they embarrassed England – at Lord's, too. Standout performers in recent years have included Roland Lefebvre, who played for Somerset and Glamorgan, and Bas Zuiderent, who had a spell with Sussex. Essex's Ryan ten Doeschate hammered four centuries in three ICC Intercontinental Cup games in 2006, and soon shot to the top of the national one-day runscoring and wicket-taking lists, while the Australian Tom Cooper, whose mother is Dutch, made a stunning start in 2010. The local players are very keen, but there are not that many of them, fans are thin on the ground, and there's really no chance of a proper first-class competition. The future might not be too bright but, for the Dutch one-day team at least, it's certainly orange.

The Netherlands' ODI records as at 23.9.10

Highest total	315-8	v Bermuda at Rotterdam 2007
Lowest total	80	v West Indies at Dublin 2007
Most runs	1234	RN ten Doeschate (avge. 68.55)
Highest score	134*	KJJ van Noortwijk v Namibia at Bloemfontein 2002-03
Most wickets	48	RN ten Doeschate (avge. 20.93)
Best bowling	4-23	E Schiferli v Kenya at Potchefstroom 2008-09
Most matches	53	B Zuiderent (1996-2010)
World Cup record	Eliminated in first round 1995-96, 2002-03 and 2006-07	
Overall ODI record	Played 57: Won 23, Lost 32, No result 2	

THE NETHERLANDS

ADEEL RAJA   August 15, 1980, Lahore, Pakistan
RHB, OB: 19 ODIs, 28 runs at 3.50, HS 8*; 17 wickets at 36.17, BB 4-42.
Returned in 2010 after failing a drugs test in 2007.

BARRESI, Wesley   May 3, 1984, Johannesburg, South Africa
RHB: 9 ODIs, 208 runs at 29.71, HS 64*.
Hard-hitting batsman who formerly played for Easterns in South Africa.

BORREN, Peter William   August 21, 1983, Christchurch, New Zealand
RHB, RM: 39 ODIs, 477 runs at 14.90, HS 96; 35 wickets at 33.25, BB 3-30.
Combative allrounder who made 105 and 96 v Canada in 2006: appointed captain in 2010.

BUKHARI, Mudassar   December 26, 1983, Gujrat, Pakistan
RHB, RFM: 27 ODIs, 283 runs at 16.64, HS 71; 33 wickets at 24.75, BB 3-17.
Primarily a bowler, he scored 71 (after opening) and took 3-24 against Ireland in July 2007.

BUURMAN, Atse F.   March 21, 1982, The Netherlands
RHB, WK: 15 ODIs, 114 runs at 16.28, HS 34; 14 ct, 3 st.
Found a permanent place after the retirement of long-serving wicketkeeper Jeroen Smits in 2009.

COOPER, Tom Lexley William   November 26, 1986, Wollongong, NSW, Australia
RHB, OB: 10 ODIs, 589 runs at 65.44, HS 101, 1×100; 5 wickets at 23.80.
Hard-hitting batsman who uniquely passed 50 in his first three ODIs, then made 101 in his fifth.

de GROOTH, Tom Nico   May 14, 1979, The Hague
RHB, OB: 22 ODIs, 387 runs at 21.50, HS 97; 1 wicket at 2.00, BB 1-2.
Made 98 (v Scotland), 196 and 97 (v Bermuda) in successive matches in August 2007.

JONKMAN, Mark Benjamin Sebastiaan   March 20, 1986, The Hague
RHB, RFM: 16 ODIs, 59 runs at 11.80, HS 16; 24 wickets at 23.54, BB 3-24.
Probably Holland's fastest bowler: his twin brother Maurits has also played for the national team.

KERVEZEE, Alexei Nicolaas   September 11, 1989, Walvis Bay, Namibia
RHB, occasional RM: 30 ODIs, 664 runs at 26.56, HS 92; 0 wickets.
World Cup debut at 17, later made 98 v Canada, and joined Worcestershire in 2007.

SCHIFERLI, Edgar   May 17, 1976, The Hague
RHB, RFM: 27 ODIs, 153 runs at 11.76, HS 41; 31 wickets at 30.12, BB 4-23.
Holland's most experienced fast bowler: missed the 2007 World Cup with a leg injury.

SEELAAR, Pieter Marinus   July 2, 1987, Schiedam
RHB, SLA: 21 ODIs, 85 runs at 21.25, HS 34*; 21 wickets at 32.80, BB 3-22.
Tidy spinner who took 5-57 in Intercontinental Cup match v Kenya at Amstelveen in 2008.

SZWARCZYNSKI, Eric Stefan   February 13, 1983, Vanderbijlpark, South Africa
RHB: 30 ODIs, 748 runs at 27.70, HS 84*.
Batsman whose favourite player is Allan Donald: made 84 v Canada in July 2010.*

ten DOESCHATE, Ryan Neil   June 30, 1980, Port Elizabeth, South Africa
RHB, RFM: 27 ODIs, 1234 runs at 68.55, HS 109*, 3×100; 48 wickets at 20.93, BB 4-31.
Allrounder who reached 1000 ODI runs quicker than anyone bar Viv Richards and Gordon Greenidge.

van BUNGE, Daan Lodewijk Samuel   October 19, 1982, Voorburg
RHB, LB: 32 ODIs, 564 runs at 21.69, HS 80; 11 wickets at 29.18, BB 3-16.
Talented batsman ... but his legspin was hit for six sixes by Herschelle Gibbs at the 2007 World Cup.

ZUIDERENT, Bastiaan   March 3, 1977, Utrecht
RHB: 53 ODIs, 1080 runs at 25.71, HS 77*.
Orthodox opener who had a spell with Sussex: has played in all Holland's World Cup matches.

SCOTLAND

Gordon Drummond

Josh Davey

Majid Haq

Cricket crept over the border from England in the mid-18th century: soldiers played it near Perth in 1750, although the first recorded match in Scotland was not till 1785. More recently there has long been a strong amateur league system in the country, although – just as in Ireland – international aspirations have always been handicapped by the absence of a proper professional set-up, which has meant that the better players have always migrated south. One of them, the Ayr-born Mike Denness, captained England, while one of the few bowlers to trouble Don Bradman in 1930 was the Scottish legspinner Ian Peebles. More recently, offspinner Peter Such (born in Helensburgh) played for England, while Gavin Hamilton (born in Broxburn) also won an England Test cap after impressing for Scotland at the 1999 World Cup. Unfortunately, Hamilton bagged a pair, and was soon back playing for Scotland: he hit his maiden ODI century in 2008. At the 2007 World Cup, Hamilton appeared alongside another former England player in Dougie Brown, the combative allrounder who had a long career with Warwickshire and played nine ODIs in 1997-98. Scotland left the auspices of the English board and joined the ICC in 1994, but they failed to win a match – or reach 200 – in any of their World Cup games in 1999 or 2007. They also competed in the English counties' limited-overs league for many years, without managing more than the occasional upset, and the team failed to qualify for the World Twenty20 in 2010 or the following year's World Cup. The main problem lying in the way of Scotland's advancement – apart from the weather – remains the lack of a sound domestic structure which might support first-class cricket; local support is also patchy, despite the sterling efforts of a few diehards. Until this is addressed – if it ever can be – Scotland will continue to suffer from a player drain to English counties.

Scotland's ODI records *as at 23.9.10*

Highest total	**293-8**	**v Canada at Mombasa 2006-07**
Lowest total	**68**	**v West Indies at Leicester 1999**
Most runs	**1231**	**GM Hamilton (avge. 35.17)**
Highest score	**123***	**RR Watson v Canada at Mombasa 2006-07**
Most wickets	**41**	**JAR Blain (avge. 28.60)**
Best bowling	**5-9**	**JH Davey v Afghanistan at Ayr 2010**
Most matches	**41**	**NFI McCallum (2006-2010)**
World Cup record		**Eliminated in first round 1999 and 2006-07**
Overall ODI record		**Played 50: Won 15, Lost 32, No result 3**

SCOTLAND

BERRINGTON, Richard Douglas April 3, 1987, Pretoria, South Africa
RHB, RFM: 16 ODIs, 292 runs at 22.46, HS 84; 10 wickets at 34.60, BB 2-14.
Handy allrounder who made 84 against the Netherlands in June 2010.

COETZER, Kyle James April 14, 1984, Aberdeen
RHB, RM: 5 ODIs, 132 runs at 26.40, HS 51; 0 wickets
Attractive batsman who is on Durham's books, and scored two first-class hundreds for them in 2007.

DAVEY, Joshua Henry August 3, 1990, Aberdeen
RHB, RM: 4 ODIs, 46 runs at 11.50, HS 24; 6 wickets at 15.66, BB 5-9.
Batsman on Middlesex's books: took 5-9 v Afghanistan at Ayr in August 2010.

DRUMMOND, Gordon David April 21, 1980, Meigle, Perthshire
RHB, RFM: 21 ODIs, 182 runs at 22.75, HS 35*; 20 wickets at 31.05, BB 4-41.
Watsonians fast bowler who took 4-41 v Canada in July 2009: appointed captain in 2010.

GOUDIE, Gordon August 12, 1987, Aberdeen
RHB, RFM: 10 ODIs, 40 runs at 8.00, HS 17*; 17 wickets at 22.00, BB 5-73.
West of Scotland fast bowler who took 5-73 against Australia in 2009.

HAQ Khan, Rana Majid February 11, 1983, Paisley
LHB, OB: 27 ODIs, 411 runs at 17.86, HS 71; 31 wickets at 33.61, BB 4-28.
Hard-hitting allrounder, who plays for Ferguslie: took 4-28 v West Indies at Clontarf in 2007.

LOCKHART, Douglas Ross January 19, 1976, Glasgow
RHB, WK: 14 ODIs, 218 runs at 24.22, HS 46; 10 ct, 0 st.
Scored 151 v Canada in 2008: returned in 2010 as first-choice wicketkeeper.

LYONS, Ross Thomas December 8, 1984, Greenock
LHB, SLA: 25 ODIs, 90 runs at 22.50, HS 28; 20 wickets at 45.05, BB 3-21.
Promising slow left-armer who dismissed Shahid Afridi in his first ODI.

McCALLUM, Neil Francis Ian November 22, 1977, Edinburgh
RHB: 41 ODIs, 977 runs at 28.73, HS 121*, 2×100.
PE teacher who made 181 v Holland in 2007, and has also hit two ODI centuries against Ireland.

MacLEOD, Calum Scott November 15, 1988, Glasgow
RHB, RFM: 4 ODIs, 12 runs at 6.00, HS 10*; 3 wickets at 46.33, BB 2-46.
Fast bowler on Warwickshire's books, whose bowling action has been under scrutiny.

MOMMSEN, Preston Luke October 14, 1987, Durban, South Africa
RHB, OB: 7 ODIs, 142 runs at 20.28, HS 80; 1 wicket at 19.00.
Prolific schoolboy batsman who qualified for Scotland in 2010.

NEL, Johann Dewald June 6, 1980, Klerksdorp, South Africa
RHB, RFM: 19 ODIs, 31 runs at 15.50, HS 11*; 14 wickets at 46.35, BB 4-25.
Fast bowler who dismissed Inzamam-ul-Haq on his ODI debut, and both Australia's openers in 2009.

POONIA, Naveed Singh May 11, 1986, Govan, Glasgow
RHB: 21 ODIs, 237 runs at 11.28, HS 67.
Stylish batsman formerly on the Warwickshire staff: he made eight centuries for their 2nd XI.

WATSON, Ryan Robert November 12, 1976, Salisbury (now Harare), Zimbabwe
RHB, RM: 35 ODIs, 956 runs at 30.83, HS 123*, 1×100; 12 wickets at 44.00, BB 3-18.
Chunky batsman, at school with SA's Graeme Smith, who hit 123 v Canada in Mombasa in 2006-07.*

WATTS, David Fraser June 5, 1979, King's Lynn, Norfolk
RHB: 32 ODIs, 884 runs at 29.46, HS 101, 1×100.
Banker-turned-batsman who scored 171 v Denmark in 2006, and 101 v Canada in July 2009.*

ZIMBABWE

Elton Chigumbura   *Ray Price*   *Christopher Mpofu*

The decline of cricket in Zimbabwe is one of the game's saddest tales – outranked, of course, by the decline of the country itself from prosperous to dangerous. Cricket was first played in what was then Rhodesia in 1891, and for years the national side took part in South Africa's Currie Cup. Several Rhodesians played for South Africa, notably Colin Bland ... and offspinner John Traicos, in 1970: he was still around 22 years later when Zimbabwe were given Test status themselves. That came after years of consistent performances, including a famous World Cup win over Australia in 1983, inspired by Duncan Fletcher, later England's Ashes-winning coach. Zimbabwe were always hampered by a small player-base, but punched above their weight thanks to a nucleus of world-class players including Dave Houghton, the Flower brothers and Heath Streak. Probably their strongest side was assembled for the 1999 World Cup, following the return of Neil Johnson (previously based in South Africa) and Murray Goodwin (Australia). Zimbabwe qualified for the second phase that year, and six of their eight Test wins came between October 1998 and November 2001. And then it all started to go wrong. At the 2003 World Cup, with the political situation at home worsening, Andy Flower and the black fast bowler Henry Olonga sported black armbands bemoaning the "death of democracy" in Zimbabwe: their reward was to be hounded out of the country. A divisive dispute over payments and selection then tore the rest of the side apart. Zimbabwe pulled out of Test cricket in 2005, just ahead of official ICC action. There was a chink of light late in 2007, when ICC's president Ray Mali optimistically claimed that Zimbabwe could top the world rankings in three years, after witnessing some encouraging performances against South Africa. The beleaguered young side has indeed shown some improvement, and there's serious talk of a return to Test cricket soon.

Zimbabwe's ODI records *as at 23.9.10*

Highest total	351-7	v Kenya at Mombasa 2008-09
Lowest total	35	v Sri Lanka at Harare 2003-04
Most runs	6786	A Flower (avge. 35.34)
Highest score	194*	CK Coventry v Bangladesh at Bulawayo 2009
Most wickets	237	HH Streak (avge. 29.81)
Best bowling	6-19	HK Olonga v England at Cape Town 1999-2000
Most matches	219	GW Flower (1992-2004)
World Cup record	Second phase 1999 and 2002-03	
Overall ODI record	Played 377: Won 98, Lost 265, Tied 5, No result 9	

Test records for Zimbabwe can be found in the 2008 Guide

ZIMBABWE

BLIGNAUT, Arnoldus Mauritius ("Andy")   August 1, 1978, Salisbury (now Harare)
LHB, RFM: 19 Tests, 886 runs (26.84), 53 wkts (37.05). 54 ODIs, 626 runs (18.96), 50 wkts (41.26).
Hard-hitting allrounder who returned to the national side after five years in 2010.

CHIBHABHA, Chamunorwa Justice   September 6, 1986, Masvingo
RHB, RM: 0 Tests. 50 ODIs, 1092 runs (21.84); 20 wkts (49.05).
Good-looking off-driver, and fine fielder: his sister Julia captained Zimbabwe's women's team.

CHIGUMBURA, Elton   March 14, 1986, Kwekwe
RHB, RFM: 6 Tests, 187 runs (15.58), 9 wkts (55.33). 113 ODIs, 2292 runs (24.38), 79 wkts (37.37).
Big-hitting allrounder, and good outfielder, who played for Northants in 2010.

COVENTRY, Charles Kevin   March 8, 1983, Kwekwe
RHB, WK: 2 Tests, 88 runs (22.00). 32 ODIs, 766 runs (27.35).
Equalled the ODI record by hammering 194* against Bangladesh at Bulawayo in 2009.

CREMER, Alexander <u>Graeme</u>   September 19, 1986, Harare
RHB, LB: 6 Tests, 29 runs (2.63), 13 wkts (45.76). 29 ODIs, 159 runs (13.25), 42 wkts (24.95).
Maturing legspinner who took 6-46 against Kenya at Harare in October 2009.

LAMB, Gregory Arthur   March 4, 1981, Harare
RHB, OB: 0 Tests. 9 ODIs, 134 runs (19.14), 8 wkts (33.37).
Handy allrounder who spent some time at Hampshire, winning the C&G Trophy in 2005.

MASAKADZA, Hamilton   August 9, 1983, Harare
RHB, LB: 15 Tests, 785 runs (27.06), 2 wkts (19.50). 95 ODIs, 2601 runs (28.58), 24 wkts (35.00).
Early-flowering batsman who made 119 on Test debut against West Indies in 2001, aged 17.

MATSIKENYERI, Stuart   May 3, 1983, Harare
RHB, OB: 8 Tests, 351 runs (23.40), 2 wkts (172.50). 109 ODIs, 2196 runs (22.63), 16 wkts (48.62).
Cheerful, diminutive allrounder who made 150 for Zimbabwe v Bangladesh Board XI in 2005.

MPOFU, Christopher Bobby   November 27, 1985, Plumtree
RHB, RFM: 6 Tests, 17 runs (2.83), 8 wkts (69.50). 42 ODIs, 29 runs (2.41), 44 wkts (38.68).
Tall seamer who took 6-52 v Kenya in Nairobi in October 2008.

PRICE, Raymond William   June 12, 1976, Salisbury (now Harare)
RHB, SLA: 18 Tests, 224 runs (9.73), 69 wkts (39.86). 79 ODIs, 296 runs (8.96), 74 wkts (35.91).
Economical spinner who played for Worcestershire between 2004 and 2007.

SIBANDA, Vusimuzi   October 10, 1983, Highfields, Harare
RHB, RM: 3 Tests, 48 runs (8.00). 84 ODIs, 1796 runs (22.17), 2 wkts (74.00).
Stylish opener who often gets out when set: made 116 in tri-series final v Bermuda in 2006.

TAIBU, Tatenda   May 14, 1983, Harare
RHB, WK: 24 Tests, 1273 runs (29.60), 1 wkt (27.00). 120 ODIs, 2466 runs (28.34), 2 wkts (30.50).
Tiny keeper, big-hearted batter: the youngest Test captain at 20, he later fell out with the Board.

TAYLOR, Brendan Ross Murray   February 6, 1986, Harare
RHB, OB, WK: 10 Tests, 422 runs (21.10), 0 wkts. 102 ODIs, 2889 runs (31.74), 9 wkts (27.11).
Occasionally brilliant batsman, with a booming cover-drive: has had disciplinary problems.

UTSEYA, Prosper   March 26, 1985, Harare
RHB, OB: 1 Test, 45 runs (22.50), 0 wkts. 111 ODIs, 749 runs (13.61), 84 wkts (45.98).
Short offspinner who keeps the runs down: appointed captain at 21 in 2006, but resigned in 2010.

VERMEULEN, Mark Andrew   March 2, 1979, Salisbury (now Harare)
RHB, OB: 8 Tests, 414 runs (25.87). 43 ODIs, 868 runs (22.25); 1 wkt (5.00).
Temperamental but occasionally brilliant batsman who made a Test century v West Indies in 2003.

OFFICIALS

ALEEM DAR

UMPIRE

Aleem Dar played 17 first-class matches as an offspinning allrounder, but never surpassed the 39 he scored in his first innings, for Railways in February 1987. He took up umpiring in 1998-99, and stood in his first ODI the following season. He officiated at the 2003 World Cup, and a year later was the first Pakistani to join the ICC's elite panel. Calm and unobtrusive, he soon established a good reputation, and it was no surprise when he was chosen to stand in the 2007 World Cup final. What was a surprise was his part in the chaos in the dark at the end, for which all the officials were excluded from the World Twenty20 championships later in the year. But he was soon back in favour, and stood in the World Twenty20 final in Barbados in 2010. Unlike most of his colleagues, he continues to play, and made 82 in a club game the day after umpiring a Test in Mumbai in November 2004.

Born *June 6, 1968, Jhang, Pakistan.* **Tests** *60,* **ODIs** *133,* **T20Is** *18*

ASAD RAUF

UMPIRE

Asad Rauf was a right-hand batsman who enjoyed a solid if unspectacular first-class career in Pakistan in the 1980s, four times making more than 600 runs in a season and scoring three centuries, the highest 130 for Railways against National Bank in November 1981. He umpired his first first-class match in 1998-99, and stood in his first ODI early in 2000. It took a bit longer to crack the Test scene, but he advanced rapidly once he did, joining the ICC's elite panel in April 2006. A former offspinner himself, he is more prepared than some to give spinners lbws when batsmen prop forward hiding bat behind pad.

Born *May 12, 1956, Lahore, Pakistan.* **Tests** *31,* **ODIs** *80,* **T20Is** *15*

TREVOR **BAYLISS**

COACH

Trevor Bayliss was a strokeplaying middle-order batsman and brilliant cover fielder for New South Wales, and replaced Steve Rixon as their coach in 2004-05. He immediately guided them to the Pura Cup title, and added the one-day cup the following year. In 2007 Bayliss, who never won a Test cap, was named to succeed another Australian, Tom Moody, as Sri Lanka's coach, and although he lost the short Test series in Australia he was then in charge for home victories over England and India, as well as a shared series in the West Indies that included Sri Lanka's first Test win there.

Born *December 21, 1962, Goulburn, NSW, Australia. Appointed Sri Lanka's coach in 2007*

BILLY **BOWDEN**

Some eccentrics are born. Others thrust eccentricity upon themselves. Brent "Billy" Bowden shot to fame with a zany array of embellished signals and a preposterous eye for showmanship. Bowden turned to umpiring after the onset of arthritis in his early twenties, and earned a reputation for giving batsmen out with a curiously bent finger. The most celebrated of his antics is the hop-on-one-leg-and-reach-for-Jesus signal for six. For all the embellishments, though his decision-making is usually spot-on.

Born *April 11, 1963, Henderson, Auckland, New Zealand.* **Tests** *62,* **ODIs** *148,* **T20Is** *18*

CHRIS **BROAD**

It was a classic case of poacher turned gamekeeper when Chris Broad became a match referee: he had several jousts with authority during a 25-Test career in the 1980s. A tall, angular left-hander, Broad did well in Australia, scoring four Test hundreds there. After a back injury hastened his retirement, he tried his hand at TV commentary, then in 2003 became a match referee keen on enforcing the Code of Conduct. His son, Stuart, made his England debut in 2006.

Born *September 29. 1957, Knowle, Bristol, England.* **Tests** *40,* **ODIs** *164,* **T20Is** *37*

JEFF **CROWE**

Jeff Crowe might have played for Australia – he had several successful Sheffield Shield seasons in Adelaide – but he eventually returned to New Zealand, winning 39 Test caps, six as captain. Although he was often overshadowed by his younger brother Martin, Jeff managed three Test centuries of his own. After retirement he had a spell as New Zealand's manager, before becoming a referee in 2003.

Born *September 14, 1958, Auckland, New Zealand.* **Tests** *42,* **ODIs** *133,* **T20Is** *19*

STEVE **DAVIS**

Steve Davis played club cricket in Adelaide before turning to umpiring. He had a rapid rise: appointed to the Australian first-class list in 1990-91, he joined the national panel two years later and stood in his first ODI the same season. He stood in three matches in the 2007 World Cup, and in the final two Tests in his native England in 2008, against South Africa, shortly after being elevated to the elite panel. He was one of the umpires in Lahore early the following year and was lucky to survive the terrorist attack on the Sri Lankan team coach.

Born *April 9, 1952, London, England.* **Tests** *27,* **ODIs** *94,* **T20Is** *14*

OFFICIALS

ASOKA **DE SILVA**

Asoka de Silva played 10 Tests and 28 one-day internationals for Sri Lanka between 1985 and 1992 as a legspinner, although he found it hard to replicate his good domestic form on the international stage. He took up umpiring in 1996-97, and soon became Sri Lanka's best-regarded official. He first stood in an ODI against Pakistan at Galle in August 1999, and umpired a Test the following year (Aravinda de Silva and Sanath Jayasuriya, who were both in de Silva's last Test as a player, were still playing for his umpiring debut). He had a spell on the ICC's elite panel before being dropped from it in 2004. But he was back for the 2007 World Cup – he also officiated in the 2003 tournament – was restored to the elite panel in the middle of 2008, and stood in the World Twenty20 in England the following year. No Sri Lankan has umpired in more Tests or ODIs.

Born *March 28, 1956, Kalutara, Sri Lanka.* **Tests** 46, **ODIs** 104, **T20Is** 9

BILLY **DOCTROVE**

Billy Doctrove played club cricket in Dominica for a number of years, but his first love was football, particularly Liverpool, which explains his odd nickname "Toshack". In 1995 he became Dominica's first FIFA referee, and officiated in a number of internationals in the Caribbean, including a World Cup qualifier between Guyana and Grenada. In 1997 he quit football to concentrate on cricket umpiring, and stood in his first Test in 2000. He joined the international panel in 2004 and the elite one in 2006, but his first forays at the highest level were uninspiring, and he found himself embroiled in the Pakistan ball-tampering furore at The Oval in 2006, as the "other umpire" to Darrell Hair. He grew in stature, though, and stood in the first two Tests of the 2009 Ashes series. The following year he umpired the final of the World Twenty20 in Barbados.

Born *July 3, 1955, Marigot, Dominica.* **Tests** 29, **ODIs** 101, **T20Is** 17

MARAIS **ERASMUS**

The solidly built Marais Erasmus was a handy allrounder for Boland in South African domestic cricket, averaging just under 30 with the bat –scoring a century against the touring Warwickshire team in 1991-92 – and also taking 131 wickets with some energetic medium-pace. That included 6 for 22 as the New Zealanders were bundled out for an embarrassing 86 on a sporting Paarl pitch in December 1994. Erasmus turned to umpiring on retirement and, once he reached the ICC's reserve list, was speedily promoted: he stood in his first ODI in Kenya in 2007, and was part of the officiating team at the World Twenty20 in 2009 and again in 2010. Earlier that year he was appointed to the ICC's elite panel, and stood in his first Test in Bangladesh in January 2010.

Born *February 27, 1964, George, Cape Province, South Africa.* **Tests** 3, **ODIs** 16, **T20Is** 11

ANDY **FLOWER**

Andy Flower was often a lone beacon of class in an underpowered Zimbabwe side. A compact left-hander strong on the sweep, Flower scored 4,794 Tests runs at 51, and nearly 7,000 in ODIs. A deep thinker, Flower was hounded out of Zimbabwe after he and Henry Olonga wore black armbands mourning the "death of democracy" there during the 2003 World Cup. Flower moved to England, where he did well for Essex, then joined the England coaching set-up, first as Peter Moores's assistant then as fulltime coach in time for the successful 2009 Ashes series.

Born *April 28, 1968, Cape Town, South Africa. Appointed England coach in 2009*

OTTIS **GIBSON**

Fast bowler Ottis Gibson was unlucky that his best years coincided with the pomp of Curtly Ambrose and Courtney Walsh: Gibson played only two Tests, and a few ODIs, in the 1990s. Still, he carved out a successful career, particularly in county cricket for Glamorgan, Leicestershire and – late in his career – for Durham. It was an inspired move: he made a career-best 155 for his new county in 2006, and the following year took all ten wickets in an innings against Hampshire. That winter he joined the England coaching staff but early in 2010 Gibson was persuaded to return home and take on the big task of returning West Indies to Test cricket's top table.

Born *March 16, 1969, Sion Hill, St Peter, Barbados. Appointed West Indies coach in 2010*

IAN **GOULD**

Ian "Gunner" Gould was a combative wicketkeeper/batsman who scored nearly 9000 runs and made more than 700 dismissals in first-class cricket. He started with Middlesex, then moved to Sussex, who he captained to the NatWest Trophy in 1986. Although he never won a Test cap, he did appear in 18 ODIs, all of them in 1983, including that year's World Cup in England. He joined the English first-class umpires' panel in 2002, was promoted to the international panel in April 2006, and joined the elite panel three years later, and immediately looked at home.

Born *August 19, 1957, Taplow, Buckinghamshire, England.* **Tests** *14,* **ODIs** *46,* **T20Is** *14*

MARK **GREATBATCH**

A beefy and charismatic left-hander, Mark "Paddy" Greatbatch was adaptable enough to block for hours to save the Perth Test of 1989-90 or to blast away at the top of the order as an early one-day pinch hitter. He started his Test career with a debut century against England in 1987-88, and finished with 2021 Test runs at 30.62. After an up-and-down time coaching at home and in England he became an advisor to New Zealand's selection panel in 2007, before the sudden resignation of Andy Moles – blamed on "player power" – saw Greatbatch promoted to the top job in January 2010.

Born *December 11, 1963, Auckland, New Zealand. Appointed New Zealand coach in 2010*

OFFICIALS

DARYL **HARPER**

Daryl Harper played club cricket in Adelaide for many years before turning to umpiring. He stood in his first first-class match in 1987-88, and joined Australia's international panel six years later. Quiet and undemonstrative, he was Australia's first representative on the ICC's international panel when it was set up in 2002, being chosen ahead of Darrell Hair and Simon Taufel, and is one of only two survivors (with Rudi Koertzen) from that original intake. He stood (along with his compatriot Simon Taufel) in the World Twenty20 final at Lord's in 2009. He likes most sports, particularly Aussie Rules football and basketball, and writes an entertaining online blog about his travels at www.cricketump.com.

Born *October 23, 1951, Adelaide, Australia.* **Tests** *90,* **ODIs** *166,* **T20Is** *10*

TONY **HILL**

Tony Hill came into umpiring without any background in first-class cricket, but soon established himself as a competent and reliable official, being appointed to the ICC's international panel in 1998 – he stood in an ODI against Zimbabwe that March – and to the full elite panel in 2009, although he had umpired the occasional Test since 2001-02. Hill was one of the umpires for the inaugural Twenty20 international, Australia's victory over New Zealand at Auckland in 2004-05, and stood in the first three World Twenty20 tournaments. He also officiated in three matches at the 2007 World Cup. At Lord's in 2010, for England's Test against Pakistan, Hill formed an all-Kiwi umpiring partnership with Billy Bowden. A keen golfer, he is a regional training officer and mentor for umpires in the Northern Districts, and runs an online question-and-answer forum for umpires of all levels.

Born *June 26, 1951, Auckland, New Zealand.* **Tests** *20,* **ODIs** *76,* **T20Is** *16*

ALAN **HURST**

A strapping fast bowler, Alan Hurst won all but one of his dozen Test caps during the World Series Cricket era, after Australia's leading players had been poached by Kerry Packer. He nonetheless took 25 wickets in the 1978-79 Ashes series, which Australia lost 5-1, before the return of Lillee and Co., and a serious back injury, put paid to his future prospects. He was also a notably bad batsman, collecting ducks in exactly half his 20 Test innings. After a spell as a teacher he joined the ICC's panel of referees in 2004. His mettle was tested in Antigua early in 2009 when poor drainage at the new Sir Vivian Richards Stadium meant a rapid move to the old Recreation Ground.

Born *July 15, 1950, Altona, Melbourne, Australia.* **Tests** *39,* **ODIs** *91,* **T20Is** *25*

GARY **KIRSTEN**

A gritty left-hander, Gary Kirsten worked out his strengths and played to them superbly in a career that brought him 7289 runs in 101 Tests for South Africa, with 21 centuries. Kirsten's methodical approach helped when he turned to coaching, first as a batting consultant, then as director of his own coaching academy in Cape Town. In December 2007 he succeeded Greg Chappell in the hot seat as coach of India.

Born *November 23, 1967, Cape Town, South Africa. Appointed India coach in 2007*

RANJAN **MADUGALLE**

A stylish right-hander, Ranjan Madugalle won 21 Test caps, the first of them in Sri Lanka's inaugural Test, against England in 1981-82, when he top-scored with 65. He also made 103 against India in Colombo in 1985, and captained Sri Lanka twice. Not long after retiring, he became one of the first match refs, and was appointed the ICC's chief referee in 2001. His easy-going exterior and charming personality are a mask for someone who has a reputation as a strict disciplinarian.

Born *April 22, 1959, Kandy, Sri Lanka.* **Tests** *119,* **ODIs** *251,* **T20Is** *44*

ROSHAN **MAHANAMA**

Roshan Mahanama was part of the winning team in the 1996 World Cup, and the following year made 225 as he and Sanath Jayasuriya put on 576, then a record Test partnership, as Sri Lanka ran up 952 for 6 (another record) against India in Colombo. An attacking right-hander who made four Test centuries, he was also a fine fielder. He was jettisoned after the 1999 World Cup and quit not long afterwards. He joined the ICC's referees panel in 2003.

Born *May 31, 1966, Colombo, Sri Lanka.* **Tests** *29,* **ODIs** *143,* **T20Is** *8*

TIM **NIELSEN**

Tim Nielsen had a hard act to follow, replacing John Buchanan after his incredibly successful stint as Australia's coach. Nielsen, a talented wicketkeeper-batsman for South Australia whose international hopes were stymied by the perpetual presence under the Baggy Green of Ian Healy, had been around for part of the Buchanan era as the assistant coach and computer analyst. Nielsen's arrival coincided with the retirements of several senior players, and his rebuilt side lost to India and South Africa before surrendering the Ashes in England in 2009.

Born *May 5, 1968, Forest Gate, London, England. Appointed Australia coach in 2007*

OFFICIALS

ANDY **PYCROFT**

A fine batsman, especially strong off the back foot, Andy Pycroft was a Zimbabwe regular throughout the 1980s, although he was slightly past his peak when they gained Test status in 1992-93. Still, he played in their first three Tests, scoring 60 against New Zealand at Harare in the last of them. The first and last of his 20 ODIs produced famous wins: over Australia in the 1983 World Cup and England in the 1991-92 one. After retiring from playing he was successively a Zimbabwean selector, team manager, and coach. He also found time to fit in the occasional spot of commentary. Outside cricket he was an attorney-at-law for 17 years, which stood him in good stead when he joined the ICC's referees' panel. His first Test as a referee was at Lord's – England v West Indies in May 2009 – and two months later he oversaw Bangladesh's victory over a makeshift West Indian side in the Caribbean.

Born *June 6, 1956, Salisbury (now Harare), Zimbabwe.* **Tests** *13,* **ODIs** *22,* **T20Is** *6*

JAMIE **SIDDONS**

A stylish, attacking batsman and a superb fielder, Jamie Siddons scored more than 10,000 runs in the Sheffield Shield (later Pura Cup), a record when he retired in 1999-2000. But he never played a Test, at a time of plenty for Australian batting, and made a solitary one-day international appearance in Pakistan in 1988-89. A severe stomach bug he picked up on that tour didn't help his Test prospects, and nor did a fractured cheekbone, courtesy of Merv Hughes, in 1991-92: "It ruined my chances of playing for Australia," said Siddons. After retiring he coached at Australia's Centre of Excellence, then accepted an offer to coach Bangladesh. The size of his task, if he didn't realise it before, was hammered home when they lost nine of his first ten Tests in charge, before beating a weakened West Indies in July 2009.

Born *April 25, 1964, Robinvale, Victoria, Australia. Appointed Bangladesh coach in 2007*

JAVAGAL **SRINATH**

Arguably the fastest bowler India has ever produced, Javagal Srinath took 236 wickets in Tests, and 315 more in ODIs. He was tall, and usually slanted the ball in. Unusually for a quick bowler, he did better in India than overseas, his bowling average of 26 at home being four runs lower than his overall one. He went out at the top: his last international match was the 2003 World Cup final. Sadly, there was no fairytale farewell – Srinath was caned (0 for 87) as Australia ran out easy winners. He was not long away from the international arena, though: after a spell as a commentator he joined the referees' panel in 2006. "I'll have to concentrate more than I did during my playing days," he observed.

Born *August 31, 1969, Mysore, Karnataka, India.* **Tests** *15,* **ODIs** *90,* **T20Is** *14*

SIMON **TAUFEL**

Simon Taufel came young to umpiring: he was only 24 when he stood in his first Sheffield Shield match, and still under 30 – and younger than some of the players – when he made his Test debut on Boxing Day 2000. He started after being forced to retire from Sydney club cricket with a back injury. Calm and collected he leaves little to chance, regularly running laps of the ground to keep fit and often standing in the nets to familiarise himself with players' techniques. He joined the ICC's elite panel in 2003, and won the award as the world's leading umpire five times running from 2004.

Born *January 21, 1971, St Leonards, Sydney, Australia.* **Tests** *64,* **ODIs** *154,* **T20Is** *22*

ROD **TUCKER**

Allrounder Rod Tucker played 100 first-class matches for Tasmania over ten years from 1988-89. His seven hundreds included a satisfying 165 against his native NSW in March 1991. He was also a handy medium-pacer who took 123 wickets. On his first morning as a first-class umpire, in December 2004, South Australia were bowled out for 29, but by January 2009 he was standing in his first ODI. He officiated in the World Twenty20s of 2009 and 2010, in between making his Test debut in New Zealand, and was appointed to the ICC's elite panel in 2010.

Born *August 28, 1964, Auburn, Sydney, Australia.* **Tests** *6,* **ODIs** *14,* **T20Is** *8*

CORRIE **VAN ZYL**

The exotically named Cornelius Johannes Petrus Gerthardus van Zyl made his first-class debut for Orange Free State in 1981-82, in the middle of the apartheid era. As a result, his international career was long delayed – he played only a couple of ODIs, in the West Indies in 1991-92, and never did win a Test cap despite an impressive career with Orange Free State. An enthusiastic fast bowler, he took 349 wickets at 23. He had a five-year spell as South Africa's assistant coach before helping the Eagles to six domestic titles. In January 2010 he was appointed national coach on an interim basis following the resignation of Mickey Arthur.

Born *October 1, 1961, Bloemfontein, South Africa. Appointed South Africa coach in 2010*

WAQAR YOUNIS

One of the most fearsome fast bowlers in world cricket in the 1990s, Waqar Younis – took 373 wickets in Tests and 416 in ODIs, many of them with his trademark inswinging yorker, which batsmen ruefully described as being "Waqared". He was also an early – and deadly – exponent of reverse swing. In March 2006 he was appointed Pakistan's bowling coach, then early in 2010 – after another calamitous tour of Australia – Waqar inherited the hot seat as national coach. A return to England, where he had had conspicuous success with Surrey, was soured when Pakistan's players were accused of "spot-fixing" during the final Test at Lord's.

Born *November 16, 1971, Vehari, Punjab, Pakistan. Appointed Pakistan coach in 2010*

OVERALL RECORDS
Test Matches

Most appearances

169	SR Tendulkar *I*
168	SR Waugh *A*
156	AR Border *A*
146	RT Ponting *A*
145	SK Warne *A*
142	R Dravid *I**
140	JH Kallis *SA**
134	MV Boucher *SA**
133	M Muralitharan *SL**
133	AJ Stewart *E*

*The records for Boucher, Dravid, Kallis and Muralitharan include one Test for the World XI

Most runs

		Avge
13837	SR Tendulkar *I*	56.02
12026	RT Ponting *A*	54.66
11953	BC Lara *WI**	52.88
11490	R Dravid *I**	52.94
11174	AR Border *A*	50.56
11126	JH Kallis *SA**	55.07
10927	SR Waugh *A*	51.06
10122	SM Gavaskar *I*	51.12
9408	DPMD J'wardene *SL*	54.06
8969	S Chanderpaul *WI*	49.28

*The records for Dravid, Kallis and Lara include one Test for the World XI

Most wickets

		Avge
800	M Muralitharan *SL**	22.72
708	SK Warne *A*	25.41
619	A Kumble *I*	29.65
563	GD McGrath *A*	21.64
519	CA Walsh *WI*	24.44
434	Kapil Dev *I*	29.64
431	RJ Hadlee *NZ*	22.29
421	SM Pollock *SA*	23.11
414	Wasim Akram *P*	23.62
405	CEL Ambrose *WI*	20.99

*Muralitharan's record includes one Test (5 wickets) for the World XI

Highest scores

400*	BC Lara	WI v Eng at St John's	2003-04
380	ML Hayden	Aust v Zim at Perth	2003-04
375	BC Lara	WI v Eng at St John's	1993-94
374	DPMD Jayawardene	SL v SA at Colombo	2006
365*	GS Sobers	WI v Pak at Kingston	1957-58
364	L Hutton	Eng v Aust at The Oval	1938
340	ST Jayasuriya	SL v India at Colombo	1997-98
337	Hanif Mohammad	Pak v WI at Bridgetown	1957-58
336*	WR Hammond	Eng v NZ at Auckland	1932-33
334*	MA Taylor	Aust v Pak at Peshawar	1998-99
334	DG Bradman	Aust v Eng at Leeds	1930

In all 23 scores of 300 or more have been made in Tests

Best innings bowling

10-53	JC Laker	Eng v Aust at Manchester	1956
10-74	A Kumble	India v Pak at Delhi	1998-99
9-28	GA Lohmann	Eng v SA at Jo'burg	1895-96
9-37	JC Laker	Eng v Aust at Manchester	1956
9-51	M Muralitharan	SL v Zim at Kandy	2001-02
9-52	RJ Hadlee	NZ v Aust at Brisbane	1985-86
9-56	Abdul Qadir	Pak v Eng at Lahore	1987-88
9-57	DE Malcolm	Eng v SA at The Oval	1994
9-65	M Muralitharan	SL v Eng at The Oval	1998
9-69	JM Patel	India v Aust at Kanpur	1959-60

There have been seven further instances of a bowler taking nine wickets in an innings

Record wicket partnerships

1st	415	ND McKenzie (226) and GC Smith (232)	South Africa v Bangladesh at Chittagong	2007-08
2nd	576	ST Jayasuriya (340) and RS Mahanama (225)	Sri Lanka v India at Colombo	1997-98
3rd	624	KC Sangakkara (287) and DPMD Jayawardene (374)	Sri Lanka v South Africa at Colombo	2006
4th	437	DPMD Jayawardene (240) and TT Samaraweera (231)	Sri Lanka v Pakistan at Karachi	2008-09
5th	405	SG Barnes (234) and DG Bradman (234)	Australia v England at Sydney	1946-47
6th	351	DPMD Jayawardene (275) and HAPW Jayawardene (154*)	Sri Lanka v India at Ahmedabad	2009-10
7th	347	DS Atkinson (219) and CC Depeiaza (122)	West Indies v Australia at Bridgetown	1954-55
8th	332	IJL Trott (184) and SCJ Broad (169)	England v Pakistan at Lord's	2010
9th	195	MV Boucher (78) and PL Symcox (108)	South Africa v Pakistan at Johannesburg	1997-98
10th	151	BF Hastings (110) and RO Collinge (68*)	New Zealand v Pakistan at Auckland	1972-73
	151	Azhar Mahmood (128*) and Mushtaq Ahmed (59)	Pakistan v South Africa at Rawalpindi	1997-98

Figures to 23.9.10. Updated records can be found at **www.cricinfo.com/ci/engine/records**

Test Matches **OVERALL RECORDS**

Most catches

Fielders

196	R Dravid	*I/World*
181	ME Waugh	*A*
172	RT Ponting	*A*
171	SP Fleming	*NZ*
164	BC Lara	*WI/World*

Most dismissals

Wicketkeepers — Ct/St

504	MV Boucher	
	SA/World	482/22
416	AC Gilchrist *A*	379/37
395	IA Healy *A*	366/29
355	RW Marsh *A*	343/12
270	PJL Dujon *WI*	265/5

Highest team totals

952-6d	**Sri Lanka** v India at Colombo	1997-98
903-7d	**Eng** v Australia at The Oval	1938
849	**Eng** v WI at Kingston	1929-30
790-3d	**WI** v Pakistan at Kingston	1957-58
765-6d	**Pak** v Sri Lanka at Karachi	2008-09
760-7d	**SL** v India at Ahmedabad	2009-10
758-8d	**Aust** v WI at Kingston	1954-55
756-5d	**Sri Lanka** v SA at Colombo	2006
751-5d	**WI** v England at St John's	2003-04
749-9d	**WI** v England at Bridgetown	2008-09

There have been nine further totals of more than 700, three by Australia and India, and one each by Pakistan, Sri Lanka and West Indies

Lowest team totals

Completed innings

26	**NZ** v Eng at Auckland	1954-55
30	**SA** v Eng at Pt Elizabeth	1895-96
30	**SA** v Eng at Birmingham	1924
35	**SA** v Eng at Cape Town	1898-99
36	**Aust** v Eng at B'ham	1902
36	**SA** v Aust at M'bourne	1931-32
42	**Aust** v Eng at Sydney	1887-88
42	**NZ** v Aust at W'ton	1945-46
42*	**India** v England at Lord's	1974
43	**SA** v Eng at Cape Town	1888-89

* One batsmen absent hurt. There have been seven further totals of less than 50, the most recent West Indies' 47 v England at Kingston in 2003-04

Best match bowling

19-90	JC Laker	Eng v Aust at Manchester	1956
17-159	SF Barnes	Eng v SA at Jo'burg	1913-14
16-136	ND Hirwani	India v WI at Madras	1987-88
16-137	RAL Massie	Aust v England at Lord's	1972
16-220	M Muralitharan	SL v England at The Oval	1998
15-28	J Briggs	Eng v SA at Cape Town	1888-89
15-45	GA Lohmann	Eng v SA at Pt Elizabeth	1895-96
15-99	C Blythe	Eng v SA at Leeds	1907
15-104	H Verity	England v Aust at Lord's	1934
15-123	RJ Hadlee	NZ v Aust at Brisbane	1985-86

Hirwani and Massie were making their Test debuts. W Rhodes (15-124) and Harbhajan Singh (15-217) also took 15 wickets in a match

Most centuries

		Tests
48	SR Tendulkar *India*	169
39	RT Ponting *Australia*	146
35	JH Kallis *South Africa/World XI*	140
34	SM Gavaskar *India*	125
34	BC Lara *West Indies/World XI*	131
32	SR Waugh *Australia*	168
30	ML Hayden *Australia*	94
29	DG Bradman *Australia*	52
29	R Dravid *India/World XI*	142
28	DPMD Jayawardene *Sri Lanka*	113

Tendulkar had scored 94 centuries in international cricket by September 2010

Test match results

	Played	Won	Lost	Drawn	Tied	% win
Australia	723	340	187	194	2	47.02
Bangladesh	68	3	59	6	0	4.41
England	903	318	260	325	0	35.21
India	440	105	138	196	1	23.86
New Zealand	359	68	145	146	0	18.94
Pakistan	352	106	99	147	0	30.11
South Africa	353	124	123	106	0	35.12
Sri Lanka	195	61	70	64	0	31.28
West Indies	465	152	154	158	1	32.68
Zimbabwe	83	8	49	26	0	9.63
World XI	1	0	1	0	0	0.00
TOTAL	1971	1285	1285	684	2	

Most appearances

444	ST Jayasuriya *SL*
442	SR Tendulkar *I*
378	Inzamam-ul-Haq *P*
356	Wasim Akram *P*
351	RT Ponting *A*
339	R Dravid *I*
337	M Muralitharan *SL*
334	M Azharuddin *I*
326	DPMD Jayawardene *SL*
325	SR Waugh *A*

Six further men have played in more than 300 ODIs, and 18 others in 250 or more

Most runs

		Avge
17598	SR Tendulkar *I*	45.12
13428	ST Jayasuriya *SL*	32.43
13072	RT Ponting *A*	42.85
11739	Inzamam-ul-Haq *P*	39.52
11363	SC Ganguly *I*	41.02
10838	JH Kallis *SA*	45.72
10765	R Dravid *I*	39.43
10405	BC Lara *WI*	40.48
9717	Mohammad Yousuf *P*	41.88
9619	AC Gilchrist *A*	35.89

AC Gilchrist (9619), M Azharuddin (9378), PA de Silva (9284) and DMPD J'wardene (9003) also reached 9000 runs

Most wickets

		Avge
515	M Muralitharan *SL*	23.07
502	Wasim Akram *P*	23.52
416	Waqar Younis *P*	23.84
400	WPUJC Vaas *SL*	27.53
393	SM Pollock *SA*	24.50
381	GD McGrath *A*	22.02
337	A Kumble *I*	30.89
324	B Lee *A*	23.01
322	ST Jayasuriya *SL*	36.72
315	J Srinath *I*	28.08

Ten other bowlers have passed 250 wickets in ODIs, and 10 more have reached 200

Highest scores

200*	SR Tendulkar	India v SA at Gwalior	2009-10
194*	CK Coventry	Zim v Bangladesh at Bulawayo	2008-09
194	Saeed Anwar	Pakistan v India at Chennai	1996-97
189*	IVA Richards	W Indies v England at Manchester	1984
189	ST Jayasuriya	Sri Lanka v India at Sharjah	2000-01
188*	G Kirsten	SA v UAE at Rawalpindi	1995-96
186*	SR Tendulkar	India v NZ at Hyderabad	1999-2000
183*	MS Dhoni	India v Sri Lanka at Jaipur	2005-06
183	SC Ganguly	India v Sri Lanka at Taunton	1999
181*	ML Hayden	Aust v N Zealand at Hamilton	2006-07
181	IVA Richards	WI v Sri Lanka at Karachi	1987-88

SR Tendulkar has scored 46 ODI centuries, RT Ponting 29, ST Jayasuriya 28, SC Ganguly 22, HH Gibbs 21 and Saeed Anwar 20

Best innings bowling

8-19	WPUJC Vaas	SL v Zimbabwe at Colombo	2001-02
7-15	GD McGrath	Aust v Namibia at P'stroom	2002-03
7-20	AJ Bichel	Aust v Eng at Port Elizabeth	2002-03
7-30	M Muralitharan	Sri Lanka v India at Sharjah	2000-01
7-36	Waqar Younis	Pakistan v England at Leeds	2001
7-37	Aqib Javed	Pakistan v India at Sharjah	1991-92
7-51	WW Davis	West Indies v Australia at Leeds	1983
6-12	A Kumble	India v West Indies at Calcutta	1993-94
6-13	BAW Mendis	Sri Lanka v India at Karachi	2008
6-14	GJ Gilmour	Australia v England at Leeds	1975
6-14	Imran Khan	Pakistan v India at Sharjah	1984-85
6-14	MF Maharoof	Sri Lanka v W Indies at Mumbai	2006-07

Waqar Younis took five in an innings 13 times and Muralitharan 10

Record wicket partnerships

1st	286	WU Tharanga (109) and ST Jayasuriya (152)	Sri Lanka v England at Leeds	2006
2nd	331	SR Tendulkar (186*) and R Dravid (153)	India v New Zealand at Hyderabad	1999-2000
3rd	237*	R Dravid (104*) and SR Tendulkar (140*)	India v Kenya at Bristol	1999
4th	275*	M Azharuddin (153*) and A Jadeja (116*)	India v Zimbabwe at Cuttack	1997-98
5th	223	M Azharuddin (111*) and A Jadeja (119)	India v Sri Lanka at Colombo	1997-98
6th	218	DPMD Jayawardene (107) and MS Dhoni (139*)	Asia XI v Africa XI at Chennai	2007
7th	130	A Flower (142*) and HH Streak (56)	Zimbabwe v England at Harare	2001-02
8th	138*	JM Kemp (110*) and AJ Hall (56*)	South Africa v India at Cape Town	2006-07
9th	126*	Kapil Dev (175*) and SMH Kirmani (24*)	India v Zimbabwe at Tunbridge Wells	1983
10th	106*	IVA Richards (189*) and MA Holding (12*)	West Indies v England at Manchester	1984

Figures to 23.9.10. Updated records can be found at **www.cricinfo.com/ci/engine/records**

One-day Internationals OVERALL RECORDS

Most catches

Fielders

168	DPMD Jayawardene	*SL*
156	M Azharuddin	*I*
152	RT Ponting	*A*
134	SR Tendulkar	*I*
133	SP Fleming	*NZ*

Most dismissals

Wicketkeepers		*Ct/St*
472	AC Gilchrist *A*	417/55
421	MV Boucher *SA*	399/22
321	KC Sangakkara *SL*	252/69
287	Moin Khan *P*	214/73
233	IA Healy *A*	194/39

Highest team totals

443-9	**SL** v N'lands at Amstelveen	2006
438-9	**SA** v Aust at Johannesburg	2005-06
434-4	**Australia** v SA at Jo'burg	2005-06
418-5	**SA** v Zim at P'stroom	2006-07
414-7	**India** v SL at Rajkot	2009-10
413-5	**Ind** v Bermuda at P-o-Spain	2006-07
411-8	**SL** v India at Rajkot	2009-10
402-2	**NZ** v Ireland at Aberdeen	2008
401-3	**India** v SA at Gwalior	2009-10
398-5	**SL** v Kenya at Kandy	1995-96

All these totals were made in 50 overs except SA's 438-9, when the winning run came off the fifth ball of the 50th over

Lowest team totals

Completed innings

35	**Zim** v SL at Harare	2003-04
36	**Canada** v SL at Paarl	2002-03
38	**Zim** v SL at Colombo	2001-02
43	**Pak** v WI at Cape Town	1992-93
44	**Zim** v B'desh at Ch'gong	2009-10
45	**Can** v Eng at Manchester	1979
45	**Nam** v Aust at P'stroom	2002-03
54	**India** v SL at Sharjah	2000-01
54	**WI** v SA at Cape Town	2003-04
55	**SL** v WI at Sharjah	1986-87

The lowest total successfully defended in a non-rain-affected ODI is 125, by India v Pakistan (87) at Sharjah in 1984-85

Most sixes

276	Shahid Afridi	*P*
270	ST Jayasuriya	*SL*
190	SC Ganguly	*I*
185	SR Tendulkar	*I*
165	CH Gayle	*WI*
157	RT Ponting	*A*
153	CL Cairns	*NZ*
149	AC Gilchrist	*A*
144	Inzamam-ul-Haq	*P*
136	Yuvraj Singh	*I*

Eleven others have hit 100 sixes

Best strike rate

Runs per 100 balls		*Runs*
113.29	Shahid Afridi *P*	6321
103.27	V Sehwag *I*	7380
99.43	IDS Smith *NZ*	1055
96.94	AC Gilchrist *A*	9619
96.66	RL Powell *WI*	2085
95.07	Kapil Dev *I*	3783
93.71	JR Hopes *A*	1326
92.44	A Symonds *A*	5088
91.22	ST Jayasuriya *SL*	13428
90.20	IVA Richards *WI*	6721

Qualification: 1000 runs

Most economical bowlers

Runs per over		*Wkts*
3.09	J Garner *WI*	146
3.28	RGD Willis *E*	80
3.30	RJ Hadlee *NZ*	158
3.32	MA Holding *WI*	142
3.37	SP Davis *A*	44
3.40	AME Roberts *WI*	87
3.48	CEL Ambrose *WI*	225
3.53	MD Marshall *WI*	157
3.54	ARC Fraser *E*	47
3.55	MR Whitney *A*	46

Qualification: 2000 balls bowled

One-day international results

	Played	Won	Lost	Tied	No result	% win
Australia	747	463	252	8	24	64.59
Bangladesh	230	57	171	0	2	25.00
England	542	263	256	5	18	50.66
India	753	365	351	3	34	50.97
Kenya	133	36	92	0	5	28.12
New Zealand	588	256	296	5	31	46.40
Pakistan	723	385	317	6	15	54.80
South Africa	439	273	149	5	12	64.51
Sri Lanka	612	286	299	3	24	48.89
West Indies	637	335	274	5	23	54.96
Zimbabwe	377	98	265	5	9	27.30
Others (see below)	313	103	198	1	11	34.27
TOTAL	3047	2920	2920	23	104	

Others: Afghanistan (P13, W8, L5), Africa XI (P6, W1, L4, NR1), Asia XI (P7, W4, L2, NR1), Bermuda (P35, W7, L28), Canada (P60, W16, L43, NR1), East Africa (P3, L3), Hong Kong (P4, L4), Ireland (P55, W27, L24, T1, NR3), Namibia (P6, L6), Netherlands (P57, W23, L32, NR2), Scotland (P50, W15, L32, NR3), UAE (P11, W1, L10), USA (P2, L2), World XI (P4, W1, L3).

Most appearances

40	BB McCullum	NZ
38	Kamran Akmal	P
37	Shahid Afridi	P
34	LRPL Taylor	NZ
33	MJ Clarke	A
33	PD Collingwood	E
32	Shoaib Malik	P
31	TM Dilshan	SL
31	DPMD Jayawardene	SL
30	ST Jayasuriya	SL
30	AB de Villiers	SA
30	Umar Gul	P

Most runs

			Avge
1100	BB McCullum	NZ	33.33
911	KP Pietersen	E	37.95
803	GC Smith	SA	32.12
760	DPMD Jayawardene	SL	28.14
733	KC Sangakkara	SL	29.32
717	TM Dilshan	SL	28.68
704	Kamran Akmal	P	23.46
644	DA Warner	A	29.27
636	Shoaib Malik	P	25.44
621	G Gambhir	I	28.22
621	ST Jayasuriya	SL	23.88

The highest batting average (min. 200 runs) is 52.00, by EJG Morgan (England)

Most wickets

		Avge
47	Umar Gul	P	13.61
47	Shahid Afridi	P	18.80
36	Saeed Ajmal	P	15.86
35	DL Vettori	NZ	16.57
35	SCJ Broad	E	21.57
34	SL Malinga	SL	20.64
33	BAW Mendis	SL	12.39
30	GP Swann	E	14.50
30	MG Johnson	A	19.53
29	DW Steyn	SA	18.31

Four further bowlers have taken 25 wickets

Highest Scores

117	CH Gayle	WI v SA at Johannesburg	2007-08
116*	BB McCullum	NZ v A at Christchurch	2009-10
101	SK Raina	India v SA at Gros Islet	2010
100	DPMD J'wardene	SL v Zim at Providence	2010
98*	RT Ponting	A v NZ at Auckland	2004-05
98*	DPMD J'wardene	SL v WI at Bridgetown	2010
98	CH Gayle	WI v India at Bridgetown	2010
96*	TM Dilshan	SL v WI at The Oval	2009
96	DR Martyn	A v SA at Brisbane	2005-06
94	LL Bosman	SA v Eng at Centurion	2009-10

Ponting's innings, in the very first such international, is the highest score on T20I debut

Best innings bowling

5-6	Umar Gul	Pakistan v NZ at The Oval	2009
5-19	R McLaren	SA v WI at N Sound	2010
5-20	NN Odhiambo	Ken v Scot at Nairobi	2009-10
5-26	DJG Sammy	WI v Zim at P-o-Spain	2009-10
4-6	SJ Benn	WI v Zim at P-o-Spain	2009-10
4-7	MR Gillespie	NZ v Kenya at Durban	2007-08
4-8	Umar Gul	Pak v Australia at Dubai	2009-10
4-9	DW Steyn	SA v WI at Port Elizabeth	2007-08
4-11	Shahid Afridi	Pak v Netherlands at Lord's	2009
4-13	RP Singh	India v SA at Durban	2007-08
4-13	WD Parnell	SA v WI at The Oval	2009
4-13	Umar Gul	Pakistan v SL at King City	2008-09

Record wicket partnerships

1st	170	GC Smith (88) and LL Bosman (94)	South Africa v England at Centurion	2009-10
2nd	166	DPMD Jayawardene (98*) and KC Sangakkara (68)	Sri Lanka v West Indies at Bridgetown	2010
3rd	120*	HH Gibbs (90*) and JM Kemp (46*)	South Africa v West indies at Johannesburg	2007-08
4th	112*	KP Pietersen (43*) and EJG Morgan (67*)	England v Pakistan at Dubai	2009-10
5th	119*	Shoaib Malik (52*) and Misbah-ul-Haq (66*)	Pakistan v Australia at Johannesburg	2007-08
6th	101*	CL White (85*) and MEK Hussey (39*)	Australia v Sri Lanka at Bridgetown	2010
7th	91	PD Collingwood (79) and MH Yardy (23*)	England v West Indies at The Oval	2007
8th	61	SK Raina (61*) and Harbhajan Singh (21)	India v New Zealand at Christchurch	2008-09
9th	44	SL Malinga (27) and CRD Fernando (21)	Sri Lanka v New Zealand at Auckland	2006-07
10th	28	JDP Oram (66*) and JS Patel (4)	New Zealand v Australia at Perth	2007-08

Figures to 23.9.10. Updated records can be found at **www.cricinfo.com/ci/engine/records**

Most catches

Fielders

22	AB de Villiers	*SA*
22	LRPL Taylor	*NZ*
18	MEK Hussey	*A*
15	GC Smith	*SA*
14	DJ Hussey	*A*
14	Shoaib Malik	*P*

Most dismissals

Wicketkeepers — Ct/St

45	Kamran Akmal	*P*	17/28
21	D Ramdin	*WI*	19/2
20	BB McCullum	*NZ*	16/4
20	KC Sangakkara	*SL*	12/8
19	MV Boucher	*SA*	18/1

Highest team totals

260-6	Sri Lanka v Kenya at Jo'burg	2007-08
241-6	SA v England at Centurion	2009-10
221-5	Aust v England at Sydney	2006-07
218-4	India v England at Durban	2007-08
215-5	Sri Lanka v India at Nagpur	2009-10
214-4	Australia v NZ at Auckland	2004-05
214-6	NZ v Aust at Christchurch	2009-10
214-4	Aust v NZ at Christchurch	2009-10
211-4	India v Sri Lanka at Mohali	2009-10
211-5	SA v Scotland at The Oval	2009

There have been nine further totals of 200 or more

Lowest team totals

Completed innings

67	Kenya v Ireland at Belfast	2008
68	Ireland v WI at Providence	2010
70	Bermuda v Can at Belfast	2008
73	Kenya v NZ at Durban	2007-08
74	India v Aus at M'bourne	2007-08
75	Can v Zim at King City	2008-09
78	B'desh v NZ at Hamilton	2009-10
79	Aust v Eng at Southampton	2005
80	Afgh v SA at Bridgetown	2010
81	Scotland v SA at The Oval	2009
81	NZ v Sri Lanka at Lauderhill	2010

West Indies scored 79-7 in 20 overs v Zimbabwe at Port-of-Spain in 2009-10

Most sixes

39	BB McCullum	*NZ*
38	Yuvraj Singh	*I*
34	CH Gayle	*WI*
31	DA Warner	*A*
31	CL White	*NZ*
29	JA Morkel	*SA*
27	DJ Hussey	*A*
26	LRPL Taylor	*NZ*
25	Kamram Akmal	*P*
24	PD Collingwood	*E*
24	KP Pietersen	*E*

Yuvraj's sixes included 6 in one over

Best strike rate

Runs per 100 balls		Runs
169.34	A Symonds *A*	337
159.82	CD McMillan *NZ*	187
153.73	Yuvraj Singh *I*	555
153.43	V Sehwag *I*	313
151.85	YK Pathan *I*	205
151.17	DA Warner *A*	644
150.32	MEK Hussey *A*	457
150.27	LL Bosman *SA*	272
148.04	Moh'd Ashraful *B*	265
146.37	CL White *A*	505

Qualification: 100 balls faced

Meanest bowlers

Runs per over		Wkts
4.68	RW Price *Z*	11
4.88	TM Odoyo *Kenya*	6
5.36	DL Vettori *NZ*	35
5.36	P Utseya *Zim*	12
5.38	GH Dockrell *Ire*	12
5.40	JAR Blain *Scot*	6
5.41	AC Botha *Ire*	21
5.45	JD Nel *Scot*	12
5.56	HA Varaiya *Ken*	5
5.60	H Osinde *Can*	6

Qualification: 120 balls bowled

Twenty20 international results

	Played	Won	Lost	Tied	No Result	% win
Australia	38	21	15	1	1	58.10
Bangladesh	16	3	13	0	0	18.75
England	34	17	15	0	2	53.12
India	27	14	11	1	1	55.76
New Zealand	40	17	20	3	0	46.25
Pakistan	40	26	13	1	0	66.25
South Africa	33	21	12	0	0	63.63
Sri Lanka	33	19	14	0	0	57.57
West Indies	28	11	15	2	0	42.85
Others (see below)	85	29	50	2	4	37.03
TOTAL	**187**	**178**	**178**	**5**	**4**	

Other teams: Afghanistan (P8, W4, L4), Bermuda (P3, L3), Canada (P11, W3, L7, T1), Ireland (P17, W7, L8, NR2), Kenya (P12, W4, L8), Netherlands (P10, W6, L3, NR1), Scotland (P12, W2, L9, NR1), Zimbabwe (P12, W3, L8, T1). Matches decided by bowlouts are shown as tied

Most appearances

39	GD McGrath	A
39	RT Ponting	A
38	ST Jayasuriya	SL
38	Wasim Akram	P
36	SR Tendulkar	I
35	PA de Silva	SL
35	Inzamam-ul-Haq	P
34	J Srinath	I
33	SP Fleming	NZ
33	Javed Miandad	P
33	SR Waugh	A

Javed Miandad played in the first six World Cup tournaments

Most runs

		Avge
1796	SR Tendulkar I	57.93
1537	RT Ponting A	48.03
1225	BC Lara WI	42.24
1165	ST Jayasuriya SL	34.26
1085	AC Gilchrist A	36.16
1083	Javed Miandad P	43.32
1075	SP Fleming NZ	35.83
1067	HH Gibbs SA	56.15
1064	PA de Silva SL	36.68
1013	IVA Richards WI	63.31

SC Ganguly (1006) and ME Waugh (1004) also passed 1000 runs in World Cup matches

Most wickets

		Avge
71	GD McGrath A	18.19
55	Wasim Akram P	23.83
53	M Muralitharan SL	19.69
49	WPUJC Vaas SL	21.22
44	J Srinath I	27.81
38	AA Donald SA	24.02
34	GB Hogg A	19.23
34	Imran Khan P	19.26
32	CZ Harris NZ	26.90
32	SK Warne A	19.50

The most wickets in one tournament in 26 by GD McGrath in 2006-07

Highest scores

188*	G Kirsten	SA v UAE at Rawalpindi	1995-96
183	SC Ganguly	India v Sri Lanka at Taunton	1999
181	IVA Richards	WI v Sri Lanka at Karachi	1987-88
175*	Kapil Dev	India v Zim at Tunbridge Wells	1983
172*	CB Wishart	Zim v Namibia at Harare	2002-03
171*	GM Turner	NZ v East Africa at Birmingham	1975
161	AC Hudson	SA v N'lands at Rawalpindi	1995-96
160	Imran Nazir	Pakistan v Zim at Kingston	2006-07
158	ML Hayden	Aust v WI at North Sound	2006-07
152	SR Tendulkar	India v Nam at P'maritzburg	2002-03

SC Ganguly, RT Ponting, SR Tendulkar and ME Waugh have all scored four centuries in the World Cup

Best bowling figures

7-15	GD McGrath	Aust v Namibia at P'stroom	2002-03
7-20	AJ Bichel	Aust v Engl at Port Elizabeth	2002-03
7-51	WW Davis	West Indies v Australia at Leeds	1983
6-14	GJ Gilmour	Australia v England at Leeds	1975
6-23	SE Bond	NZ v Aust at Port Elizabeth	2002-03
6-23	A Nehra	India v England at Durban	2002-03
6-25	WPUJC Vaas	SL v B'desh at P'maritzburg	2002-03
6-39	KH MacLeay	Australia v India at Nottingham	1983
5-14	GD McGrath	Australia v WI at Manchester	1999
5-18	AJ Hall	SA v England at Bridgetown	2006-07

Record wicket partnerships

1st	194	Saeed Anwar (113*) and Wajahatullah Wasti (84)	Pakistan v New Zealand at Manchester	1999
2nd	318	SC Ganguly (183) and R Dravid (145)	India v Sri Lanka at Taunton	1999
3rd	237*	R Dravid (104) and SR Tendulkar (140*)	India v Kenya at Bristol	1999
4th	204	MJ Clarke (93*) and BJ Hodge (123)	Australia v Netherlands at Basseterre	2006-07
5th	148	RG Twose (80*) and CL Cairns (60)	New Zealand v Australia at Cardiff	1999
6th	161	MO Odumbe (82) and AV Vadher (73*)	Kenya v Sri Lanka at Southampton	1999
7th	98	RR Sarwan (75) and RD Jacobs (50)	West Indies v New Zealand at Port Elizabeth	2002-03
8th	117	DL Houghton (142) and IP Butchart (54)	Zimbabwe v New Zealand at Hyderabad	1987-88
9th	126*	Kapil Dev (175*) and SMH Kirmani (24*)	India v Zimbabwe at Tunbridge Wells	1983
10th	71	AME Roberts (37*) and J Garner (37)	West Indies v India at Manchester	1983

Figures to 23.9.10. Updated records can be found at **www.cricinfo.com/ci/engine/records**

World Cup 1975-2007 **OVERALL RECORDS**

Most catches

Fielders

25	**RT Ponting** *A*	
18	**ST Jayasuriya** *SL*	
16	**CL Cairns** *NZ*	
16	**Inzamam-ul-Haq** *P*	
16	**BC Lara** *WI*	

Most dismissals

Wicketkeepers		*Ct/St*
52	**AC Gilchrist** *A*	45/7
32	**KC Sangakkara** *SL*	26/6
31	**MV Boucher** *SA*	31/0
30	**Moin Khan** *P*	23/7
23	**BB McCullum** *NZ*	22/1
23	**AJ Stewart** *E*	21/2

Highest team totals

413-5	**Ind** v Bermuda at P-o-Spain	2006-07
398-5	**SL** v Kenya at Kandy	1995-96
377-6	**Aust** v SA at Basseterre	2006-07
373-6	**India** v Sri Lanka at Taunton	1999
363-5	**NZ** v Canada at Gros Islet	2006-07
360-4	**WI** v Sri Lanka at Karachi	1987-88
359-2	**Aust** v India at Jo'burg	2002-03
358-5	**Aust** v N'lands at Basseterre	2006-07
356-4	**SA** v WI at St George's	2006-07
353-3	**SA** v N'lands at Basseterre	2006-07

Australia's 359-2 was scored in the final.
In 1975, 1979 and 1983 the innings were of 60 overs; since then the maximum has been 50

Lowest team totals

Completed innings

36	**Canada** v SL at Paarl	2002-03
45	**Can** v Eng at Manchester	1979
45	**Nam** v Aust at P'stroom	2003-03
68	**Scotland** v WI at Leicester	1999
74	**Pak** v Eng at Adelaide	1991-92
77	**Ire** v SL at St George's	2006-07
78	**Berm** v SL at P-o-Spain	2006-07
84	**Nam** v Pak at Kimberley	2002-03
86	**SL** v WI at Manchester	1975
91	**Ire** v Aust at Bridgetown	2006-07

There have been four other all-out scores of under 100, one each by East Africa, England, West Indies and Zimbabwe

Most expensive bowling

12-1-105-2	**MC Snedden**	New Zealand v England at The Oval	1983
10-0-97-1	**ALF de Mel**	Sri Lanka v West Indies at Karachi	1987-88
10-0-96-1	**RDM Leverock**	Bermuda v India at Port-of-Spain	2006-07
10-0-92-0	**RJ van Vuuren**	Namibia v Australia at P'stroom	2002-03
10-0-89-1	**PW Borren**	Netherlands v Australia at Basseterre	2006-07
10-0-87-0	**J Srinath**	India v Australia at Johannesburg	2002-03
9-0-86-1	**DR Brown**	Scotland v Australia at Basseterre	2006-07
10-0-86-1	**Abdur Razzak**	Bangladesh v Sri Lanka at Port-of-Spain	2006-07
9-0-85-1	**MA Suji**	Kenya v Sri Lanka at Kandy	1995-96
10-0-84-1	**WPUJC Vaas**	Sri Lanka v India at Taunton	1983

The most economical full spell is BS Bedi's 12-8-6-1 for India v East Africa at Leeds in 1975

Best strike rate

Runs per 100 balls		*Runs*
115.14	**Kapil Dev** *I*	669
101.18	**Wasim Akram** *P*	426
98.01	**AC Gilchrist** *A*	1085
92.93	**ML Hayden** *A*	987
90.66	**ST Jayasuriya** *SL*	1165
88.21	**SR Tendulkar** *I*	1796
87.84	**JN Rhodes** *SA*	354
87.38	**HH Gibbs** *SA*	1067
86.57	**PA de Silva** *SL*	1064
86.26	**BC Lara** *WI*	1225

Qualification: 20 innings

World Cup finals

		Man of the Match
1975	**West Indies** (291-8) beat Australia (274) by 17 runs at Lord's	CH Lloyd
1979	**West Indies** (286-9) beat England (194) by 92 runs at Lord's	IVA Richards
1983	**India** (183) beat West Indies (140) by 43 runs at Lord's	M Amarnath
1987-88	**Australia** (253-5) beat England (246-8) by 7 runs at Calcutta	DC Boon
1991-92	**Pakistan** (249-6) beat England (227) by 22 runs at Melbourne	Wasim Akram
1995-96	**Sri Lanka** (245-3) beat Australia (241-7) by 7 wickets at Lahore	PA de Silva
1999	**Australia** (133-2) beat Pakistan (132) by 8 wickets at Lord's	SK Warne
2002-03	**Australia** (359-2) beat India (234) by 125 runs at Johannesburg	RT Ponting
2006-07	**Australia** (281-4) beat Sri Lanka (215-8) by 53 runs* at Bridgetown	AC Gilchrist

* Duckworth/Lewis Method

AUSTRALIA
Test Match Records

Most appearances

168	SR Waugh	
156	AR Border	
146	RT Ponting	
145	SK Warne	
128	ME Waugh	
124	GD McGrath	
119	IA Healy	
107	DC Boon	
105	JL Langer	
104	MA Taylor	

ML Hayden (103) also won more than 100 caps

Most runs

		Avge
12026	RT Ponting	54.66
11174	AR Border	50.56
10927	SR Waugh	51.06
8625	ML Hayden	50.73
8029	ME Waugh	41.81
7696	JL Langer	45.27
7525	MA Taylor	43.49
7422	DC Boon	43.65
7110	GS Chappell	53.86
6996	DG Bradman	99.94

RN Harvey (6149) also reached 6000 Test runs

Most wickets

		Avge
708	SK Warne	25.41
563	GD McGrath	21.64
355	DK Lillee	23.92
310	B Lee	30.81
291	CJ McDermott	28.63
259	JN Gillespie	26.13
248	R Benaud	27.03
246	GD McKenzie	29.78
228	RR Lindwall	23.03
216	CV Grimmett	24.21

MG Hughes (212), SCG MacGill (208) & JR Thomson (200) also reached 200

Highest scores

380	ML Hayden	v Zimbabwe at Perth	2003-04
334*	MA Taylor	v Pakistan at Peshawar	1998-99
334	DG Bradman	v England at Leeds	1930
311	RB Simpson	v England at Manchester	1964
307	RM Cowper	v England at Melbourne	1965-66
304	DG Bradman	v England at Leeds	1934
299*	DG Bradman	v South Africa at Adelaide	1931-32
270	DG Bradman	v England at Melbourne	1936-37
268	GN Yallop	v Pakistan at Melbourne	1983-84
266	WH Ponsford	v England at The Oval	1934

At the time of his retirement in 1948 DG Bradman had made eight of Australia's highest ten Test scores

Best innings bowling

9-121	AA Mailey	v England at Melbourne	1920-21
8-24	GD McGrath	v Pakistan at Perth	2004-05
8-31	FJ Laver	v England at Manchester	1909
8-38	GD McGrath	v England at Lord's	1997
8-43	AE Trott	v England at Adelaide	1894-95
8-53	RAL Massie	v England at Lord's	1972
8-59	AA Mallett	v Pakistan at Adelaide	1972-73
8-61	MG Johnson	v South Africa at Perth	2008-09
8-65	H Trumble	v England at The Oval	1902
8-71	GD McKenzie	v West Indies at Melbourne	1968-69
8-71	SK Warne	v England at Brisbane	1994-95

Trott and Massie were making their Test debuts

Record wicket partnerships

1st	382	WM Lawry (210) and RB Simpson (205)	v West Indies at Bridgetown	1964-65
2nd	451	WH Ponsford (266) and DG Bradman (244)	v England at The Oval	1934
3rd	315	RT Ponting (206) and DS Lehmann (160)	v West Indies at Port-of-Spain	2002-03
4th	388	WH Ponsford (181) and DG Bradman (304)	v England at Leeds	1934
5th	405	SG Barnes (234) and DG Bradman (234)	v England at Sydney	1946-47
6th	346	JHW Fingleton (136) and DG Bradman (270)	v England at Melbourne	1936-37
7th	217	KD Walters (250) and GJ Gilmour (101)	v New Zealand at Christchurch	1976-77
8th	243	MJ Hartigan (116) and C Hill (160)	v England at Adelaide	1907-08
9th	154	SE Gregory (201) and JM Blackham (74)	v England at Sydney	1894-95
10th	127	JM Taylor (108) and AA Mailey (46*)	v England at Sydney	1924-25

Figures to 23.9.10. Updated records can be found at **www.cricinfo.com/ci/engine/records**

Most catches

Fielders

181	ME Waugh	
172	RT Ponting	
157	MA Taylor	
156	AR Border	
128	ML Hayden	

Most dismissals

Wicketkeepers — Ct/St

416	AC Gilchrist	379/37
395	IA Healy	366/29
355	RW Marsh	343/12
187	ATW Grout	163/24
130	WAS Oldfield	78/52

Highest team totals

758-8d	v West Indies at Kingston	1954-55
735-6d	v Zimbabwe at Perth	2003-04
729-6d	v England at Lord's	1930
701	v England at The Oval	1934
695	v England at The Oval	1930
674-6d	v England at Cardiff	2009
674	v India at Adelaide	1947-48
668	v West Indies at Bridgetown	1954-55
659-8d	v England at Sydney	1946-47
656-8d	v England at Manchester	1964

Australia have reached 600 on 29 occasions, 16 of them against England

Lowest team totals

Completed innings

36	v England at Birmingham	1902
42	v England at Sydney	1887-88
44	v England at The Oval	1896
53	v England at Lord's	1896
58*	v England at Brisbane	1936-37
60	v England at Lord's	1888
63	v England at The Oval	1882
65	v England at The Oval	1912
66*	v England at Brisbane	1928-29
68	v England at Manchester	1886

One or more batsmen absent. Australia's lowest total against anyone other than England is 75, v South Africa at Durban in 1949-50

[handwritten] ※ 47 v SA at Cape Town 2011

Best match bowling

16-137	RAL Massie	v England at Lord's	1972
14-90	FR Spofforth	v England at The Oval	1882
14-199	CV Grimmett	v South Africa at Adelaide	1931-32
13-77	MA Noble	v England at Melbourne	1901-02
13-110	FR Spofforth	v England at Melbourne	1878-79
13-148	BA Reid	v England at Melbourne	1990-91
13-173	CV Grimmett	v South Africa at Durban	1935-36
13-217	MG Hughes	v West Indies at Perth	1988-89
13-236	AA Mailey	v England at Melbourne	1920-21
12-87	CTB Turner	v England at Sydney	1887-88

Massie was playing in his first Test, Grimmett (1935-36) in his last – he took 10 or more wickets in each of his last three

Hat-tricks

FR Spofforth	v England at Melbourne	1878-79
H Trumble	v England at Melbourne	1901-02
H Trumble	v England at Melbourne	1903-04
TJ Matthews	v South Africa at Manchester	1912
TJ Matthews	v South Africa at Manchester	1912
LF Kline	v South Africa at Cape Town	1957-58
MG Hughes	v West Indies at Perth	1988-89
DW Fleming	v Pakistan at Rawalpindi	1994-95
SK Warne	v England at Melbourne	1994-95
GD McGrath	v West Indies at Perth	2000-01

Fleming was playing in his first Test, Trumble (1903-04) in his last. Matthews, a legspinner, uniquely took a hat-trick in both innings of the same Test

Australia's Test match results

	Played	Won	Lost	Drawn	Tied	% win
v Bangladesh	4	4	0	0	0	100.00
v England	321	132	99	90	0	41.12
v India	76	34	18	23	1	44.73
v New Zealand	50	26	7	17	0	52.00
v Pakistan	57	28	12	17	0	49.12
v South Africa	83	47	18	18	0	56.62
v Sri Lanka	20	13	1	6	0	65.00
v West Indies	108	52	32	23	1	48.14
v Zimbabwe	3	3	0	0	0	100.00
v World XI	1	1	0	0	0	100.00
TOTAL	**723**	**340**	**187**	**194**	**2**	**47.02**

Figures to 23.9.10. Updated records can be found at **www.cricinfo.com/ci/engine/records**

AUSTRALIA
One-day International Records

Most appearances

350	RT Ponting	
325	SR Waugh	
286	AC Gilchrist	
273	AR Border	
249	GD McGrath	
244	ME Waugh	
232	MG Bevan	
208	DR Martyn	
198	A Symonds	
193	SK Warne	

A total of 24 Australians have played in more than 100 ODIs

Most runs

		Avge
12957	RT Ponting	42.62
9595	AC Gilchrist	35.93
8500	ME Waugh	39.35
7569	SR Waugh	32.90
6912	MG Bevan	53.58
6524	AR Border	30.62
6131	ML Hayden	44.10
6068	DM Jones	44.61
5964	DC Boon	37.04
5509	MJ Clarke	43.03

DR Martyn (5346) and A Symonds (5088) also reached 5000 runs

Most wickets

		Avge
380	GD McGrath	21.98
324	B Lee	23.01
291	SK Warne	25.82
203	CJ McDermott	24.71
195	SR Waugh	34.67
174	NW Bracken	24.36
156	GB Hogg	26.84
142	JN Gillespie	25.42
134	DW Fleming	25.38
133	A Symonds	37.25

Five further Australians have taken 100 wickets

Highest scores

181*	ML Hayden	v New Zealand at Hamilton	2006-07
173	ME Waugh	v West Indies at Melbourne	2000-01
172	AC Gilchrist	v Zimbabwe at Hobart	2003-04
164	RT Ponting	v South Africa at Johannesburg	2005-06
158	ML Hayden	v West Indies at North Sound	2006-07
156	A Symonds	v New Zealand at Wellington	2005-06
154	AC Gilchrist	v Sri Lanka at Melbourne	1998-99
151	A Symonds	v Sri Lanka at Sydney	2005-06
149	AC Gilchrist	v Sri Lanka at Bridgetown	2006-07
146	ML Hayden	v Pakistan at Nairobi	2002-03

Gilchrist's 149 against Sri Lanka is the highest score in a World Cup final

Best innings bowling

7-15	GD McGrath	v Namibia at Potchefstroom	2002-03
7-20	AJ Bichel	v England at Port Elizabeth	2002-03
6-14	GJ Gilmour	v England at Leeds	1975
6-39	KH MacLeay	v India at Nottingham	1983
5-13	SP O'Donnell	v New Zealand at Christchurch	1989-90
5-14	GD McGrath	v West Indies at Manchester	1999
5-14	JR Hopes	v Ireland at Dublin	2010
5-15	GS Chappell	v India at Sydney	1980-81
5-16	CG Rackemann	v Pakistan at Adelaide	1983-84
5-17	TM Alderman	v New Zealand at Wellington	1981-82

DK Lillee took 5-34 against Pakistan at Leeds in the 1975 World Cup, the first five-wicket haul in ODIs

Record wicket partnerships

1st	212	GR Marsh (104) and DC Boon (111)	v India at Jaipur	1986-87
2nd	252*	SR Watson (136*) and RT Ponting (111*)	v England at Centurion	2009-10
3rd	234*	RT Ponting (140*) and DR Martyn (88*)	v India at Johannesburg	2002-03
4th	237	RT Ponting (124) and A Symonds (151)	v Sri Lanka at Sydney	2005-06
5th	220	A Symonds (156) and MJ Clarke (82*)	v New Zealand at Wellington	2005-06
6th	165	MEK Hussey (109*) and BJ Haddin (70)	v West Indies at Kuala Lumpur	2006-07
7th	123	MEK Hussey (73) and B Lee (57)	v South Africa at Brisbane	2005-06
8th	119	PR Reiffel (58) and SK Warne (55)	v South Africa at Port Elizabeth	1993-94
9th	77	MG Bevan (59*) and SK Warne (29)	v West Indies at Port-of-Spain	1998-99
10th	63	SR Watson (35*) and AJ Bichel (28)	v Sri Lanka at Sydney	2002-03

Figures to 23.9.10. Updated records can be found at **www.cricinfo.com/ci/engine/records**

AUSTRALIA

Most catches

Fielders

151	RT Ponting	
127	AR Border	
111	SR Waugh	
108	ME Waugh	
82	MEK Hussey/A Symonds	

Most dismissals

Wicketkeepers   Ct/St

470	AC Gilchrist	416/54
233	IA Healy	194/39
124	RW Marsh	120/4
97	BJ Haddin	90/7
49	WB Phillips	42/7

Highest team totals

434-4	v South Africa at Johannesburg	2005-06
377-6	v South Africa at Basseterre	2006-07
368-5	v Sri Lanka at Sydney	2005-06
359-2†	v India at Johannesburg	2002-03
359-5	v India at Sydney	2003-04
358-5	v Netherlands at Basseterre	2006-07
350-4	v India at Hyderabad	2009-10
349-6	v New Zealand at St George's	2006-07
348-6	v New Zealand at C'church	1999-2000
347-2	v India at Bangalore	2003-04
347-5	v New Zealand at Napier	2004-05

† In World Cup final. All scores made in 50 overs

Lowest team totals

Completed innings

70	v England at Birmingham	1977
70	v New Zealand at Adelaide	1985-86
91	v West Indies at Perth	1986-87
93	v S Africa at Cape Town	2005-06
101	v England at Melbourne	1978-79
101	v India at Perth	1991-92
107	v W Indies at Melbourne	1981-82
109	v England at Sydney	1982-83
120	v Pakistan at Hobart	1996-97
124	v New Zealand at Sydney	1982-83

Australia scored 101-9 in a 30-overs match against West Indies at Sydney in 1992-93 – and won

Most sixes

154	RT Ponting
148	AC Gilchrist
103	A Symonds
87	ML Hayden
68	SR Waugh
64	DM Jones
63	MEK Hussey
57	ME Waugh
50	SR Watson
47	BJ Haddin

Ponting (3) and Gilchrist (1) also hit sixes for the World XI

Best strike rate

Runs per 100 balls   Runs

96.89	AC Gilchrist	9595
93.71	JR Hopes	1326
92.44	A Symonds	5504
88.48	MEK Hussey	4287
88.46	DJ Hussey	598
88.16	IJ Harvey	715
87.51	BJ Hodge	516
85.71	WB Phillips	852
85.08	CJ Ferguson	599
84.35	SR Watson	2982

Qualification: 500 runs

Most economical bowlers

Runs per over   Wkts

3.37	SP Davis	44
3.55	MR Whitney	46
3.58	DK Lillee	103
3.65	GF Lawson	88
3.65	TM Alderman	88
3.87	GD McGrath	380
3.92	PR Reiffel	106
3.94	CG Rackemann	82
3.94	RM Hogg	85
4.03	CJ McDermott	203

Qualification: 2000 balls bowled

Australia's one-day international results

	Played	Won	Lost	Tied	No Result	% win
v Bangladesh	16	15	1	0	0	93.75
v England	106	61	41	2	2	59.61
v India	103	61	34	0	8	64.21
v New Zealand	123	84	34	0	5	71.18
v Pakistan	85	52	29	1	3	64.02
v South Africa	77	39	35	3	0	52.59
v Sri Lanka	68	46	20	0	2	69.69
v West Indies	125	63	57	2	3	52.45
v Zimbabwe	27	25	1	0	1	96.15
v others *(see below)*	17	17	0	0	0	100.00
TOTAL	**747**	**463**	**252**	**8**	**24**	**64.59**

Other teams: Canada (P1, W1), Ireland (P2, W2), Kenya (P4, W4), Namibia (P1, W1), Netherlands (P2, W2), Scotland (P3, W3), USA (P1, W1), World XI (P3, W3).

BANGLADESH *Test Match Records*

Most appearances

55	Mohammad Ashraful
50	Habibul Bashar
44	Khaled Mashud
40	Javed Omar
36	Mashrafe Mortaza
33	Mohammad Rafique
29	Shahadat Hossain
24	Rajin Saleh
23	Mushfiqur Rahim
21	Shakib Al Hasan
21	Tapash Baisya

Habibul Bashar missed only two of Bangladesh's first 52 Tests

Most runs

		Avge
3026	Habibul Bashar	30.87
2306	Mohammad Ashraful	22.38
1720	Javed Omar	22.05
1445	Tamim Iqbal	40.13
1409	Khaled Mashud	19.04
1179	Shakib Al Hasan	31.02
1141	Rajin Saleh	25.93
1140	Mushfiqur Rahim	27.14
1059	Mohammad Rafique	18.57
942	Junaid Siddique	26.91

Habibul Bashar reached 2000 runs for Bangladesh before anyone else had made 1000

Most wickets

		Avge
100	Mohammad Rafique	40.76
78	Mashrafe Mortaza	41.52
75	Shakib Al Hasan	32.13
66	Shahadat Hossain	45.33
41	Enamul Haque jnr	39.24
36	Tapash Baisya	59.36
28	Manjural Islam	57.32
22	Mahmudullah	36.31
20	Mohammad Ashraful	59.40
18	Enamul Haque snr	57.05

Mohammad Rafique completed the 1000-run 100-wicket double in his last Test

Highest scores

158*	Moh'd Ashraful	v India at Chittagong	2004-05
151	Tamim Iqbal	v India at Mirpur	2009-10
145†	Aminul Islam	v India at Dhaka	2000-01
138	Shahriar Nafees	v Australia at Fatullah	2005-06
136	Moh'd Ashraful	v Sri Lanka at Chittagong	2005-06
129*	Moh'd Ashraful	v Sri Lanka at Colombo	2007
128	Tamim Iqbal	v West Indies at Kingstown	2009
121	Nafees Iqbal	v Zimbabwe at Dhaka	2004-05
119	Javed Omar	v Pakistan at Peshawar	2003-04
115	Mahmudullah	v New Zealand at Hamilton	2009-10

† On debut. Mohammad Ashraful scored five Test centuries, Tamim Iqbal four, and Habibul Bashar three

Best innings bowling

7-36	Shakib Al Hasan	v NZ at Chittagong	2008-09
7-95	Enamul Haque jnr	v Zimbabwe at Dhaka	2004-05
6-27	Shahadat Hossain	v South Africa at Dhaka	2007-08
6-45	Enamul Haque jnr	v Zim at Chittagong	2004-05
6-77	Moh'd Rafique	v South Africa at Dhaka	2002-03
6-81	Manjural Islam	v Zim at Bulawayo	2000-01
6-99	Shakib Al Hasan	v SA at Centurion	2008-09
6-122	Moh'd Rafique	v New Zealand at Dhaka	2004-05
6-132	Naimur Rahman	v India at Dhaka	2000-01
5-36	Moh'd Rafique	v Pakistan at Multan	2003-04

Mohammad Rafique and Shakib Al Hasan took five wickets in an innings on seven occasions, Shahadat Hossain four, and Enamul Haque jnr three

Record wicket partnerships

1st	185	Tamim Iqbal (103) and Imrul Kayes (75)	v England at Lord's	2010
2nd	200	Tamim Iqbal (151) and Junaid Siddique (55)	v India at Mirpur	2009-10
3rd	130	Javed Omar (119) and Mohammad Ashraful (77)	v Pakistan at Peshawar	2003-04
4th	120	Habibul Bashar (77) and Manjural Islam Rana (35)	v West Indies at Kingstown	2004
5th	144	Mehrab Hossain jnr (83) and Mushfiqur Rahim (79)	v New Zealand at Chittagong	2008-09
6th	191	Mohammad Ashraful (129*) and Mushfiqur Rahim (80)	v Sri Lanka at Colombo	2007
7th	145	Shakib Al Hasan (87) and Mahmudullah (115)	v New Zealand at Hamilton	2009-10
8th	113	Mushfiqur Rahim (79) and Naeem Islam (38)	v England at Chittagong	2009-10
9th	77	Mashrafe Mortaza (79) and Shahadat Hossain (31)	v India at Chittagong	2006-07
10th	69	Mohammad Rafique (65) and Shahadat Hossain (3*)	v Australia at Chittagong	2005-06

Figures to 23.9.10. Updated records can be found at **www.cricinfo.com/ci/engine/records**

Test Match Records — **BANGLADESH**

Most catches

Fielders

24	Mohammad Ashraful
22	Habibul Bashar
14	Rajin Saleh
12	Imrul Kayes
12	Shahriar Nafees

Most dismissals

Wicketkeepers — Ct/St

87	Khaled Mashud	78/9
38	Mushfiqur Rahim	31/7
4	Mohammad Salim	3/1
2	Mehrab Hossain	2/0

Highest team totals

488	v Zimbabwe at Chittagong	2004-05
427	v Australia at Fatullah	2005-06
419	v England at Mirpur	2009-10
416	v West Indies at Gros Islet	2004
413	v Sri Lanka at Mirpur	2008-09
408	v New Zealand at Hamilton	2009-10
400	v India at Dhaka	2000-01
382	v England at Lord's	2010
361	v Pakistan at Peshawar	2003-04
345	v West Indies at Kingstown	2009

The 400 against India came in Bangladesh's inaugural Test

Lowest team totals

Completed innings

62	v Sri Lanka at Colombo	2007
86	v Sri Lanka at Colombo	2005-06
87	v West Indies at Dhaka	2002-03
89	v Sri Lanka at Colombo	2007
90	v Sri Lanka at Colombo	2001-02
91	v India at Dhaka	2000-01
96	v Pakistan at Peshawar	2003-04
97	v Australia at Darwin	2003
102	v South Africa at Dhaka	2002-03
104	v Eng at Chester-le-Street	2005

The lowest all-out total by the opposition is 154, by Zimbabwe at Chittagong in 2004-05 (Bangladesh's first Test victory)

Best match bowling

12-200	Enamul Haque jnr	v Zimbabwe at Dhaka	2004-05
9-97	Shahadat Hossain	v South Africa at Dhaka	2007-08
9-115	Shakib Al Hasan	v NZ at Chittagong	2008-09
9-160	Moh'd Rafique	v Australia at Fatullah	2005-06
8-110	Mahmudullah	v W Indies at Kingstown	2009
8-129	Shakib Al Hasan	v W Indies at St George's	2009
7-105	Khaled Mahmud	v Pakistan at Multan	2003-04
7-116	Moh'd Rafique	v Pakistan at Multan	2003-04
7-174	Shakib Al Hasan	v India at Chittagong	2009-10
6-77	Moh'd Rafique	v South Africa at Dhaka	2002-03

Khaled Mahmud took only six other wickets in 11 more Tests

Hat-tricks

Alok Kapali	v Pakistan at Peshawar	2003-04

Alok Kapali's figures were 2.1-1-3-3; he ended Pakistan's innings by dismissing Shabbir Ahmed, Danish Kaneria and Umar Gul. He took only three other Test wickets.

Two bowlers have taken hat-tricks against Bangladesh: AM Blignaut for Zimbabwe at Harare in 2003-04, and JEC Franklin for New Zealand at Dhaka in 2004-05.

Shahadat Hossain took an ODI hat-trick for Bangladesh against Zimbabwe at Harare in 2006

Bangladesh's Test match results

	Played	Won	Lost	Drawn	Tied	% win
v Australia	4	0	4	0	0	0.00
v England	8	0	8	0	0	0.00
v India	7	0	6	1	0	0.00
v New Zealand	9	0	8	1	0	0.00
v Pakistan	6	0	6	0	0	0.00
v South Africa	8	0	8	0	0	0.00
v Sri Lanka	12	0	12	0	0	0.00
v West Indies	6	2	3	1	0	33.33
v Zimbabwe	8	1	4	3	0	12.50
TOTAL	68	3	59	6	0	4.41

Figures to 23.9.10. Updated records can be found at **www.cricinfo.com/ci/engine/records**

BANGLADESH One-day International Records

Most appearances

161	Mohammad Ashraful	
126	Khaled Mashud	
123	Mohammad Rafique	
111	Habibul Bashar	
111	Mashrafe Mortaza	
103	Abdur Razzak	
94	Shakib Al Hasan	
85	Aftab Ahmed	
85	Tamim Iqbal	
77	Khaled Mahmud	

Habibul Bashar captained in 69 ODIs, Mohammad Ashraful in 38, Khaled Mashud in 30

Most runs

		Avge
3354	Moh'd Ashraful	23.61
2478	Tamim Iqbal	29.15
2465	Shakib Al Hasan	32.86
2168	Habibul Bashar	21.68
1954	Aftab Ahmed	24.73
1857	Shahriar Nafees	33.76
1818	Khaled Mashud	21.90
1319	Mushfiqur Rahim	23.14
1312	Javed Omar	23.85
1190	Moh'd Rafique	13.52

Alok Kapali (1190), Mashrafe Mortaza (1125), Raqibul Hasan (1103) and Rajin Saleh (1005) also passed 1000 runs

Most wickets

		Avge
144	Abdur Razzak	28.41
142	Mashrafe Mortaza	30.29
119	Mohammad Rafique	38.75
109	Shakib Al Hasan	30.73
67	Khaled Mahmud	42.76
61	Syed Rasel	33.62
59	Tapash Baisya	41.55
42	Shahadat Hossain	43.42
38	Nazmul Hossain	32.15
29	Hasibul Hossain	46.13

Mohammad Rafique completed the 1000-run/100-wicket double in ODIs as well as Tests

Highest scores

154	Tamim Iqbal	v Zimbabwe at Bulawayo	2009
134*	Shakib Al Hasan	v Canada at St John's	2006-07
129	Tamim Iqbal	v Ireland at Dhaka	2007-08
125	Tamim Iqbal	v England at Mirpur	2009-10
123*	Shahriar Nafees	v Zimbabwe at Jaipur	2006
118*	Shahriar Nafees	v Zimbabwe at Harare	2006-07
115	Alok Kapali	v India at Karachi	2008
109	Moh'd Ashraful	v UAE at Lahore	2008
108*	Rajin Saleh	v Kenya at Fatullah	2005-06
108	Shakib Al Hasan	v Pakistan at Multan	2007-08

Nine further centuries have been scored for Bangladesh, by Imrul Kayes, Junaid Siddique, Mehrab Hossain, Mohammad Ashraful (2), Shahriar Nafees (2) and Shakib Al Hasan (2)

Best bowling figures

6-26	Mashrafe Mortaza	v Kenya at Nairobi	2006
5-29	Abdur Razzak	v Zimbabwe at Mirpur	2009-10
5-31	Aftab Ahmed	v NZ at Dhaka	2004-05
5-33	Abdur Razzak	v Zimbabwe at Bogra	2006-07
5-42	Farhad Reza	v Ireland at Dhaka	2007-08
5-47	Moh'd Rafique	v Kenya at Fatullah	2005-06
4-16	Tapash Baisya	v West Indies at Kingstown	2004
4-16	Rajin Saleh	v Zimbabwe at Harare	2006
4-19	Khaled Mahmud	v Zimbabwe at Harare	2003-04
4-22	Syed Rasel	v Kenya at Nairobi	2006

Aftab Ahmed took only seven more wickets in 84 other matches

Record wicket partnerships

1st	170	Shahriar Hossain (68) and Mehrab Hossain (101)	v Zimbabwe at Dhaka	1998-99
2nd	160	Imrul Kayes (66) and Junaid Siddique (97)	v Pakistan at Dambulla	2010
3rd	141	Mohammad Ashraful (109) and Raqibul Hassan (83)	v United Arab Emirates at Lahore	2008
4th	175*	Rajin Saleh (108*) and Habibul Bashar (64*)	v Kenya at Fatullah	2005-06
5th	119	Shakib Al Hasan (52) and Raqibul Hassan (63)	v South Africa at Dhaka	2007-08
6th	123*	Al Sahariar (62*) and Khaled Mashud (53*)	v West Indies at Dhaka	1999-2000
7th	101	Mushfiqur Rahim (86) and Naeem Islam (43)	v New Zealand at Dunedin	2009-10
8th	70*	Khaled Mashud (35*) and Mohammad Rafique (41*)	v New Zealand at Kimberley	2002-03
9th	97	Shakib Al Hasan (108) and Mashrafe Mortaza (38)	v Pakistan at Multan	2007-08
10th	54*	Khaled Mashud (39*) and Tapash Baisya (22*)	v Sri Lanka at Colombo	2005-06

Figures to 23.9.10. Updated records can be found at **www.cricinfo.com/ci/engine/records**

Most catches

Fielders

35	Mashrafe Mortaza	
33	Mohammad Ashraful	
29	Aftab Ahmed	
28	Mohammad Rafique	
26	Habibul Bashar	

Highest team totals

320-8	v Zimbabwe at Bulawayo	2009
313-6	v Zimbabwe at Bulawayo	2009
301-7	v Kenya at Bogra	2005-06
300-8	v UAE at Lahore	2008
296-6	v India at Mirpur	2009-10
293-7	v Ireland at Dhaka	2007-08
285-7	v Pakistan at Lahore	2007-08
283-6	v India at Karachi	2008
278-5	v Canada at St John's	2006-07
278-6	v Scotland at Dhaka	2006-07

Bangladesh passed 300 for the first time in their 119th one-day international

Lowest team totals

Completed innings

74	v Australia at Darwin	2008
76	v Sri Lanka at Colombo	2002
76	v India at Dhaka	2002-03
77	v NZ at Colombo	2002-03
86	v NZ at Chittagong	2004-05
87*	v Pakistan at Dhaka	1999-2000
92	v Zimbabwe at Nairobi	1997-98
93	v S Africa at Birmingham	2004
93	v NZ at Queenstown	2007-08
94	v Pakistan at Moratuwa	1985-86

* One batsman absent hurt

Most dismissals

Wicketkeepers

		Ct/St
126	Khaled Mashud	91/35
67	Mushfiqur Rahim	50/17
13	Dhiman Ghosh	9/4
4	Jahurul Islam	4/0

Most sixes

49	Aftab Ahmed
39	Mashrafe Mortaza
32	Tamim Iqbal
29	Mohammad Ashraful
29	Mohammad Rafique
18	Shakib Al Hasan
14	Abdur Razzak
14	Mushfiqur Rahim
12	Naeem Islam
10	Alok Kapali
10	Habibul Bashar

Best strike rate

Runs per 100 balls

		Runs
85.61	Mashrafe Mortaza	1125
83.04	Aftab Ahmed	1954
78.66	Tamim Iqbal	2478
75.75	Shakib Al Hasan	2465
71.81	Mohammad Rafique	1190
70.83	Mohammad Ashraful	3354
70.64	Junaid Siddique	864
70.43	Abdur Razzak	548
69.68	Shahriar Nafees	1857
68.90	Mahmudullah	997

Qualification: 500 runs

Most economical bowlers

Runs per over

		Wkts
4.19	Shakib Al Hasan	109
4.39	Mohammad Rafique	119
4.42	Mushfiqur Rahman	19
4.52	Abdur Razzak	144
4.59	Mashrafe Mortaza	142
4.63	Syed Rasel	61
4.84	Manjural Islam	24
4.95	Naimur Rahman	10
4.97	Naeem Islam	27
5.07	Khaled Mahmud	67

Qualification: 1000 balls bowled

Bangladesh's one-day international results

	Played	Won	Lost	Tied	No Result	% win
v Australia	16	1	15	0	0	6.25
v England	14	1	13	0	0	7.14
v India	22	2	20	0	0	9.09
v New Zealand	17	1	16	0	0	5.88
v Pakistan	26	1	25	0	0	3.84
v South Africa	13	1	12	0	0	7.69
v Sri Lanka	29	2	27	0	0	6.89
v West Indies	16	3	11	0	2	21.42
v Zimbabwe	47	25	22	0	0	53.19
v others (see below)	30	20	10	0	0	66.66
TOTAL	230	57	171	0	2	25.00

Other teams: Bermuda (P2, W2), Canada (P2, W1, L1), Hong Kong (P1, W1), Ireland (P6, W4 L2), Kenya (P14, W8, L6), Netherlands (P1, L1), Scotland (P3, W3), UAE (P1, W1).

ENGLAND
Test Match Records

Most appearances

133	AJ Stewart
118	GA Gooch
117	DI Gower
115	MA Atherton
114	MC Cowdrey
108	G Boycott
102	IT Botham
100	GP Thorpe
96	N Hussain
95	APE Knott

Cowdrey was the first man to reach 100 Tests, in 1968

Most runs

		Avge
8900	GA Gooch	42.58
8463	AJ Stewart	39.54
8231	DI Gower	44.25
8114	G Boycott	47.72
7728	MA Atherton	37.69
7624	MC Cowdrey	44.06
7249	WR Hammond	58.45
6971	L Hutton	56.67
6806	KF Barrington	58.67
6744	GP Thorpe	44.66

ME Trescothick (5825), DCS Compton (5807), N Hussain (5764) and MP Vaughan (5719) also passed 5500 runs

Most wickets

		Avge
383	IT Botham	28.40
325	RGD Willis	25.20
307	FS Trueman	21.57
297	DL Underwood	25.83
252	JB Statham	24.84
248	MJ Hoggard	30.50
236	AV Bedser	24.89
234	AR Caddick	29.91
229	D Gough	28.39
222	SJ Harmison	31.94

A Flintoff (219) and JA Snow (202) also took more than 200 wickets

Highest scores

364	L Hutton	v Australia at The Oval	1938
336*	WR Hammond	v New Zealand at Auckland	1932-33
333	GA Gooch	v India at Lord's	1990
325	A Sandham	v West Indies at Kingston	1929-30
310*	JH Edrich	v New Zealand at Leeds	1965
287	RE Foster	v Australia at Sydney	1903-04
285*	PBH May	v West Indies at Birmingham	1957
278	DCS Compton	v Pakistan at Nottingham	1954
262*	DL Amiss	v West Indies at Kingston	1973-74
258	TW Graveney	v West Indies at Nottingham	1957

Foster was playing in his first Test, Sandham in his last

Best innings bowling

10-53	JC Laker	v Australia at Manchester	1956
9-28	GA Lohmann	v South Africa at Johannesburg	1895-96
9-37	JC Laker	v Australia at Manchester	1956
9-57	DE Malcolm	v South Africa at The Oval	1994
9-103	SF Barnes	v S Africa at Johannesburg	1913-14
8-7	GA Lohmann	v S Africa at Port Elizabeth	1895-96
8-11	J Briggs	v South Africa at Cape Town	1888-89
8-29	SF Barnes	v South Africa at The Oval	1912
8-31	FS Trueman	v India at Manchester	1952
8-34	IT Botham	v Pakistan at Lord's	1978

Botham also scored 108 in England's innings victory

Record wicket partnerships

1st	359	L Hutton (158) and C Washbrook (195)	v South Africa at Johannesburg	1948-49
2nd	382	L Hutton (364) and M Leyland (187)	v Australia at The Oval	1938
3rd	370	WJ Edrich (189) and DCS Compton (208)	v South Africa at Lord's	1947
4th	411	PBH May (285*) and MC Cowdrey (154)	v West Indies at Birmingham	1957
5th	254	KWR Fletcher (113) and AW Greig (148)	v India at Bombay	1972-73
6th	281	GP Thorpe (200*) and A Flintoff (137)	v New Zealand at Christchurch	2001-02
7th	197	MJK Smith (96) and JM Parks (101*)	v West Indies at Port-of-Spain	1959-60
8th	332	IJL Trott (184) and SCJ Broad (169)	v Pakistan at Lord's	2010
9th	163*	MC Cowdrey (128*) and AC Smith (69*)	v New Zealand at Wellington	1962-63
10th	130	RE Foster (287) and W Rhodes (40*)	v Australia at Sydney	1903-04

Figures to 23.9.10. Updated records can be found at **www.cricinfo.com/ci/engine/records**

Test Match Records

Most catches

Fielders

120	IT Botham	
120	MC Cowdrey	
110	WR Hammond	
105	GP Thorpe	
103	GA Gooch	

Most dismissals

Wicketkeepers		*Ct/St*
269	APE Knott	250/19
241	AJ Stewart	227/14
219	TG Evans	173/46
174	RW Taylor	167/7
165	RC Russell	153/12

Highest team totals

903-7d	v Australia at The Oval	1938
849	v West Indies at Kingston	1929-30
658-8d	v Australia at Nottingham	1938
654-5	v South Africa at Durban	1938-39
653-4d	v India at Lord's	1990
652-7d	v India at Madras	1984-85
636	v Australia at Sydney	1928-29
633-5d	v India at Birmingham	1979
629	v India at Lord's	1974
627-9d	v Australia at Manchester	1934

England have made six other totals of 600 or more

Lowest team totals

Completed innings		
45	v Australia at Sydney	1886-87
46	v WI at Port-of-Spain	1993-94
51	v WI at Kingston	2008-09
52	v Australia at The Oval	1948
53	v Australia at Lord's	1888
61	v Aust at Melbourne	1901-02
61	v Aust at Melbourne	1903-04
62	v Australia at Lord's	1888
64	v NZ at Wellington	1977-78
65*	v Australia at Sydney	1894-95

*One batsman absent

Best match bowling

19-90	JC Laker	v Australia at Manchester	1956
17-159	SF Barnes	v S Africa at Johannesburg	1913-14
15-28	J Briggs	v S Africa at Cape Town	1888-89
15-45	GA Lohmann	v S Africa at Port Elizabeth	1895-96
15-99	C Blythe	v South Africa at Leeds	1907
15-104	H Verity	v Australia at Lord's	1934
15-124	W Rhodes	v Australia at Melbourne	1903-04
14-99	AV Bedser	v Australia at Nottingham	1953
14-102	W Bates	v Australia at Melbourne	1882-83
14-144	SF Barnes	v South Africa at Durban	1913-14

Barnes took ten or more wickets in a match a record seven times for England

Hat-tricks

W Bates	v Australia at Melbourne	1882-83
J Briggs	v Australia at Sydney	1891-92
GA Lohmann	v S Africa at Port Elizabeth	1895-96
JT Hearne	v Australia at Leeds	1899
MJC Allom	v New Zealand at Christchurch	1929-30
TWJ Goddard	v S Africa at Johannesburg	1938-39
PJ Loader	v West Indies at Leeds	1957
DG Cork	v West Indies at Manchester	1995
D Gough	v Australia at Sydney	1998-99
MJ Hoggard	v West Indies at Bridgetown	2003-04
RJ Sidebottom	v New Zealand at Hamilton	2007-08

Allom was playing in his first match

England's Test match results

	Played	Won	Lost	Drawn	Tied	% win
v Australia	321	99	132	90	0	30.84
v Bangladesh	8	8	0	0	0	100.00
v India	99	34	19	46	0	34.34
v New Zealand	94	45	8	41	0	47.87
v Pakistan	71	22	13	36	0	30.98
v South Africa	138	56	29	53	0	40.57
v Sri Lanka	21	8	6	7	0	38.09
v West Indies	145	43	53	49	0	29.65
v Zimbabwe	6	3	0	3	0	50.00
TOTAL	**903**	**318**	**260**	**325**	**0**	**35.21**

Figures to 23.9.10. Updated records can be found at **www.cricinfo.com/ci/engine/records**

ENGLAND
One-day International Records

Most appearances

189	PD Collingwood
170	AJ Stewart
158	D Gough
138	A Flintoff
133	JM Anderson
125	GA Gooch
123	ME Trescothick
122	AJ Lamb
120	GA Hick
116	IT Botham

Five further men played 100 or more ODIs for England

Most runs

		Avge
4978	PD Collingwood	36.07
4677	AJ Stewart	31.60
4335	ME Trescothick	37.37
4290	GA Gooch	36.98
4010	AJ Lamb	39.31
3846	GA Hick	37.33
3692	AJ Strauss	35.50
3637	NV Knight	40.41
3314	KP Pietersen	43.03
3293	A Flintoff	31.97

DI Gower (3170) also passed 3000 runs, and seven others reached 2000

Most wickets

		Avge
234	D Gough	26.29
179	JM Anderson	30.32
168	A Flintoff	23.61
145	IT Botham	28.54
124	SCJ Broad	25.70
115	PAJ DeFreitas	32.82
106	PD Collingwood	38.63
80	RGD Willis	24.60
76	JE Emburey	30.86
76	SJ Harmison	32.64

Nine further bowlers have taken 50 wickets in ODIs for England

Highest scores

167*	RA Smith	v Australia at Birmingham	1993
158	DI Gower	v New Zealand at Brisbane	1982-83
154	AJ Strauss	v Bangladesh at Birmingham	2010
152	AJ Strauss	v Bangladesh at Nottingham	2005
142*	CWJ Athey	v New Zealand at Manchester	1986
142	GA Gooch	v Pakistan at Karachi	1987-88
137	DL Amiss	v India at Lord's	1975
137	ME Trescothick	v Pakistan at Lord's	2001
136	GA Gooch	v Australia at Lord's	1989
131	KWR Fletcher	v New Zealand at Nottingham	1975

Trescothick scored 12 centuries in ODIs, Gooch 8, Gower and KP Pietersen 7

Best innings bowling

6-31	PD Collingwood	v B'desh at Nottingham	2005
5-15	MA Ealham	v Zim at Kimberley	1999-2000
5-19	A Flintoff	v WI at Gros Islet	2008-09
5-20	VJ Marks	v NZ at Wellington	1983-84
5-21	C White	v Zim at Bulawayo	1999-2000
5-23	SCJ Broad	v S Africa at Nottingham	2008
5-23	JM Anderson	v SA at Port Elizabeth	2009-10
5-26	RC Irani	v India at The Oval	2002
5-28	GP Swann	v Aust at Chester-le-Street	2009
5-31	M Hendrick	v Australia at The Oval	1980

Collingwood also scored 112 in the same match. All Ealham's five wickets were lbw, an ODI record*

Record wicket partnerships

1st	200	ME Trescothick (114*) and VS Solanki (106)	v South Africa at The Oval	2003
2nd	250	AJ Strauss (154) and IJL Trott (110)	v Bangladesh at Birmingham	2010
3rd	213	GA Hick (86*) and NH Fairbrother (113)	v West Indies at Lord's	1991
4th	226	AJ Strauss (100) and A Flintoff (123)	v West Indies at Lord's	2004
5th	174	A Flintoff (99) and PD Collingwood (79*)	v India at The Oval	2004
6th	150	MP Vaughan (90*) and GO Jones (80)	v Zimbabwe at Bulawayo	2004-05
7th	110	PD Collingwood (100) and C White (48)	v Sri Lanka at Perth	2002-03
8th	99*	RS Bopara (43*) and SCJ Broad (45*)	v India at Manchester	2007
9th	100	LE Plunkett (56) and VS Solanki (39*)	v Pakistan at Lahore	2005-06
10th	50*	D Gough (46*) and SJ Harmison (11*)	v Australia at Chester-le-Street	2005

Figures to 23.9.10. Updated records can be found at www.cricinfo.com/ci/engine/records

Most catches

Fielders

105	PD Collingwood	
64	GA Hick	
49	AJ Strauss	
46	A Flintoff	
45	GA Gooch/ME Tres'thick	

Most dismissals

Wicketkeepers — *Ct/St*

163	AJ Stewart	148/15
72	GO Jones	68/4
63	MJ Prior	59/4
47	RC Russell	41/6
43	CMW Read	41/2

Highest team totals

391-4	v Bangladesh at Nottingham	2005
363-7	v Pakistan at Nottingham	1992
347-7	v Bangladesh at Birmingham	2010
340-6	v New Zealand at Napier	2007-08
334-4	v India at Lord's	1975
333-9	v Sri Lanka at Taunton	1983
328-7	v West Indies at Birmingham	2004
327-4	v Pakistan at Lahore	2005-06
325-5	v India at Lord's	2002
323-8	v South Africa at Centurion	2009–10

England have reached 300 on 14 other occasions

Lowest team totals

Completed innings

86	v Australia at Manchester	2001
88	v SL at Dambulla	2003-04
89	v NZ at Wellington	2001-02
93	v Australia at Leeds	1975
94	v Aust at Melbourne	1978-79
101	v NZ at Chester-le-Street	2004
103	v SA at The Oval	1999
104	v SL at Colombo	2007-08
107	v Zim at Cape Town	1999-2000
110	v Aust at Melbourne	1998-99
110	v Aust at Adelaide	2006-07

The lowest totals against England are 45 by Canada (1979), and 70 by Australia (1977)

Most sixes

92	A Flintoff*
72	PD Collingwood
59	KP Pietersen*
44	IT Botham
41	GA Hick
41	ME Trescothick
30	AJ Lamb
26	OA Shah
26	AJ Stewart
22	DI Gower
22	RA Smith

*Also hit one six for the World XI

Best strike rate

Runs per 100 balls — *Runs*

90.90	LJ Wright	600
89.70	EJG Morgan	1054
89.14	A Flintoff	3293
86.66	KP Pietersen	3314
85.21	ME Trescothick	4335
83.83	PAJ DeFreitas	690
79.89	AJ Strauss	3692
79.10	IT Botham	2113
78.67	OA Shah	1834
78.21	GO Jones	815

Qualification: 500 runs

Most economical bowlers

Runs per over — *Wkts*

3.28	RGD Willis	80
3.54	ARC Fraser	47
3.79	GR Dilley	48
3.84	AD Mullally	63
3.96	IT Botham	145
3.96	PAJ DeFreitas	115
4.01	AR Caddick	69
4.08	MA Ealham	67
4.10	JE Emburey	76
4.17	GC Small	58

Qualification: 2000 balls bowled

England's one-day international results

	Played	Won	Lost	Tied	No result	% win
v Australia	106	41	61	2	2	40.38
v Bangladesh	14	13	1	0	0	92.85
v India	70	30	38	0	2	44.11
v New Zealand	70	29	35	2	4	45.45
v Pakistan	68	38	28	0	2	57.57
v South Africa	44	18	23	1	2	44.04
v Sri Lanka	44	23	21	0	0	52.27
v West Indies	82	37	41	0	4	47.43
v Zimbabwe	30	21	8	0	1	72.41
v others (see below)	14	13	0	0	1	92.85
TOTAL	**542**	**263**	**256**	**5**	**18**	**50.66**

Other teams: Canada (P2, W2), East Africa (P1, W1), Ireland (P3, W3), Kenya (P2, W2), Namibia (P1, W1), Netherlands (P2, W2), Scotland (P2, W1, NR1), United Arab Emirates (P1, W1).

INDIA *Test Match Records*

Most appearances

169	SR Tendulkar
141	R Dravid
132	A Kumble
131	Kapil Dev
125	SM Gavaskar
116	DB Vengsarkar
113	SC Ganguly
113	VVS Laxman
99	M Azharuddin
91	GR Viswanath

Gavaskar played 106 consecutive matches between 1974-75 and 1986-87

Most runs

		Avge
13837	SR Tendulkar	56.02
11467	R Dravid	53.33
10122	SM Gavaskar	51.12
7415	VVS Laxman	47.22
7212	SC Ganguly	42.17
6956	V Sehwag	54.34
6868	DB Vengsarkar	42.13
6215	M Azharuddin	45.03
6080	GR Viswanath	41.74
5248	Kapil Dev	31.05

Tendulkar has scored 48 centuries, Gavaskar 34, Dravid 29, Azharuddin 22, Selwag 21

Most wickets

		Avge
619	A Kumble	29.65
434	Kapil Dev	29.64
357	Harbhajan Singh	31.62
266	BS Bedi	29.74
242	BS Chandrasekhar	29.74
242	Z Khan	32.98
236	J Srinath	30.49
189	EAS Prasanna	30.38
162	MH Mankad	32.32
156	S Venkataraghavan	36.11

In all 16 Indians have reached 100 wickets

Highest scores

319	V Sehwag	v South Africa at Chennai	2007-08
309	V Sehwag	v Pakistan at Multan	2003-04
293	V Sehwag	v Sri Lanka at Mumbai	2009-10
281	VVS Laxman	v Australia at Kolkata	2000-01
270	R Dravid	v Pakistan at Rawalpindi	2003-04
254	V Sehwag	v Pakistan at Lahore	2005-06
248*	SR Tendulkar	v Bangladesh at Dhaka	2004-05
241*	SR Tendulkar	v Australia at Sydney	2003-04
239	SC Ganguly	v Pakistan at Bangalore	2007-08
236*	SM Gavaskar	v West Indies at Madras	1983-84

Sehwag has scored six double-centuries, Dravid and Tendulkar five, and Gavaskar four

Best innings bowling

10-74	A Kumble	v Pakistan at Delhi	1998-99
9-69	JM Patel	v Australia at Kanpur	1959-60
9-83	Kapil Dev	v WI at Ahmedabad	1983-84
9-102	SP Gupte	v W Indies at Kanpur	1958-59
8-52	MH Mankad	v Pakistan at Delhi	1952-53
8-55	MH Mankad	v England at Madras	1951-52
8-61	ND Hirwani	v W Indies at Madras	1987-88
8-72	S Venkataraghavan	v N Zealand at Delhi	1964-65
8-75	ND Hirwani	v W Indies at Madras	1987-88
8-76	EAS Prasanna	v NZ at Auckland	1975-76

Hirwani's two performances were in the same match, his Test debut

Record wicket partnerships

1st	413	MH Mankad (231) and P Roy (173)	v New Zealand at Madras	1955-56
2nd	344*	SM Gavaskar (182*) and DB Vengsarkar (157*)	v West Indies at Calcutta	1978-79
3rd	336	V Sehwag (309) and SR Tendulkar (194*)	v Pakistan at Multan	2003-04
4th	353	SR Tendulkar (241*) and VVS Laxman (178)	v Australia at Sydney	2003-04
5th	376	VVS Laxman (281) and R Dravid (180)	v Australia at Calcutta	2000-01
6th	298*	DB Vengsarkar (164*) and RJ Shastri (121*)	v Australia at Bombay	1986-87
7th	259*	VVS Laxman (143*) and MS Dhoni (132*)	v South Africa at Kolkata	2009-10
8th	161	M Azharuddin (109) and A Kumble (88)	v South Africa at Calcutta	1996-97
9th	149	PG Joshi (52*) and RB Desai (85)	v Pakistan at Bombay	1960-61
10th	133	SR Tendulkar (248*) and Z Khan (75)	v Bangladesh at Dhaka	2004-05

Figures to 23.9.10. Updated records can be found at **www.cricinfo.com/ci/engine/records**

Test Match Records

INDIA

Most catches

Fielders

195	R Dravid	
118	VVS Laxman	
108	SM Gavaskar	
106	SR Tendulkar	
105	M Azharuddin	

Most dismissals

Wicketkeepers — Ct/St

198	SMH Kirmani	160/38
139	MS Dhoni	119/20
130	KS More	110/20
107	NR Mongia	99/8
82	FM Engineer	66/16

Highest team totals

726-9d	v Sri Lanka at Mumbai	2009-10
707	v Sri Lanka at Colombo	2010
705-7d	v Australia at Sydney	2003-04
676-7	v Sri Lanka at Kanpur	1986-87
675-5d	v Pakistan at Multan	2003-04
664	v England at The Oval	2007
657-7d	v Australia at Kolkata	2000-01
644-7d	v West Indies at Kanpur	1978-79
643-6d	v South Africa at Kolkata	2009-10
642	v Sri Lanka at Kanpur	2009-10

India have reached 600 on 12 further occasions

Lowest team totals

Completed innings

42*	v England at Lord's	1974
58	v Australia at Brisbane	1947-48
58	v England at Manchester	1952
66	v S Africa at Durban	1996-97
67	v Aust at Melbourne	1947-48
75	v West Indies at Delhi	1987-88
76	v SA at Ahmedabad	2007-08
81*	v NZ at Wellington	1975-76
81	v W Indies at Bridgetown	1996-97
82	v England at Manchester	1952

*One or more batsmen absent

Best match bowling

16-136	ND Hirwani	v West Indies at Madras	1987-88
15-217	Harbhajan Singh	v Australia at Chennai	2000-01
14-124	JM Patel	v Australia at Kanpur	1959-60
14-149	A Kumble	v Pakistan at Delhi	1998-99
13-131	MH Mankad	v Pakistan at Delhi	1952-53
13-132	J Srinath	v Pakistan at Calcutta	1998-99
13-181	A Kumble	v Australia at Chennai	2004-05
13-196	Harbhajan Singh	v Australia at Kolkata	2000-01
12-104	BS Chandrasekhar	v Australia at Melbourne	1977-78
12-108	MH Mankad	v England at Madras	1951-52

Hirwani's feat was on his Test debut

Hat-tricks

Harbhajan Singh   v Australia at Kolkata   2000-01

The wickets of RT Ponting, AC Gilchrist and SK Warne, as India fought back to win after following on.

IK Pathan   v Pakistan at Karachi   2005-06

Salman Butt, Younis Khan and Mohammad Yousuf with the fourth, fifth and sixth balls of the match – Pakistan still won the match by 341 runs.

India have never conceded a hat-trick in a Test match

India's Test match results

	Played	Won	Lost	Drawn	Tied	% win
v Australia	76	18	34	23	1	23.68
v Bangladesh	7	6	0	1	0	85.71
v England	99	19	34	46	0	19.19
v New Zealand	47	15	9	23	0	31.91
v Pakistan	59	9	12	38	0	15.25
v South Africa	24	6	11	7	0	25.00
v Sri Lanka	35	14	6	15	0	40.00
v West Indies	82	11	30	41	0	13.41
v Zimbabwe	11	7	2	2	0	63.63
TOTAL	**440**	**105**	**138**	**196**	**1**	**23.86**

Figures to 23.9.10. Updated records can be found at **www.cricinfo.com/ci/engine/records**

INDIA
One-day International Records

Most appearances

442	SR Tendulkar
335	R Dravid
334	M Azharuddin
308	SC Ganguly
269	A Kumble
251	Yuvraj Singh
229	J Srinath
225	Kapil Dev
218	V Sehwag
210	Harbhajan Singh

Robin Singh played 136 ODIs for India – but only one Test match

Most runs

		Avge
17598	SR Tendulkar	45.12
11221	SC Ganguly	40.95
10644	R Dravid	39.42
9378	M Azharuddin	36.92
7328	Yuvraj Singh	36.64
7102	V Sehwag	34.98
5559	MS Dhoni	50.08
5359	A Jadeja	37.47
4413	NS Sidhu	37.08
4091	K Srikkanth	29.01

Kapil Dev (3783), DB Vengsarkar (3508), G Gambhir (3351), RJ Shastri (3108) and SM Gavaskar (3092) also reached 3000

Most wickets

		Avge
334	A Kumble	30.83
315	J Srinath	28.08
288	AB Agarkar	27.85
253	Kapil Dev	27.45
238	Harbhajan Singh	32.97
228	Z Khan	30.63
196	BKV Prasad	32.30
157	M Prabhakar	28.87
154	SR Tendulkar	44.26
152	IK Pathan	29.91

A Nehra (142), RJ Shastri (129) and SC Ganguly (100) also reached 100 wickets

Highest scores

200*	SR Tendulkar	v South Africa at Gwalior	2009-10
186*	SR Tendulkar	v N Zealand at Hyderabad	1999-2000
183*	MS Dhoni	v Sri Lanka at Jaipur	2005-06
183	SC Ganguly	v Sri Lanka at Taunton	1999
175*	Kapil Dev	v Zimbabwe at Tunbridge Wells	1983
175	SR Tendulkar	v Australia at Hyderabad	2009-10
163*	SR Tendulkar	v NZ at Christchurch	2008-09
159*	D Mongia	v Zimbabwe at Guwahati	2001-02
153*	M Azharuddin	v Zimbabwe at Cuttack	1997-98
153*	SC Ganguly	v New Zealand at Gwalior	1999-2000
153	R Dravid	v N Zealand at Hyderabad	1999-2000

Tendulkar scored 46 centuries, Ganguly 22, Sehwag 13

Best bowling figures

6-12	A Kumble	v West Indies at Calcutta	1993-94
6-23	A Nehra	v England at Durban	2002-03
6-27	M Kartik	v Australia at Mumbai	2007-08
6-42	AB Agarkar	v Australia at Melbourne	2003-04
6-55	S Sreesanth	v England at Indore	2005-06
6-59	A Nehra	v Sri Lanka at Colombo	2005
5-6	SB Joshi	v South Africa at Nairobi	1999-2000
5-15	RJ Shastri	v Australia at Perth	1991-92
5-16	SC Ganguly	v Pakistan at Toronto	1997-98
5-21	Arshad Ayub	v Pakistan at Dhaka	1988-89
5-21	N Chopra	v West Indies at Toronto	1999-2000

Agarkar took four wickets in an ODI innings 12 times

Record wicket partnerships

1st	258	SC Ganguly (111) and SR Tendulkar (146)	v Kenya at Paarl	2001-02
2nd	331	SR Tendulkar (186*) and R Dravid (153)	v New Zealand at Hyderabad	1999-2000
3rd	237*	R Dravid (104*) and SR Tendulkar (140*)	v Kenya at Bristol	1999
4th	275*	M Azharuddin (153*) and A Jadeja (116*)	v Zimbabwe at Cuttack	1997-98
5th	223	M Azharuddin (111*) and A Jadeja (119)	v Sri Lanka at Colombo	1997-98
6th	158	Yuvraj Singh (120) and MS Dhoni (67*)	v Zimbabwe at Harare	2005-06
7th	102	HK Badani (60*) and AB Agarkar (53)	v Australia at Melbourne	2003-04
8th	84	Harbhajan Singh (49) and P Kumar (40*)	v Australia at Vadodara	2009-10
9th	126*	Kapil Dev (175*) and SMH Kirmani (24*)	v Zimbabwe at Tunbridge Wells	1983
10th	64	Harbhajan Singh (41*) and L Balaji (18)	v England at The Oval	2004

Figures to 23.9.10. Updated records can be found at **www.cricinfo.com/ci/engine/records**

One-day International Records

Most catches

Fielders

156	M Azharuddin
134	SR Tendulkar
124	R Dravid
99	SC Ganguly
85	A Kumble

Most dismissals

Wicketkeepers   *Ct/St*

219	MS Dhoni	167/52
154	NR Mongia	110/44
90	KS More	63/27
86	R Dravid	72/14

Highest team totals

414-7	v Sri Lanka at Rajkot	2009-10
413-5	v Bermuda at Port-of-Spain	2006-07
401-3	v South Africa at Gwalior	2009-10
392-4	v N Zealand at Christchurch	2008-09
387-5	v England at Rajkot	2008-09
376-2	v N Zealand at Hyderabad	1999-2000
374-4	v Hong Kong at Karachi	2008
373-6	v Sri Lanka at Taunton	1999
363-5	v Sri Lanka at Colombo	2008-09
356-9	v Pakistan at Visakhapatnam	2004-05

All scored in 50 overs

Lowest team totals

Completed innings

54	v Sri Lanka at Sharjah	2000-01
63	v Australia at Sydney	1980-81
78	v Sri Lanka at Kanpur	1986-87
79	v Pakistan at Sialkot	1978-79
88	v NZ at Dambulla	2010
91	v South Africa at Durban	2006-07
100	v WI at Ahmedabad	1993-94
100	v Australia at Sydney	1999-2000
103	v Sri Lanka at Colombo	2008-09
103	v Sri Lanka at Dambulla	2010

*The lowest score against India is
Zimbabwe's 65 at Harare in 2005-06*

Most sixes

189	SC Ganguly
185	SR Tendulkar
134	Yuvraj Singh
116	V Sehwag
112	MS Dhoni
85	A Jadeja
77	M Azharuddin
67	Kapil Dev
55	SK Raina
44	NS Sidhu

Dhoni hit 10 sixes in one innings

Best strike rate

Runs per 100 balls   *Runs*

103.34	V Sehwag	7102
95.07	Kapil Dev	3783
91.92	RV Uthappa	786
89.43	SB Joshi	584
89.22	SK Raina	2444
88.02	Yuvraj Singh	7328
87.55	MS Dhoni	5559
86.26	SR Tendulkar	17598
84.72	G Gambhir	3351
82.17	SM Patil	1005

Qualification: 500 runs

Most economical bowlers

Runs per over   *Wkts*

3.71	Kapil Dev	253
3.95	Maninder Singh	66
4.05	Madan Lal	73
4.21	RJ Shastri	129
4.27	M Prabhakar	157
4.29	Harbhajan Singh	238
4.29	A Kumble	334
4.33	M Amarnath	46
4.36	SLV Raju	63
4.44	SB Joshi	69
4.44	J Srinath	315

Qualification: 2000 balls bowled

India's one-day international results

	Played	Won	Lost	Tied	No result	% win
v Australia	103	34	61	0	8	35.78
v Bangladesh	22	20	2	0	0	90.90
v England	70	38	30	0	2	55.88
v New Zealand	83	41	37	0	5	52.56
v Pakistan	119	46	69	0	4	40.00
v South Africa	60	22	36	0	2	37.93
v Sri Lanka	128	67	50	0	11	57.26
v West Indies	95	38	54	1	2	41.39
v Zimbabwe	51	39	10	2	0	78.43
v others (see below)	22	20	2	0	0	90.90
TOTAL	**753**	**365**	**351**	**3**	**34**	**50.97**

*Other teams: Bermuda (P1, W1), East Africa (P1, W1), Hong Kong (P1, W1), Ireland (P1, W1), Kenya (P13, W11, L2), Namibia
(P1, W1), Netherlands (P1, W1), Scotland (P1, W1), United Arab Emirates (P2, W2).*

NEW ZEALAND
Test Match Records

Most appearances

111	SP Fleming
99	DL Vettori
86	RJ Hadlee
82	JG Wright
81	NJ Astle
78	AC Parore
77	MD Crowe
63	IDS Smith
62	CL Cairns
61	BE Congdon

Vettori also played one Test for the World XI against Australia in October 2005

Most runs

		Avge
7172	SP Fleming	40.06
5444	MD Crowe	45.36
5334	JG Wright	37.82
4702	NJ Astle	37.02
3954	DL Vettori	30.89
3448	BE Congdon	32.22
3428	JR Reid	33.28
3320	CL Cairns	33.53
3124	RJ Hadlee	27.16
3116	CD McMillan	38.46

Crowe scored 17 Test centuries, Wright 12 and Astle 11

Most wickets

		Avge
431	RJ Hadlee	22.29
324	DL Vettori	33.62
218	CL Cairns	29.40
181	CS Martin	35.03
160	DK Morrison	34.68
130	BL Cairns	32.92
123	EJ Chatfield	32.17
116	RO Collinge	29.25
111	BR Taylor	26.60
102	JG Bracewell	35.81

RC Motz (100) also took 100 Test wickets. Vettori also took one wicket for the World XI

Highest scores

299	MD Crowe	v Sri Lanka at Wellington	1990-91
274*	SP Fleming	v Sri Lanka at Colombo	2002-03
267*	BA Young	v Sri Lanka at Dunedin	1996-97
262	SP Fleming	v South Africa at Cape Town	2005-06
259	GM Turner	v West Indies at Georgetown	1971-72
239	GT Dowling	v India at Christchurch	1967-68
230*	B Sutcliffe	v India at Delhi	1955-56
224	L Vincent	v Sri Lanka at Wellington	2004-05
223*	GM Turner	v West Indies at Kingston	1971-72
222	NJ Astle	v England at Christchurch	2001-02

There have been five other double-centuries, two by MS Sinclair and one each by MP Donnelly, SP Fleming and JD Ryder

Best innings bowling

9-52	RJ Hadlee	v Australia at Brisbane	1985-86
7-23	RJ Hadlee	v India at Wellington	1975-76
7-27	CL Cairns	v West Indies at Hamilton	1999-2000
7-52	C Pringle	v Pakistan at Faisalabad	1990-91
7-53	CL Cairns	v Bangladesh at Hamilton	2001-02
7-65	SB Doull	v India at Wellington	1998-99
7-74	BR Taylor	v West Indies at Bridgetown	1971-72
7-74	BL Cairns	v England at Leeds	1983
7-87	SL Boock	v Pakistan at Hyderabad	1984-85
7-87	DL Vettori	v Australia at Auckland	1999-2000

Hadlee took five or more wickets in an innings 36 times: the next-best for New Zealand is 18, by DL Vettori

Record wicket partnerships

1st	387	GM Turner (259) and TW Jarvis (182)	v West Indies at Georgetown	1971-72
2nd	241	JG Wright (116) and AH Jones (143)	v England at Wellington	1991-92
3rd	467	AH Jones (186) and MD Crowe (299)	v Sri Lanka at Wellington	1990-91
4th	271	LRPL Taylor (151) and JD Ryder (201)	v India at Napier	2008-09
5th	222	NJ Astle (141) and CD McMillan (142)	v Zimbabwe at Wellington	2000-01
6th	339	MJ Guptill (189) and BB McCullum (185)	v Bangladesh at Hamilton	2009-10
7th	225	CL Cairns (158) and JDP Oram (90)	v South Africa at Auckland	2003-04
8th	256	SP Fleming (262) and JEC Franklin (122*)	v South Africa at Cape Town	2005-06
9th	136	IDS Smith (173) and MC Snedden (22)	v India at Auckland	1989-90
10th	151	BF Hastings (110) and RO Collinge (68*)	v Pakistan at Auckland	1972-73

Figures to 23.9.10. Updated records can be found at **www.cricinfo.com/ci/engine/records**

Test Match Records — NEW ZEALAND

Most catches

Fielders

171	SP Fleming	
71	MD Crowe	
70	NJ Astle	
64	JV Coney	
55	DL Vettori	

Most dismissals

Wicketkeepers		Ct/St
201	AC Parore	194/7
176	IDS Smith	168/8
172	BB McCullum	161/11
96	KJ Wadsworth	92/4
59	WK Lees	52/7

Highest team totals

671-4	v Sri Lanka at Wellington	1990-91
630-6d	v India at Chandigarh	2003-04
619-9d	v India at Napier	2008-09
595	v South Africa at Auckland	2003-04
593-8d	v South Africa at Cape Town	2005-06
586-7d	v Sri Lanka at Dunedin	1996-97
563	v Pakistan at Hamilton	2003-04
561	v Sri Lanka at Napier	2004-05
553-7d	v Australia at Brisbane	1985-86
553-7d	v Bangladesh at Hamilton	2009-10

671-4 is the record score in any team's second innings in a Test match

Lowest team totals

Completed innings		
26	v England at Auckland	1954-55
42	v Australia at Wellington	1945-46
47	v England at Lord's	1958
54	v Australia at Wellington	1945-46
65	v England at Christchurch	1970-71
67	v England at Leeds	1958
67	v England at Lord's	1978
70	v Pakistan at Dacca	1955-56
73	v Pakistan at Lahore	2001-02
74	v W Indies at Dunedin	1955-56
74	v England at Lord's	1958

26 is the lowest total by any team in a Test match

Best match bowling

15-123	RJ Hadlee	v Australia at Brisbane	1985-86
12-149	DL Vettori	v Australia at Auckland	1999-2000
12-170	DL Vettori	v Bangladesh at Chittagong	2004-05
11-58	RJ Hadlee	v India at Wellington	1975-76
11-102	RJ Hadlee	v West Indies at Dunedin	1979-80
11-152	C Pringle	v Pakistan at Faisalabad	1990-91
11-155	RJ Hadlee	v Australia at Perth	1985-86
11-169	DJ Nash	v England at Lord's	1994
11-180	CS Martin	v South Africa at Auckland	2003-04
10-88	RJ Hadlee	v India at Bombay	1988-89

Hadlee took 33 wickets at 12.15 in the three-Test series in Australia in 1985-86

Hat-tricks

PJ Petherick	v Pakistan at Lahore	1976-77
JEC Franklin	v Bangladesh at Dhaka	2004-05

Petherick's hat-trick was on Test debut: he dismissed Javed Miandad (who had made 163 on his debut), Wasim Raja and Intikhab Alam. Petherick won only five more Test caps.

Franklin is one of only five men to have scored a century and taken a hat-trick in Tests: the others are J Briggs of England, Abdul Razzaq and Wasim Akram of Pakistan, and IK Pathan of India

New Zealand's Test match results

	Played	Won	Lost	Drawn	Tied	% win
v Australia	50	7	26	17	0	14.00
v Bangladesh	9	8	0	1	0	88.88
v England	94	8	45	41	0	8.51
v India	47	9	15	23	0	19.14
v Pakistan	48	7	22	19	0	14.58
v South Africa	35	4	20	11	0	11.42
v Sri Lanka	26	9	7	10	0	34.61
v West Indies	37	9	10	18	0	24.32
v Zimbabwe	13	7	0	6	0	53.84
TOTAL	**359**	**68**	**145**	**146**	**0**	**18.94**

Figures to 23.9.10. Updated records can be found at www.cricinfo.com/ci/engine/records

NEW ZEALAND *One-day International Records*

Most appearances

279	SP Fleming
251	DL Vettori
250	CZ Harris
223	NJ Astle
214	CL Cairns
197	CD McMillan
179	AC Parore
171	BB McCullum
157	SB Styris
149	JG Wright

Fleming (1), Vettori (4) and Cairns (1) also played in official ODIs for the World XI

Most runs

		Avge
8007	SP Fleming	32.41
7090	NJ Astle	34.92
4881	CL Cairns	29.22
4707	CD McMillan	28.18
4704	MD Crowe	38.55
4379	CZ Harris	29.00
4056	SB Styris	32.70
3891	JG Wright	26.46
3569	BB McCullum	29.01
3314	AC Parore	25.68

Astle scored 16 centuries: Fleming is next with eight. Fleming also scored 30 runs and Cairns 69 for the World XI

Most wickets

		Avge
260	DL Vettori	31.49
203	CZ Harris	37.50
200	CL Cairns	32.78
170	KD Mills	26.02
158	RJ Hadlee	21.56
147	SE Bond	20.88
142	JDP Oram	30.52
140	EJ Chatfield	25.84
128	SB Styris	34.87
126	DK Morrison	27.53

MC Snedden (114), GR Larsen (113), DR Tuffey (106) and C Pringle (103) also took 100 wkts. Vettori also took 8 wkts, and Cairns 1, for the World XI

Highest scores

172	L Vincent	v Zimbabwe at Bulawayo	2005-06
171*	GM Turner	v East Africa at Birmingham	1975
166	BB McCullum	v Ireland at Aberdeen	2008
161	JAH Marshall	v Ireland at Aberdeen	2008
145*	NJ Astle	v USA at The Oval	2004
141	SB Styris	v Sri Lanka at Bloemfontein	2002-03
140	GM Turner	v Sri Lanka at Auckland	1982-83
141	SB Styris	v Sri Lanka at Bloemfontein	2002-03
139	JM How	v England at Napier	2007-08
131	BB McCullum	v Pakistan at Abu Dhabi	2009-10

Turner's 171 was the highest score in the first World Cup*

Best bowling figures

6-19	SE Bond	v India at Bulawayo	2005-06
6-23	SE Bond	v Australia at Port Elizabeth	2002-03
6-25	SB Styris	v West Indies at Port-of-Spain	2001-02
5-7	DL Vettori	v Bangladesh at Queenstown	2007-08
5-22	MN Hart	v West Indies at Margao	1994-95
5-22	AR Adams	v India at Queenstown	2002-03
5-23	RO Collinge	v India at Christchurch	1975-76
5-23	SE Bond	v Australia at Wellington	2006-07
5-25	RJ Hadlee	v Sri Lanka at Bristol	1983
5-25	SE Bond	v Australia at Adelaide	2001-02
5-25	KD Mills	v South Africa at Durban	2007-08

In all Hadlee took five wickets in an ODI on five occasions

Record wicket partnerships

1st	274	JAH Marshall (161) and BB McCullum (166)	v Ireland at Aberdeen	2008
2nd	156	L Vincent (102) and NJ Astle (81)	v West Indies at Napier	2005-06
3rd	181	AC Parore (96) and KR Rutherford (108)	v India at Baroda	1994-95
4th	190	LRPL Taylor (95) and SB Styris (89)	v India at Dambulla	2010
5th	148	RG Twose (80*) and CL Cairns (60)	v Australia at Cardiff	1999
6th	165	CD McMillan (117) and BB McCullum (86*)	v Australia at Hamilton	2006-07
7th	123	NT Broom (71) and JDP Oram (83)	v Bangladesh at Napier	2009-10
8th	79	SB Styris (63) and DL Vettori (47)	v Zimbabwe at Harare	2005-06
9th	83	KD Mills (54) and TG Southee (32)	v India at Christchurch	2008-09
10th	65	MC Snedden (40) and EJ Chatfield (19*)	v Sri Lanka at Derby	1983

Figures to 23.9.10. Updated records can be found at www.cricinfo.com/ci/engine/records

Most catches

Fielders

132	SP Fleming	
96	CZ Harris	
83	NJ Astle	
67	DL Vettori	
66	CL Cairns	

Most dismissals

Wicketkeepers		*Ct/St*
196	BB McCullum	183/13
136	AC Parore	111/25
85	IDS Smith	80/5
37	TE Blain	36/1
30	LK Germon	21/9
30	WK Lees	28/2

Highest team totals

402-2	v Ireland at Aberdeen	2008
397-5	v Zimbabwe at Bulawayo	2005-06
363-5	v Canada at St Lucia	2006-07
350-9	v Australia at Hamilton	2006-07
349-9	v India at Rajkot	1999-2000
348-8	v India at Nagpur	1995-96
347-4	v USA at The Oval	2004
340-5	v Australia at Auckland	2006-07
340-7	v England at Napier	2007-08
338-4	v Bangladesh at Sharjah	1989-90

The 397-5 came from 44 overs; all the others were from 50, except 350-9 (49.3), and 340-5 (48.4)

Lowest team totals

Completed innings

64	v Pakistan at Sharjah	1985-86
73	v Sri Lanka at Auckland	2006-07
74	v Aust at Wellington	1981-82
74	v Pakistan at Sharjah	1989-90
94	v Aust at Christchurch	1989-90
97	v Aust at Faridabad	2003-04
105	v Aust at Auckland	2005-06
108	v Pakistan at Wellington	1992-93
110	v Pakistan at Auckland	1993-94
112	v Aust at Port Elizabeth	2002-03

The lowest score against New Zealand is 70, by Australia at Adelaide in 1985-86

Most sixes

151	CL Cairns	
105	BB McCullum	
86	NJ Astle	
84	CD McMillan	
71	JDP Oram	
63	SP Fleming	
63	SB Styris	
55	LRPL Taylor	
43	CZ Harris	
41	BL Cairns	

CL Cairns also hit 2 for the World XI

Best strike rate

Runs per 100 balls		*Runs*
104.88	BL Cairns	987
99.43	IDS Smith	1055
93.26	JD Ryder	637
87.86	BB McCullum	3569
84.82	JDP Oram	2203
83.76	CL Cairns	4881
82.38	MJ Guptill	959
82.38	DL Vettori	1843
81.84	LRPL Taylor	2376
79.07	SB Styris	4056

Qualification: 500 runs

Most economical bowlers

Runs per over		*Wkts*
3.30	RJ Hadlee	158
3.57	EJ Chatfield	140
3.76	GR Larsen	113
4.06	BL Cairns	89
4.13	DL Vettori	260
4.14	W Watson	74
4.17	DN Patel	45
4.17	JV Coney	54
4.28	SE Bond	147
4.28	CZ Harris	203

Qualification: 2000 balls bowled

New Zealand's one-day international results

	Played	Won	Lost	Tied	No result	% win
v Australia	123	34	84	0	5	28.81
v Bangladesh	17	16	1	0	0	94.11
v England	70	35	29	2	4	54.54
v India	83	37	41	0	5	47.43
v Pakistan	82	32	48	1	1	40.12
v South Africa	51	17	30	0	4	36.17
v Sri Lanka	72	35	32	1	4	52.20
v West Indies	51	20	24	0	7	45.45
v Zimbabwe	28	19	7	1	1	72.22
v others (see below)	11	11	0	0	0	100.00
TOTAL	**588**	**256**	**296**	**5**	**31**	**46.40**

Other teams: Canada (P2, W2), East Africa (P1, W1), Ireland (P2, W2), Kenya (P1, W1), Netherlands (P1, W1), Scotland (P2, W2), United Arab Emirates (P1, W1), United States of America (P1, W1).

PAKISTAN
Test Match Records

Most appearances

124	Javed Miandad
119	Inzamam-ul-Haq
104	Wasim Akram
103	Salim Malik
90	Mohammad Yousuf
88	Imran Khan
87	Waqar Younis
81	Wasim Bari
78	Zaheer Abbas
76	Mudassar Nazar

Inzamam-ul-Haq also played one Test for the World XI

Most runs

		Avge
8832	Javed Miandad	52.57
8829	Inzamam-ul-Haq	50.16
7530	Mohammad Yousuf	52.29
5768	Salim Malik	43.69
5260	Younis Khan	50.09
5062	Zaheer Abbas	44.79
4114	Mudassar Nazar	38.09
4052	Saeed Anwar	45.52
3931	Majid Khan	38.92
3915	Hanif Mohammad	43.98

Mohammad Yousuf was known as Yousuf Youhana until September 2005

Most wickets

		Avge
414	Wasim Akram	23.62
373	Waqar Younis	23.56
362	Imran Khan	22.81
261	Danish Kaneria	34.79
236	Abdul Qadir	32.80
208	Saqlain Mushtaq	29.83
185	Mushtaq Ahmed	32.97
178	Shoaib Akhtar	25.69
177	Sarfraz Nawaz	32.75
171	Iqbal Qasim	28.11

Five further bowlers have taken 100 wickets

Highest scores

337	Hanif Mohammad	v WI at Bridgetown	1957-58
329	Inzamam-ul-Haq	v NZ at Lahore	2001-02
313	Younis Khan	v Sri Lanka at Karachi	2008-09
280*	Javed Miandad	v India at Hyderabad	1982-83
274	Zaheer Abbas	v Eng at Birmingham	1971
271	Javed Miandad	v NZ at Auckland	1988-89
267	Younis Khan	v India at Bangalore	2004-05
260	Javed Miandad	v England at The Oval	1987
257*	Wasim Akram	v Zim at Sheikhupura	1996-97
240	Zaheer Abbas	v England at The Oval	1974

Wasim Akram's innings included 12 sixes, a record for any Test innings

Best innings bowling

9-56	Abdul Qadir	v England at Lahore	1987-88
9-86	Sarfraz Nawaz	v Australia at Melbourne	1978-79
8-58	Imran Khan	v Sri Lanka at Lahore	1981-82
8-60	Imran Khan	v India at Karachi	1982-83
8-69	Sikander Bakht	v India at Delhi	1979-80
8-164	Saqlain Mushtaq	v England at Lahore	2000-01
7-40	Imran Khan	v England at Leeds	1987
7-42	Fazal Mahmood	v India at Lucknow	1952-53
7-49	Iqbal Qasim	v Australia at Karachi	1979-80
7-52	Intikhab Alam	v NZ at Dunedin	1972-73
7-52	Imran Khan	v Eng at Birmingham	1982

Wasim Akram took five or more wickets in a Test innings on 25 occasions, Imran Khan 23, Waqar Younis 22

Record wicket partnerships

1st	298	Aamer Sohail (160) and Ijaz Ahmed (151)	v West Indies at Karachi	1997-98
2nd	291	Zaheer Abbas (274) and Mushtaq Mohammad (100)	v England at Birmingham	1971
3rd	451	Mudassar Nazar (231) and Javed Miandad (280*)	v India at Hyderabad	1982-83
4th	350	Mushtaq Mohammad (201) and Asif Iqbal (175)	v New Zealand at Dunedin	1972-73
5th	281	Javed Miandad (163) and Asif Iqbal (166)	v New Zealand at Lahore	1976-77
6th	269	Mohammad Yousuf (223) and Kamran Akmal (154)	v England at Lahore	2005-06
7th	308	Waqar Hasan (189) and Imtiaz Ahmed (209)	v New Zealand at Lahore	1955-56
8th	313	Wasim Akram (257*) and Saqlain Mushtaq (79)	v Zimbabwe at Sheikhupura	1996-97
9th	190	Asif Iqbal (146) and Intikhab Alam (51)	v England at The Oval	1967
10th	151	Azhar Mahmood (128*) and Mushtaq Ahmed (59)	v South Africa at Rawalpindi	1997-98

Figures to 23.9.10. Updated records can be found at **www.cricinfo.com/ci/engine/records**

Test Match Records

PAKISTAN

Most catches

Fielders

93	Javed Miandad	
81	Inzamam-ul-Haq	
67	Younis Khan	
66	Majid Khan	
65	Mohammad Yousuf	
65	Salim Malik	

Most dismissals

		Ct/St
Wicketkeepers		
228	Wasim Bari	201/27
206	Kamran Akmal	184/22
147	Moin Khan	127/20
130	Rashid Latif	119/11
104	Salim Yousuf	91/13

Highest team totals

765-6d	v Sri Lanka at Karachi	2008-09
708	v England at The Oval	1987
699-5	v India at Lahore	1989-90
679-7d	v India at Lahore	2005-06
674-6	v India at Faisalabad	1984-85
657-8d	v West Indies at Bridgetown	1957-58
652	v India at Faisalabad	1982-83
643	v New Zealand at Lahore	2001-02
636-8d	v England at Lahore	2005-06
624	v Australia at Adelaide	1983-84

Pakistan have made four other scores of 600 or more, and one of 599-7d

Lowest team totals

Completed innings

53*	v Australia at Sharjah †	2002-03
59	v Australia at Sharjah †	2002-03
62	v Australia at Perth	1981-82
72	v Australia at Perth	2004-05
72	v England at Birmingham	2010
74	v England at Lord's	2010
77*	v West Indies at Lahore	1986-87
80	v England at Nottingham	2010
87	v England at Lord's	1954
90	v England at Manchester	1954
90	v Sri Lanka at Colombo	2009

* One batsman retired hurt or absent hurt.

† Same match

Best match bowling

14-116	Imran Khan	v Sri Lanka at Lahore	1981-82
13-101	Abdul Qadir	v England at Lahore	1987-88
13-114	Fazal Mahmood	v Australia at Karachi	1956-57
13-135	Waqar Younis	v Zimbabwe at Karachi	1993-94
12-94	Fazal Mahmood	v India at Lucknow	1952-53
12-94	Danish Kaneria	v Bangladesh at Multan	2001-02
12-99	Fazal Mahmood	v England at The Oval	1954
12-100	Fazal Mahmood	v West Indies at Dacca	1958-59
12-130	Waqar Younis	v NZ at Faisalabad	1990-91
12-165	Imran Khan	v Australia at Sydney	1976-77

Imran Khan took ten or more wickets in a match six times, Abdul Qadir, Waqar Younis and Wasim Akram five each

Hat-tricks

Wasim Akram	v Sri Lanka at Lahore	1998-99
Wasim Akram	v Sri Lanka at Dhaka	1998-99
Abdul Razzaq	v Sri Lanka at Galle	1999-2000
Mohammad Sami	v Sri Lanka at Lahore	2001-02

Wasim Akram's hat-tricks came in successive matches: he also took Pakistan's first two hat-tricks in one-day internationals.

RS Kaluwitharana was the first victim in both Wasim Akram's first hat-trick and in Abdul Razzaq's

Pakistan's Test match results

	Played	Won	Lost	Drawn	Tied	% win
v Australia	57	12	28	17	0	21.05
v Bangladesh	6	6	0	0	0	100.00
v England	71	13	22	36	0	18.30
v India	59	12	9	38	0	20.33
v New Zealand	48	22	7	19	0	45.83
v South Africa	16	3	8	5	0	18.75
v Sri Lanka	37	15	9	13	0	40.54
v West Indies	44	15	14	15	0	34.09
v Zimbabwe	14	8	2	4	0	57.14
TOTAL	352	106	99	147	0	30.11

*Figures to 23.9.10. Updated records can be found at **www.cricinfo.com/ci/engine/records***

PAKISTAN
One-day International Records

Most appearances

375	Inzamam-ul-Haq
356	Wasim Akram
296	Shahid Afridi
283	Salim Malik
280	Mohammad Yousuf
262	Waqar Younis
250	Ijaz Ahmed
247	Saeed Anwar
239	Abdul Razzaq
233	Javed Miandad

Moin Khan (219) and Younis Khan (202) also played in more than 200 ODIs

Most runs

		Avge
11701	Inzamam-ul-Haq	39.53
9551	Mohammad Yousuf	42.26
8824	Saeed Anwar	39.21
7381	Javed Miandad	41.70
7170	Salim Malik	32.88
6564	Ijaz Ahmed	32.33
6284	Shahid Afridi	24.16
5841	Rameez Raja	32.09
5765	Younis Khan	32.57
5188	Shoaib Malik	34.35

Aamer Sohail (4780) and Abdul Razzaq (4677) also passed 4000 runs

Most wickets

		Avge
502	Wasim Akram	23.52
416	Waqar Younis	23.84
288	Saqlain Mushtaq	21.78
280	Shahid Afridi	35.08
257	Abdul Razzaq	31.09
229	Shoaib Akhtar	23.77
182	Aqib Javed	31.43
182	Imran Khan	26.61
161	Mushtaq Ahmed	33.29
134	Shoaib Malik	36.29

Six further bowlers have taken 100 wickets for Pakistan ODIs

Highest scores

194	Saeed Anwar	v India at Chennai	1996-97
160	Imran Nazir	v Zimbabwe at Kingston	2006-07
144	Younis Khan	v Hong Kong at Colombo	2004
143	Shoaib Malik	v India at Colombo	2004
141*	Mohammad Yousuf	v Zim at Bulawayo	2002-03
140	Saeed Anwar	v India at Dhaka	1997-98
139*	Ijaz Ahmed	v India at Lahore	1997-98
137*	Inzamam-ul-Haq	v N Zealand at Sharjah	1993-94
137	Ijaz Ahmed	v England at Sharjah	1998-99
136	Salman Butt	v Bangladesh at Karachi	2007-08

Saeed Anwar scored 20 centuries, Mohammad Yousuf 15, Ijaz Ahmed and Inzamam-ul-Haq 10

Best innings bowling

7-36	Waqar Younis	v England at Leeds	2001
7-37	Aqib Javed	v India at Sharjah	1991-92
6-14	Imran Khan	v India at Sharjah	1984-85
6-16	Shoaib Akhtar	v New Zealand at Karachi	2001-02
6-18	Azhar Mahmood	v W Indies at Sharjah	1999-2000
6-26	Waqar Younis	v Sri Lanka at Sharjah	1989-90
6-27	Naved-ul-Hasan	v India at Jamshedpur	2004-05
6-30	Waqar Younis	v N Zealand at Auckland	1993-94
6-35	Abdul Razzaq	v Bangladesh at Dhaka	2001-02
6-38	Shahid Afridi	v Australia at Dubai	2008-09

Waqar Younis took five or more wickets in an innings 13 times (the ODI record), Saqlain Mushtaq and Wasim Akram 6

Record wicket partnerships

1st	204	Saeed Anwar (110) and Rameez Raja (109*)	v Sri Lanka at Sharjah	1992-93
2nd	263	Aamer Sohail (134) and Inzamam-ul-Haq (137*)	v New Zealand at Sharjah	1993-94
3rd	230	Saeed Anwar (140) and Ijaz Ahmed (117)	v India at Dhaka	1997-98
4th	206	Shoaib Malik (128) and Mohammad Yousuf (87)	v India at Centurion	2009-10
5th	176	Younis Khan (89) and Umar Akmal (102*)	v Sri Lanka at Colombo	2009
6th	144	Imran Khan (102*) and Shahid Mahboob (77)	v Sri Lanka at Leeds	1983
7th	124	Mohammad Yousuf (91*) and Rashid Latif (66)	v Australia at Cardiff	2001
8th	100	Fawad Alam (63*) and Sohail Tanvir (59)	v Hong Kong at Karachi	2008
9th	73	Shoaib Malik (52*) and Mohammad Sami (46)	v South Africa at Centurion	2006-07
10th	103	Mohammad Aamer (73*) and Saeed Ajmal (33)	v New Zealand at Abu Dhabi	2009-10

Figures to 23.9.10. Updated records can be found at www.cricinfo.com/ci/engine/records

PAKISTAN

Most catches

Fielders

113	Inzamam-ul-Haq
102	Younis Khan
100	Shahid Afridi
90	Ijaz Ahmed
88	Wasim Akram

Most dismissals

Wicketkeepers		Ct/St
287	Moin Khan	214/73
220	Rashid Latif	182/38
145	Kamran Akmal	124/21
103	Salim Yousuf	81/22
62	Wasim Bari	52/10

Highest team totals

385-7	v Bangladesh at Dambulla	2010
371-9	v Sri Lanka at Nairobi	1996-97
353-6	v England at Karachi	2005-06
351-4	v South Africa at Durban	2006-07
349	v Zimbabwe at Kingston	2006-07
347-5	v Zimbabwe at at Karachi	2007-08
344-5	v Zimbabwe at Bulawayo	2002-03
344-8	v India at Karachi	2003-04
343-5	v Hong Kong at Colombo	2004
338-5	v Sri Lanka at Swansea	1983

Pakistan have reached 300 on 42 further occasions

Lowest team totals

Completed innings

43	v W Indies at Cape Town	1992-93
71	v W Indies at Brisbane	1992-93
74	v England at Adelaide	1991-92
75	v Sri Lanka at Lahore	2008-09
81	v West Indies at Sydney	1992-93
85	v England at Manchester	1978
87	v India at Sharjah	1984-85
89	v S Africa at Mohali	2006-07
107	v S Africa at Cape Town	2006-07
108	v Australia at Nairobi	2002-03

Against India in 1984-85 Pakistan were chasing only 126 to win

Most sixes

274	Shahid Afridi
143	Inzamam-ul-Haq
121	Wasim Akram
112	Abdul Razzaq
97	Saeed Anwar
87	Ijaz Ahmed
87	Mohammad Yousuf
61	Moin Khan
59	Shoaib Malik
50	Younis Khan

Afridi hit 2 other sixes in official ODIs

Best strike rate

Runs per 100 balls		Runs
113.20	Shahid Afridi	6284
89.60	Manzoor Elahi	741
88.33	Wasim Akram	3717
85.58	Kamran Akmal	2577
84.80	Zaheer Abbas	2572
84.51	Naved-ul-Hasan	524
82.93	Umar Akmal	724
81.30	Moin Khan	3266
81.22	Misbah-ul-Haq	1523
81.01	Imran Nazir	1895

Qualification: 500 runs

Most economical bowlers

Runs per over		Wkts
3.63	Sarfraz Nawaz	63
3.71	Akram Raza	38
3.89	Imran Khan	182
3.89	Wasim Akram	502
4.06	Abdul Qadir	132
4.14	Arshad Khan	56
4.14	Tauseef Ahmed	55
4.24	Mudassar Nazar	111
4.26	Mushtaq Ahmed	161
4.28	Aqib Javed	182

Qualification: 2000 balls bowled

Pakistan's one-day international results

	Played	Won	Lost	Tied	No result	% win
v Australia	85	29	52	1	3	35.97
v Bangladesh	26	25	1	0	0	96.15
v England	68	28	38	0	2	42.42
v India	119	69	46	0	4	60.00
v New Zealand	82	48	32	1	1	59.87
v South Africa	52	16	35	0	1	31.37
v Sri Lanka	120	70	46	1	3	60.25
v West Indies	114	48	64	2	0	42.98
v Zimbabwe	40	36	2	1	1	93.58
v others (see below)	17	16	1	0	0	94.11
TOTAL	**723**	**385**	**317**	**6**	**15**	**54.80**

Other teams: Canada (P1, W1), Hong Kong (P2, W2), Ireland (P1, L1), Kenya (P5, W5), Namibia (P1, W1), Netherlands (P3, W3), Scotland (P2, W2), United Arab Emirates (P2, W2).

SOUTH AFRICA *Test Match Records*

Most appearances

139	JH Kallis	
133	MV Boucher	
108	SM Pollock	
101	G Kirsten	
101	M Ntini	
90	HH Gibbs	
85	GC Smith	
72	AA Donald	
70	DJ Cullinan	
68	WJ Cronje	

Kallis, Boucher and Smith all also played one Test for the World XI against Australia

Most runs

		Avge
11043	JH Kallis	54.94
7289	G Kirsten	45.27
7158	GC Smith	51.12
6167	HH Gibbs	41.95
5154	MV Boucher	31.23
4554	DJ Cullinan	44.21
4232	AB de Villiers	45.50
3781	SM Pollock	32.31
3714	WJ Cronje	36.41
3471	B Mitchell	48.88

Kallis (83 runs), Smith (12) and Boucher (17) also played one Test for the World XI against Australia

Most wickets

		Avge
421	SM Pollock	23.11
390	M Ntini	28.82
330	AA Donald	22.25
265	JH Kallis	31.56
211	DW Steyn	23.13
170	HJ Tayfield	25.91
134	PR Adams	32.87
123	TL Goddard	26.22
123	A Nel	31.86
116	PM Pollock	24.18

NAT Adcock (104) and N Boje (100) also took 100 wickets. Kallis also took one wicket for the World XI

Highest scores

277	GC Smith	v England at Birmingham	2003
275*	DJ Cullinan	v New Zealand at Auckland	1998-99
275	G Kirsten	v England at Durban	1999-2000
274	RG Pollock	v Australia at Durban	1969-70
259	GC Smith	v England at Lord's	2003
255*	DJ McGlew	v New Zealand at Wellington	1952-53
253*	HM Amla	v India at Nagpur	2009-10
236	EAB Rowan	v England at Leeds	1951
232	GC Smith	v Bangladesh at Chittagong	2007-08
231	AD Nourse	v Australia at Johannesburg	1935-36

Smith's 277 and 259 were in consecutive matches

Best innings bowling

9-113	HJ Tayfield	v England at Johannesburg	1956-57
8-53	GB Lawrence	v N Zealand at Johannesburg	1961-62
8-64	L Klusener	v India at Calcutta	1996-97
8-69	HJ Tayfield	v England at Durban	1956-57
8-70	SJ Snooke	v England at Johannesburg	1905-06
8-71	AA Donald	v Zimbabwe at Harare	1995-96
7-23	HJ Tayfield	v Australia at Durban	1949-50
7-29	GF Bissett	v England at Durban	1927-28
7-37	M Ntini	v W Indies at Port-of-Spain	2004-05
7-51	DW Steyn	v India at Nagpur	2009-10

Klusener was making his Test debut

Record wicket partnerships

1st	415	ND McKenzie (226) and GC Smith (232)	v Bangladesh at Chittagong	2007-08
2nd	315*	HH Gibbs (211*) and JH Kallis (148*)	v New Zealand at Christchurch	1998-99
3rd	429*	JA Rudolph (222*) and HH Dippenaar (177*)	v Bangladesh at Chittagong	2002-03
4th	249	JH Kallis (177) and G Kirsten (137)	v West Indies at Durban	2003-04
5th	267	JH Kallis (147) and AG Prince (131)	v West Indies at St John's	2004-05
6th	271	AG Prince (162*) and MV Boucher (117)	v Bangladesh at Centurion	2008-09
7th	246	DJ McGlew (255*) and ARA Murray (109)	v New Zealand at Wellington	1952-53
8th	150	ND McKenzie (103) and SM Pollock (111)	v Sri Lanka at Centurion	2000-01
	150	G Kirsten (130) and M Zondeki (59)	v England at Leeds	2003
9th	195	MV Boucher (78) and PL Symcox (108)	v Pakistan at Johannesburg	1997-98
10th	103	HG Owen-Smith (129) and AJ Bell (26*)	v England at Leeds	1929

Figures to 23.9.10. Updated records can be found at **www.cricinfo.com/ci/engine/records**

Test Match Records **SOUTH AFRICA**

Most catches

Fielders

155	JH Kallis	
111	GC Smith	
94	HH Gibbs	
83	G Kirsten	
76	AB de Villiers	

Most dismissals

Wicketkeepers		Ct/St
502	MV Boucher	480/22
152	DJ Richardson	150/2
141	JHB Waite	124/17
56	DT Lindsay	54/2
51	HB Cameron	39/12

Highest team totals

682-6d	v England at Lord's	2003
658-9d	v West Indies at Durban	2003-04
651	v Australia at Cape Town	2008-09
622-9d	v Australia at Durban	1969-70
621-5d	v New Zealand at Auckland	1998-99
620-7d	v Pakistan at Cape Town	2002-03
620	v Australia at Johannesburg	1966-67
604-6d	v West Indies at Centurion	2003-04
600-3d	v Zimbabwe at Harare	2001-02
595	v Australia at Adelaide	1963-64

The 620 was scored in the second innings of the match

Lowest team totals

Completed innings

30	v Eng at Port Elizabeth	1895-96
30	v Eng at Birmingham	1924
35	v Eng at Cape Town	1898-99
36	v Aust at Melbourne	1931-32
43	v Eng at Cape Town	1888-89
45	v Aust at Melbourne	1931-32
47	v Eng at Cape Town	1888-89
58	v England at Lord's	1912
72	v Eng at Johannesburg	1956-57
72	v Eng at Cape Town	1956-57

South Africa's lowest total since their return to Test cricket in 1991-92 is 84 against India at Johannesburg in 2006-07

Best match bowling

13-132	M Ntini	v W Indies at Port-of-Spain	2004-05
13-165	HJ Tayfield	v Australia at Melbourne	1952-53
13-192	HJ Tayfield	v England at Johannesburg	1956-57
12-127	SJ Snooke	v England at Johannesburg	1905-06
12-139	AA Donald	v India at Port Elizabeth	1992-93
12-181	AEE Vogler	v England at Johannesburg	1909-10
11-112	AE Hall	v England at Cape Town	1922-23
11-113	AA Donald	v Zimbabwe at Harare	1995-96
11-127	AA Donald	v England at Jo'burg	1999-2000
11-150	EP Nupen	v England at Jo'burg	1930-31

Hall was making his Test debut. His performance, and Vogler's, were at the old Wanderers ground in Johannesburg

Hat-tricks

GM Griffin	v England at Lord's	1960

Griffin achieved the feat in his second and final Test (he was no-balled for throwing in the same match).

GA Lohmann (for England at Port Elizabeth in 1895-96), TJ Matthews (twice in the same match for Australia in Manchester in 1912) and TWJ Goddard (for England at Johannesburg in 1938-39) have taken Test hat-tricks against South Africa

South Africa's Test match results

	Played	Won	Lost	Drawn	Tied	% win
v Australia	83	18	47	18	0	21.68
v Bangladesh	8	8	0	0	0	100.00
v England	138	29	56	53	0	21.01
v India	24	11	6	7	0	45.83
v New Zealand	35	20	4	11	0	57.14
v Pakistan	16	8	3	5	0	50.00
v Sri Lanka	17	8	4	5	0	47.05
v West Indies	25	16	3	6	0	64.00
v Zimbabwe	7	6	0	1	0	85.71
TOTAL	**353**	**124**	**123**	**106**	**0**	**35.12**

*Figures to 23.9.10. Updated records can be found at **www.cricinfo.com/ci/engine/records***

SOUTH AFRICA One-day International Records

Most appearances

298	JH Kallis
294	SM Pollock
287	MV Boucher
248	HH Gibbs
245	JN Rhodes
188	WJ Cronje
185	G Kirsten
172	M Ntini
171	L Klusener
164	AA Donald

Pollock (9), Kallis (5), Boucher (5) and Ntini (1) also appeared in official ODIs for composite teams

Most runs

		Avge
10809	JH Kallis	46.59
8094	HH Gibbs	36.13
6798	G Kirsten	40.95
5935	JN Rhodes	35.11
5732	GC Smith	40.36
5565	WJ Cronje	38.64
4501	MV Boucher	28.66
3860	DJ Cullinan	32.99
3576	L Klusener	41.10
3466	AB de Villiers	44.43

Kallis (29 runs), Smith (0), Boucher (163) and de Villiers (150) also appeared in official ODIs for composite teams

Most wickets

		Avge
387	SM Pollock	24.31
272	AA Donald	21.78
265	M Ntini	24.53
250	JH Kallis	32.12
192	L Klusener	29.95
114	WJ Cronje	34.78
106	A Nel	27.68
95	N Boje	35.27
95	PS de Villiers	27.74
95	AJ Hall	26.47

Pollock (6 wickets), Ntini (1), Kallis (4) and Boje (1) also appeared in official ODIs for composite teams

Highest scores

188*	G Kirsten	v UAE at Rawalpindi	1995-96
175	HH Gibbs	v Australia at Johannesburg	2005-06
169*	DJ Callaghan	v N Zealand at Verwoerdburg	1994-95
161	AC Hudson	v Netherlands at Rawalpindi	1995-96
153	HH Gibbs	v B'desh at Potchefstroom	2002-03
147*	MV Boucher	v Zimbabwe at Potchefstroom	2006-07
146	AB de Villiers	v West Indies at St George's	2006-07
143	HH Gibbs	v N Zealand at Johannesburg	2002-03
141	GC Smith	v England at Centurion	2009-10
140	HM Amla	v Bangladesh at Benoni	2008-09

Gibbs has scored 21 one-day hundreds, Kallis 17 and Kirsten 13

Best bowling figures

6-22	M Ntini	v Australia at Cape Town	2005-06
6-23	AA Donald	v Kenya at Nairobi	1996-97
6-35	SM Pollock	v W Indies at East London	1998-99
6-49	L Klusener	v Sri Lanka at Lahore	1997-98
5-18	AJ Hall	v England at Bridgetown	2006-07
5-20	SM Pollock	v Eng at Johannesburg	1999-2000
5-21	L Klusener	v Kenya at Amstelveen	1999
5-21	N Boje	v Australia at Cape Town	2001-02
5-21	M Ntini	v Pakistan at Mohali	2006-07
5-23	SM Pollock	v Pakistan at Johannesburg	2006-07

Klusener has taken five wickets in an ODI innings six times, Pollock five and Ntini four

Record wicket partnerships

1st	235	G Kirsten (115) and HH Gibbs (111)	v India at Kochi	1999-2000
2nd	209	G Kirsten (124) and ND McKenzie (131*)	v Kenya at Cape Town	2001-02
3rd	186	JA Morkel (97) and AB de Villiers (107)	v Zimbabwe at Harare	2007
4th	232	DJ Cullinan (124) and JN Rhodes (121)	v Pakistan at Nairobi	1996-97
5th	183*	JH Kallis (109*) and JN Rhodes (94*)	v Pakistan at Durban	1997-98
6th	137	WJ Cronje (70*) and SM Pollock (75)	v Zimbabwe at Johannesburg	1996-97
7th	114	MV Boucher (68) and L Klusener (75*)	v India at Nagpur	1999-2000
8th	138*	JM Kemp (100*) and AJ Hall (56*)	v India at Cape Town	2006-07
9th	65	WD Parnell (49) and DW Steyn (35)	v India at Jaipur	2009-10
10th	67*	JA Morkel (23*) and M Ntini (42*)	v New Zealand at Napier	2003-04

Figures to 23.9.10. Updated records can be found at www.cricinfo.com/ci/engine/records

One-day International Records SOUTH AFRICA

Most catches

Fielders

115	JH Kallis	
108	HH Gibbs	
105	JN Rhodes	
104	SM Pollock	
81	GC Smith	

Most dismissals

Wicketkeepers | | | Ct/St |
|---|---|---|
| 412 | MV Boucher | 391/21 |
| 165 | DJ Richardson | 148/17 |
| 23 | AB de Villiers | 23/0 |
| 9 | SJ Palframan | 9/0 |

Highest team totals

438-9	v Australia at Johannesburg	2005-06
418-5	v Zimbabwe at Potchefstroom	2006-07
392-6	v Pakistan at Centurion	2006-07
365-2	v India at Ahmedabad	2009-10
363-3	v Zimbabwe at Bulawayo	2001-02
358-4	v Bangladesh at Benoni	2008-09
356-4	v West Indies at St George's	2006-07
354-3	v Kenya at Cape Town	2001-02
354-6	v England at Cape Town	2009-10
353-3	v Netherland at Basseterre	2006-07

438-9 was the highest total in all ODIs at the time, and came from 49.5 overs; all the others above were scored in 50 overs, apart from 353-3 (40)

Lowest team totals

Completed innings

69	v Australia at Sydney	1993-94
83	v England at Nottingham	2008
101*	v Pakistan at Sharjah	1999-2000
106	v Australia at Sydney	2001-02
107	v England at Lord's	2003
107	v England at Lord's	2003
108	v NZ at Mumbai	2006-07
119	v Eng at Port Elizabeth	2009-10
123	v Aust at Wellington	1994-95
129	v Eng at East London	1995-96

* One batsman retired hurt

Most sixes

128	HH Gibbs	
128	JH Kallis	
94	WJ Cronje	
81	MV Boucher	
76	L Klusener	
55	SM Pollock	
54	AB de Villiers	
52	JM Kemp	
47	JN Rhodes	
36	GC Smith	

Boucher (2), Pollock (3), Kemp (1) and de Villiers (4) also hit sixes for the Africa XI

Best strike rate

Runs per 100 balls		Runs
102.92	JA Morkel	599
89.91	L Klusener	3576
89.35	AB de Villiers	3466
89.29	N Boje	1410
88.56	HM Amla	1371
85.55	SM Pollock	3193
84.62	MV Boucher	4501
83.61	PL Symcox	694
83.26	HH Gibbs	8094
82.94	GC Smith	5732

Qualification: 500 runs

Most economical bowlers

Runs per over		Wkts
3.57	PS de Villiers	95
3.65	SM Pollock	387
3.94	CR Matthews	79
4.15	AA Donald	272
4.15	PL Symcox	72
4.28	BM McMillan	70
4.44	WJ Cronje	114
4.50	RP Snell	44
4.51	N Boje	95
4.51	AJ Hall	95
4.51	M Ntini	265

Qualification: 2000 balls bowled

South Africa's one-day international results

	Played	Won	Lost	Tied	No result	% win
v Australia	77	35	39	3	0	47.40
v Bangladesh	13	12	1	0	0	92.30
v England	44	23	18	1	2	55.95
v India	60	36	22	0	2	62.06
v New Zealand	51	30	17	0	4	63.82
v Pakistan	52	35	16	0	1	68.62
v Sri Lanka	46	22	22	1	1	50.00
v West Indies	50	37	12	0	1	75.51
v Zimbabwe	29	26	2	0	1	92.85
v others (see below)	17	17	0	0	0	100.00
TOTAL	**439**	**273**	**149**	**5**	**12**	**64.51**

Other teams: Canada (P1, W1), Ireland (P2, W2), Kenya (P10, W10), Netherlands (P2, W2), Scotland (P1, W1), United Arab Emirates (P1, W1).

SRI LANKA

Test Match Records

Most appearances

132	M Muralitharan
113	DPMD Jayawardene
111	WPUJC Vaas
110	ST Jayasuriya
93	PA de Silva
93	A Ranatunga
91	KC Sangakkara
90	MS Atapattu
83	HP Tillakaratne
63	TM Dilshan

Ranatunga uniquely played in his country's first Test and their 100th

Most runs

		Avge
9408	DPMD Jayawardene	54.06
8016	KC Sangakkara	56.85
6973	ST Jayasuriya	40.07
6361	PA de Silva	42.97
5502	MS Atapattu	39.02
5105	A Ranatunga	35.69
4545	HP Tillakaratne	42.87
4244	TT Samaraweera	53.72
3906	TM Dilshan	43.40
3089	WPUJC Vaas	24.32

RS Mahanama (2576) and AP Gurusinha (2452) also reached 2000 runs

Most wickets

		Avge
795	M Muralitharan	22.67
355	WPUJC Vaas	29.58
101	SL Malinga	33.15
98	ST Jayasuriya	34.34
89	CRD Fernando	35.82
85	GP Wickremasinghe	41.87
73	RJ Ratnayake	35.10
71	HMRKB Herath	37.88
69	HDPK Dharmasena	42.31
64	DNT Zoysa	33.70

Muralitharan also took 5 wickets for the World XI

Highest scores

374	DPMD Jayawardene	v SA at Colombo	2006
340	ST Jayasuriya	v India at Colombo	1997-98
287	KC Sangakkara	v SA at Colombo	2006
275	DPMD Jayawardene	v Ind at Ahmedabad	2009-10
270	KC Sangakkara	v Zim at Bulawayo	2003-04
267	PA de Silva	v NZ at Wellington	1990-91
253	ST Jayasuriya	v Pak at Faisalabad	2004-05
249	MS Atapattu	v Zim at Bulawayo	2003-04
242	DPMD Jayawardene	v India at Colombo	1998-99
240	DPMD Jayawardene	v Pak at Karachi	2008-09

Jayawardene made 28 Test centuries, Sangakkara 23, de Silva 20, Atapattu 16 and Jayasuriya 14

Best innings bowling

9-51	M Muralitharan	v Zimbabwe at Kandy	2001-02
9-65	M Muralitharan	v England at The Oval	1998
8-46	M Muralitharan	v West Indies at Kandy	2005
8-70	M Muralitharan	v England at Nottingham	2006
8-83	JR Ratnayeke	v Pakistan at Sialkot	1985-86
8-87	M Muralitharan	v India at Colombo	2001-02
7-46	M Muralitharan	v England at Galle	2003-04
7-71	WPUJC Vaas	v West Indies at Colombo	2001-02
7-84	M Muralitharan	v South Africa at Galle	2000-01
7-94	M Muralitharan	v Zimbabwe at Kandy	1997-98

Muralitharan took five or more wickets in an innings a record 67 times

Record wicket partnerships

1st	335	MS Atapattu (207*) and ST Jayasuriya (188)	v Pakistan at Kandy	2000
2nd	576	ST Jayasuriya (340) and RS Mahanama (225)	v India at Colombo	1997-98
3rd	624	KC Sangakkara (287) and DPMD Jayawardene (374)	v South Africa at Colombo	2006
4th	437	DPMD Jayawardene (240) and TT Samaraweera (231)	v Pakistan at Karachi	2008-09
5th	280	TT Samaraweera (138) and TM Dilshan (168)	v Bangladesh at Colombo	2005-06
6th	351	DPMD Jayawardene (275) and HAPW Jayawardene (154*)	v India at Ahmedabad	2009-10
7th	223*	HAPW Jayawardene (120*) and WPUJC Vaas (100*)	v Bangladesh at Colombo	2007
8th	170	DPMD Jayawardene (237) and WPUJC Vaas (69)	v South Africa at Galle	2004-05
9th	118	TT Samaraweera (83) and BAW Mendis (78)	v India at Colombo	2010
10th	79	WPUJC Vaas (68*) and M Muralitharan (43)	v Australia at Kandy	2003-04

Figures to 23.9.10. Updated records can be found at **www.cricinfo.com/ci/engine/records**

Test Match Records

SRI LANKA

Fielders

161	DPMD Jayawardene	
89	HP Tillakaratne	
78	ST Jayasuriya	
70	M Muralitharan	
62	MS Atapattu	

Most dismissals

Wicketkeepers		*Ct/St*
151	KC Sangakkara	131/20
119	RS Kaluwitharana	93/26
88	HAPW Jayawardene	66/22
35	HP Tillakaratne	33/2
34	SAR Silva	33/1

Highest team totals

952-6d	v India at Colombo	1997-98
760-7d	v India at Ahmedabad	2009-10
756-5d	v South Africa at Colombo	2006
713-3d	v Zimbabwe at Bulawayo	2003-04
644-7d	v Pakistan at Karachi	2008-09
642-4d	v India at Colombo	2010
628-8d	v England at Colombo	2003-04
627-9d	v West Indies at Colombo	2001-02
610-6d	v India at Colombo	2001-02
606	v Pakistan at Lahore	2008-09

952-6d is the highest total in all Tests. In all Sri Lanka have reached 500 on 27 occasions

Lowest team totals

Completed innings

71	v Pakistan at Kandy	1994-95
73*	v Pakistan at Kandy	2005-06
81	v England at Colombo	2000-01
82	v India at Chandigarh	1990-91
93	v NZ at Wellington	1982-83
95	v S Africa at Cape Town	2000-01
97	v N Zealand at Kandy	1983-84
97	v Australia at Darwin	2004
101	v Pakistan at Kandy	1985-86
109	v Pakistan at Kandy	1985-86

* One batsman absent hurt

Best match bowling

16-220	M Muralitharan	v England at The Oval	1998
14-191	WPUJC Vaas	v West Indies at Colombo	2001-02
13-115	M Muralitharan	v Zimbabwe at Kandy	2001-02
13-171	M Muralitharan	v South Africa at Galle	2000
12-82	M Muralitharan	v Bangladesh at Kandy	2007
12-117	M Muralitharan	v Zimbabwe at Kandy	1997-98
12-225	M Muralitharan	v South Africa at Colombo	2006
11-93	M Muralitharan	v England at Galle	2003-04
11-110	M Muralitharan	v India at Colombo	2008
11-132	M Muralitharan	v England at Nottingham	2006

Muralitharan took ten or more wickets in a match a record 22 times; the only others to do it for Sri Lanka are Vaas (twice), UDU Chandana and BAW Mendis

Hat-tricks

DNT Zoysa	v Zimbabwe at Harare	1999-2000

He dismissed TR Gripper, MW Goodwin and NC Johnson with the first three balls of his first over, the second of the match.

Four hat-tricks have been taken against Sri Lanka in Tests, all of them for Pakistan: two by Wasim Akram (in successive Tests in the Asian Test Championship at Lahore and Dhaka in 1998-99), Abdul Razzaq (at Galle in 2000-01) and Mohammad Sami (at Lahore in 2001-02)

Sri Lanka's Test match results

	Played	Won	Lost	Drawn	Tied	% win
v Australia	20	1	13	6	0	5.00
v Bangladesh	12	12	0	0	0	100.00
v England	21	6	8	7	0	28.57
v India	35	6	14	15	0	17.14
v New Zealand	26	7	9	10	0	26.92
v Pakistan	37	9	15	13	0	24.32
v South Africa	17	4	8	5	0	23.52
v West Indies	12	6	3	3	0	50.00
v Zimbabwe	15	10	0	5	0	66.66
TOTAL	**195**	**61**	**70**	**64**	**0**	**31.28**

Figures to 23.9.10. Updated records can be found at **www.cricinfo.com/ci/engine/records**

SRI LANKA *One-day International Records*

Most appearances

440	ST Jayasuriya
330	M Muralitharan
321	DPMD Jayawardene
321	WPUJC Vaas
308	PA de Silva
269	KC Sangakkara
269	A Ranatunga
268	MS Atapattu
213	RS Mahanama
200	HP Tillakaratne

In all 19 Sri Lankans have played more than 100 ODIs

Most runs

		Avge
13362	ST Jayasuriya	32.59
9284	PA de Silva	34.90
8734	DPMD Jayawardene	32.22
8529	MS Atapattu	37.57
8251	KC Sangakkara	36.67
7456	A Ranatunga	35.84
5162	RS Mahanama	29.49
4860	TM Dilshan	35.73
3950	RP Arnold	35.26
3902	AP Gurusinha	28.27

Jayasuriya (66), Jayawardene (269) and Sangakkara (259) all scored runs in ODIs for composite teams

Most wickets

		Avge
504	M Muralitharan	23.06
399	WPUJC Vaas	27.45
319	ST Jayasuriya	36.64
172	CRD Fernando	30.43
151	UDU Chandana	31.72
138	HDPK Dharmasena	36.21
121	MF Maharoof	25.89
109	GP Wickremasinghe	39.64
108	DNT Zoysa	29.75
106	PA de Silva	39.40
106	SL Malinga	27.32

Murali (11), Vaas (1), Jayasuriya (3) and Fernando (4) took wkts for other teams

Highest scores

189	ST Jayasuriya	v India at Sharjah	2000-01
160	TM Dilshan	v India at Rajkot	2009-10
157	ST Jayasuriya	v Netherlands at Amstelveen	2006
152	ST Jayasuriya	v England at Leeds	2006
151*	ST Jayasuriya	v India at Mumbai	1996-97
145	PA de Silva	v Kenya at Kandy	1995-96
140	ST Jayasuriya	v N Zealand at Bloemfontein	1994-95
138*	KC Sangakkara	v India at Jaipur	2005-06
137*	TM Dilshan	v Pakistan at Lahore	2008-09
134*	ST Jayasuriya	v Pakistan at Lahore	1997-98
134	PA de Silva	v Pakistan at Sharjah	1996-97
134	ST Jayasuriya	v Pakistan at Singapore	1995-96

Jayasuriya scored 28 ODI centuries

Best bowling figures

8-19	WPUJC Vaas	v Zimbabwe at Colombo	2001-02
7-30	M Muralitharan	v India at Sharjah	2000-01
6-13	BAW Mendis	v India at Karachi	2008
6-14	MF Maharoof	v West Indies at Mumbai	2006-07
6-20	AD Mathews	v India at Colombo	2008-09
6-25	WPUJC Vaas	v B'desh at P'maritzburg	2002-03
6-27	CRD Fernando	v England at Colombo	2007-08
6-29	ST Jayasuriya	v England at Moratuwa	1992-93
6-29	BAW Mendis	v Zimbabwe at Harare	2008-09
5-9	M Muralitharan	v New Zealand at Sharjah	2001-02

Vaas's 8-19 are the best bowling figures in all ODIs. In his 6-25 Vaas took a hat-trick with the first three balls of the match, and four wickets in all in the first over

Record wicket partnerships

1st	286	WU Tharanga (109) and ST Jayasuriya (152)	v England at Leeds	2006
2nd	170	S Wettimuny (74) and RL Dias (102)	v India at Delhi	1982-83
	170	ST Jayasuriya (120) and HP Tillakaratne (81*)	v New Zealand at Bloemfontein	2002-03
3rd	226	MS Atapattu (102*) and DPMD Jayawardene (128)	v India at Sharjah	2000-01
4th	171*	RS Mahanama (94*) and A Ranatunga (87*)	v West Indies at Lahore	1997-98
5th	166	ST Jayasuriya (189) and RP Arnold (52*)	v India at Sharjah	2000-01
6th	159	LPC Silva (67) and CK Kapugedera (95)	v West Indies at Port-of-Spain	2007-08
7th	126*	DPMD Jayawardene (94*) and UDU Chandana (44*)	v India at Dambulla	2005-06
8th	91	HDPK Dharmasena (51*) and DK Liyanage (43)	v West Indies at Port-of-Spain	1996-97
9th	76	RS Kalpage (44*) and WPUJC Vaas (33)	v Pakistan at Colombo	1994-95
10th	51	RP Arnold (103) and KSC de Silva (2*)	v Zimbabwe at Bulawayo	1999-2000

Figures to 23.9.10. Updated records can be found at **www.cricinfo.com/ci/engine/records**

One-day International Records — **SRI LANKA**

Most catches

Fielders

162	DPMD Jayawardene	
126	M Muralitharan	
123	ST Jayasuriya	
109	RS Mahanama	
95	PA de Silva	

Most dismissals

Wicketkeepers — Ct/St

312	KC Sangakkara	246/66
206	RS Kaluwitharana	131/75
45	HP Tillakaratne	39/6
34	DSBP Kuruppu	26/8
30	RG de Alwis	27/3

Highest team totals

443-9	v Netherlands at Amstelveen	2006
411-8	v India at Rajkot	2009-10
398-5	v Kenya at Kandy	1995-96
357-9	v Bangladesh at Lahore	2008
349-9	v Pakistan at Singapore	1995-96
343-5	v Australia at Sydney	2002-03
339-4	v Pakistan at Mohali	1996-97
332-8	v Bangladesh at Karachi	2008
329	v West Indies at Sharjah	1995-96
324-2	v England at Leeds	2006

The 324-2 was scored in 37.3 overs

Lowest team totals

Completed innings

55	v W Indies at Sharjah	1986-87
78*	v Pakistan at Sharjah	2001-02
86	v W Indies at Manchester	1975
91	v Australia at Adelaide	1984-85
96	v India at Sharjah	1983-84
98	v S Africa at Colombo	1993-94
98	v India at Sharjah	1998-99
99	v England at Perth	1998-99
102	v W Indies at Brisbane	1995-96
105	v SA at Bloemfontein	1997-98

* One batsman absent hurt

Most sixes

268	ST Jayasuriya
102	PA de Silva
64	A Ranatunga
49	DPMD Jayawardene
42	AP Gurusinha
35	KC Sangakkara
30	TM Dilshan
27	CK Kapugedera
22	UDU Chandana
22	MF Maharoof
22	WPUJC Vaas

Jayasuriya also hit 2 for the Asia XI

Best strike rate

Runs per 100 balls — Runs

91.28	ST Jayasuriya	13362
87.36	TM Dilshan	4860
86.80	RJ Ratnayake	612
85.19	MF Maharoof	984
81.13	PA de Silva	9284
79.07	AD Mathews	563
77.91	A Ranatunga	7456
77.70	RS Kaluwitharana	3711
77.00	M Muralitharan	663
76.68	DPMD Jayawardene	8734

Qualification: 500 runs

Most economical bowlers

Runs per over — Wkts

3.92	M Muralitharan	504
4.18	WPUJC Vaas	399
4.18	SD Anurasiri	32
4.27	HDPK Dharmasena	138
4.29	CPH Ramanayake	68
4.29	VB John	34
4.37	BAW Mendis	78
4.50	DS de Silva	32
4.50	RS Kalpage	73
4.52	DNT Zoysa	108
4.52	KMDN Kulasekara	94

Qualification: 2000 balls bowled

Sri Lanka's one-day international results

	Played	Won	Lost	Tied	No result	% win
v Australia	68	20	46	0	2	30.30
v Bangladesh	29	27	2	0	0	93.10
v England	44	21	23	0	0	47.72
v India	128	50	67	0	11	42.73
v New Zealand	72	32	35	1	4	47.79
v Pakistan	120	46	70	1	3	39.74
v South Africa	46	22	22	1	1	50.00
v West Indies	46	18	26	0	2	40.90
v Zimbabwe	46	38	7	0	1	84.44
v others (see below)	13	12	1	0	0	92.30
TOTAL	**612**	**286**	**299**	**3**	**24**	**48.89**

Other teams: Bermuda (P1, W1), Canada (P1, W1), Ireland (P1, W1), Kenya (P5, W4, L1), Netherlands (P3, W3), United Arab Emirates (P2, W2).

WEST INDIES
Test Match Records

Most appearances

132	CA Walsh
130	BC Lara
126	S Chanderpaul
121	IVA Richards
116	DL Haynes
110	CH Lloyd
108	CG Greenidge
102	CL Hooper
98	CEL Ambrose
93	GS Sobers

Sobers played 85 successive Tests between 1954-55 and 1971-72

Most runs

		Avge
11912	BC Lara	53.17
8969	S Chanderpaul	49.28
8540	IVA Richards	50.23
8032	GS Sobers	57.78
7558	CG Greenidge	44.72
7515	CH Lloyd	46.67
7487	DL Haynes	42.29
6227	RB Kanhai	47.53
6007	CH Gayle	40.31
5949	RB Richardson	44.39

Greenidge and Haynes put on 6482 runs together, the Test record by any pair of batsmen

Most wickets

		Avge
519	CA Walsh	24.44
405	CEL Ambrose	20.99
376	MD Marshall	20.94
309	LR Gibbs	29.09
259	J Garner	20.97
249	MA Holding	23.68
235	GS Sobers	34.03
202	AME Roberts	25.61
192	WW Hall	26.38
161	IR Bishop	24.27

In all 18 West Indians have reached 100 Test wickets

Highest scores

400*	BC Lara	v England at St John's	2003-04
375	BC Lara	v England at St John's	1993-94
365*	GS Sobers	v Pakistan at Kingston	1957-58
317	CH Gayle	v South Africa at St John's	2004-05
302	LG Rowe	v England at Bridgetown	1973-74
291	IVA Richards	v England at The Oval	1976
291	RR Sarwan	v England at Bridgetown	2008-09
277	BC Lara	v Australia at Sydney	1992-93
270*	GA Headley	v England at Kingston	1934-35
261*	RR Sarwan	v Bangladesh at Kingston	2003-04
261	FMM Worrell	v England at Nottingham	1950

Lara scored 34 Test centuries, Sobers 26, Richards 24

Best innings bowling

9-95	JM Noreiga	v India at Port-of-Spain	1970-71
8-29	CEH Croft	v Pakistan at Port-of-Spain	1976-77
8-38	LR Gibbs	v India at Bridgetown	1961-62
8-45	CEL Ambrose	v England at Bridgetown	1989-90
8-92	MA Holding	v England at The Oval	1976
8-104	AL Valentine	v England at Manchester	1950
7-22	MD Marshall	v England at Manchester	1988
7-25	CEL Ambrose	v Australia at Perth	1992-93
7-37	CA Walsh	v New Zealand at Wellington	1994-95
7-49	S Ramadhin	v England at Birmingham	1957

Valentine was playing in his first Test, Croft and Noreiga in their second

Record wicket partnerships

1st	298	CG Greenidge (149) and DL Haynes (167)	v England at St John's	1989-90
2nd	446	CC Hunte (260) and GS Sobers (365*)	v Pakistan at Kingston	1957-58
3rd	338	ED Weekes (206) and FMM Worrell (167)	v England at Port-of-Spain	1953-54
4th	399	GS Sobers (226) and FMM Worrell (197*)	v England at Bridgetown	1959-60
5th	322	BC Lara (213) and JC Adams (94)	v Australia at Kingston	1998-99
6th	282*	BC Lara (400*) and RD Jacobs (107*)	v England at St John's	2003-04
7th	347	DS Atkinson (219) and CC Depeiaza (122)	v Australia at Bridgetown	1954-55
8th	148	JC Adams (101*) and FA Rose (69)	v Zimbabwe at Kingston	1999-2000
9th	161	CH Lloyd (161*) and AME Roberts (68)	v India at Calcutta	1983-84
10th	106	CL Hooper (178*) and CA Walsh (30)	v Pakistan at St John's	1992-93

Figures to 23.9.10. Updated records can be found at **www.cricinfo.com/ci/engine/records**

Most catches

Fielders

164	BC Lara	
122	IVA Richards	
115	CL Hooper	
109	GS Sobers	
96	CG Greenidge	

Most dismissals

Wicketkeepers   *Ct/St*

270	PJL Dujon	265/5
219	RD Jacobs	207/12
189	DL Murray	181/8
122	D Ramdin	119/3
101	JR Murray	98/3

Highest team totals

790-3d	v Pakistan at Kingston	1957-58
751-5d	v England at St John's	2003-04
749-9d	v England at Bridgetown	2008-09
747	v South Africa at St John's	2004-05
692-8d	v England at The Oval	1995
687-8d	v England at The Oval	1976
681-8d	v England at Port-of-Spain	1953-54
660-5d	v New Zealand at Wellington	1994-95
652-8d	v England at Lord's	1973
644-8d	v India at Delhi	1958-59

West Indies have passed 600 in Tests on nine further occasions

Lowest team totals

Completed innings

47	v England at Kingston	2003-04
51	v Aust at Port-of-Spain	1998-99
53	v Pakistan at Faisalabad	1986-87
54	v England at Lord's	2000
61	v England at Leeds	2000
76	v Pakistan at Dacca	1958-59
77	v NZ at Auckland	1955-56
78	v Australia at Sydney	1951-52
82	v Australia at Brisbane	2000-01
86*	v England at The Oval	1957

One batsman absent hurt

Best match bowling

14-149	MA Holding	v England at The Oval	1976
13-55	CA Walsh	v N Zealand at Wellington	1994-95
12-121	AME Roberts	v India at Madras	1974-75
11-84	CEL Ambrose	v England at Port-of-Spain	1993-94
11-89	MD Marshall	v India at Port-of-Spain	1988-89
11-107	MA Holding	v Australia at Melbourne	1981-82
11-120	MD Marshall	v N Zealand at Bridgetown	1984-85
11-126	WW Hall	v India at Kanpur	1958-59
11-134	CD Collymore	v Pakistan at Kingston	2004-05
11-147	KD Boyce	v England at The Oval	1973

Marshall took ten or more wickets in a Test four times, Ambrose and Walsh three

Hat-tricks

WW Hall   v Pakistan at Lahore   1958-59
The first Test hat-trick not for England or Australia.

LR Gibbs   v Australia at Adelaide   1960-61
Gibbs had taken three wickets in four balls in the previous Test, at Sydney.

CA Walsh   v Australia at Brisbane   1988-89
The first Test hat-trick to be split over two innings.

JJC Lawson   v Australia at Bridgetown   2002-03
Also split over two innings

West Indies' Test match results

	Played	Won	Lost	Drawn	Tied	% win
v Australia	108	32	52	23	1	29.62
v Bangladesh	6	3	2	1	0	50.00
v England	145	53	43	49	0	36.55
v India	82	30	11	41	0	36.58
v New Zealand	37	10	9	18	0	27.02
v Pakistan	44	14	15	15	0	31.81
v South Africa	25	3	16	6	0	12.00
v Sri Lanka	12	3	6	3	0	25.00
v Zimbabwe	6	4	0	2	0	66.66
TOTAL	**465**	**152**	**154**	**158**	**1**	**32.68**

Figures to 23.9.10. Updated records can be found at **www.cricinfo.com/ci/engine/records**

WEST INDIES *One-day International Record.*

295	BC Lara	
261	S Chanderpaul	
238	DL Haynes	
227	CL Hooper	
224	RB Richardson	
217	CH Gayle	
205	CA Walsh	
187	IVA Richards	
176	CEL Ambrose	
169	PJL Dujon	

25 West Indians have played more than 100 ODIs. Lara and Gayle also played for the World XI

Most runs

		Avge
10348	BC Lara	40.90
8648	S Chanderpaul	41.77
8648	DL Haynes	41.37
7830	CH Gayle	39.74
6721	IVA Richards	47.00
6248	RB Richardson	33.41
5761	CL Hooper	35.34
5134	CG Greenidge	45.03
5098	RR Sarwan	43.94
3675	PV Simmons	28.93

Gayle and Lara scored 19 centuries, Haynes 17, Greenidge and Richards 11

Most wickets

		Avge
227	CA Walsh	30.47
225	CEL Ambrose	24.12
193	CL Hooper	36.05
157	MD Marshall	26.96
156	CH Gayle	34.21
146	J Garner	18.84
142	MA Holding	21.36
130	M Dillon	32.44
129	DJ Bravo	28.84
118	IR Bishop	26.50
118	IVA Richards	35.83

WKM Benjamin (100) and RA Harper (100) also reached 100 wickets

Highest scores

189*	IVA Richards	v England at Manchester	1984
181	IVA Richards	v Sri Lanka at Karachi	1987-88
169	BC Lara	v Sri Lanka at Sharjah	1995-96
157*	XM Marshall	v Canada at King City	2008-09
156	BC Lara	v Pakistan at Adelaide	2004-05
153*	IVA Richards	v Australia at Melbourne	1979-80
153*	CH Gayle	v Zimbabwe at Bulawayo	2003-04
153	BC Lara	v Pakistan at Sharjah	1993-94
152*	DL Haynes	v India at Georgetown	1988-89
152*	CH Gayle	v S Africa at Johannesburg	2003-04
152	CH Gayle	v Kenya at Nairobi	2001-02

S Chanderpaul scored 150 v SA at East London in 1998-99

Best bowling figures

7-51	WW Davis	v Australia at Leeds	1983
6-15	CEH Croft	v England at Kingstown	1980-81
6-22	FH Edwards	v Zimbabwe at Harare	2003-04
6-29	BP Patterson	v India at Nagpur	1987-88
6-41	IVA Richards	v India at Delhi	1989-90
6-50	AH Gray	v Aust at Port-of-Spain	1990-91
5-1	CA Walsh	v Sri Lanka at Sharjah	1986-87
5-17	CEL Ambrose	v Australia at Melbourne	1988-89
5-22	AME Roberts	v England at Adelaide	1979-80
5-22	WKM Benjamin	v Sri Lanka at Bombay	1993-94

Edwards's feat was in his first ODI; he had earlier taken 5-36 on his Test debut

Record wicket partnerships

1st	200*	SC Williams (78*) and S Chanderpaul (109*)	v India at Bridgetown	1996-97
2nd	221	CG Greenidge (115) and IVA Richards (149)	v India at Jamshedpur	1983-84
3rd	195*	CG Greenidge (105*) and HA Gomes (75*)	v Zimbabwe at Worcester	1983
4th	226	S Chanderpaul (150) and CL Hooper (108)	v South Africa at East London	1998-99
5th	154	CL Hooper (112*) and S Chanderpaul (67)	v Pakistan at Sharjah	2001-02
6th	154	RB Richardson (122) and PJL Dujon (53)	v Pakistan at Sharjah	1991-92
7th	115	PJL Dujon (57*) and MD Marshall (66)	v Pakistan at Gujranwala	1986-87
8th	84	RL Powell (76) and CD Collymore (3)	v India at Toronto	1999-2000
9th	77	RR Sarwan (65) and IDR Bradshaw (37)	v New Zealand at Christchurch	2005-06
10th	106*	IVA Richards (189*) and MA Holding (12*)	v England at Manchester	1984

Figures to 23.9.10. Updated records can be found at **www.cricinfo.com/ci/engine/records**

Most catches

Fielders

120	CL Hooper	
117	BC Lara	
100	IVA Richards	
94	CH Gayle	
75	RB Richardson	

Most dismissals

Wicketkeepers — *Ct/St*

204	PJL Dujon	183/21
189	RD Jacobs	160/29
114	D Ramdin	109/5
68	CO Browne	59/9
51	JR Murray	44/7

Highest team totals

360-4	v Sri Lanka at Karachi	1987-88
347-6	v Zimbabwe at Bulawayo	2003-04
339-4	v Pakistan at Adelaide	2004-05
333-6	v Zimbabwe at Georgetown	2005-06
333-7	v Sri Lanka at Sharjah	1995-96
333-8	v India at Jamshedpur	1983-84
324-4	v India at Ahmedabad	2002-03
324-8	v India at Nagpur	2006-07
319	v India at Kingston	2009
316-4	v Canada at Kingston	2009-10

All these totals came from 50 overs except the 333-8 (45)

Lowest team totals

Completed innings

54	v S Africa at Cape Town	2003-04
80	v Sri Lanka at Mumbai	2006-07
87	v Australia at Sydney	1992-93
91	v Zimbabwe at Sydney	2000-01
93	v Kenya at Pune	1995-96
103	v Pak at Melbourne	1996-97
110	v Australia at Manchester	1999
111	v Pak at Melbourne	1983-84
113	v Aust at Kuala Lumpur	2006-07
114	v Pak at Pt-of-Spain	1999-2000

The 87 was in a match reduced to 30 overs: Australia made 101-9

Most sixes

164	CH Gayle
133	BC Lara
126	IVA Richards
83	S Chanderpaul
81	CG Greenidge
75	RL Powell
65	CL Hooper
54	RB Richardson
53	DL Haynes
51	RR Sarwan

XM Marshall (12) holds the West Indian record for sixes in an innings

Best strike rate

Runs per 100 balls — *Runs*

97.26	DR Smith	925
96.66	RL Powell	2085
95.66	DJG Sammy	508
94.22	KA Pollard	538
90.20	IVA Richards	6721
83.71	CH Gayle	7830
82.13	DJ Bravo	1715
81.22	CH Lloyd	1977
79.62	BC Lara	10348
77.70	D Ramdin	899

Qualification: 500 runs

Most economical bowlers

Runs per over — *Wkts*

3.09	J Garner	146
3.32	MA Holding	142
3.40	AME Roberts	87
3.48	CEL Ambrose	225
3.53	MD Marshall	157
3.83	CA Walsh	227
3.97	RA Harper	100
4.00	CE Cuffy	41
4.09	EAE Baptiste	36
4.15	WKM Benjamin	100

Qualification: 2000 balls bowled

West Indies' one-day international results

	Played	Won	Lost	Tied	No result	% win
v Australia	125	57	63	2	3	47.54
v Bangladesh	16	11	3	0	2	78.57
v England	82	41	37	0	4	52.56
v India	95	54	38	1	2	58.60
v New Zealand	51	24	20	0	7	54.54
v Pakistan	114	64	48	2	0	57.01
v South Africa	50	12	37	0	1	24.48
v Sri Lanka	46	26	18	0	2	59.09
v Zimbabwe	41	31	9	0	1	77.50
v others (see below)	17	15	1	0	1	88.23
TOTAL	**637**	**335**	**274**	**5**	**23**	**54.96**

Other teams: Bermuda (P1, W1), Canada (P4, W4), Ireland (P3, W2, NR1), Kenya (P6, W5, L1), Netherlands (P1, W1), Scotland (P2, W2).

INTERNATIONAL SCHEDULE 2010-11

	Tests	ODIs	T20Is
October 2010			
India v Australia	2	3	–
Bangladesh v New Zealand	–	5	–
South Africa v Zimbabwe	–	3	2
Pakistan v South Africa in UAE	2	5	2
November 2010			
Australia v Sri Lanka	–	3	1
India v New Zealand	3	5	–
Australia v England	5	7	2
Sri Lanka v West Indies	3	5	–
December 2010			
South Africa v India	3	5	1
New Zealand v Pakistan	2	6	3
Bangladesh v Zimbabwe	–	5*	–
February 2011			
World Cup in Asia	–	49	–
March 2011			
World Cup in Asia			
(final April 2)	–	–	–
April 2011			
West Indies v India	4	5	–
Bangladesh v Australia	2	3	–
May 2011			
England v Sri Lanka	3	5	1
West Indies v Pakistan	2	5	–

	Tests	ODIs	T20Is
June 2011			
Australia v Zimbabwe	–	3*	–
July 2011			
England v India	4	5	1
Zimbabwe v Bangladesh	–	5*	–
August 2011			
Sri Lanka v Australia	3	5	–
September 2011			
India v Australia	3	5	–
Zimbabwe v Pakistan	–	3*	–
October 2011			
South Africa v Australia	3	5	–
India v England	–	5	1
Pakistan v Sri Lanka	3	5	–
Bangladesh v West Indies	2	3	–
November 2011			
Australia v New Zealand	2	–	–
India v West Indies	3	5	–
December 2011			
Australia v India	4	–	–
Bangladesh v Pakistan	2	3	–
New Zealand v Zimbabwe	–	3*	–
South Africa v Sri Lanka	3	5	–

Details subject to change. Some tours may continue into the month after the one shown above. An asterisk signifies that the number of matches is unconfirmed. Twenty20 internationals may well be added to some of the later tours.